Linguistic Imperialism

Robert Phillipson

Oxford University Press

OXFORD

UNIVERSITY PRESS

Great Clarendon Street, Oxford OX2 6DP

Oxford University Press is a department of the University of Oxford.
It furthers the University's objective of excellence in research, scholarship,
and education by publishing worldwide in

Oxford New York

Auckland Bangkok Buenos Aires Cape Town Chennai
Dar es Salaam Delhi Hong Kong Istanbul Karachi Kolkata
Kuala Lumpur Madrid Melbourne Mexico City Mumbai
Nairobi São Paulo Shanghai Taipei Tokyo Toronto

OXFORD and OXFORD ENGLISH are registered trade marks of
Oxford University Press in the UK and in certain other countries

ISBN 0 19 437146 8

Typeset by Pentacor plc
in 10 on 12 pt Sabon

Printed in China

Acknowledgements

I am extremely grateful to those who kindly agreed to be interviewed in 1986 for the purposes of this book: Roger Bowers, Chris Brumfit, Neville Grant, Bernard Lott, George Perren, Sir Randolph Quirk, Peter Strevens, and Henry Widdowson. Their insights, recollections, and assessments were invaluable for me in clarifying many of the policy issues, past and present, and in elucidating a wealth of factual details. They all (with one exception) agreed to let me tape the discussions, which has permitted me to quote them verbatim. It is customary in introductory acknowledgements to thank named individuals for their assistance and exonerate them for any shortcomings or errors. Such declarations would not be to the point here, as the people interviewed and quoted are in no way responsible for the text. They had a general idea of the purpose of my investigation, expressed their views, and these I have drawn on. I sincerely hope a constructive dialogue with them will continue, irrespective of whether or not they agree with my analysis.

I am also greatly indebted to George Perren for unearthing a substantial number of invaluable papers from the immediate post-war period and the 1960s. He generously reacted to an earlier version of the text by writing a lengthy and informative critique. I have referred to this in the text by (Perren, ms). His enthusiasm for historically based work in this field because 'it is important that an impartial record should be made where there is so much folklore being invented to explain or justify present discontents and deficiencies' and the example of his own insightful scholarship have been a real source of inspiration and encouragement.

I am grateful to many British Council staff in the English Language and Literature Division, the English-Teaching Information Centre, the Resource Centre, the Registry, and Archives, for their help and efficiency in tracing written material for me. I owe particular thanks to Roger Bowers for facilitating these visits, and for providing much useful comment on the first draft of the manuscript.

An earlier version of this book was accepted as a doctoral thesis at the University of Amsterdam in 1990. I am very grateful to the seven professors who acted as assessors: Chris Mullard, chair, Memet Alkan, Teun van Dijk, Henk Heeren (all four from Amsterdam), Antje-Katrin Menk (Bremen), Jacob Mey (Odense), and Wilfried Stölting-Richert (Oldenburg). I should also like to record my long-standing professional debt to Chris Mullard, Teun van Dijk, Jacob Mey, and Jim Cummins for their distinguished example as critical scholars.

My sincere thanks, too, to those readers who assessed the manuscript for Oxford University Press, and made valuable suggestions for improving it; to Cristina Whitecross for her dedication and commitment as publisher; and to Ann Hunter for an immensely thorough and thoughtful revision of the text.

My greatest debt of all is to my wife, Tove Skutnabb-Kangas. In the past decade we have written over a dozen joint articles on topics related to the theme of this book. Her immense erudition, commitment, capacity to see the conventional in a new light, and urge to develop and apply theory, have made working with her challenging and stimulating. Chapter 9 is a revised version of what was initially a joint paper at the World Sociology Congress in Delhi in 1986, published in Phillipson and Skutnabb-Kangas 1986a. Tove has ensured that the long gestation period of this book has not been a solitary one, but one during which I have received constant support and encouragement, incisive and harsh but constructive criticism, all to a far greater extent than professional interest or the commitment to combat imperialism would demand. She has my love and gratitude—while I, of course, have responsibility for the final product.

I should also like to acknowledge my profound debt to my parents, Jane and Henry Phillipson, and my children, Caspar, Thomas, and Louise. They have in their several supportive ways been decisive in nurturing my love of language and in promoting an awareness of the complexity of language as a social force.

The author and publishers would like to thank the following for permission to reproduce the material below that falls within their copyright:

Her Britannic Majesty's Stationery Office, for permission to quote from the 'Report of the Official Committee on the

Teaching of English Overseas' (Ministry of Education 51352, 23 March 1956).

The British Council, for permission to quote from the British Council internal report on the 'Anglo-American Conference on English Teaching Abroad', June 1961.

Braj Kachru for extracts from 'The power and politics of English', *World Englishes* 1986.

Textual source material written in Danish, French, German, Norwegian, and Swedish has been quoted in English, in my translation.

Contents

1 ELT: Taking stock of a world commodity

The aims of this book

This book explores the contemporary phenomenon of English as a world language and sets out to analyse how the language became so dominant and why. It looks at the spread of English historically, in order to ascertain whether the language has been actively promoted as an instrument of the foreign policy of the major English-speaking states, and if so, in what ways. It looks at the language policies that Third World countries inherited from colonial times, and considers how well 'aid', in the form of support for educational development and English learning in particular, has served the interests of the receiving countries and the donors, and assesses whether it has contributed to perpetuating North-South inequalities and exploitation. It looks specifically at the ideology transmitted with, in, and through the English language, and the role of language specialists in the cultural export of English.

To put things more metaphorically, whereas once Britannia ruled the waves, now it is English which rules them. The British empire has given way to the empire of English. This book attempts to contribute to an understanding of the ways in which English rules, who makes the rules, and what role the English teaching profession plays in promoting the 'rules' of English and the rule of English.

Among the questions it attempts to shed light on are the following: What role does English play in Third World countries? Why have other languages, with few exceptions, not prospered? How and why has the position of English been strengthened? What has been the role of foreign experts on language, in promoting this development? What arguments have been used to justify the continued use of the former colonial languages? Whose interests do the present policies on language in education serve? What kind of long-term accountability is there for projects involving educational aid? How can one relate

the micro level of ELT (English Language Teaching) professionalism to the macro level of global inequality? What ethical issues
are raised by the ELT profession attempting to span the North-
South divide, in a world characterized by an acutely unjust
division of the fruits of the earth and of the products of human
labour? How can we, in a theoretically informed way, relate the
global role of English, and the way in which language pedagogy
supports the spread and promotion of the language, to the
political, economic, military, and cultural pressures that propel
it forward? How can analysis probe beyond individual experience and reflection to the processes and structures which are in
operation at the international, national, group, and personal levels?

In order to provide a basis for tentative answers to these
questions, the first two chapters set the scene descriptively by
looking at English as the international language *par excellence*,
at professional and ethical aspects of aid, at English in different
parts of the world, at how international languages are promoted,
and at opposition to the dominance of English. The following
two chapters present the theoretical framework for the analysis:
Chapter 3 deals with the theory of linguistic imperialism, and
presents the key concept linguicism; Chapter 4 reviews earlier
work in this area.

One of my reasons for writing this book is the belief that
language pedagogy, the scientific study of language learning and
language teaching, has been isolated from the social sciences for
too long, and that ELT needs to be situated in a macro-societal
theoretical perspective.[1] The book aims therefore at unearthing
some of the historical, political, and intellectual roots of the
language pedagogy profession. This means that a major concern
of the empirical parts of the book is the colonial linguistic
inheritance, and the developments of the 1950s and early 1960s
which helped applied linguistics and ELT to expand at the time
and in the manner they did—the winds of change of
decolonization blew life into the infant profession.

I am fully aware of the inherent difficulty of probing into such
a complex set of problems. I have attempted to narrow the field
so that certain aspects can be studied in depth, while clarifying
the over-arching concerns. The analysis inevitably reflects the
bias of the particular ways in which I have been involved in ELT
for a quarter of a century in a variety of contexts, in Western
Europe, communist south-east Europe, and the Third World,
particularly Africa.[2] Although it is particularly the British

experience of ELT that is the main focus of attention, with rather less coverage of American source material and activities, it is hoped that the theoretical apparatus, and the main thrust of the analysis, for instance of pedagogic principles and the structure of aid, is of wide applicability and relevance.

The book also reflects the fact that professionally and personally I am multilingual and live in Denmark, where English is a 'foreign' language. Here one cannot help appreciating that English is the medium for a massive impact from a variety of sources—some benign, some pernicious.

A serious constraint has been the limitations of available theory. Any philosophy of science paradigm inevitably reflects value judgements about the ethical and ultimately political purposes of scientific activity, however much the individual strives for objectivity and scientific impartiality in dealing with the material. The theoretical framework elaborated for this book involves drawing on and synthesizing traditions in a number of disciplines, both in the social sciences (in particular imperialism theories and concepts derived from them in the analysis of international cultural phenomena, the sociology of language, theories of the state and hegemony) and in the humanities (in particular theories of language learning and teaching, educational language planning, and linguistic human rights).

My theoretical approach has been substantially influenced by working for a decade with Tove Skutnabb-Kangas on theorizing language and power, relationships between dominant and dominated groups, and minority education. Our work has attempted to integrate the perspectives of those dominated (female, immigrant, mother tongue a 'small' language) and the dominant (male, dominant group, mother tongue an 'expansionist' language), and where the goal of such scientific work is both a theoretically-based understanding of each perspective and analysis which can promote increased justice for both groups. Undoubtedly the book would have benefited if it had drawn on more specialist input from sociology, political science, economics, development studies, and social psychology, particularly if these had been merged into an integrated, inter-disciplinary approach. In being multidisciplinary and exploratory, the book conforms to what the Norwegian peace researcher Johan Galtung writes (1988: 151) about social science research, where 'analysis, exploration, means entering something messy with messy tools—probably the only way of doing it.'

As we shall see, English is one of several languages which are promoted internationally in similar ways. I shall explore why English has become the dominant international language and how language pedagogy has contributed to its hegemony. A more specific reason triggering my interest in analysing the international consolidation of English and the role of language teaching in that process, has been my involvement in support work for SWAPO of Namibia (one product of which is Phillipson, Skutnabb-Kangas, and Africa 1985). In order to contribute constructively to educational language planning and curriculum development work for Namibia, it seemed essential to look at the role of English in comparable countries, at the processes by which English has retained its dominant role, and the consequences for other languages. A theoretically explicit and critical analysis of the record elsewhere was a vital preliminary before assisting Namibians to implement English as a medium of education in schools. Otherwise we might have been aiding in the incorporation of Namibia into a neo-colonialist structure of dependence on foreign expertise, know-how, and products. This is a very real dilemma, to which I hope to contribute theoretical clarification of benefit to practical involvement. A case study of one aspect of language planning for Namibia is included in Chapter 9.

In order to provide for a wider basis of assessments of the role of British ELT, I was fortunate enough to be able to interview eight ELT policy makers who have been influential as academics, administrators, and writers over a period of thirty years (see Acknowledgements). The interviews covered the origins and nature of British support for ELT, training and research in Britain, and English in the global context. The purpose of the interviews was to elicit the views of the informants on the dominant ELT paradigm and their assessment of the strengths and weaknesses of experience to date.

ELT has boomed over the past 30 years, and seen a proliferation of university departments, language schools, publi-cations, conferences, and all the paraphernalia of an established profession. ELT is also a billion-pound business, described in an *Economist Intelligence Unit* study of English as a 'world commodity', in a report written to promote strategies for capitalizing further on this growth industry (McCallen 1989). However, this 'frequently lucrative' business (ibid.: 117) does not generally pay the majority of its teachers well (these being described as having a job rather than a career—one which is far from secure or attractive). A similar pattern is diagnosed in a study of the career paths of EFL (English as a Foreign Language) teachers (Centre for British Teachers 1989). This notes major structural imbalances between the professional aspirations of recruits to the profession, the output of MA graduates, and market forces which are more characteristic of an industry than a profession (ibid.: 30). It is also ironical that this transnational business has its headquarters in Britain and the USA, countries which are renowned for their backwardness in foreign language learning. In spite of this, the professionalism and sophistication of much of the ELT business is a reality. All the more reason for taking stock, and seeking answers to a range of questions about the power of English and the power of English teaching.

English for all?

English has also become a lingua franca to the point that any literate educated person is in a very real sense deprived if he does not know English. Poverty, famine, and disease are instantly recognized as the cruellest and least excusable forms of deprivation. Linguistic deprivation is a less easily noticed condition, but one nevertheless of great significance.
(Burchfield 1985: 160)

This comment on the global reach of English by the influential editor of *The Oxford English Dictionary* seems to equate linguistic deprivation with ignorance of English. While there is a sense in which Burchfield is making a valid observation, as an unqualified generalization it is patently false. There are many millions of highly literate people in the world who are happily and quite justifiably ignorant of English.

What is more challenging about his claim is the question of the links between the worldwide spread of English and the occurrence of poverty, famine, and disease. There is clearly no simple causal relationship between them, but to deny that there could be any link would be to ignore the fact that the language has accompanied the slave trade and imperialism round the world, as did several other European languages. (It should also be pointed out that English has featured prominently in the struggle to abolish slavery and colonialism.) At the present time English, to a much greater extent than any other language is the language in which the fate of most of the world's millions is decided. English has, in the twentieth century, become the international language *par excellence.*

English has a dominant position in science, technology, medicine, and computers; in research, books, periodicals, and software; in transnational business, trade, shipping, and aviation; in diplomacy and international organizations; in mass media entertainment, news agencies, and journalism; in youth culture and sport; in education systems, as the most widely learnt foreign language (an estimated 115 million learners at school level by the early 1970s, Gage and Ohannessian 1974; and in the wake of the disintegration of communist states, an estimated 100,000 new teachers of English are needed for 30 million learners in Central and Eastern Europe in the 1990s, *British Council Annual Report*, 1989/90: 17). This non-exhaustive list of the domains in which English has a dominant, though not of course exclusive, place is indicative of the functional load carried by English.

Whereas in earlier historical periods other languages have spread over large areas for certain purposes (often commercial or religious), the spread of English is unique, both in terms of its geographical reach and as regards the depth of its penetration. The novelty and distinctiveness of the increasing spread of English in recent decades is analysed as follows by the first director of the Center for Applied Linguistics in Washington.

> The spread of English is as significant in its way as is the modern use of computers. When the amount of information needing to be processed came to exceed human capabilities, the computer appeared on the scene, transforming the processes of planning and calculation. When the need for global communication came to exceed the limits set by language barriers, the spread of English accelerated, transforming existing patterns of international communication. (Ferguson 1983: ix)

What this extract does not refer to is the forces—economic, political, intellectual, and social—which have propelled English forward. The spread of English has not been left to chance, and language pedagogy has played a part in this process. One of Ferguson's successors as Director of the Center for Applied Linguistics explains the development thus:

From a minor language in 1600, English has in less than four centuries come to be the leading language of international communication in the world today. This remarkable development is ultimately the result of 17th, 18th, and 19th century British successes in conquest, colonization, and trade, but it was enormously accelerated by the emergence of the United States as the major military world power and technological leader in the aftermath of World War II. The process was also greatly abetted by the expenditure of large amounts of government and private foundation funds in the period 1950–1970, perhaps the most ever spent in history in support of the propagation of a language.
(Troike 1977: 2)

English has been successfully promoted, and has been eagerly adopted in the global linguistic marketplace. One symptom of the impact of English is *linguistic borrowing*. English intrudes on all the languages that it comes into contact with. As Calvet has indicated (1987: 235), the technical terms 'borrowing' and 'loan word' are misleading, since speakers of a language who borrow words from another have no intention of returning anything. The transaction is purely unidirectional, and reflects the desirability of the product to the consumer. The only constraint on use is intelligibility—though states may attempt to ban certain foreign forms and implement measures to devise indigenous neologisms. Borrowing is a phenomenon that has offended users of other languages for more than a century (for a sample French protest against 'anglomania' in 1853, see Fishman 1972: 240). It has also generated an extensive literature on linguistic borrowing from English (Viereck and Bald 1986; for African languages see Bokamba 1983, for European languages see Filipović 1982, for Indian languages see Kachru 1983a). British English absorbs a large number of words of American origin, often without the source being noticed (Foster 1968). Many languages borrow gastronomic and *haute couture* terms from French; in the same way there is a carry-over from the use of English in many of the domains listed above into the vocabulary of other languages. The English linguistic invasion has been so pervasive that some governments, representing both small linguistic communities, for instance Slovenia (Paternost 1985) and large ones, for instance France (Calvet 1987), have adopted measures to stem the tide and shore up their own languages, particularly in the area of neologisms for technical concepts. Such measures, which are likely to be only partially successful, reflect an anxiety that essential cultural and linguistic values are at risk.

In language pedagogy, the connections between the English language and political, economic, and military power are seldom pursued. Language pedagogy tends to focus on what goes on in the classroom, and related organizational and methodological matters. In professional English teaching circles, English tends to be regarded as an incontrovertible boon, as does language policy and pedagogy emanating from Britain and the USA. It is felt that while English was imposed by force in colonial times,[3] contemporary language policies are determined by the state of the market ('demand') and the force of argument (rational planning in the light of the available 'facts'). The discourse accompanying and legitimating the export of English to the rest of the world has been so persuasive that English has been equated with progress and prosperity. In the view of the Ford Foundation's language projects officer, 'English as a Second Language (ESL) was believed to be a vital key to development by both the United States and by countries like Indonesia, the Philippines, Thailand, India, Turkey, Afghanistan, Pakistan, Egypt, Nigeria, Colombia, and Peru.' (Fox 1975: 36)

The arguments in favour of English are intuitively commonsensical, but only in the Gramscian sense of being based on beliefs which reflect the dominant ideology (Gramsci 1971). Hegemonic ideas tend to be internalized by the dominated, even though they are not objectively in their interest. Thus it will be seen that many of the tenets adhered to in educational language planning at the end of the colonial era, though apparently 'commonsensical', were scientifically fallacious (see Chapter 7). Similarly, many of the arguments used to promote English internationally are suspect, despite being intuitively sensible (see Chapter 9). Part of the explanation for this is that the majority of those working in the ELT field tend to confine themselves, by choice and training, to linguistic, literary, or pedagogical matters. ELT is however an international activity with political, economic, military, and cultural implications and ramifications.

A huge demand has been created for English and for teachers of the language. As the director of a dynamic worldwide chain of English language schools puts it: 'Once we used to send gunboats and diplomats abroad; now we are sending English teachers'. (International House brochure, 1979). 'Africa is hungry for the English language . . . Support to the English language is and must remain an integral part of Britain's technical assistance to Anglophone Africa.' (The Director-General of the British Council, quoted in Clarke 1988: 25) 'The worldwide demand for high-quality English teaching is expanding fast.' (*British Council Annual Report*, 1989/90: 13)

The demand for English is articulated not only by partisan Anglo-Americans but also by leaders in all parts of the world. The Danish Minister of Education has declared that English has advanced from being Denmark's first foreign language to being the 'second mother tongue' of Danes,[4] a claim that many Danes would be alarmed to hear. Bernard Lott, in charge of British Council ELT operations from the mid-1960s to the mid-1970s, states that the promotion of English was unnecessary. It was more a question of saying to foreign governments 'Sorry, we can't let you have 100 teachers, we can let you have two.' (Lott, interview).[5] The same still holds true today.

A government Minister from Sri Lanka has suggested that the teaching of English throughout Asia, Africa, and the Pacific should be placed on the same level as the World Health Organization or Unesco (*English Today* 1985/4: 22). We might presumably then see the UN move on from proclaiming 'Education for all' to 'English for all'. The Minister is quoted as saying that 'for one tenth of the money they pay for "star wars" the Americans can get the whole of Asia listening to their president. English teaching is a bigger weapon in the armoury of the English-speaking peoples than star wars'. The analogy is revealing, and not so far-fetched as might at first appear. The Minister seems to be implying that if Third World peoples do not voluntarily accept American hegemony, the imperial power might have recourse to force, and that the establishment of a sister organization to WHO and Unesco could obviate the need for military might. The parallel is paradoxical, given that the USA (followed by Thatcher's Britain) left Unesco precisely because it could no longer impose its will on that organization.

The Minister's improbable suggestion was made at a high level conference on English teaching.[6] The very fact that English can be regarded as an educational and social panacea or that the teaching of English can be credited with such universal, supranational goals as those of WHO and Unesco confirms how securely English is established. It could also indicate that the language is promoted in an uncritical and partisan manner.

The notion that English is in fact an essential cornerstone of the global capitalist system needs to be examined in greater depth, but on the face of it the hypothesis is a strong one. That the interests of capitalism are global is patently clear, as a succinct policy statement from one of its leading representatives, Caspar Weinburger demonstrates:

> There is no corner of the world so remote, no nation so insignificant, that it does not represent a vital interest of the United States.
> (*Guardian Weekly*, 20 May 1984)

In a similar vein, the British government greeted the collapse of communism in Eastern Europe by allowing the Foreign Secretary to proclaim in May 1990 that Britain aims to replace Russian with English as the second language throughout Eastern Europe. Presumably British government motives in doing so are not exclusively altruistic.

The vital underlying question is what purposes English is being learnt for, what 'needs' it responds to. Joshua Fishman, in his pioneer research on the sociology of language, propagated the idea of the purportedly neutral, tool-like image of English in much of the non-English-mother-tongue world, English being described as 'ethnically and ideologically unencumbered' (Fishman 1977: 118). A decade later he argues for additional testing and refinement of the original generalization[7] and writes:

> The relative unrelatedness of English to ideological issues in much of the Third World today must not be viewed as a phenomenon that requires no further qualification. Western-ization, modernization, the spread of international youth culture, popular technology and consumerism are all ideo-logically encumbered and have ideological as well as behavi-oral and econo-technical consequences.
> (Fishman 1987: 8)

Manfred Görlach, in a review entitled 'English as a world language—the state of the art'[8], has also identified the need for research in this area (1988: 23):

> The political role of English (of a national or international type) must be defined, especially for ESL/EFL countries of the Third World, many of which are too small, or too poor, or both, to develop a national language of their own. Arguments

in favour of expanding the use of English that are based on economic and technological advantage or alleged necessity must be weighed against concern about educational and social inequality deriving from a continued use of English in official functions.

Fishman saw this dilemma earlier (1976: 49), when he asked whether English, the linguistic *eminence grise*, would continue to spread as a second language the world over, as a benevolent bonus or creeping cancer of modernity. This book cannot hope to provide an answer to this question, but will attempt to clarify some of the forces behind the spread of English as a second or foreign language, and some of the ways in which it is legitimated. It will particularly concentrate on the formative years of the ELT profession and on contexts where 'aid' is provided to education systems in foreign countries.

Professional and ethical aspects of ELT 'aid'

One characteristic of the majority of Third World countries in which English is a dominant language is that the wealth that English provides access to is very inequitably distributed. Such countries have economics which are relatively weak in the international balance of power, and the gap between them and the West has been widening in recent decades, despite aid of all kinds. One form of aid from Britain and the USA (with Canada, Australia, and New Zealand playing minor roles) is support for the promotion of English and related teacher training and curriculum development activities. English has been marketed as the language of development, modernity, and scientific and technological advance. It has also held out a promise which so far has been only marginally fulfilled.

When ELT figures in an aid context, it has been financed for specific purposes, such as the learning of English for science and technology in higher education, for supporting English as a medium of education in schools, or to permit technical training for particular developmental goals (Iredale 1986: 44). A second goal, according to the British donor, is that 'Naturally, when people learn English, for whatever purpose and by whatever method, they acquire something of the flavour of our culture, our institutions, our ways of thinking and communicating.' (ibid.) Aid thus operates at several levels, and cannot be divorced from its social context, either at the micro level of project realization or at the macro level of donor-recipient relations and the nature of the links that unite them, and the agendas, overt and covert, of the parties involved.

Aid is constantly being reviewed, by donor governments striving for greater efficiency (such as the British government's Efficiency Unit, see Clarke 1988), by the transnational funding giants (the World Bank analysis of Education in Sub-Saharan Africa, World Bank 1988), by reformists (the Brandt reports 1980 and 1983), as well as by academic critics (Hayter and Watson 1985). Some of the evidence is disturbing: almost half of the multi-billion dollar development assistance budgets is spent on financing experts (in Africa alone there are an estimated 80,000 foreign 'experts'—a larger number of expatriates than in the colonial period); their life-style contrasts grotesquely with that of the poor whose needs they are supposed to be serving; and many projects fail to meet their goals (Hancock 1989). A study of education systems in Asian and African countries concludes that if structures continue unchanged, the economy of such countries will remain shackled and 'the only political result of education is to "keep the macabre circulation of parasitical élites going"' (Hanf *et al.* 1975). It is highly relevant therefore to scrutinize aid in the form of the international promotion of English and to relate this to the structural functions served by English nationally and internationally.

There are also strong reasons for a long, hard look at what has happened in the field of ELT and language-related aid. A Ford Foundation review of aid projects in the field of language and education concluded as follows:

> If a single theme emerges from this survey, it is that the Western models that served as the basis for developmental assistance in pre-university education were in fact not adequate. At their best, at the university level, they were minimally transferable. At other levels, attempts to apply such models to developing societies often created more problems than were solved. What was missing was detailed knowledge among American and British aid agencies of how the educational systems worked in the countries they were attempting to assist and the language setting that surrounded those systems.
>
> (Fox 1975: 86)

An analysis of research issues and perspectives in language in education in Africa draws an equally bleak conclusion on the contribution of research to this field. Despite 'a vast array of urgent research questions', the research community is small, the research outcome disappointing, and even marginal. (Obura 1986: 415)

A scholar who is generally extremely sober and generous in his views also pronounces a disturbingly damning verdict on the international TESL (Teaching of English as a Second Language) community:

> The role of English in the sociolinguistic context of each English-using Third World country is not properly under-stood, or is conveniently ignored. The consequences of this attitude are that the Third World countries are slowly realizing that, given the present attitude of TESL specialists, it is difficult to expect from such specialists any theoretical insights and professional leadership in this field which would be contextually, attitudinally and pragmatically useful to the Third World countries.
> (Kachru 1986a: 101)

When speculating, in a different paper, about the reasons why ESL and EFL orthodoxies have not delivered the goods, he is more explicit about the causes of such shortcomings: 'A harsher interpretation is that our profession has not been able to shake off the earlier evangelical and rather ethnocentric approaches to its task.' (Kachru 1985: 29)

It therefore seems to be essential for those concerned with the teaching and learning of English to question the language pedagogy professionalism we have inherited. This is of course what many are doing, in their research and teaching. Here are some of the most relevant critiques:

- Widdowson (1968) contains a devastating critique of a British Council-promoted scheme for reforming ELT in part of southern India, a project which was intellectually and pedagogically unsound.
- Day looks at the history of American language policy on Pacific islands, the inadequacies of ESL programmes, and asks ' . . . are Peace Corps Volunteers who teach English merely teachers, or are they agents of linguistic, and cultural imperialism—an imperialism which may conceivably result in linguistic and cultural genocide?' (1981: 78)

- Rogers (1982) protests against the promotion of English creating false expectations among the mass of educational push-outs (a more honest and correct term than drop-outs) in the Third World, and refers to the poor cost-efficiency of English teaching and the lack of attention to the social context in which it takes place.
- Hayes (1983) writes of unused, and possibly by implication unusable, syllabi and textbooks written by expatriate 'experts'.
- Richards (1984) is sceptical of the communicative language teaching bandwaggon, and pleads for greater accountability and evaluation in the area of innovation in language teaching methods, and more rigorous scientific analysis of the issues: this is needed in view of the 'often irrelevant claims of methods promoters' (ibid.: 14), which he feels the British Council and their American counterparts have made.
- Brumfit (1985b) is concerned that the ELT professional methodologists seem to be committed to the notion that process is content, and that they ignore the social and ideological messages expressed in language learning situations. There are also criticisms of current practice in Brumfit 1986.
- Sridhar and Sridhar (1986) complain that second language acquisition researchers over-emphasize constructs derived from a monolingual setting and ignore the fact that the reality and goal of their learners is bilingualism.
- Krasnick (1986) identifies three ELT images which stigmatize learners as being deficient: they are in need of remediation ('special education'); they are treated as non-students (in need of language not content); and they need re-socializing (so that they can behave properly). ELT training focuses little on the educational and sociological fields that could equip its professionals to function more adequately.
- Prodromou (1988) is scathing about the teaching fads that have been energetically promoted in recent years, and wonders why 'a particular piece of "authentic" material may fall flat in the classroom; why the functional syllabus does not always function; why communicative methodology does not produce much communication; why Council of Europe Needs Analysis has not met the Greek learners' needs', and considers that the reason is that the teaching material, ideological messages, and pedagogy which are part of a globally marketed ELT, are culturally inappropriate.

– Pennycook (1990) pleads for a critical applied linguistics, because language teaching that refuses to explore the cultural and political aspects of language learning has more to do with assimilating learners than empowering them.

All these evaluative criticisms raise not only intellectual questions about the nature, premises, and practice of the ELT profession, but also ethical issues about the responsibility of the West for what we have contributed to the Third World.

When Edward Said, the American/Palestinian scholar, was invited to advise the English Department of a national university in one of the Gulf States, he found that the English literature being studied was anachronistic, and that English had been reduced to 'the level of a technical language almost totally stripped of expressive and aesthetic characteristics but also denuded of any critical or self-conscious dimension' (Said 1990:3).

Norms in English literature, and the functions of literature teaching will be referred to at several points in this book, as language and literature interlock in significant ways, but the main concentration will be on the language teaching profession. The title, *Linguistic Imperialism*, refers to a particular theory for analysing relations between dominant and dominated cultures, and specifically the way English language learning has been promoted.

In order to understand where the ELT profession stands now, and how we got there, we need to look at the historical roots from which it has grown. I shall be looking particularly at the structure and ideology of the ELT profession in its formative days, and at various aspects of ELT activities, in particular ELT research, training, and teaching in relation to aid. This involves asking awkward and difficult questions about the role of the English teaching profession internationally and about some of the possibly unquestioned ideological tenets of our work.

Notes

1 'Social scientists, unlike linguists, have been somewhat indifferent to language pedagogy and have hardly recognized the importance of theories and descriptions of society and culture for language teaching. Instead some educational linguists and a few language teachers have boldly moved into the social science arena.' (Stern 1983: 284)

2 I was employed by the British Council from 1964–1973, with ELT posts in Algeria, Yugoslavia, and London. Since 1973 I have taught English, Development Studies, and International Cultural Studies at Roskilde University, Denmark, where studies are multi-disciplinary and project-oriented.

3 The nature of the 'force' used is analysed in Chapter 5, which will show that the statement is compatible with a widespread wish on the part of subjects in colonies to learn English.

4 The Minister, Bertel Haarder, stated this to the journal of Danish foreign language teachers, *Sproglæreren*, spring 1990.

5 'Interview' in the text refers to the interviews conducted with the named individual in April 1986.

6 The Minister's proposal probably reflects concern about communal strife in Sri Lanka, which has since erupted into civil war, and dissatisfaction with the educational policies of earlier governments. These had reduced the role of English and encouraged education through Lankan languages.

7 A recent study of the role of English in France and attitudes to it, which specifically investigated Fishman's original claim concludes, not surprisingly, that for some French people English is 'encumbered by the ideological baggage of both the American and British realms' and that Fishman's claim is refuted (Flaitz 1988: 201).

8 Görlach sees a need for research into the forms of English in different contexts, linguistic change, attitudes to different variants of English, and contrastive study of the impact of English on different languages. He pleads for 'English as a World Language' to be investigated in relation to cross-cultural interaction, using both Western and non-Western traditions of scholarship. He would also like to see the spread of English compared with that of other languages of wider communication, such as French, Spanish, or Arabic, and their political functions. In his description of the state of the art in relation to the political role of English he has very few references, and is rather dismissive of the one study which does integrate the use and learning of English into a wider political analysis, a study of English and Creole languages in the Caribbean (Devonish 1986).

2 English, the dominant language

This chapter discusses English as a dominant language, language promotion, and opposition to the dominance of English. The historical spread of English is examined first in relation to *core English-speaking countries*. This term covers Britain and the USA, Canada, Australia, and New Zealand. All are countries in which the dominant group are native speakers of English. Indeed, the countries are often thought of as exclusively English-speaking, despite the linguistic diversity within their borders. As the ancestors of the dominant group came from Europe, such countries can be described as Europeanized societies (Mullard 1985).

I shall then discuss the role of English in *periphery-English countries*.[1] The periphery-English countries are of two types: countries which require English as an international link language (Scandinavia, Japan), and countries on which English was imposed in colonial times, and where the language has been successfully transplanted and still serves a range of intranational purposes (India, Nigeria).[2] The countries are English-peripheral in the sense that they generally attempt to follow the linguistic norms of the core English-speaking countries.

The core-periphery metaphor is inspired by the use of these terms in analyses of the relationship between the dominant rich countries and dominated poor ones.

English in core English-speaking countries

The use of one language generally implies the exclusion of others, although this is by no means logically necessary. Functional bilingualism or multilingualism at the individual and societal level is common throughout the world. However the pattern in core English-speaking countries has been one of increasing monolingualism. This is so at least in official statistics, but perhaps less so in practice. The advance of English, whether in Britain, North America, South Africa, Australia, or New Zealand has invariably been at the expense of other languages.

Although English has dominated other languages, both indigenous and immigrant in such Europeanized societies, it needs to be recalled that the relationship between the languages is never a static one.

The trend towards monolingualism has been partially checked in some parts of the Western world. For instance in Canada the supremacy of English has been successfully challenged and has given way over the past 30 years to a comprehensive French-English bilingual policy throughout the country, with special support given to French in Quebec (Bourhis 1984). In recent years some official support has also been given to the maintenance and cultivation of Canada's many 'heritage' languages, of both immigrant and indigenous minorities (Cummins and Danesi 1990; Stairs 1988).

In Wales the rapid demise of the Welsh language over the past century has been arrested and the language is now more actively used in the education system—from nursery to university level, the media, and the law courts (Lewis 1982; Williams 1990). In both Canada and Wales, defying the might of English involved a protracted political struggle, with loss of life on occasion, before the dominant group would concede language rights to the dominated group.

A struggle against the odds was necessary because the consolidation of English and the suppression or neglect of other languages was official policy in Great Britain, as in other core English-speaking countries. The policy has had even more devastating effects on indigenous languages in Scotland and Ireland than in Wales (on Celtic languages see Trudgill 1984, Price 1985, on Irish language issues see Hindley 1990; on the dominance of English in Britain, Grillo 1989). His Majesty's Inspector of Schools, Matthew Arnold (also an influential poet and thinker), saw the issue thus in 1852, in what amounts to a prescription for linguicide:

> Whatever encouragement individuals may think it desirable to give to the preservation of the Welsh language on grounds of philological or antiquarian interest, it must be the desire of a government to render its dominions, as far as possible, homogeneous, and to break down barriers to the freest intercourse between the different parts of them. Sooner or later, the difference of language between Wales and England will probably be effaced, as has happened with the difference of language between Cornwall and the rest of England.
> (quoted in Sutherland 1973: 23)

The Cornish language did in fact die out, though there may still have been some Cornish-speakers in Arnold's times, and the language has since been revived (Shield 1984). The speakers of Welsh who survived the onslaught on their language have (only recently) acquired greatly increased language rights. However, the future of all the Celtic languages in the British Isles, including Welsh, is extremely uncertain despite strenuous efforts to maintain the languages and resist the encroachment of English (Williams 1990). Adequate theoretical frameworks for analysing how to reverse language shift are emerging (Fishman 1990) in tandem with optimistic reports on the revival of threatened languages (for instance, Scottish Gaelic, MacKinnon 1990).

Such efforts on behalf of indigenous minority languages have been significantly encouraged by developments at the supranational level. Several European Parliament resolutions advocate the use of indigenous minority languages throughout education, in the media, and in dealings with public authorities (most recently the Kuijpers resolution, passed in October 1987, see the bulletin of the European Community-financed European Bureau for Lesser Used Languages, *Contact* 4/3: 1987–8, 1). The Council of Europe's proposed European Charter for Regional and Minority Languages (Resolution 192, 1988, of the Standing Conference of Local and Regional Authorities of Europe) has similar goals, and states in its preamble that it is false to regard the promotion of minority languages as representing an obstacle to national languages. Of 24 member countries of the Council of Europe, only three have had major reservations about such a policy—France, Greece, and Turkey.[3]

Monolingualism has a long pedigree. Its roots can be traced back at least to the Greek stigmatization of speakers of other languages as 'barbarian', which originally meant one who uttered meaningless sounds, a non-language. Colonial policy in Ireland involved the imposition of English and the relegation of Irish beyond the pale from the early 16th century. In the late eighteenth century, when there was talk of French as a 'universal' language because it was the language of the European aristocracy, less than half the population of France was French-speaking. Even the influence of more democratic social ideas resulting from the French Revolution was filtered through monolingualism. The ideologues of the French Revolution believed that their ideals would best be achieved by imposing a single language on all, a linguicidal policy which they then proceeded to follow (Calvet 1974: 165). This policy is still largely in force.[4]

Speakers of *immigrant minority languages* in Britain have brought greater linguistic diversity to Britain with them (Rosen and Burgess 1982), but are still fighting for language rights (*Linguistic Minorities Project* 1985). Recent expressions of official policy on the educational needs and attainments of ethnic minority groups such as the Swann Report (Swann 1985), see bilingualism as a problem rather than as a resource, and equate multicultural education with assimilation to traditional British educational values and the English language. There is widespread awareness among those professionally concerned with teaching English to linguistic minority groups that 'learning English cannot be disassociated from attitudes to ethnicity, racism, social aspirations and concepts of the nature of multicultural societies' (Brumfit 1985c). However, the policy advocated in the Swann Report does not confront the institutional racism of British schools *vis-à-vis* minorities or the cultural racism of a monolingual curriculum and of most current English as a Second Language teaching (Khan 1985; National Council for Mother Tongue Teaching 1985; Verma 1986; Usher 1989; see also Tosi 1984 and 1986). The representatives of the English-speaking dominant group seem to be unable to appreciate that linguistic and cultural diversity, bilingualism, and biculturalism are assets to the individual and society. As a result, there will continue to be discrimination against British people with mother tongues other than English.

In recent years there has been heated debate in the British media on declining standards of English, and a flurry of official language planning reports. The Kingman Report (1988) was about English language in the English mother tongue curriculum, the Cox Report (1989) about teaching English as a mother tongue in the National Curriculum (for a critique see Cameron and Bourne 1989). That current official British reports are basically assimilationist and monolingual can be seen from the fact that linguistic minorities were excluded from consideration in the Kingman report, while the ministerial directions to the Cox Committee decreed that 'The group should take account of the ethnic diversity of the school population and society at large, bearing in mind the cardinal point that English should be the first language and medium of instruction for all pupils in England' (quoted in Stubbs forthcoming). This seems to indicate that for speakers of English as a second language the new National Curriculum has the task of ensuring that English becomes a first language.

In the United States the content of the melting pot was also monolingual, though there, too, the ethnic ingredients tenaciously resisted losing their distinctiveness. In the 1960 census, 11 per cent of Americans declared that a language other than English was their mother tongue (Fishman 1972:109). Since then, there have been large numbers of Asian and Latin American immigrants. According to the 1980 census, more than 23 million Americans spoke languages other than English in their homes; there are eight million children of school age living in minority language families (King and Vallejo 1986). There is currently a major unresolved struggle between protagonists of a monolingual English-speaking USA (with a body called 'US English' lobbying for a change in the US Constitution to enshrine English alone) and those who see bilingualism as an individual right that the community should support and benefit from (see Hernández-Chávez 1988; the thematic issue of the *International Journal of the Sociology of Language*, 60, 1986, on Language Rights and the English Language Amendment; Fishman 1989b, and Adams and Brink 1990).

There is nothing new about this tension in attitudes to language in the USA.

In its early period, the US valued diversity of language and maintained the English legal custom of not regulating language officially or denying personal liberties in language. However, the late nineteenth century gave rise to the promotion of a monolingual tradition and emphasis on standard English as the mark of reason, ethics, and esthetics; the tolerance of diversity which had characterized the early national history declined sharply. An English-only, standard-English-preferred policy was institutionalized though not legalized. (Heath and Mandabach 1983:102)

The decisive agent in this socialization process was the school, with the teacher of English playing a pre-eminent role in promoting the assimilation of linguistically and culturally diverse children to Anglo norms (Hernández-Chávez 1978).

The impact on the cultures and languages of the indigenous peoples of a monolingual policy has been devastating:

Navajo children are taught in a foreign language: they are taught concepts which are foreign, they are taught values that

are foreign, they are taught lifestyles which are foreign, and they are taught by human models which are foreign. The intention behind this kind of schooling is to mold the Navajo child (through speech, action, thought) to be like members of the predominant Anglo-Saxon mainstream culture. The apparent assumption seemingly being that people of other ethnic groups cannot be human unless they speak English, and behave according to the values of a capitalistic society based on competition and achievement. The children grow up in these schools with a sense of: (1) confusion regarding the values, attitudes and behaviour taught at home. (2) Loss of self-identity and pride concerning their selfhood—their Navajo-ness. (3) Failure in classroom learning activities. (4) Loss of their own Navajo language development and loss of in-depth knowledge of their own Navajo culture.
(Pfeiffer 1975: 133)

Attitudes to bilingualism and multilingualism can change radically, as they did in Canada. The same is true of Australia, which has in recent years seen an upsurge of activity and official report-writing encouraging the retention of a bilingual and bicultural identity for the many ethnic groups represented in Australia (Clyne 1982 and 1986; the journal *Vox*). Australia has commissioned a national language policy (Lo Bianco 1987), which outlines the principles that should guide a policy for all Australian languages, the relationship between English and other languages, language services, and a description of how the goals can be achieved. How far there will be greater power-sharing between English and other languages is still an open question (Smolicz in press), but the hegemony of English is now definitely disputed.

Similar steps have been taken in New Zealand to formulate a national languages policy (Hollis 1990). This affirms the right of all New Zealanders, of whatever linguistic origins, to have access to both English and Maori. It also stresses the importance of the minority languages of immigrants and refugees, and the need to learn the languages of trading partners, increasingly from the Asian and Pacific region (ibid.). Both English and Maori have the status of official languages. There has been an upsurge in Maori-language pre-schools; government departments are gradually adding Maori to their repertoires; there is a Maori Language Commission with a mandate to 'contribute to a New Zealand society where the Maori and English languages share equal legal status, where New Zealanders are free to use either Maori or English in all public contexts; to promote and maintain the Maori language as a living language so that it is used as an everyday means of communication' (untitled planning paper, Maori Language Commission, 1988). To this end a major programme of language development and training is being implemented (for an assessment of the size of this task, see Karetu forthcoming; for comparison of language revival efforts in Ireland and New Zealand, see Benton 1986).

The central issue here is not that there is a straight choice between English and one other language. That would be to accept uncritically the monolingual Western norm which has falsely claimed that monolingualism is a necessary condition for modernization, and that a multiplicity of languages is a nuisance. The politics of language has been bedevilled by myths and binary over-simplifications in many countries, not least in India (Pattanayak 1985: 402, and 1986a: 6; see also Lenin 1951: 10). 'Those who juxtapose English against Hindi or any other Indian language and take an "either-or" position in a linear scale understand neither the sociocultural dynamics of India nor do they understand the role and function of language in society' (Pattanayak 1981: 160). English needs to be seen as one language in a multilingual framework, both internationally and within each core English-speaking country.

The English language has become immensely powerful, but it is arguable that the monolingualism of the Anglo-American establishment blinds its representatives to the realities of multilingualism in the contemporary world and gives them a limiting and false perspective. Their monolingualism has a 'major negative impact' on them (Fishman 1976: 50). Yet these are the people whose language is spreading worldwide and whose universities produce an increasing number of 'experts' on language teaching.

English in periphery-English countries

English is no longer only of concern to those who live in relatively small islands in north-west Europe or who have emigrated to North America or the antipodes. English is now entrenched worldwide, as a result of British colonialism, international interdependence, 'revolutions' in technology, transport, communications and commerce, and because English is the language of the USA, a major economic, political, and military force in the contemporary world. It is not only Britain which has gravitated towards linguistic homogeneity, but a significant portion of the entire world.

Whereas it is estimated that 400 years ago there were between five and seven million speakers of English, the number of *native* speakers of English (those in core English-speaking countries, plus a sprinkling elsewhere) now remains constant at about 315 million. The number of users of English as a *second* or *foreign* language (in periphery-English countries) is increasing dramatically: these are estimated at 300 and 100 million people, respectively (Crystal 1985: 7). Such guesstimates are inevitably based on a loose definition of proficiency, and much higher figures are sometimes quoted (up to one and a half billion users of English as a foreign language, Crystal in *Dunford Seminar Report* 1987, 1988: 102).

The conventional definition of ESL countries is countries in which English is not a native language but where it is used widely as a medium of communication in domains such as education and government. This is so in Nigeria or Singapore. The term ESL is also standard in the USA to describe programmes teaching English to people with a language other than English as their mother tongue. In EFL countries, English is not a medium of instruction or government, but is learnt at school, as is the case in France or Japan, for communicating with speakers of the language, or for reading texts in the language (definitions from Richards, Platt, and Weber 1985). There are (or should be) quite different teaching needs and strategies in ESL and EFL situations because of the differing degree of exposure to the language outside school, and the different roles for English both within the education system and in the wider community. Throughout this book, the term ELT is used to cover both types of teaching.

In fact the dividing-line between ESL and EFL fluctuates, and a strict definition may confuse social and educational issues. For instance Bangladesh would be categorized as an ESL country, but the amount of English that Bangladeshi children are exposed to may be so small that teaching should be organized as for an EFL situation. The town/country variable may also be decisive, as in Malaysia: 'For many rural Malaysians, English remains an entirely foreign language. By contrast it is very much an everyday language of the large cities' (Benson 1990: 20). In the

Nordic countries (Scandinavia and Finland), a shift is under way from EFL to ESL, and this has implications both for school teaching and for society as a whole: success or failure in English at school may be decisive for educational and career prospects, meaning that English has a social stratificational function within the country; textbooks written in English are used in virtually all university degree programmes, meaning that English is a pre-condition for higher educational qualifications; much inter-Scandinavian academic discourse, at conferences and in journals, takes place in English, meaning that English is domestically a necessary professional skill. Major Scandinavian corporations increasingly use English as the in-company language (Hollqvist 1984). Many programmes from core English-speaking countries are shown on television, with the original soundtrack. Consumers need to be able to read product descriptions and instructions in English.[5] Newspapers regularly use words borrowed from English, and even though their statistical frequency is not very high, the degree of their integration into the Scandinavian languages and the ways in which the loans are used result in a feeling that the English language is conspicuous (Chrystal 1988). Unquestionably the number of domains where English is becoming indispensable in Scandinavia is increasing constantly. In a real sense English can be regarded as a second language rather than a foreign language in the Nordic countries.

Statistics for the number of speakers of English are not in themselves particularly revealing unless we look at the functions which English serves and at the relationship between English and other languages. ESL and EFL countries have provisionally been grouped together as periphery-English countries. They are peripheral in the sense that norms for the language are regarded as flowing from the core English-speaking fountainheads. The target in language teaching is English as it is spoken in one of the core-English speaking countries. This may however be an unattainable and irrelevant target in many English-teaching situations. Some ESL periphery-English countries are in the process of establishing their own norms, for Indian English, West African English, and so on (see Wong 1982; Kachru 1986a). Each variant functions in its own multilingual ecosystem (Thumboo 1985) and has its own formal and functional characteristics.

The essential question then is the nature of the relationship between the standard English of core English-speaking countries and periphery-English variants. Do they form one language or are there now several 'Englishes', as the title of the journal, *World Englishes* unambiguously proclaims? The political, social, and pedagogical implications of any declaration of linguistic independence by periphery-English variants are considerable. Randolph Quirk has, in a succession of papers, dubbed such efforts as 'liberation linguistics' and insists on standard British English, as endorsed in the Kingman report, being the target for English learning worldwide (1989, 1990). Braj Kachru (1991) regards the issue of international standardization as 'an unprecedented challenge to language policy makers' but feels that Quirk's 'deficit linguistics' approach ignores the sociolinguistic and pragmatic realities of the huge range of contexts in which English is used as a second and foreign language, and is therefore misguided. This debate raises important issues: linguistic and pedagogic standards, language variation, the status of indigenized varieties of English, and the norms that should hold for learners of English in a variety of contexts. These issues are of central concern, as is the underlying question of *who* has the power to impose a particular norm and *why*.

There is a similar divide in the realm of literature written in English. There are writers from many parts of the periphery-English world who have refashioned the English language so as to meet their own cultural and linguistic needs. It appears that their capacity to draw on English and other local languages, and to blend their own culture with the canons of certain genres has not resulted in attempts to reassert a global standard, meaning one that conformed to British or American expectations. Significantly the title of the book celebrating the fiftieth anniversary of the British Council refers to a single language but plural literatures: *English in the world: Teaching and Learning the Language and Literatures* (Quirk and Widdowson 1985).

A good example of the need to see dominant languages in terms of power is provided by the familiar expression 'English-speaking African countries'. English is indeed an official language in the countries in which nearly 60 per cent of Africa's population live. But as in many other periphery-English countries, only a minute proportion of the population actually speak English. This aspect of the multilingual African reality is obscured by the term. The language of power (the language of the former colonial power) is referred to, and the powerless languages, even those with large numbers of speakers, are passed over in silence.

Among a small but growing number of Western-educated Africans, the trend is to use English as the language of the home. This was observed in Ghana in the early 1960s (Chinebuah 1981: 19), and has led one East African scholar to predict that 'By the year 2000 there will probably be more black people in the world who speak English as their *native tongue* than there will be British people' (Mazrui 1975: 9). The pull of English is remarkably strong in periphery-English areas, not only among the élites who benefit directly from their proficiency in English but also among the masses, who appreciate that the language provides access to power and resources, whether in the slums of Bombay, where the English-medium school is a prestige symbol (Rajyashree 1986: 46) or in Kenya, where parents have 'an acute understanding of the competitive nature of life chances' (Obura 1986: 421). In Kachru's image (1986a), those in possession of English benefit from an alchemy which transmutes into material and social gain and advantage. Not surprisingly, attitudes to the language tend to be very favourable.

Globally, what we are experiencing is that English is both *replacing* other languages, as in Mazrui's example, and *displacing* them, as is happening in Scandinavia (Fishman 1977; Skutnabb-Kangas and Phillipson 1985b and 1986a). Displacement occurs when English takes over in specific domains, whether in computers or entertainment.[6] In many former colonies there is a diglossic or triglossic situation, with the colonial language still being used in high status activities, a dominant local language (for example, Swahili) being used for less prestigious functions, and local languages used for other purposes.

When the Organization of African Unity was founded in 1963, one article in its charter stipulated that the official use of foreign languages—the former colonial languages—would be only provisionally tolerated. An OAU Inter-African Bureau of Languages was set up to 'assist and encourage the use of indigenous African languages for educational, commercial and communication purposes on a national, regional and continental level' (see Kalema 1980: 1). However, these goals have only been realized to a very small extent. The dominance of European languages is still virtually complete. With few exceptions

(Swahili and Somali are the best examples, see Scotton 1981)
African languages tend to be marginalized and lose out in the
competition with European languages. Proficiency in the latter is
essential for upward social mobility and privileged positions in
society. Just as schools were the principal instrument for
alienating indigenous minorities from their languages and
traditional cultures (as in the case of the Welsh, the American
native peoples, and the Australian aborigines, Jordan 1987a and
b, 1988), it is schools in Africa which are stifling local languages
and imposing alien tongues and values. 'The foreign colonial
languages are more favoured now than they were before
independence', writes the director of the Inter-African Bureau of
Languages (Mateene 1980: vii). 'The use of vernaculars in
education has been gradually phased out' (Bokamba and Tlou
1980: 49). There has been a gradual shift 'in the direction of
europeanisation of the media of instruction with a concomitant
neglect of the teaching of African languages' (ibid.: 49). In 1986
the OAU's Inter-African Bureau of Languages was disbanded,
ostensibly for financial reasons, but doubtless the bureau's
championing of indigenous languages, following the spirit and
the letter of the OAU Charter, was a thorn in the flesh of
political leaders whose destiny is viscerally linked to proficiency
in the colonial languages.

The trend is not exclusively away from indigenous languages.
For instance, a considerable amount of experimental work in
introducing African languages in francophone Africa has been
undertaken (see Treffgarne 1986 for a review), and in Kenya
there are indications of an increased emphasis on Swahili and
less on English (Njoroge 1986: 349), although many factors
impede this development (Obura 1986). In Tanzania, English is
still favoured in secondary and higher education, despite the fact
that Swahili is used for most social and official purposes
(Rubagumya 1990). The general picture is one of massive
dominance of the European languages in formal domains.

The relationship between the learning of languages in educational establishments and the use of languages for a range of
societal purposes is not a simple one, but there is no doubt that
education is of paramount importance in transmitting values
and modes of thought from one generation to the next. English
has retained its privileged position in the educational process in
Asia as well as Africa.

Singapore has four official languages, Chinese, Tamil, Malay, and English, but virtually all children are educated through the medium of English and are expected to study their mother tongue, the language of their ethnic affiliation, as a second language (Kuo and Jernudd 1988: 13–14). University education is now no longer offered in Chinese and is only available through the medium of English. In fact, although Malay is the sole national language, the medium of education at the National University of Singapore is English. It is government policy to establish English as the language of Singapore's public, industrial, and modern business sectors, which means that people in their thirties feel handicapped by their limited English, as compared with those who have been at school more recently (ibid.: 3). English is being promoted as a supra-ethnic language of national integration, and it is claimed that this accounts for the lack of inter-ethnic friction in Singapore. Officially there is a policy of pragmatic multilingualism, with a commitment to maintaining Malay and promoting Mandarin Chinese, but effectively English appears to have been established as the language of power.

In Hong Kong there is an increasing realization, among some analysts, that language policy to date has not been based on the realities of language use in the colony and that the products of an English-dominated education system emerge as 'cultural eunuchs . . . with insufficient command or literacy in either English or Chinese' (Lord and T'sou 1985: 17). These writers feel that Hong Kong is sitting on a 'language bomb', which can only be defused by the adoption of a bilingual education policy which strengthens the teaching of Chinese and delays the introduction of English as a medium of instruction in secondary schools until as late as possible (ibid.: 22).

Throughout India, at the secondary school stage a student has to learn at least three languages, one of which is English (Annamalai 1988: 9). The medium of instruction in higher education is generally English, despite efforts to reduce its importance. The quality of tertiary education in the humanities in India is sharply criticized (Kachru 1975 and Pattanayak 1981), among other things for excessive adherence to the academic tradition inherited from the colonizers. English functions as a Pan-Indian language, particularly among élite groups, despite the impressive spread of Hindi since independence in many parts of the country and in spite of the consolidation of the dominant languages in each state (Khubchandani 1983). English is also the mother tongue of the relatively small group of Anglo-Indians, who, like all Indians, are bilingual or often multilingual (Bayer 1986).

The privileged position of English is in part perpetuated by the dominance of English in the media. Although two or three per cent of the population is literate in English and 35 per cent literate in Indian languages (Kelly and Altbach 1978: 37), 42 per cent of the books published in India in 1982 were in English—a total of about 7,000 titles (Annamalai 1988: 13). India is the third largest publisher of books in English after the USA and Britain. According to Indian government figures for the late 1970s, 20 per cent of the registered newspapers were written in English, accounting for 22 per cent of circulation, compared with 23.8 per cent for Hindi (Kachru 1983a: 71). There has since been a decline in the proportion of English language newspapers, primarily because of developments in computer technology, which has made it possible to print newspapers cheaply in Indian languages. However, the English language press is still highly influential, and reaches the more affluent sectors of the population, as indicated by a 53 per cent share of advertising revenue, as compared with 15 per cent for Hindi newspapers.

The importance of English in such African and Asian periphery-English countries is twofold. English has a dominant role *internally*, occupying space that other languages could possibly fill. English is also the key *external* link, in politics, commerce, science, technology, military alliances, entertainment, and tourism. The relationship between English and other languages is an unequal one, and this has important consequences in almost all spheres of life.

Prior to 1949, English also had a privileged role internally in China, as it was the medium of education at universities run by British and American missionaries in Beijing and Shanghai (Pride and Ru-Shan 1988: 42). Since China opened up to the West in the late 1970s, English has been extensively studied—an estimated 50 million are currently learning English (ibid.: 44). At tertiary level institutions, extensive use of English is encouraged (ibid.: 51). Academic apologists for the spread of English estimate that the time has come when the use of English should be 'extended from almost exclusively international communication to communication among the Chinese people themselves . . . a foundation can be laid for societal bilingualism in Chinese and English' (ibid.: 67–8). This proposal is put forward in the pages of a scientific journal, and reveals applied linguists actively involved in marketing English, in attempting to entrench English as a second language in China, ostensibly in order to facilitate the learning of the language.

Language promotion

The present distribution throughout the world of the major international languages—Arabic, Chinese, English, French, Russian, and Spanish is evidence of conquest and occupation, followed by adoption of the invader's language because of the benefits that accrue to speakers of the language when the dominant language has been imposed. Language spread invariably occurs in conjunction with forces such as religion or trade, which are seen by some as extra-linguistic, but the significance of language as a tool for unification has long been recognized.

In the very year that Columbus set off for another continent—1492—Queen Isabella of Spain was presented with a plan for establishing Castilian as 'a tool for conquest abroad and a weapon to suppress untutored speech at home' (quoted in Illich 1981: 35). For its author, Nebrija, 'Language has always been the consort of empire, and forever shall remain its mate' (ibid.: 34). In order to counteract the centripetal force of the many vernaculars of Spain, the queen's tongue was to be codified into the first grammar of a modern European language and then taught as a standard in an education system. Illich regards this event as momentous for the creation of the modern state: 'Here the first modern language expert advises the Crown on the way to make, out of a people's speech and lives, tools that befit the state and its pursuits' (ibid.: 43). (There are affinities between Nebrija's arguments for the use of Castilian as a domestic and international norm and Quirk's endorsement of the Kingman Report as a norm for Britain and worldwide.) There is some controversy as to how far Nebrija's project was ever implemented, in Spain itself, except under the extreme monolingual policy of the fascist period, or in the new world (Bierbach 1989).

It would doubtless be fascinating to undertake a comparative study of the distinctive characteristics of empires, and the role played by language in their establishment and maintenance from ancient to modern times. It would also be of more than historical interest to study the promotion of the Russian language throughout the Soviet Union and Eastern Europe, and the

relationship of Russian to other languages. Such studies unfortunately lie outside the scope of this book.[7] British colonial
language policy will be contrasted with the policy of the major
competing imperialist power, France, and an assessment of their
significance for the contemporary world will be made. Initially
we shall consider some of the ways in which Western powers
promote their languages. A few examples will serve to illustrate
how they have jostled for linguistic and political influence.

Many of the missionaries who descended on Africa in the
nineteenth century were strongly nationalistic as well as being
interested in the souls of the natives. For instance, the naval
officer in charge of French Gabon in 1882 reported to the French
Foreign Ministry that American missionaries were unwelcome
because they were incapable of teaching in French; and the
apostolic mission in the French Congo reported in 1890 that to
do their humanitarian work properly required preventing the
English, Germans, and Belgians from extending their influence in
the area (Moussirou-Mouyama 1985: 79). Promotion of religon,
language, and national economic and political interests have
often gone hand in hand, even when the exertions of the
missionaries revolved around the triad of the church, the
dispensary, and the school.

The same pattern is largely true in the contemporary world.
The missionary activity of the Summer Institute of Linguistics
(SIL) has been severely criticized in several Latin American
countries, because of suspicion that they are paving the way for
American commercial interests, and failing to meet the needs of
the indigenous groups they are ostensibly helping via a programme of alphabetization and conversion (Hvalkof and Aaby
1981; Calvet 1987; Patthey 1989; the German journal *Pogrom*
1988/144). Even if the SIL is nominally independent and does
not have formalized links with the CIA, it is certain that the USA
is held up as the ideal in their work, which involves conditioning
indigenous people for participation in a 'modern' world. The
language teaching programmes are transitional, literacy in the
mother tongue being merely a stepping-stone on the path
towards incorporation into mainstream society and literacy in
the official language of the state.

The other dominant language, French, was unchallenged as
the international language of diplomacy until the peace talks at
the conclusion of the 1914–1918 war, when parity between
English and French was agreed. The fact that the two languages

were accorded equal validity at the peace conferences and that the Treaty of Versailles was drawn up in both French and English led to these two languages becoming the official languages of the League of Nations and of the Permanent Court of International Justice (Lieberson 1982: 42). The French were adamantly opposed to the upgrading of English, but the presence of the Americans at the peace conferences was decisive. The French were well aware that the recognition of equal status for English marked the end of the era of French linguistic pre-eminence.

French overseas language promotion has a long history. The *Alliance Française pour la propagation de la langue française dans les colonies et à l'étranger* was established in 1883. In view of the rapid expansion of English in the post-World War II period, the French stepped up efforts to strengthen French internationally by the creation of appropriate bodies such as the Haut Comité pour la Défense et l'Expansion de la Langue Française (1966) and the promotion and encouragement of *francophonie*. The French still devote a substantial part of their overseas representation budget to cultural and linguistic affairs, and see a need to step up efforts along a broad front (particularly in education systems, the media, technical and scientific collaboration—see Haut Conseil de la Francophonie 1986; Coste 1984). The French are also concerned at the diminished use of French in international organizations and are attempting to reverse this trend. In point of fact, there are now more speakers of French as a first and second language than at any time in the past (Calvet 1987: 263), from which one can conclude that the French are relatively successful in promoting their language abroad—except when this is compared with the advance of English. For a comparative study of competition between English and French globally see Wardhaugh 1987 (but for a critical analysis see Chapter 4 below).

The Germans are also anxious for German not to lose ground to other languages, and therefore campaign, with some measure of success, for German to have equal status with the more visible international languages in newly established international organizations, for instance the Conference on Confidence-building Measures and Disarmament in Europe, and the Centre for Medium-range Weather Forecasts (Bericht 1985: 16). It is German government policy to strengthen the position of German as a school subject around the world because it is recognized that space on a school timetable indicates respect for the cultural, commercial, and political potential of the country where the language is spoken (ibid.: 7). The same argument holds for English and French as foreign languages, but as German is slightly in recession (ibid.: 6), a more deliberate policy needs to be articulated. The government report referred to contains an extensive rationale for language promotion as a tool of diplomacy. There is nothing new about such strategies. Nazi Germany resented the intrusion of English into areas such as Scandinavia, where German used to be the first foreign language (Thierfelder 1940: 14).

Political leaders are dismayed at seeing their languages being displaced or underused, whether in intranational or international settings. In European Community (EC) institutions, equal rights are nominally accorded to the official languages of all its member countries. French was *de facto* the dominant language until 1972, when Denmark, Great Britain, and Ireland joined the EC. Now the primary working languages are French and English. This has serious implications for the languages of the smaller powers and their influence. Germany felt obliged in September 1984 to insist that German has not only the right to equal use but that it should in fact be so used (Bericht 1985: 17). Judging by an editorial in *The Guardian*, entitled 'Just stick to English' (29 June 1986), the British are convinced that negotiating in their mother tongue gives them an advantage and hope that they will be able to continue to compete on (unequal) terms that favour English.

Recent attempts to ensure that all western European children learn two foreign languages at school need to be seen in the light of European concern at the dominance of English. It is hoped that if continental children learn at least one foreign language in addition to English, this will strengthen linguistic and cultural links between Europeans of different nations. The British refused to agree to this plan in May 1989. This indicates that even when language promotion has been taken on board by a supranational body, in this case the European Community with its 'Lingua' programme (there is an equivalent programme promoting higher education mobility, 'Erasmus'), it is national interests, and the promotion of official national languages, which are prime motive sources for the programmes.

The British were not galvanized into setting up a special agency for the promotion of English outside the British empire until they needed to counteract cultural propaganda on the part of Nazi Germany and Fascist Italy, who were particularly active in the Middle East, Latin America, and south-east Europe. The British Council was established in 1934 to serve this purpose (see Chapter 6 below). The *Annual Reports* of the British Council refer to 'competition' in winning friends abroad: for instance the Chairman stresses in the 1982–83 report that Britain's 'competitors' spend far more money than the British on cultural diplomacy.

Britain, the United States, France, Germany, and, on a smaller scale, many other countries promote their languages by similar means, among them the following: training and research, for natives and non-natives, in the 'mother country'; scholarships for longer or shorter periods, courses, specialist visits; the production and promotion of textbooks, audiovisual materials, etc; library services and gifts of books; the supply of teachers overseas and experts in curriculum development, advisory work, and in-service training; and cultural manifestations.

There are therefore essential similarities in the way that western nations promote the continued use of their languages abroad, both in education and in society at large. A study of the promotion of English will therefore in many ways reveal processes which apply to most languages which are cultivated as an international asset.

Opposition to the dominance of English

To the thesis of the increased dominance of English needs to be added the antithesis of opposition to the advance of English. Opposition has come from many parts. Those protesting include colonized people, European parliamentarians, political enemies of core-English nations, guardians of the purity of languages that English intrudes on, and intellectuals from core and periphery-English countries. What the protesters have in common is a recognition of evidence of linguistic imperialism and dominance, and a desire to combat it. The following brief examples provide an indication of some of the sources and types of protest:

- leaders of oppressed groups like Gandhi (1927), who protested against the alienation induced by English in India, the intoxication, denationalization, and mental slavery which the language brought with it, in public and private life. He also held English responsible for distorting education, where

because of the time spent learning English the standard reached in other subjects was 'pitifully inadequate';
- theoretical and empirical work on the ideology of colonizers and on the colonized consciousness of Third World subjects, in particular the role of language in causing colonized people to internalize the norms of the colonizers, which leads to cultural deracination (Fanon 1952 and 1961). This work has been of central importance in the development of racism studies (Mullard 1985; Gilroy 1987);
- analysis of the forms and psychology of contemporary imperialism, for instance the work of Ngũgĩ wa Thiong'o, who, in a series of fictional and philosophical writings, analyses neocolonialism in Kenya, a typical periphery-English country, and shows how English serves to uphold the domination of a small élite and of the foreign interests that they are allied with (Ngũgĩ 1981, 1982, 1983, 1985, and 1986);
- denunciations of cultural imperialism, for instance a Nazi critique of the British Council, which identified the advance of English with the destruction of western civilization (Thierfelder 1940), and a recent official French study which sees the worldwide extension of English in almost identical terms, as the imposition of a linguistic uniformity which is intellectually and spiritually cramping and a threat to cultural and creative values (Haut Conseil de la Francophonie 1986: 341);
- anti-imperialist studies, such as Soviet analyses of English as the language of world capitalism and world domination (references in Goodman 1968);
- political measures, for instance initiatives taken as a result of the concern of some European parliamentarians that the preponderance of English in economic life, and science and technology represents a threat to the languages and cultures of the European Community, and the concepts and modes of thought embodied in these (*European Parliament Working Document* 1–83/84/B: 27). Equivalent concerns have influenced the policy of Quebec and also of Mexico, a country which is, as one of its Presidents said, 'so far from God and so close to the USA'.[8]

The continued advance of English involves the suppression (displacement and replacement) of other languages and the defeat of competing imperialist languages. A full understanding of the mechanisms of the spread of English cannot be undertaken without considering thesis and antithesis, and the legitimacy of the arguments of both those who promote English and those who protest against it.

Notes

1 For an attempt at a taxonomy of English-using societies, with substantial descriptive coverage, see Moag 1982.
2 The core English-speaking countries correspond to Kachru's 'inner' circle of English users, the periphery-English countries to his 'expanding' and 'outer' circles (Kachru 1985: 12).
3 Turkey operates a blatantly linguicidal policy, enshrined in the constitution and other legislation, against its citizens of Kurdish origin. See Skutnabb-Kangas and Phillipson 1990, a report prepared for Kurdish refugee organizations for submission to Unesco in connection with 1990—UN International Literacy Year. See also Skutnabb-Kangas and Bucak (forthcoming).
4 On French language policy, including the ideology of the French language as a defining feature of citizenship, see the contributions to Giordan (1992).
5 The European Parliament has passed a resolution designed to ensure that consumers are provided with publicity and trade documentation in their national language (*European Parliament Working Documents* 1980–1981, document 1–514/ 81). The preamble rails against a 'patois-jargon' which is supposed to be English but has no relation to Anglo-Saxon. For discussion of the relationship between national legislation and EEC Directives on product labelling see de Witte 1991.
6 For a study of the spread of English as the international language of medicine, and its use in domestic Japanese contexts, see Maher 1986.
7 Useful starting-points for such a study would be Achard 1986; Anderson 1983; Calvet 1974; Fishman 1989a; Lowenberg 1988. See also the references in Chapter 5. On Soviet language policies see Bromley and Kozlov 1981; Lewis 1982; Krag 1983; Phillipson, Skutnabb-Kangas, and Africa 1985; Guboglo 1986a; Viikberg 1990; Rannut (forthcoming).
8 I am grateful to Rainer Enrique Hamel for this sample of Mexican political humour.

3 Linguistic imperialism: theoretical foundations

A cautionary word on terminology

Many of the basic terms used in analyses of language and imperialism are ideologically loaded. They reflect a European way of conceptualizing the issues, and tend to reinforce eurocentric myths and stereotypes. It is therefore imperative to clarify a few central terms before proceeding to the theoretical analysis and historical narrative.

Many eurocentric concepts conform to the pattern of how racism is affirmed, namely by means of 1) self-exaltation on the part of the dominant group which creates an idealistic image of itself, 2) the devaluation of the dominated group, and the suppression and stagnation of its culture, institutions, life-styles and ideas, and 3) systematic rationalization of the relationships between both groups, always favourable to the dominant group (Preiswerk 1980).

Two of the most central labels in colonialist cultural mythology are *tribe* and *dialect*. They both express the way the dominant group differentiates itself from and stigmatizes the dominated group. They therefore form part of an essentially racist ideology. The rule is that *we* are a nation with a language whereas *they* are tribes with dialects. This has applied irrespective of the numbers involved. It is assumed to apply to communities which by Europeans are perceived as being trapped in 'primarily local self-concepts, concerns and integrative bonds' whereas 'nations' have got beyond this (Fishman 1989: 106). A comment by a Ugandan political scientist stresses the eurocentric nature of the terms:

> One might further ask what a tribe is. There was a time when the word possessed scientific content, when it characterized social formations that did not possess a state structure—the communal, classless societies, as, for example, the Germanic tribes. Today, however, every single ethnic group in Africa is referred to as a tribe regardless of the nature of its social

development. What is it that makes two million Norwegians[1] a people and just as many Baganda a tribe? A few hundred thousand Icelanders a people and fourteen million Hausa-Fulanis a tribe? There is only one explanation: racism.
(Mamdani 1976: 3)

Calvet makes a similar point in his study of language and colonialism, in which he concludes that traditionally linguistics has failed to define rigorously enough such concepts as language and dialect in relation to social power. For him 'a dialect is never anything other than a defeated language, and a language is a dialect which has succeeded politically' (Calvet 1974: 54). In colonial discourse all African languages were classified as dialects or *patois* (Calvet 1974: 51 and 1979: 127). Calvet refuses to use the binary opposition *language* and *dialect*, because colonial discourse abused the terms and because his analysis requires terms which express the power relationship between competing languages. He therefore refers to the *dominant language* and *dominated languages* (Calvet 1974: 54 and 1987). This usage will generally be followed throughout this book, even though the terms are not exact parallels to language and dialect.

In some circumstances *mother tongue* may be preferred, for which the defining criteria are origin, function, competence, self-identification, and identification by others (Skutnabb-Kangas 1984a), and the assumption is that the individual can have more than one mother tongue. The term itself is not unambiguous, as a 'mother' tongue may be the language of the biological mother or father, or a local vehicular language (Calvet 1987: Chapter 6). (For a study of the theoretical and sociopolitical construction of the concept 'mother tongue' see Skutnabb-Kangas and Phillipson 1989.)

The mother tongue/language/dialect concepts are not simple to operate, and criteria adopted in one context may be less relevant in another. In the Nigerian Rivers Readers Project it was decided that 'the single most determining factor in determining what is to be a language from the point of view of the project is the expressed feeling of a group of people that it constitutes a distinct and internally coherent linguistic community, although the acceptable internal coherence differs widely from one area to another' (Williamson 1972: 2). This criterion has the virtue of focusing on the self-identification of the people in question.

Concepts can be revitalized and redefined. In Canada the

indigenous people refer to themselves as the First Nations (Longboat 1984, quoted in Jordan 1988). The indigenous North Americans have broken with the eurocentric label 'Red Indians', with its racist associations, and now call themselves 'native American peoples'. This term destigmatizes 'native',[2] much as 'black' is now a positive ascription. If the label 'tribe' is to be retained, it needs to be purged of the myths and overtones it evokes. Kashoki (1982) criticizes much western research for regarding the tribe as a static monolingual group, and quotes evidence from a number of sociolinguistic surveys in several African countries which shows that the norm in Africa is for individuals and communities, urban and rural, to be bilingual or multilingual. He concludes that 'the present conception of African languages as essentially tribal tools of communication might have little basis in fact' (ibid.: 163). It seems unlikely however at present that the word 'tribe' can be stripped of its colonialist ideological load.[3]

Vernacular is another loaded term. The word comes from an Indo-Germanic root meaning 'rootedness' and 'abode'. As a Latin word it referred to whatever was homebred, homegrown, or homemade, as opposed to what was obtained in formal exchange. Varro used this distinction in classifying language: vernacular language is made up of the words and patterns grown on the speaker's own ground, as opposed to what is grown elsewhere and then transported (Illich 1981: 57). 'Vernacular' is now generally used, both in its technical sense and in popular speech, to mean a localized nonstandard or substandard language in contrast to a literary, cultured, or foreign language (Webster's *Third New International Dictionary*). The term therefore stigmatizes certain languages and holds others up as the norm. At the Unesco conference on African Languages and English in Education, Jos, Nigeria, 1953, participants were unable to agree on a definition of a vernacular and used the label 'African languages' (Tiffen 1968: 104). The Unesco monograph on 'The use of vernacular languages in education' defines a vernacular language as 'a language which is the mother tongue of a group which is socially or politically dominated by another group speaking a different language. We do not consider the language of a minority in one country as a vernacular if it is an official language in another country' (Unesco 1953: 46).

The Unesco report also has useful definitions of two terms which are often confused. A *national language* is 'the language of a political, social, and cultural entity', and an *official language* is 'a language used in the business of government—legislative, executive, and judicial' (ibid.: 46). It follows that the same language or languages may serve either or both these purposes. The terms are widely but inconsistently used, in part because of competing and ambiguous presuppositions. 'While the designation *national* tends to stand for past, present, or hoped for sociocultural authenticity in the ethnic realm (nationality being a broader level of integration growing out of coalescences between earlier and more localized ethnicities) the designation *official* tends to be associated primarily with current political-operational needs . . . The term national language . . . designates that language (or those languages) whose use is viewed as furthering sociocultural integration at the nationwide (hence 'national') level' (Fishman 1972: 215). Mateene has pointed out (1985b: 18) how problematic these terms are, and the reality behind them, when African linguistic resources are neglected: ' . . . in Africa very few national languages are official languages, and the usual practice of the majority of our states is to honour the foreign European languages with the exclusive status of official languages'. The result is that the linguistic heritage of the nation is undervalued and marginalized.

The term *lingua franca* is also an ambivalent one, where the historical development of the term is revealing. The term is now frequently applied to dominant international languages which happen to be the former colonial languages—for instance 'English as the lingua franca of international scientific contact'. In colonial times, by contrast, English and French were placed at the apex of a linguistic hierarchy and the vernaculars at the bottom, while lingua franca was restricted to dominant African languages. Thus French was not considered a lingua franca in the Belgian Congo, and also ceased being designated as a 'vehicular language' when four local languages emerged as the key languages of interethnic communication, education, and labour relations. They ultimately radiated as mother tongues in this multilingual community (see Fabian's detailed study of the appropriation of Swahili in the Belgian Congo 1880–1938, Fabian 1986). In the Report on the Conference on the Teaching of English as a Second Language, held at Makerere, Uganda, in 1961, a lingua franca is defined, for the purposes of the report, as 'any non-English language which is widely used, or taught in schools for use, between nationals of the same country, but which is not the mother tongue of all' (*Makerere Report* 1961: 5). The restriction of lingua franca to country-internal uses is bizarre, but the placing of English in a category of its own, superior to all other languages which are merely lingua francas or vernaculars, is a clear example of colonialist discourse, being used here as the neo-colonialist order was ushered in.

A contemporary dictionary definition is as follows: a lingua franca is 'a language that is used for communication between different groups of people, each speaking a different language. The lingua franca could be an internationally used language of communication (e.g. English), it could be the native language of one of the groups, or it could be a language which is not spoken natively by any of the groups but has a simplified sentence structure and vocabulary and is often a mixture of two or more languages' (Richards, Platt, and Weber 1985).

The pendulum has now swung the other way, and the tendency is to promote English as the *only* lingua franca which can serve modern purposes. This discourse also puts English into a class of its own. This reinforces the dominant ideology, which presupposes that English is the most eligible language for virtually all significant purposes. On the other hand, usage is not entirely consistent: there is a tendency in academic discourse to label European languages as 'international' and non-European ones as lingua francas (Calvet 1987).

There is also a fundamental problem with terminology dealing with the social phenomena under investigation. The label *underdeveloped* evolved as a euphemistic reformulation of the colonialist epithets *backward* and *primitive*. 'Underdeveloped' was still an ethnocentric term, as it was premised on the belief that other cultures should follow along a Darwinian line towards the technical heights of western 'civilization'. In like fashion, the liberal neologisms *developing* and *emergent*, even though they appear to be more positive terms, are ethnocentric because they hold up ourselves as the norm. They are implicitly racist in that they assume that the countries to which the labels are applied have lived in darkness and lack any past worth knowing about. However, 'underdeveloped' can also be used in an active sense as a term to refer to the colonial process of subjugating the economies of colonized countries to European interests. It is here a scientific term for describing a particular historical phenomenon, namely *underdevelopment* (Frank 1967; Rodney 1972). This term specifies the active agents of underdevelopment, namely colonial and post-colonial economic, political, and ideological interests. Colonized societies had their economies actively underdeveloped in order to provide the raw materials and labour necessary for the 'development' of western economies. In the present world, the western powers are still able to maintain their supplies of food and raw materials, and the gap between them and underdeveloped countries (the North-South divide) has progressively increased. It is in this sense that I shall use the term 'underdeveloped'.

The awareness generated by using the word in this way naturally makes one suspicious of the apparently innocuous term *development*. In non-technical language it has a purely positive ring to it. In the study of the post-colonial world, development, however, refers to a particular vision of economic and technical advance. It generally embraces all aspects of society, implying social and cultural as well as economic and technical change. At times it refers to the abolition of poverty, the progressive equalization of living standards, and a process of national and international integration (Open University 1983). The term is a misnomer in that it is now an economic fact that the expectations created by the development message have not been fulfilled for the so-called 'developing' countries (see Brandt 1980, 1983). Development is therefore in a symbiotic relationship to underdevelopment, and the term needs to be understood accordingly. A further critique of 'development' is the feminist analysis of it as implying a patriarchal notion of goals, which exclude most of the ideals embodied in a 'feminine principle' (French 1986).

A similar problem arises with the analogous term *modernization*. 'Modernization' is used as a technical term to describe the 'development' process, the transition from traditional to so-called modern principles of economic, political, and social organization. The traditionalism-modernity dichotomy is a continuum with behavioural, attitudinal, and valuational elements. Modernization implies westernization in the sense of socio-cultural and politico-economic developments which were initially set in motion and have been most continuously developed in western nations (Fishman 1972: 216). The term is therefore based on western experience and ideology (for a critique, see Leys 1982).

A slightly different terminological problem arises with the term *Third World*, a concept which assumes some degree of homogeneity among an immensely varied group of nations. The term 'Third World' originally arose as a metaphor for countries which were not part of the rich capitalist world or the Communist world, and which hoped to improve their lot by finding an unaligned 'third way'. The term was first used in 1952 by a French demographer, Alfred Sanuy (Worsley 1990: 83). Economists now classify groups of countries as 'newly industrializing', 'oil-producing', 'low income' and 'middle income' countries, which underscores the need for differentiation. Unesco classifies countries according to the extent of educational provision rather than gross national product. The assessment of relative economic prosperity is a complex operation, relating as it does to indebtedness, the distribution of wealth within the country, the traditional non-market economy, and the role of transnational corporations, quite apart from social indicators. Any of the following six characteristics may be involved in the classification of a country as belonging to the Third World: non-aligned, non-industrial, ex-colonial, poor, populist, and peripheral/marginal/dependent (Open University 1983). A further characteristic is that they are exporters of labour to North countries, both of qualified labour (the 'brain drain') and unqualified (the immigrant proletariat). The optimism of the 1950s has faded, as no easy third way solutions have been found, so it is more appropriate for those countries which find themselves in the lower section of the North-South divide to be called 'underdeveloped'. Of course, when this blanket term is used, the considerable diversity among such countries needs to be borne in mind.

The same need for terminological clarification arises with *imperialism*. Ambiguity can arise from uncertainty as to whether the term is being used in a technical sense, most often in relation to an economic system, or in a more general political sense. This ambiguity can be traced back to the nineteenth century, when imperialism embraced both an economic order and wider 'civilizing' goals. Hobson's classic study of imperialism (1902) is divided into two parts, one on the economics and one on the politics of imperialism.

The imperialist powers ascribed to themselves a missionary role which was based on explicitly racist premises. This ideology is encapsulated in Earl Grey's remarks in 1899:

> Probably everyone would agree that an Englishman would be right in considering his way of looking at the world and at life better than that of the Maori or the Hottentot, and no one will

object in the abstract to England doing her best to impose her
better and higher view on these savages . . . Can there be any
doubt that the white man must, and will, impose his superior
civilization on the coloured races?
(Quoted in Hobson 1902: 158)

Part of that 'civilization' was, needless to say, language.

Raymond Williams unravels some of the competing meanings
of imperialism:

If imperialism, as normally defined in late 19th century
England, is primarily a political system in which colonies are
governed from an imperial centre, for economic but also for
other reasons held to be important, then the subsequent grant
of independence or self-government to these colonies can be
described, as indeed it widely has been, as 'the end of
imperialism'. On the other hand, if imperialism is understood
primarily as an economic system of external investment and
the penetration and control of markets and sources of raw
materials, political changes in the status of colonies or former
colonies will not greatly affect description of the continuing
economic system as imperialist. In current political argument
the ambiguity is often confusing. This is especially the case
with 'American imperialism', where the primarily political
reference is less relevant, especially if it carries the 19th
century sense of direct government from an imperial centre,
but where the primarily economic reference, with implications
of consequent indirect or manipulated political and military
control, is still exact. Neo-imperialism and especially neo-
colonialism have been widely used, from the middle of the
20th century, to describe this latter type of imperialism.
(Williams 1976: 159)

Lenin is a key theorist of imperialism, building on earlier work
by Kautsky and Hobson, whom he quotes, largely with
approval. In *Imperialism, the Highest Stage of Capitalism* he
wrote: 'If it were necessary to give the briefest possible definition
of imperialism we should have to say that imperialism is the
monopoly stage of capitalism' (Lenin 1973: 49, written in
1916). His theory and empirical documentation are primarily
economic. An essential feature of imperialism is rivalry between
great powers, a competition that culminated in the First World
War. Lenin wrote in 1915 that the Europeans were fighting
about colonial power: 'they are fighting a war for the purpose of

retaining the colonies they have grabbed and robbed. . . . Britain is grabbing at Germany's colonies' (ibid.: 39). (Germany's colonies were indeed confiscated.)

Though much analysis of imperialism has been primarily economic, later versions of imperialism theory also encompass the political, social, and ideological dimensions of exploitation, and integrate all these strands into a coherent whole. The theories attempt to account for the structure which perpetuates inequality in the world.

Imperialism theory will be expounded more fully later. Prior to that, a cautionary note is needed on the implications of using a label such as 'imperialism' as a technical term. It follows from what has already been said about imperialism that individuals with possibly the most altruistic motives for their work may nevertheless function in an imperialist structure. This might for instance apply to anyone concerned with educational aid ('aid', 'educated', and many additional western concepts need to be used with critical caution). That the individuals in question would be disconcerted at being classified as cultural or linguistic imperialists is to be expected. Whereas for most of this century many Europeans were proud to be imperialists, confidently participating in the radiation of their culture, most would resent being accused of imperialism now—even if they represent a dominant culture and their role is to disseminate it. There is likely to be a gut reaction against an accusation of involvement in any form of imperialism, linguistic or otherwise. This is because there is an element of the unethical and morally reprehensible attached to the term, as there is with the words 'racism' and 'sexism'. In order for analysis of the issue to go beyond the level of individual perceptions, roles, and self-image, it is essential to dig down to the underlying structures which support (or counteract) individual efforts. This highlights the need for the elaboration of an adequate theory for this purpose, preferably one which also elucidates how individual actors can influence the structure so as to change it.

A working definition of English linguistic imperialism

I shall now suggest a working definition of English linguistic imperialism and relate it to imperialism as a broad theory enabling us to understand exploitation. We live in a world characterized by inequality—of gender, nationality, race, class, income, and language. To trace and understand the linkages between English linguistic imperialism and inequality in the political and economic spheres will require us to look at the rhetoric and legitimation of ELT (for instance, at protestations that it is a 'neutral', 'non-political' activity) and relate what ELT claims to be doing to its structural functions.

A working definition of *English linguistic imperialism* is that *the dominance of English is asserted and maintained by the establishment and continuous reconstitution of structural and cultural inequalities between English and other languages.* Here *structural* refers broadly to material properties (for example, institutions, financial allocations) and *cultural* to immaterial or ideological properties (for example, attitudes, pedagogic principles). English linguistic imperialism is one example of *linguicism*, which is defined as 'ideologies, structures, and practices which are used to legitimate, effectuate, and reproduce an unequal division of power and resources (both material and immaterial) between groups which are defined on the basis of language' (the definition is an elaboration of variants evolved over several years, see Skutnabb-Kangas 1988, first published in Phillipson and Skutnabb-Kangas 1986; Phillipson 1988). English lingusitic imperialism is seen as a sub-type of linguicism.

The structural and cultural inequalities ensure the continued allocation of more material resources to English than to other languages and benefit those who are proficient in English. Linguicism occurs, for instance, if there is a policy of supporting several languages, but if priority is given in teacher training, curriculum development, and school timetables to one language. This was the familiar pattern in core English-speaking countries, and one which was exported to the periphery. One forum in which the legitimation of this linguicism takes place is in political discourse on language issues. Another forum in which linguicism is legitimated is in language pedagogy. The legitimation of English linguistic imperialism makes use of two main mechanisms in relation to educational language planning, one in respect of language and culture (anglocentricity), the other in respect of pedagogy (professionalism).

The term *anglocentricity* has been coined by analogy with ethnocentricity, which refers to the practice of judging other cultures by the standards of one's own. There is a sense in which we are inescapably committed to the ethnocentricity of our own world view, however much insight and understanding we have of other cultures (for a philosophical analysis see MacCabe 1985). Anglocentricity takes the forms and functions of English, and the promise of what English represents or can lead to, as the norm by which all language activity or use should be measured. It simultaneously devalues other languages, either explicitly or implicitly. For the concepts ethnocentricity or anglocentricity to be anything more than useful cultural relativist terms they need to be integrated with structural power.

Professionalism refers to seeing methods, techniques, and procedures followed in ELT, including the theories of language learning and teaching adhered to, as sufficient for understanding and analysing language learning. I would argue that ELT professionalism excludes broader societal issues, the prerequisites and consequences of ELT activity, from its professional purview.

Anglocentricity and professionalism *legitimate* English as the dominant language by rationalizing activities and beliefs which contribute to the structural and cultural inequalities between English and other languages. The professional discourse around ELT *disconnects* culture from structure by limiting the focus in language pedagogy to technical matters, that is, language and education in a narrow sense, to the exclusion of social, economic, and political matters.

These working definitions have been formulated so as to attempt to see whether ELT contributes in education systems to the reproduction and distribution of political, economic, and cultural power, and if so, how. If we were studying the role of American films in cultural and linguisitic imperialism, we would need to focus on matters other than anglocentricity and (ELT) professionalism. In order to illustrate the relationship between global language promotion and economic and political interests on the one hand, and English linguistic imperialism in educational language planning and in the classroom on the other, I shall now give some brief examples of ELT activities. They shed some light on where the 'power' of English comes from, an issue I shall return to later.

In the contemporary world, ELT seems to be marketable worldwide. There is a demand for material products and resources (books, jobs for English teachers, space on timetables) and for immaterial resources (ideas, teaching principles). This is of significance to Britain, as the Director-General of the British Council stated in the 1987/88 *Annual Report* (page 8): 'Britain's real black gold is not North Sea oil but the English language. It has long been at the root of our culture and now is fast becoming the global language of business and information. The challenge facing us is to exploit it to the full.' ELT therefore has economic as well as ideological aspects. It is concerned with culture and structure.

When China shows a BBC English teaching series on television (there were an estimated 100 million viewers for the series *Follow me* in the mid-1980s), the way language is presented and practised ('culture' in the definition of English linguistic imperialism) is one level of an operation that also demands financial investment and may have economic consequences ('structure'). That this type of language pedagogy export is considered a good political investment can be seen by the fact that the United States Information Agency felt prompted to begin work on an equivalent multi-media English teaching series aimed at false beginners, in collaboration with the Macmillan Publishing Company (United States Advisory Commission on Public Diplomacy 1986: 39).

An earlier example of ELT professionalism in operation was the American audiolingual doctrine which was widely disseminated in the postwar period. The doctrine was available (a pedagogical method had been worked out), as were the material resources for disseminating it (books, teachers, aid projects). It is unthinkable that audiolingualism would have had such a significant impact globally without American economic might behind it. It is also possible that it would never have taken the form it did without its genesis in the Defence Language Institute, set up to teach foreign languages to US armed forces: learners were under military discipline and their promotion depended on success, which does wonders for motivation. The impact of audiolingualism was great in countries which were themselves economically weak and lacked an effective pedagogical counterweight, that is, in underdeveloped countries, whereas western European countries were largely sceptical and either resisted or modified audiolingualism. The propagation of audiolingualism was itself the result of a combination of cultural and structural factors, including a military element, and it had both cultural and structural implications.

A key issue in ELT at present, which is a test case for anglocentricity and professionalism, is what norms learners of English in underdeveloped countries should aim at (mentioned earlier as the dispute between liberation linguistics and deficit linguistics). Are learners supposed to have standard British English as the target, or a local educated variety of English? The conflicting answers to this controversial question provide revealing insight into the nature of professionalism at the local level, as well as at the international 'expert' level. Classroom practice may, of course, continue oblivious of the niceties of academic policy formation, but the answers have implications for the official policy on classroom practice, choice of teaching materials, and learning strategies. The answers also reveal what kind of relationship there is between the core English-speaking area, from which 'international' norms are derived, and the periphery-English areas in question. Key questions are raised: why should norms from Britain be considered 'global' at all? Why should 'experts' from the core English-speaking areas be listened to rather than local people? It is likely that adherence to a British global norm is symptomatic of dependence rather than self-sufficiency. It is also probable that dependence in the ideological sphere is matched and to some extent caused by dependence in the technical, economic, and political spheres. There is a clear link between the target norm that a periphery-English teacher aims at (a vital question at the micro level) and the relative power of the core country in the periphery (a macro-level structural question).

The issues touched on here will be analysed in greater depth later, particularly in Chapters 7 and 8.

Linguistic imperialism and linguicism

As indicated earlier, there are essentially two competing paradigms for understanding North-South links, modernization theory and imperialism theory. Development aid inspired by western modernization ideals has had to concede that the vision of underdeveloped countries retracing the steps of western democracies on a guaranteed route to prosperity has not come about. This sobering realization applies equally to the massive education 'aid' inspired by human capital theory and the belief that South countries could be galvanized from the top downwards. These empirical facts serve to discredit the modernization paradigm, and possibly to strengthen the claims of imperialism theories which focus on political economy, class structure, the dynamics of capital accumulation within a global matrix, and the transformation of precapitalist societies by colonial and neo-colonial capitalism. But there are other possible interpretations too which, while accepting many of the claims of imperialism theory, at the same time question some of the underlying assumptions of both theories. Galtung (1988) does this from a comparative philosophical humanistic point of view, criticizing both theories for economism, and suggesting orientally-inspired, more flexible theories which put basic human needs in focus. French (1986) arrives at similar conclusions from a feminist point of view. The science paradigm criticism of Harding (1986) and others can be used to further undermine the credibility of some of the basic unquestioned assumptions of both modernization and imperialism theories. In choosing Galtung's version of imperialism theory as the main starting point and developing notions about linguistic imperialism, I have tried to incorporate some of this criticism and to avoid some of the most obvious reductionist fallacies.

In practical 'aid' terms, the realization that the hopes of the 1960s have not been fulfilled means that the focus of such key bodies as the World Bank and the International Monetary Fund has shifted to attempting to supply the 'basic needs' of the underprivileged (Hayter and Watson 1985; Hoogveldt 1982), and more recently, to enforcing 'structural adjustment'. How this is experienced by the poor countries is expressed by ex-President Nyerere of Tanzania, who is quoted in the Danish journal *Kontakt* as saying in a speech in London in 1985:

> Instead of gunboats, economic power is used one-sidedly to push through the will of the powerful. The International Monetary Fund has more or less become the rich countries' instrument for the economic and ideological control of the poor countries.

In the elaboration of a theory of linguistic imperialism that follows, a primary source will be Galtung's theoretical work, as this represents an attempt to integrate all the various dimensions of imperialism, and therefore permits linguistic imperialism to be situated in relation to other types of imperialism. Galtung's theory does not refer to linguistic imperialism, but this can be seen as a sub-type of what he refers to as cultural imperialism. Other theorists of cultural imperialism will be drawn on, namely a theory dealing with global incorporation and theories of other sub-types of cultural imperialism, such as media and educational imperialism. These are relevant in relation to the dissemination of the fundamental teaching norms of ELT, where there is an intermeshing of language and pedagogy.

Galtung's *imperialism theory* posits six mutually interlocking types of imperialism: *economic, political, military, communicative* (here meaning communication and transport), *cultural,* and *social* (1980: 128). Imperialism is 'a type of relationship whereby one society (or collectivity in more general terms) can dominate another' (ibid.: 107). It is propelled by four mechanisms, the most essential of which is exploitation, the others being penetration, fragmentation, and marginalization. Exploitation involves asymmetric interaction between parties which exchange goods on unequal terms.

Galtung's goal is 'an image of imperialism rich enough to capture a wide variety of phenomena, yet specific enough not to be a tautology' (ibid.: 127). The theory operates with a division of the world into a dominant Centre (the powerful western countries and interests), and dominated Peripheries (the underdeveloped countries). There are centres of power in the Centre and in the Periphery. The Peripheries in both the Centre and the Periphery are exploited by their respective Centres. Elites in the Centres of both the Centre and the Periphery are linked by shared interests within each type of imperialism and, it is claimed here, by language. The norms, whether economic, military, or linguistic, are dictated by the dominant Centre and have been internalized by those in power in the Periphery. The interlocking of the various types of imperialism can be seen in the way cultural imperialism serves to reproduce the material conditions for exploitation (an economic-reproductive function) and to legitimate exploitation (an ideological-reproductive function).

In the early colonial phase of imperialism, the élites in the Periphery consisted of the colonizers themselves, whether settlers or administrators. In present-day neo-colonialism, the élites are to a large extent indigenous, but most of them have strong links with the Centre. Many of them have been educated in Centre countries and/or through the medium of the Centre language, the old colonial language. In this phase international organizations play a key role. These organizations are economic (private or governmental transnational corporations), political (supranational governmental organizations), military (various systems of alliance, treaties), communicational (shipping and air companies, news agencies), and cultural (film companies, book publishers).

In the next phase of imperialism, neo-neo-colonialism, Centre-Periphery interaction will be increasingly by means of international communications. Computer technology will obviate the need for the physical presence of the exploiters. New communications technology will step up the Centre's attempt to control people's consciousness. This will play an ever-increasing role in order to strengthen control over the means of production. For this to be effective requires the Centre's cultural and linguistic penetration of the Periphery.

The progression from one type of imperialist control to another parallels the way power can be exerted by means of sticks (impositional force), carrots (bargaining), and ideas (persuasion). Language is the primary means for communicating ideas. Therefore an increased linguistic penetration of the Periphery is essential for completing the move away from crude means, the sticks of colonial times, and even the more discreet means of the neo-colonialist phase of assymetrical bargaining, to neo-neo-colonialist control by means of ideas.

Galtung mentions the dissemination of Centre languages in the Periphery and the role of governmental organizations in promoting dominant languages. For our purposes it is necessary to establish *linguistic imperialism* as a distinct type of imperialism, in order to be able to assess its role within an imperialist structure as a whole. Linguistic imperialism permeates all the types of imperialism, for two reasons. The first has to do with form (language as a medium for transmitting ideas), the second with content. As regards the first, language is the primary medium of communication for links in all fields—indeed language is a precondition for most forms of contact other than brute force. Communication presupposes mutual understanding on the basis of a shared code. It is hardly surprising therefore that it is the Centre's language which is used. Secondly, linguistic imperialism dovetails with other types of imperialism and is an integral part of them. Linguistic imperialism is a primary component of cultural imperialism, though it must be remembered that cultural dissemination can also take non-linguistic forms (German music, Italian painting) and can occur in translation (ranging from highbrow works to Walt Disney comics).[4] Linguistic imperialism is also central to social imperialism, which relates to the transmission of the norms and behaviour of a model social structure, and these are embedded in language. This occurs wherever a socializing influence is exerted, for instance from the example set by 'aid' personnel in the field. It also occurs wherever English plays a major role in the education system of an underdeveloped country and transmits social values.

Individuals who operate internationally, whether by working abroad or through the dissemination of their ideas in books and other media, can be described as *inter-state actors* (Preiswerk 1978). English language teachers working abroad and applied linguists in their writings both fall into this category.

The working definition of English linguistic imperialism attempts to capture the way one language dominates others, with anglocentricity and professionalism as the central ELT mechanisms operating within a structure in which unequal power and resource allocation is effected and legitimated. *Linguicism* is the central concept here. Linguicism is distinct from other '-isms' such as sexism and racism, in so far as it is language rather than gender or race which is the crucial criterion in the beliefs and structure which result in unequal power and resource allocation.

Sexism has been defined as 'words or actions that arbitrarily assign roles or characteristics to people on the basis of sex. Originally used to refer to practices that discriminated against women, the term now includes any usage that unfairly delimits the aspirations or attributes of either sex' (from the *Guidelines for Nonsexist Use of Language in Publications of the National Association of Teachers of English in the USA*, Nilsen *et al.* 1977: 182). *Racism* involves a similar process of ascription, racialization. One definition of racism is that it is 'both a structural and ideological form in terms of a race relations structure in which the inequalities and differentiation inherent in the wider social structure are related to physical and cultural criteria of an ascriptive kind and are rationalized in terms of deterministic belief systems which tend to make reference to biological science' (Mullard 1980: 7). Miles (1989: 38) notes how the crystallization of racism in the colonial period, drawing on centuries of historical representations of the Other, 'entails a dialectic of representational inclusion and exclusion. By attributing a population with certain characteristics in order to categorize and differentiate it as an Other, those who do so also establish criteria by which they themselves are represented'.

Linguicism involves representation of the dominant language, to which desirable characteristics are attributed, for purposes of inclusion, and the opposite for dominated languages, for purposes of exclusion. The binary opposition language/dialect and the set international language/lingua franca/vernacular already noted are characteristic examples of linguicist discourse. Sample specimens of linguicist discourse, both in the colonial period and in more recent times, will be analysed later.

English linguistic imperialism is one sub-type of *linguicism*. Linguistic imperialism on the part of the speakers of any language exemplifies linguicism. Linguicism may be in operation simultaneously with sexism, racism, or classism, but linguicism refers exclusively to ideologies and structures where language is the means for effecting or maintaining an unequal allocation of power and resources. This could apply, for instance, in a school in which the mother tongues of some children, from an immigrant or indigenous minority background, are ignored, and this has consequences for their learning. Linguicism is also in operation if a teacher stigmatizes the local dialect spoken by the children and this has consequences of a structural kind, that is, there is an unequal division of power and resources as a result. But for linguicism also to constitute *linguistic imperialism* presupposes that the actors in question are supported by an imperialist structure of exploitation of one society or collectivity by another. Thus it is linguistic imperialism if the English language is imposed (by sticks, carrots, or ideas) on the Welsh or the Ugandans, and linguicism is in operation. In the neo-colonial phase of imperialism inter-state actors from the Centre and representatives of the élite in the Periphery (their counterparts and collaborators) are the key agents of this linguistic imperialism. Like racism, linguicism may be conscious or unconscious on the part of the actors, and overt or covert. It may be of an abstract kind (regulations for the use of particular languages) or more concrete (resource allocation to one language but not others).

There is no reason to restrict linguicism to matters of ideology alone, as Miles (1989) does in relation to racism. In order to shed light on the relationship between ELT and imperialism, it is important to identify the structures which are upheld by linguicism as well as linguicist ideologies. Thus, if an African university has 20 posts in English and a minute number in the indigenous languages of the country, then there is prima facie

evidence of a linguicist structure, which may well be underpinned by linguicist beliefs. If the country/collectivity in question
is part of the global imperialist structure, then linguistic
imperialism is in operation. In Galtung's terms, imperialism is
effected by penetration and the establishment of a bridgehead,
for instance the establishment of a colonialist education system,
within an exploitative structure. As English is also used widely
for supranational and international links, English linguistic
imperialism operates globally as a key medium of Centre-
Periphery relations.

Even if the definitions of linguicism and of English linguistic
imperialism are explicit and unambiguous enough to permit
identification of what is linguicist or linguistic imperialist in a
given historically-determined context, this does not mean that
English linguistic imperialism and linguicism are straightforward
and invariably functional. They operate within a wider socio-
political structure which is always itself full of contradictions.
Just as Miles regards racism as 'a necessarily contradictory
phenomenon rather than that it is functional to the mode of
production' (ibid.: 129), linguicism is a set of practices and
beliefs which represent an attempt by those involved in language
matters to give signification to a complex segment of reality,
which itself meshes with political, ideological, and other factors.

Few authors have attempted to define linguistic imperialism.
Calvet (1987) refers to linguistic racism, but he does so in a
general sense without defining it. The Ghanaian sociolinguist,
Gilbert Ansre, describes linguistic imperialism as:

> The phenomenon in which the minds and lives of the speakers
> of a language are dominated by another language to the point
> where they believe that they can and should use only that
> foreign language when it comes to transactions dealing with
> the more advanced aspects of life such as education, philo-
> sophy, literature, governments, the administration of justice,
> etc. . . . Linguistic imperialism has a subtle way of warping the
> minds, attitudes, and aspirations of even the most noble in a
> society and of preventing him from appreciating and realizing
> the full potentialities of the indigenous languages.[5]
> (Ansre 1979: 12–13)

Ansre's description has the merit of specifying the types of belief
that characterize linguistic imperialism. It fleshes out and
animates anglocentricity, and describes the consequences for the

dominant and dominated languages and for the individual. His description is reminiscent of the way in which racism is affirmed and stresses the tenacity of this form of ideological reproduction. The references to the lives of those who have internalized linguistic imperialism and the institutions typically affected stretch the description beyond that of a set of beliefs to the practices involved, and implicitly to structure. On the other hand Ansre's detailed description of linguistic imperialism is not concerned with language pedagogy and imperialism, and it is the particular logic of this professional world that needs scrutiny here.

Cultural imperialism in science, the media, and education

We can now revert to the insights from other areas of imperialism theory which can support the study of English linguistic imperialism. Galtung exemplifies cultural imperialism by a sub-type which he calls *scientific imperialism*:

> If the Center always provides the teachers and the definition of what is worthy of being taught (from the gospels of Christianity to the gospels of Technology and Science), and the Periphery always provides the learners, then there is a pattern of imperialism . . . a pattern of scientific teams from the Center who go to Periphery nations to collect data (raw material) in the form of deposits, sediments, flora, fauna, archaeological findings, attitudes, opinions, behavioral patterns, and so on for data processing, data analysis, and theory formation (like industrial processing in general). This takes place in the Center universities (factories), in order to send the finished product, a journal, a book (manufactured goods) back for consumption in the center of the Periphery, first having created a demand for it through demonstration effect, training in the Center country, and some degree of low-level participation in the data-collection team. This parallel is not a joke, it is a structure.
> (Galtung 1980: 130)

Most of the benefits and spin-offs of this relationship accrue to the Centre, while the Periphery remains in a dependent situation. Linguicism is in operation if the Centre language is always used, and Periphery languages are not accorded enough resources to develop so that the same functions could be performed in them.

The imperialist structure ensures that the West has a near monopoly of scientific research, whether into technological questions, Third World development issues, or English language pedagogy. The structural resources of the Centre (universities, research institutions, publishers, funding agencies) are vastly greater than those available in Periphery countries. The cultural resources of the Centre (ideas, theories, experience) are constantly renewed, partly also through scientific imperialism, with the Periphery remaining in a dependent situation. This structure is the framework within which the relationship between the core English-speaking countries and periphery-English countries in the ELT field needs to be seen.

Cultural imperialism has also been analysed as 'the sum of processes by which a society is brought into the modern world system and how its dominating stratum is attracted, pressured, forced, and sometimes bribed into shaping social institutions to correspond to, or even promote, the values and structures of the dominating center of the system' (Schiller 1976: 9). The means used for this purpose are manifold: commercial products of all kinds, films, television serials (the USA dominates telecommunications and satellite communications worldwide), advertising agencies abroad (the majority of which are American), youth culture; the entire battery of activities in cultural diplomacy (in the sense of government-financed operations), among them such key items as study in the Centre country, ensuring the place of the dominant language as a school subject or even as the medium of education, the stationing of inter-state actors abroad, and the export of books and other reading matter (referred to, in relation to subsidized textbooks for higher education, as 'literary colonialism' by Altbach 1975); examinations ensuring international 'standards', higher education links, educational 'aid' projects, etc. Many of these could be classified as educational imperialism.

If the concept 'culture' is defined broadly, economic, political and military imperialist links all have ideological implications and consequences. They can therefore be considered as having a cultural imperialist dimension. Schiller's definition of cultural imperialism is necessarily a broad one, as he is describing the global process of structural and ideological incorporation. His definition meshes usefully with the definition of English linguistic imperialism: English is the language in which this incorporation is taking place (form), and the structures and ideologies connected with English operate globally (content). If 'Americanization' or 'Westernization' is what Schiller is describing, then English is the key medium for this process.

Schiller's focus on global incorporation into the norms of the Centre is relevant for a language which has to some extent a 'global' reach. It is less relevant when describing the kind of dislocation that occurs when one language advances at the expense of others in a more restricted local context. Thus in Tanzania, English is a dominant language *vis-à-vis* Swahili, which in turn dominates the other languages. A linguistic hierarchy of this kind is found in many other contexts, for instance French remains the language of power in post-independence Mali, and the recent advance of Bambara, including widespread literacy in it, has been at the expense of other Malian languages (Calvet 1979). In such cases there is clear evidence of linguicism, but whether there is a situation of linguistic and cultural imperialism would depend on the links between the language(s) in question and a wider framework of exploitation.

English linguistic imperialism is often advanced by such cultural activities as film, videos, and television. For instance, besides pop music, television is the greatest source of the considerable amount of English that children in the Nordic countries know before they meet the language as a school subject: television accounts for Finnish children knowing such existential lexical items as 'shoot', 'kill', and 'hands up' (Palmberg 1985). A considerable proportion of programme time on television in the Nordic countries is of foreign origin, largely from English-speaking countries, and broadcast in the original language.

There are studies of loans from English into Danish (Sørensen 1973), Finnish (Sajavaara 1983), Norwegian (Vinje 1977), and Swedish (Ljung 1982; Jones 1983), and a wide range of European languages (Filipović 1982). These studies are generally restricted to study of the forms of language and do not analyse the processes or structure of linguistic or cultural imperialism. This exemplifies the principle, noted in connection with the definition of English linguistic imperialism, that language specialists disconnect culture from structure. Sajavaara's Finnish study has also investigated attitudes to the imperialist language, but in a form which attitude studies often take, namely investigating ideological phenomena only rather than both these and their structural connections. There is a Danish study of the Americanization of Danish cultural life in the decade following 1945, in particular the ideology of comics, paperbacks, and the Danish-language version of the *Reader's Digest*, and the considerable social impact these had (Christensen *et al.* 1983). Although the role of language or language pedagogy is not covered in this study, it is clear that the socio-cultural shift inherent in and triggered by Americanization facilitates English linguistic imperialism. Their study also demonstrates clearly that no aspect of imperialism can be analysed in isolation from imperialism as an all-embracing, multifaceted phenomenon.

Many cultural imperialist activities are engaged in by private enterprise for profit. Government agencies also assist the private sector when this serves their political goals. For instance in the immediate post-war years, *Reader's Digest*, *Time*, and *Life* were provided with a substantial US government subsidy so as to assist their establishment in the European market and to accustom Europeans to American tastes and ideas (for details see Christensen *et al.* 1983). The same strategy has been successful in underdeveloped countries, where choice of informed reading matter tends to be restricted. 'African intellectuals read *Time* and *Newsweek*', is the terse comment from one eminent African (Achebe 1975: 38).

A similar example of cultural imperialism is the promotion of the British book trade by government finance. This is primarily designed to boost the Centre's commerce with the Periphery and the dissemination of the Centre's ideas and language. While many books are of undoubted relevance, it also appears that books can be offloaded in the Periphery, like pharmaceuticals and pesticides which are banned, suspect, or no longer wanted in the Centre. The British Council's *Annual Report* 1987/88 (page 12) states that on 'April 21, 1988 the Minister for Overseas Development, Chris Patten, announced the Textbooks for Africa Project, designed to get surplus British textbooks into African schools.'

In northern Scandinavia in the 1930s, a similar pattern, with more explicitly ideological goals was followed. Free books and journals in Norwegian and Swedish were given to Finnish and Sami indigenous minority groups as part of the Norwegian and Swedish governments' policy to assimilate these communities linguistically and culturally. Minority groups were provided with cheaper radio licenses. The radio programmes were, of

course, in the dominant languages only. As late as the 1950s
there was a ban in the relevant part of Sweden on importing
Finnish-language books and journals, and libraries were for-
bidden to buy them (Eriksen and Niemi 1981: 241–5).

A central feature of the imperialist structure is that the
interaction is *asymmetrical*. This can be clearly seen in *media
imperialism*, one of the branches of cultural imperialism which
has been extensively researched, and which has affinities with
linguistic imperialism in education systems. Media imperialism
has been defined as follows:

> The term refers to the process whereby the ownership,
> structure, distribution, or content of the media in any country
> are singly or together subject to substantial external pressures
> from the media interests of any other country or countries
> without proportionate reciprocation of influence by the
> country so affected.
> (Boyd-Barrett 1977: 117)

There is a trickle of products, ideas, and influence from the
Periphery to the Centre, but the overwhelming flow is from
Centre to Periphery. For instance, many underdeveloped countries and Scandinavia are dependent for their overseas news on
Reuter's. The flow in the opposite direction is minimal. Finnish
research indicates that Reuter's, a London-based private agency,
has operated as 'the window to the world' for Finland (Kivikuru
1985: 20). This phrase must have a familiar ring to those versed
in the arguments advanced for the use of English as an
'international' language. Many politicians and applied linguists
credit English with this 'window' function. In both instances, the
news agency and the language, the window serves as the medium
for information, and the phrase does not refer either to content
or to the filtering processes involved. Nor does it disclose that
visibility through the window is asymmetrical.

In the process referred to as *cultural synchronization* (Hamelink 1983: 5), the Centre cultural products serve as models for
the Periphery, and many aspects of local cultural creativity and
social inventiveness, evolved over centuries, are thrown into
confusion or destroyed. The sequence of events is for the new
mode to be adopted in its alien form initially and to be gradually
transformed. This is akin to what happens when loan words are
adopted and used initially in their foreign form—typically in a
fast-developing field like computers—until a neologism in the

borrowing language is coined, or else the word is partially modified in the direction of the linguistic norms of the host language. *Modelling* is the term used for following a foreign recipe and transforming it into a local production. It is so widespread in the media that the figures for 'foreign' and 'domestic' production (of, for instance, television programmes) are only partially revealing, in that much of the indigenous output follows a foreign model.

This description of the processes involved in media imperialism could also apply to such aspects of ELT as curriculum design or textbook-writing. Professionalism is a key element in ELT, as it is in broadcasting and journalism. The mechanisms of professional transfer to underdeveloped countries in media imperialism have been described as threefold: *institutional transfer* (in the case of British colonies, export of BBC principles and practices), *training and education*, and the *diffusion of occupational ideologies* (Golding 1977). Dependence on the technology and professionalism of the Centre, and the availability of relatively cheap products from the Centre, serve to ensure the reproduction in the Periphery of the institutions and practices of the Centre and militate against finding more appropriate local solutions. In view of the absence of the self-regulating autonomy which characterizes professions in the Centre, what effectively is transferred is the ideology rather than the practice of professionalism (ibid.: 293).

It is highly likely that the professionalism of ELT has a similar pedigree. The same mechanisms of professional transfer have operated: the transfer of Centre institutions as models for those in the Periphery (in underdeveloped countries 'the organization of education systems, from kindergarten to research institute, reflects western models', Altbach 1982: 472). Training and education is what most ELT 'aid' has been about. ELT has aimed at the diffusion of an occupational ideology, an accepted definition of what legitimate behaviour, skills, and knowledge characterize the profession at its various levels. The mechanisms of professional transfer from Centre to Periphery thus seem to a large extent to be identical to those described in media imperialism. Likewise, dependence on the technology and professionalism of Centre ELT, and the availability of relatively cheap products (the most significant of which is books), serves to facilitate the reproduction in the Periphery of the institutions and practices of the Centre and militates against finding (more appropriate) local solutions. One can classify this structure as forming part of *educational imperialism.*

The imperialism theory I have elaborated tries to avoid reductionism by recognizing that what happens in the Periphery is not irrevocably determined by the Centre. The efforts of the Centre do not mesh in precisely with what the Periphery's needs are understood to be. Nor are the Periphery representatives passive spectators. They have a variety of motives, at the state and the personal level, as do the Centre inter-state actors. Periphery decision-makers have some freedom of manoeuvre in negotiating with the Centre, in deciding whether to accept 'aid', and under what conditions. A conspiracy theory is therefore inadequate as a means of grasping the role of the key actors in Centre or Periphery. The conspiracy explanation tends to be too vague and undifferentiated to merit being called a theory. It also ignores the structure within which the actors operate. The extent to which individual actors can influence the structure is a more open question, and one of major importance for those who seek change.

The mixed experience of educational 'aid' efforts demonstrates clearly how the Centre improvises within a general strategy of extending influence. 'The history of educational "aid" agencies shows the difficulty of both the diagnosis of the problems to be solved and the selection of remedies for them. There is little agreement even as to the broad purposes of educational "aid". As we move through the objectives, strategies, rationales, and tactics of the programmes, their overall coherence, (and frequently their internal coherence) rapidly decreases. Far from the conspiracy theorists' nightmare of planned capitalist seduction, the realities are much more of *ad hoc* and flexible programmes whose original coherence is among the first thing to go as they come under the pressures of implementation' (Dale and Wickham 1984: 43).

This does not however reduce the impact of Centre aid agencies. American foundations have spent vast funds on education in underdeveloped countries, the impact of which has, for instance, been analysed in relation to Africa (Berman 1982a and 1982b) and India (Sancheti 1984). (See also the *World Bank Report* on Education in Sub-Saharan Africa, 1988, analysed in a thematic issue of *Comparative Education Review*, February 1989.) These analyses indicate that one of the most significant outcomes of educational imperialism has been that the parameters

of educational reform and innovation in recipient nations
have been to a large extent defined by the Centre. This creates
continued dependence on the Centre. The international aid
organizations have occupied the available space. The fact that
they have had ambiguous or unclear goals, some of which were
unquestionably humanitarian, or that there has been a dialogue
between donor and recipient, does not alter the basic structure.
Even if an organization such as the British Council is guided in
its work by principles of 'reciprocity and mutual respect' (Burgh
1985: vii), the relationship between the participants is asymmetrical and the resources available to each party unequal. The
flow of funds and ideas is predominantly unidirectional.
Reciprocity is in fact a myth that serves to uphold western
hegemony. A Nigerian scholar's review for the World Bank of
African curriculum research concludes unambiguously: 'The
current trend in African countries of creating curriculum
development centres is a result of the impact of educational ideas
and practice from the United States of America . . . The direction
of research is . . . heavily influenced by the policies and
orientations of the donor agencies' (Yoloye 1986: 41–2).

ELT aid consists of the transfer of a language, a preferred
approach to teaching and learning the language, a certain type of
training, know-how, and skills. It merges elements of linguistic
and educational imperialism, and spans structure and culture. It
is comparable to the transfer of technology in the sphere of
economic production. In both areas—education and production
—there is serious concern about the viability of the exercise. One
can therefore have doubts as to the extent to which ELT
professionalism has in effect been successfully transferred, for
instance whether Periphery ELT people have become adept at
writing textbooks or syllabuses or handling classroom work
according to Centre professional norms. Irrespective of the
degree of 'success' of such an operation, if English is adopted as
a school subject, and particularly where English is the medium of
education, serious consequences ensue both for English and for
local languages. These consequences are of a structural kind,
affecting publishing, jobs in schools and higher education, and
the relationship between education and the community around
it. There are also consequences of a cultural kind, among them
attitudes to different languages, and the norms, values, and
activities of the classroom. These micro-level consequences are
intimately related to the macro-level of a global imperialist

structure and the relationship between Centre countries and Periphery countries.

To sum up the presentation of theory thus far, imperialism theory provides a conceptual framework within which English linguistic imperialism, the dominance of English worldwide, and efforts to promote the language can be understood. Scientific imperialism, media imperialism, and educational imperialism are all sub-types of cultural imperialism. So is linguistic imperialism. Linguistic imperialism also permeates all the other types of imperialism, since language is the means used to mediate and express them. Each is a theoretical construct forming part of imperialism as a global theory which is concerned with the structural relations between rich and poor countries and the mechanisms by which the inequality between them is maintained. Each type overlaps and interweaves with the others and must be seen as aspects of imperialism as an over-arching world structure. Activities in each area contribute to the incorporation of the Periphery into the 'modern' world system. They all involve 'modelling', presenting a norm and an example for the Periphery to follow, the transfer of institutions, ideals of training and education, and occupational ideologies. In each area the relationship between Centre and Periphery is asymmetrical, that is, it lacks reciprocity. It is in relation to such concepts and the general theory of imperialism that some aspects of English linguistic imperialism will be explored.

The State, hegemony, and ELT

A basic question that needs to be confronted is how ELT serves the interests of the core-English State. The issue will be explored by analysing the contribution of education systems to social reproduction, and probing into the complex concept of hegemony, and relating ELT to these.

A practical starting point would be to ask whether members of the ELT profession regard their work as non-political. This has been a widely held view, though there may be a variety of answers to the question, partly depending on how the concept 'political' itself is understood. The question has been raised mainly because the non-political ideal was explicitly invoked in a conference report which was seminal for the growth of ELT. This was the report of the Commonwealth Conference on the Teaching of English as a Second Language, held at the University

College of Makerere,[6] Uganda in 1961, and attended by delegates from 23 Commonwealth countries. The conference played a key role in crystallizing the principles which were to govern ELT aid in the immediate post-colonial period. In the assessment of a Ford Foundation review (written by a retired senior British Council officer), the Makerere conference was 'undoubtedly the most important landmark' of the period of ELT expansion (Cawson 1974:395).

In the opening address by the conference chairman (Michael Grant, President and Vice-Chancellor of the Queen's University, Belfast), the non-political nature of the conference was asserted. Whereas English had, in many countries inside and outside the Commonwealth, become a political issue, the delegates at Makerere were not 'in any way concerned with politics' (*Makerere Report* 1961: 46). A possible objection is deftly parried when the text continues: 'Nor can there be any question of believing that we propose, by our efforts, to supersede or weaken or dilute any of the cultures of Asia and Africa' (ibid.). This is an implicit rebuttal of any possible charge of cultural imperialism or, to use the chairman's term, 'cultural nationalism' (ibid.: 47). Drawing a clear dividing-line between the technical concerns of the conference and 'political' issues is such an important premiss for the conference (as it is for the ELT field in general) that the introduction to the conference report picks up the same point, namely that there is no clash between meeting the demand for English and the requirements of Asian and African cultures (ibid.: 10).

However, educational aid *has* lent itself to the achievement of political goals by ostensibly non-political means, as studies of American foundations indicate.

> There can be little doubt that the Ford Foundation, Carnegie Corporation, and Rockefeller Foundation have used their largesse since 1945 to ensure the controlled growth and development of African societies through the strengthening of strategic cultural and political institutions. The primary means to accomplish this has been through support for African education, as well as complementary social science research and public training institutes . . . The emphasis on the provision of a commodity which ostensibly had no political overtones and which is in great demand has enabled founda-tion personnel to appear in the guise of disinterested humanit-arians . . . Education was perceived as the opening wedge

ensuring an American presence in those African nations considered of strategic and economic importance to the governing and business élite of the United States.
(Berman 1982b: 225)

The belief that ELT is non-political serves to *disconnect culture from structure*. It assumes that educational concerns can be divorced from social, political, and economic realities. It exonerates the experts who hold the belief from concerning themselves with these dimensions. It encourages a technical approach to ELT, divorced even from wider educational issues. It permits the English language to be exported as a standard product without the requirements of the local market being considered except in a superficial way. (The aspects of the local culture or languages which are referred to in the Makerere Report are limited to such matters as sound patterns which can influence pronunciation, *Makerere Report* 1961: 12).

Virtually all the delegates at Makerere were government employees, either directly as civil servants or indirectly as academics, but this is not seen as being inconsistent with the claim of political purity. Most, if not all of them, must have felt that their participation in the conference was in their pay-masters' interests, and that the education they were planning was such as governments would wish to support. In that sense the conference was in the interests of the states represented (some independent, some still colonies). The more general questions that then arise are whose interests the state serves, and what the role of state-organized education is.

In liberal political science and popular belief derived from it, the national *State* is regarded as being raised above particular interests, so as to serve the interests of all. This fails to explain how social inequality is reproduced, in which process the State education system plays a decisive role. In classical Marxist political science, the capitalist State is regarded as emerging from the relations of production, and serves to protect and reproduce the dominance of the bourgeoisie, in part by mediating class conflicts (Carnoy 1982: 83). In neo-Marxist theories which address the issue of the role of education in capitalist societies, the State is regarded not as an institution but as a relation by means of which the class structure is reproduced (ibid.: 95, summarizing Poulantzas). The State is heavily and actively involved in the economy (and thus not distinct from it) by financing operations (defence) and by regulating production.

Schools contribute to the continuation of a mode of production by allocating learners to different occupational roles, that is, by distributing and producing knowledge which is useful and marketable. *Education* serves the State by fulfilling three functions. These are economic-reproductive (a process of qualification for work in the economy), ideological (the inculcation of attitudes and values), and repressive (the imposition of sanctions for not complying with the demands of school. In many countries there is no alternative to the education offered by the State) (ibid.: 116).

ELT is mostly funded and organized by the State, in the Centre and the Periphery. The specific functions performed by ELT within State education systems are fairly simple to place within Carnoy's analytical framework. First, part of the widespread legitimation for English is to qualify people to build up the nation, to operate the technology that English provides access to, and which the State has decided to embrace. It therefore has an *economic-reproductive* function. This is what language skills, such as those specified in syllabuses, are to be used for. This is an argument which 'aid' work in more recent years has specifically endorsed.

Secondly, English is also supposed to bring 'modern' ideas with it, to be a channel for interpersonal, social, and cultural values. It therefore has an *ideological* function. English was legitimated at Makerere in terms of two criteria or promises, the one a goal, namely material advance, the other a means, namely efficiency. English was supposed to represent 'a gateway to better communications, better education, and so a higher standard of living and better understanding' (*Makerere Report* 1961: 47). Efficiency in ELT was regarded as so uncontentious a principle as to need no justification (ibid.: 46). It was a cornerstone of imperialist ideology, and is, of course, a central ideological pillar of the capitalist, patriarchal mode of production. The ideological goals of ELT are sometimes specified, mostly in very general terms, in official regulations. Thus in the Danish school system one of the goals of the subject English is as follows: 'The teaching should enable pupils to become well informed about the life and culture of the countries where the language is spoken, so that they acquire a more solid foundation for international understanding' (quoted in Færch, Haastrup, and Phillipson 1984: 224, where the subject-specific regulations are related to the overall aims of schooling).

Thirdly, English has a *repressive* function, in that there is no choice other than to use the language in English classes. This has substantial implications if English is used as the medium of education for other subjects. (There may be more visibly repressive uses of English, when English is the only permitted language in courts of law, in detention, dealings with the authorities, and so on.)[7]

The examples given here of the functions of education, and the way ELT fulfills them, have all been of the formal, explicit curriculum. In addition, the socializing effect of the hidden curriculum (the 'tacit teaching of social and economic norms and expectations to students in schools', Apple 1979: 44) permeates each of the three functions.

The State not only ensures that certain types of knowledge and skill are generated or reproduced in schools. It also, to an increasing degree, commissions the knowledge it needs from higher education research institutions. This in turn is a reflection of the fact that over the past 50 years the State has taken a progressively more active role in many domains of life, so as to attempt to manage the crises of the capitalist system. Most research activities serve that purpose, and are increasingly under the direct financial control of the State (Carnoy 1982: 99). Intellectual activities, such as those engaged in by researchers and educational planners, are divorced from manual work, the process of direct production. The role of the planners tends to be confined to that of purveyors of technocratic 'facts', and ideological legitimation of a particular type of society, and its forms of production and reproduction.

What has been said so far about the role of the State and education is abstract and general, and may have given the impression that the whole system functions smoothly and is without contradictions. This is not the case. The needs of capital fluctuate, and the demands made on education systems reflect this. There are genuine conflicts and clashes of interest at many levels, although they may not be apparent. There is a constant dialectic between the national State, capital (which is international), and civil society (Dale and Wickham 1984). The goals of each of these are constantly being readjusted to adapt to an ongoing situation.

An example of manifest contradictions in education is that many teachers and educational administrators are genuinely motivated by a wish to help people. However, generated out of educators' common sense assumptions of what constitutes normal and abnormal behaviour, and important and unimportant knowledge are forms of action that have latent functions. These functions relate to economic and cultural power in society. Many such connections are not immediately obvious, even to educators (Apple 1979). Structural inequalities of power and access to resources are reinforced and reproduced by schools through curricular, pedagogical, and evaluative activities. This does not imply a conspiracy to keep the lower classes in their place. But granted that education is pyramidically structured, in western and underdeveloped societies education serves to condemn underprivileged groups to less rewarding positions in society. As schools focus on individual responsibility and employ a rhetoric of freedom of choice, it is the victim who gets the blame for failure, rather than the structure which generates failure or the society which is permeated by hegemonic ideas which make this state of affairs appear natural and unavoidable, and possibly even just.

There is a wealth of educational research on reproduction in education, some of it more economically oriented, some more culturally (see Apple 1979 and 1982). The issues are more complex when it comes to exploring reproduction and dependency in education in a Centre-Periphery relationship. There is little theory-building specifically on the role of education in creating or maintaining dependence, but a considerable amount of data and analysis of the issues exist (Dale 1982b; Altbach, Arnove, and Kelly 1982; Treffgarne 1984a and b). Much of what western researchers 'discovered' in the 1970s about the psychological dependence of the Periphery on the Centre ('academic colonialism', 'servitude of the mind', Altbach 1978 and 1982) was the subject of intense debate within the Periphery long before (Sancheti 1984: 5). The nature of the consciousness of the colonizer and the colonized had been penetratingly analysed by Fanon (1961), and had indeed been anticipated by Edward Blyden in West Africa a century earlier. He wrote that in subjecting the African to 'unmodified European training', the missions were producing a slavery 'far more subversive of the real welfare of the race than the ancient physical fetters' (quoted in Ashby 1966: 153).

The analysis of dependence in education can benefit from being integrated into an imperialism theory, but the theory must not be so rigid or simplistic as not to allow for the substantial complexities of operations in this area. At the same time the theory must be able to reveal the structural functions of educational activities. There is a risk of the latent effects of ELT, like those of any other activity in the Periphery, not being immediately obvious, and of the dominant ideology making us blind to structural realities.

The relationship between an ELT operation and its latent or structural functions can be demonstrated by considering the hypothesis that *ELT is neo-colonialist* in relation to the work of one scholar who analyses neo-colonialism in education, namely Altbach, a comparative educationalist. One dictionary definition of the term is that neo-colonialism is 'the use of economic, political, or other means of obtaining or retaining influence over former colonies' (*Concise Oxford Dictionary* 1976). Neo-colonialism, according to Altbach, is related to the Centre-Periphery and dependency concepts, in that it is based on inequalities between nations, and for him it also posits a conscious policy on the part of the Centre nations to maintain their influence and power over the Third World (Altbach 1982: 471). Altbach suggests that there is an element of choice on the part of both donor and recipient as to whether aid should be given or not, and that it is difficult to prove whether donor nations are neo-colonialist or not when they attempt to meet the declared development needs of receiving countries. Foreign policy goals may be explicit or covert. Altbach is reluctant to brand activities as neo-colonial in a field which is 'complex, politically sensitive, and necessarily controversial'. However he marshals a massive amount of evidence of dependency in education, publishing, and research, all of which indicates that the prevailing structure is imperialist.

> The impact of the industrialized powers extends throughout the intellectual life of Third World Nations. The organization of education systems, from kindergarten to research institute, reflects western models. In many Third World nations, especially those that were under colonial domination, the language of education and intellectual discourse is that of the colonial power and change to indigenous languages has been slow and awkward. The administrative structures of schools and universities reflect Western traditions.
> (Altbach 1982: 472)

It therefore does not seem to be unduly censorious or unscientific to classify the outcomes, if not the activities, of Centre policies as neo-colonialist. That being so, the motives of the donor governments are irrelevant, as they can scarcely be unaware of the outcomes, and they probably have no illusions about the structure within which the aid takes place, nor about the degree to which they are pursuing their own interests in their aid policies. In fact Altbach's insertion of a consciousness criterion (one which much research, for instance in pedagogy or psycholinguistics, has difficulties in handling) into his conceptualization of neo-colonialism is spurious and diverts attention away from the issue of structural power. Neo-colonialism is therefore the present-day form that imperialism takes *vis-à-vis* former colonies. In view of the evidence compiled by Altbach (corroborating the findings of other researchers) there is a very strong case for claiming that some forms of ELT and the intellectual tradition behind it are neo-colonialist.

Just as imperialism does not depend for its functioning on wicked people, cultural reproduction is not 'caused (in the strong sense of the term) by an elite group of managers who sat or now sit around tables plotting ways to "do in" their workers at both the workplace and the school' (Apple 1979: 40). The values and norms of dominant groups are transmitted by hegemonic processes. *Hegemony* has been a significant construct in critical social theory in recent decades, building particularly on the ideas of Gramsci (1971, see also Bocock 1986). Hegemony can be defined as 'a whole body of practices and expectations: our assignments of energy, our ordinary understanding of man and his (*sic*) world. It is a set of meanings and values which as they are experienced as practices appear as reciprocally confirming. It thus constitutes a reality for most people in society, a sense of absolute because experienced reality beyond which it is very difficult for most members of society to move in most areas of their lives' (Williams 1973).

Hegemony refers to dominant ideas that we take for granted. English has a hegemonic position in many former colonies, with the result that, for instance in Zambia, 'language teaching has come to mean English language teaching' (Chishimba 1981: 169). Because of the investment in teacher training and publications, and because of the acceptance of ideas which legitimate a dominant role for English, this comes to be accepted as the natural state of affairs rather than a choice which reflects particular interests.

Hegemony sees 'the relations of domination and subordination, in their forms as practical consciousness, as in effect a saturation of the whole process of living—not only of political and economic activity, nor only of manifest social activity, but of the whole substance of lived identities and relationships, to such a depth that the pressures and limits of what can ultimately be seen as a specific economic, political, and cultural system seem to most of us the pressures and limits of simple experience and common sense' (Williams 1977: 110).

The notions of hegemony, legitimation, and ideology are closely intertwined, but need to be distinguished one from the other.

The advantage of hegemony over ideology is that whether or not ideology is taken as intentionally distorting, it tends to have about it some notion of contrivance, of deliberate manipulation, and at the same time of having an identifiable source, of being devised to forward or protect a particular interest. Legitimation has rather more of a negative connotation. Its role typically seems to be of a *post hoc* compensatory or remedial character; it fills in for shortcomings in the desired course of events.
(Dale 1982a: 147)

English linguistic hegemony can be understood as referring to the explicit and implicit values, beliefs, purposes, and activities which characterize the ELT profession and which contribute to the maintenance of English as a dominant language. Hegemony is a more useful term for this set of practices and experience than is ideology, for the reasons given by Dale above. The hegemonic ideas associated with ELT are not simply a crude 'deliberate manipulation' but a much more complex and diverse set of personal and institutional norms and experienced 'meanings and values' (Williams 1973). The source of these can be found in both base and superstructure, as they derive from the economic foundations on which ELT activity rests (institutions, project funds, publishing houses, and ultimately the mode of production which these are an outcome of) and from the consciousness of the ELT profession (the ideas and practices which are its intellectual manifestations, and which evolve in dialectic interaction with the economic base).

The legitimation of ELT is embodied in arguments used to justify the use of English or the learning of English in given contexts. Such arguments can be grouped according to whether they refer to the 'intrinsic' qualities of the language (what English *is*), its 'extrinsic' qualities (what English *has*—material and personal resources), and the use to which English is put (what English *does*) (Phillipson and Skutnabb-Kangas 1985; Skutnabb-Kangas and Phillipson 1986b). Whereas Dale (op. cit.) seems to restrict legitimation to a reactive role, here it is seen as covering the explicit verbalization of arguments for a particular language policy, and may be proactive. It therefore applies to any description of the capacities of English which can be used as advocacy for the language.

Hegemony is not a simple matter of manipulation or indoctrination. 'It has continually to be renewed, recreated, defended, and modified. It is also continually resisted, limited, altered, challenged by pressures not all its own . . . The reality of any hegemony, in the extended political and cultural sense, is that, while by definition it is always dominant, it is never either total or exclusive' (Williams 1977: 112–3). Hegemony does not imply a conspiracy theory, but a competing and complementary set of values and practices, with those in power better able to legitimate themselves and to convert their ideas into material power.

Bocock, in his analysis of hegemony stresses that a major component in Gramsci's theory is the capacity of the dominant group (the ruling class or alliance of classes, or class fractions) to provide intellectual, moral, and philosophical leadership and to pursue policies which are not in the direct, narrow interest of capitalists but rather which can be presented plausibly as being in the interests of the whole people, of the nation (1986: 63). The focus on moral and philosophical values and goals is important when studying the structure of a scientific-educational activity, such as the dominant paradigm in ELT and applied linguistics. These are bearers of value judgements which reflect political and socio-historical determinants, though positivistic science attempts to exclude such matters from its purview at its peril. Non-authoritarian hegemonic leadership in a nation is able to tap the emotional commitment of citizens, who sympathize with overall goals which are reproduced and renewed in the media, religion, and other sites of civil society. An educational discipline is on the borderline between civil society in which norms are negotiated, and the coercive power of the State which dictates policy. ELT projects values over and above those of the discipline proper, and these values are typically what is referred to in legitimatory discourse. An ideology of the superiority of a language, or of the superior skills of a particular professionalism is similar to a hegemonic political philosophy. We can thus predict that ELT is projected as being in the interests of the entire nation rather than particular interests.

In analysing ELT and imperialism we are therefore inevitably concerned with values. (One aspect of this was raised in Chapter 1, namely the ethical aspects of aid.) Making values explicit raises epistemological problems. It can also raise hackles and lead to unfruitful debate.

> The problem with values being introduced, from the outside as it were, into a social science, is that they appear to be arbitrary, the personal whim of the author, and can easily be rejected by someone who disagrees with that particular set of values. To counteract this kind of perception, the re-introduction of philosophical, rational discussion of values and politics into social theory and the social sciences is necessary. This needs to be embedded within social theory rather than left outside the discourse.
> (Bocock 1986: 123)

What we should therefore aim at is contributing to 'rational, scientifically-based discourse' on the issues, in the hope that those who react defensively or have an alternative view of ELT and imperialism will make their value judgements explicit, and also in the hope that an adequate, theoretically explicit foundation for analysing the issues has been provided.

Inspiration for the study of the ELT profession, its academic and political roots, can be found in Said's study of orientalism (1978). Said links up the micro-level of academic norms and practices in a specific discipline with macro-level historical developments. He demonstrates how an image of the oriental was created in the west. Orientalism was a multi-faceted way of 'coming to terms with the Orient that is based on the Orient's special place in European western experience' (ibid.: 1), with roots in conceptions of 'the Other' going back centuries. For Said, 'orientalism' is a label covering a vast range of hegemonic beliefs and practices by means of which a dominant group could shape a dominated group, with the academic world playing a decisive role (as it did in racism, Miles 1989). Most relevant for this study, Said documents that in the immediate post-1945 period 'Oriental studies were to be thought of not so much as scholarly activities but as instruments of national policy towards the newly independent, and possibly intractable, nations of the postcolonial world' (Said 1978: 275). A central issue in this book is the relationship between the scholarship of ELT and its function as an instrument of national policy in the post-colonial period.

Several studies of the sociology of science and the sociology of knowledge distinguish between the *internal* and *external* constraints which influence how a particular science is established and develops. *Externalism* refers to the social factors which influence the cognitive structure of a science, either strongly or weakly. *Internalism* refers to the intrinsic determination of a science, the pursuit of knowledge for intellectual, personal motives. Haberland 1988 briefly reviews the establishment of sociolinguistics as a distinct branch of academia in the light of this distinction, and such factors as degree of professionalism (when the subject becomes independent of the judgement of outsiders), the degree of autonomy of the researcher, and institutional frameworks. He considers the growth of socio-linguistics in two key areas, the global national interest of the USA, and the American disadvantaged, and concludes that 'the real battlefield is not so much research, but the area where experts really are indispensible: the preparation of teaching materials, the development of teaching programs, and the actual teaching . . . much more money is spent on "development" than on "hard-core research" ' (ibid.: 1822).

The existence of *alternatives* to the prevailing hegemony provides openings both for influencing the dominant order and for challenging it. For a description of a successful challenge to the establishment orthodoxy in the area of research into race relations, within an explicit framework for analysing competing ideologies, see Mullard 1985. The English language and English language teaching are hegemonic if they uphold the values of dominant groups, and if the pre-eminence of English is legitimated as being a 'common sense' social fact, thus concealing whose interests are being served by the dominant ideology and dominant professional practice. Analysing English linguistic imperialism in a context of hegemony, with its reproduction under continuous contestation and with its own internal contradictions, holds open the possibility of change.

Notes

1　The population of Norway is in fact 4.1 million, but this slip does not invalidate the argument.

2　On 'native' and 'native speaker', see *English Today* 7, July 1986: 14–15.

3　In Indian official and academic discourse, 'tribe' and 'tribal' are widely used, even by those who are working for increased rights for such people.

4　Walt Disney comics are produced in 18 different languages, including four Spanish-language editions. The content remains basically the same. See Dorman and Mattelart 1975.

5　Ansre's significant contribution to unmasking the illegitimate arguments used by such people to preserve the position of the dominant language, and the privileges that go with it, will be analysed in Chapter 9.

6　Pronounced with stress on the second syllable.

7　An example from Nigeria from Ayo Bamgbose (personal communication): 'In my own country, there are no legally enshrined language rights, and hardly any concessions are made to citizens who cannot speak the country's official language. The situation even becomes absurd when an accused person or plaintiff in court has to have his evidence interpreted into English when he/she and the judge may share the same indigenous language!'

4 Earlier work relevant to linguistic imperialism

In analysing theoretical approaches which can shed light on English linguistic imperialism, the next step is to ask what help can be obtained from language-related fields of study, such as language spread, the sociology of language, language planning, theories of language teaching and learning, and linguistic human rights, and to see what contribution they can make.

Language spread

Language spread is a metaphor for the adoption of a given language by individuals. Language spread can be defined as 'an increase, over time, in the proportion of a communication network that adopts a given language or language variety for a given communicative function' (Cooper 1982b: 6). Sociolinguistic studies of language spread analyse who adopts what language, when, why, and how (ibid.: 30), concentrating mainly on three aspects—form, function, and pervasiveness.

A considerable number of factors are involved in any language spread situation. Lewis groups them into four sets (1982: 215):

1 language attitudes, for instance the strength of efforts to maintain a threatened language or to restrict the functions of an indigenous language;

2 the nature of the between-group interaction, e.g. geographical contiguity, ease of communication, conquest, colonization, the nature of the relationship between the colonizing Centre and the Periphery;

3 modernization, including the intensity of economic development, the degree of external exploitation of indigenous resources, urbanization, demographical features such as the degree of education of mobile and stable population groups;

4 the political theories and religious and cultural characteristics associated with a language, especially the distance between the spreading language and other languages in

contact with it with respect to these theories and characteristics.

These factors interact in complex ways, as can be seen from a
few examples related to the spread of English. Attitudinal factors
(Lewis's first set), for instance strong adherence to the mother
tongue, may be relatively powerless in the face of structural
inequalities which favour English. Thus strong identification
with and loyalty to the mother tongue in Ghana does not reduce
the impact of English, which is structurally favoured (Ansre
1975). Ghana is a multilingual society, in which English benefits
from the ideological and structural association with modernization (Lewis's third set). The material and social benefits which
accrue to speakers of English elude those restricted to other
languages.

In social interaction in East Africa, use of English symbolizes
education and authority, whereas use of Swahili or a local
language symbolizes solidarity or local ethnicity (Scotton 1982).
In practice in such countries few other than the educated élites
learn to use English effectively. As in India, it is only bilingualism
or multilingualism of the élite kind that is produced by formal
learning in schools (Annamalai 1986). Since socio-economic
integration in countries such as Kenya and India is restricted,
learning English may not on its own guarantee access to privilege
(something that is clearly visible in high levels of the 'educated'
unemployed in underdeveloped countries, see Foster 1975 and
1977 for Ghana, Adiseshiah 1980 for Asia, and Coombs 1985
for a general assessment), whereas proficiency in other local
lingua francas is essential for low-level employment and interaction, and this contributes to a positive attitude towards them.
In the terms of Lewis's fourth set, there is too wide a distance
between the underprivileged masses and the message of English,
and schooling through the medium of English does little to
alleviate this. The prestige and prosperity linked with English are
beyond the reach of those whose home background does not
support the acquisition of English. This does not hinder parents
from articulating a demand for education in which English is
given pride of place, even though this is probably not appropriate for their children (Obura 1986).

As these examples show, language spread theory can provide a
useful framework for analysing processes of language spread
and for synthesizing the results of such studies. It is however
little more than a heuristic formula and not specifically concerned

with analysing structural forces in society. It is therefore of limited scope for our purposes.

Durmüller (1984) has investigated by means of questionnaires and interviews the extent to which English is used for intranational purposes in multilingual Switzerland. Among the findings are that young adults prefer speaking English to speaking their second language (French or German) and that a clear majority of the public do not resent the presence of English in their everyday lives. Also included in the project are statistical analyses of the language of radio music, films, and mural graffiti.

A study of the spread of English in France and the extent to which the language is 'ideologically unencumbered' also uses interviews as a means of gauging attitudes, and collects statistical data on language borrowing, the status of English in school education and adult education, use in the television, cinema, the press, science, and business and industry (as measured in job advertisements) (Flaitz 1988). While accumulating a great deal of useful information on trends, her concluding remarks indicate the limitations of this type of study. 'The notion that English carries an ideological message has been suggested, not proven, through the findings of this research. Correlational studies of this kind can only point to relationships between variables. They do not imply cause and effect' (ibid.: 203).

Attitudinal factors are accorded great importance by Kachru in 'The power and politics of English' (1986b: 130). He tabulates the parameters of the power of English as follows:

Demographical and numerical: unprecedented spread across cultures and languages; on practically every continent (see e.g. Fishman *et al.*: 1970; and Crystal 1985).

Functional: provides access to most important scientific, technological, and cross-cultural domains of knowledge and interaction.

Attitudinal: symbolizes—certainly to a large group across cultures—one or more of the following: neutrality, liberalism, status and progressivism.

Accessibility: provides *intra*national accessibility in the Outer Circle and international mobility across regions (cf. 'link language,' and 'complementary language').

Pluricentricity: this has resulted in the nativization and acculturation of the language. These two are, then, responsible for the 'assimilation' of English across cultures.

Material: a tool for mobility, economic gains, and social status.

Kachru's paper is an exploratory one, identifying theoretical and empirical landmarks, rather than producing an integrated account of the spread of English. He seeks inspiration in Foucault's theories and stresses that hitherto work in this field has not tackled the issue of linguistic power *per se*. He underlines the extent to which the pluricentricity of English has diversified the language so that it is no longer only an exponent of the Judeo-Christian tradition and western concepts (an issue which he analyses elsewhere in relation to literary creativity). Periphery-English élites (his 'Outer Circle' of English) seem to be hooked onto English, to the detriment of other languages. He identifies psychological factors, particularly strong emotional attachment to the language, which in turn is propelled by the message of ideological change associated with the language, as being of decisive importance for the current spread of English.

Kachru identifies four basic areas in which the power of English manifests itself (ibid.: 132). These are *linguistic*, the question of norms referred to earlier; *literary*, likewise a question of the competing norms of the Centre and its Peripheries; *attitudinal*, the question of linguistic identity; and *pedagogical*, in which he identifies a number of key sites for hegemonic control. These are:

> (a) the model for the teaching of English and its sociological and pragmatic validity; (b) the bandwagons of methods (often commercially motivated), which seldom take into consideration the local needs and various limitations in the Outer Circle; (c) the teacher-training programs for ESL which have been developed in the Inner Circle (the core-English Centre) for the training of 'specialists'; (d) the fast developing industry of tests for evaluating competence and proficiency in English, and the underlying culturally biased assumptions for the construction of such tests; and (e) the approaches and research paradigms for English for Special Purposes (ESP).
> (Kachru 1986b:133)

He also points out that there is an economic dimension to each of the four areas, particularly the pedagogical one.

Kachru's paper identifies many of the issues already singled out in Chapter 1 as being in need of research. His paper concludes with an insightful prompt to further research (ibid.: 137):

> This paper essentially raises questions and does not necessarily provide answers. Concerning the global functions of English,

as yet not many meaningful questions have been asked. It is not that one does not think of such questions since most of these are rather obvious. It seems to me that perhaps in the suppression of such questions, if one looks very carefully, one might find an interplay of 'power' and 'politics'.

So far as Foucault (as a source of theoretical inspiration) is concerned, it is probably his emphasis on the way power is established in discourse which is most helpful. This is particularly so when conceptualizing the discourse of academic professionalism, as illustrated in his detailed study of the medical profession. Texts about language, language policy, and language planning can be seen as exemplars of discourse. They can be studied for the way they reveal power issues being dynamically worked out. The issue here is less one of language spread than the spread of a particular scientific tradition. What needs analysis is the anatomy of the discourse of one particular example of scientific imperialism.

Of considerable potential relevance for the analysis of linguistic imperialism is the new field of *language spread policy*, which concentrates on government promotion of a language abroad. A thematic issue of the *International Journal of the Sociology of Language*, number 95, 1992, edited by Ulrich Ammon, attempts to elaborate on the concept 'language spread policy'. This is defined in a planning paper for the volume as comprising 'all endeavours, directed or supported by institutions of a state, which either aim at spreading a language beyond its present area and domains or which aim at preventing the retraction of a language from its present area and domains . . . The objectives for the volume are twofold: (i) to gather and present some comparative data on language spread policy, (ii) to contribute to the development of a general framework of analysis of language spread policy.'

The sociology of language

The sociology of language offers relatively richer theories and empirical data than language spread theory. For instance, the factors impelling underdeveloped countries to opt for English or another *language of wider communication as a national language*, either permanently or transitionally, have been analysed by Fishman in a heuristic model which postulates three types of decision (Fishman 1972). Choice of a national language or national languages in periphery-English countries is determined by the need of local élites to promote socio-cultural integration. Choice of national language depends on whether there exists locally a Great Tradition (for instance Arabic/Islam or many of the oriental languages/cultures), in which case this is opted for, nationalism can build on it, and a fusion of traditional and modern spheres is attempted. English is adopted for modern functions, and it is intended that this should only be transitional pending the evolution of the indigenous language. Secondly, there may be competing Great Traditions within the same nation (as is the case in India) requiring a compromise between political integration and separate authenticities. English is adopted here as a unifying compromise within a national and regional pattern of bilingualism. Thirdly, where there is no Great Tradition at the national level, selection of a national language is governed by considerations of political integration (which Fishman has termed 'nationism'). English is adopted as a permanent national symbol, and the goal is modernity, with English replacing local languages. In the first two cases a substantial language planning effort goes into modernizing respectively one and several local languages, in the third no such effort is undertaken with respect to local languages, and the norms of the metropolitan language are accepted as being valid locally. In such countries the decision to favour the former colonial language and the modernization-oriented élite is 'justified by the basic need to obtain and retain as much tangible aid, as much trained personnel and as much influence abroad as possible in order to meet the immediate operational demands of nationhood' (ibid.: 193). Fishman concludes that 'Languages of wider communication seem likely to retain long-term significance under all three types of decisions' (ibid.: 207). He sees no prospect of them being ultimately dislodged in the third type (exemplified by Kenya or Ghana) or the second type (exemplified by India or Sri Lanka), whereas in the case of the first type (where Fishman's examples are Israel, Thailand, Somalia, and Ethiopia. Tanzania, perhaps surprisingly, is not included), the language of wider communication continues to serve as a vital language in certain more modern domains, but it may be hoped that they can ultimately and ideally be dislodged.

The purpose of Fishman's analysis is to evolve a theoretical framework in which specific dimensions can permit valid comparisons and anlysis, preferably of a quantitative kind. The dimensions identified by Fishman are the factors that influence decisions on language policy. Some have to do with the *goals of decision-makers*—perceived socio-cultural integration needs, bilingualism goals, and biculturism goals. Others reflect the status quo—the existence of pre-colonial and colonial traditions. One factor, namely language planning concerns, is a *consequence* of the decisions taken. The pressures on leaders to take decisions of one type rather than another are diverse and complex. 'Expert' professional advice on language planning has tended to be western-inspired and based on Western experience, which is of dubious relevance in multilingual Third World contexts. Whether the decisions taken serve the interests of the mass of the population as well as the élites will depend on the nature of the state in question, and the degree of popular participation in decision-making.

Several sociological studies on the *spread of English* have been undertaken (Fishman, Cooper, and Conrad 1977). A wealth of data documents the use of English worldwide in education systems and the printed word, and the number of foreign students in the core-English countries (Conrad and Fishman 1977: 55). The use of English in 102 non-English mother-tongue countries has been correlated with a range of economic, educational, and demographic variables (Fishman, Cooper, and Rosenbaum 1977: 105). Not surprisingly, there is a positive correlation between English and military imposition, duration of authority (colonial rule), linguistic diversity in a given country, material advantages (particularly exports), urbanization, economic development, and religious composition. It was also found that poorer countries are more likely to depend on English as a medium of instruction than were richer nations. Complex cross-tabulation of the statistics shows, among other things, that the level of educational development does not contribute much independently of the other variables.

While all such data are usefully informative, they seem to be short on explanatory power. For instance, the education variable covers quantitative expansion, but not the issue of education as a bridgehead for western cultural or linguistic influence, a bridgehead being a symptom of imperialist penetration. Such analyses can therefore not begin to clarify the contribution of language pedagogy to the global diffusion of English. The sociology of language has sophisticated measures for analysing language maintenance and language shift, the extent to which different languages are used for different functions, and the role of attitudes to language, as well as stimulating reflections on the socio-cultural processes affecting the diffusion of English (Fishman 1977: 113 ff.). Fishman is illuminating in describing the many factors involved, and the insight to be expected from specific types of sociological research, but his approach has weaknesses. As we saw in Chapter 1, he has recently modified his position on the relative 'neutrality' of English, but a major collection of his writings (Fishman 1989) reproduces work from the mid-1970s on the spread of English in relation to language maintenance and language shift, and his primary book (Fishman *et al.* 1977) on the spread of English is still the undisputed benchmark. It does, therefore, need critical analysis.

Fishman regards English as not being 'imposed' (ibid.: 114), but relegates discussion of non-military means of compulsion to a footnote and future research (ibid.: 128). He lends credence to the idea of English being 'neutral', though acknowledging its role in facilitating access to power. He eloquently champions dominated languages, but seems to be confident that English is not replacing other languages in the Third World, and that the present global displacement is no cause for alarm. He claims that the spread of English has been assisted by the language being seen as ethnically and ideologically unencumbered. 'It is part of the relative good fortune of English as an additional language that neither its British nor its American fountainheads have been widely or deeply viewed in an ethnic or ideological context *for the past quarter century or so.*' (ibid.: 118), but recognizes that the language has been associated with nationalism, nationism, development, modernity, efficiency (which he treats as process variables), western civilization, and many other culturally-loaded values, all of which are features of contemporary capitalism. There are pleas for more research and for language planning at the international level (ibid.: 126), but there is little attempt to come to grips with global inequality and its structural determinants. Perhaps of greatest relevance (though sobering in view of the considerable effort that Fishman and his associates have put into this field) is the observation that 'we still have no study encompassing all of these factors and viewing the acquisition of English as an additional language as a process which interacts with the major social, cultural, economic, and political processes of the national (let alone the international) context' (ibid.: 116).

Language planning

Language planning has traditionally been concerned with harnessing the skills of linguists and others to the solution of problems of the status and corpus of languages in situations where it was felt that language engineering could help. Language planning theory has recently attempted to incorporate wider social, economic, and political concerns, and to explode the myth of objectivity in such activities (Neustupny 1983; Haarmann 1990). Dissatisfaction with the principles of the technocratic approach of the 1970s has led to new labels for the activity, 'language policy' (Kachru 1981), and 'language management' (Jernudd and Neustupny 1986), but these have not yet been widely adopted. The paradigm advocated by Neustupny (op. cit.) assumes that for language treatment to be regarded as a language planning activity, as opposed to colonialist or imperialist language imposition, it must be informed by a theory of language planning. The key elements of his theory are identification of a language *problem* (at any level from the phonetic to the societal) and language *correction* to remedy the problem (using methods integrating macrolinguistics and microlinguistics and situating language problems in discourse). His theory requires language planners to identify the socio-economic determinants and consequences of language problems and to contribute actively to their solution. The value judgements of language planners have to be made explicit—'Any theory of language planning must provide a full account of all political values involved in language planning processes' (ibid.: 3); 'The criterion of "development", which favours those who control the process of economic production is receding in favour of the criterion of "equal access" to resources, in other words to the criterion of "democratization". The issue includes language rights of ethnic minorities, the disadvantaged and those discriminated against' (ibid.). The theory recognizes that western conceptions are not automatically valid for the Third World. Neustupny also criticizes western social scientists for tending to view their own perceptions and values as universally valid.

This paradigm for language planning combines the technical aspects of earlier models (typologies and techniques for various levels of problem) with increased political and social sensitivity. One aspect of this must be greater insight into the role of the state and its agencies. Another could be the role of international organizations active in the language field.

An expansion of language planning to cover 'acquisition planning' in addition to corpus and status planning has been proposed by Cooper (1988). His goal is partly the micro-level goal of including decisions by teachers on choice of teaching materials within the reach of language planning (this empowers teachers to contribute to language policy), and partly the macro-level goal of including within language planning the contribution of education systems to spreading or maintaining particular languages. In Cooper's view, language planning can be viewed as superordinate or subordinate to applied linguistics, but language planning and linguistics cannot be entirely separated from each other.

Educational language planning is logically a sub-type of language planning. It would clearly benefit from a requirement that the socio-economic determinants and consequences of language planning decisions, and the value judgements of language planners should be identified. This is particularly important in language teaching situations where policy is subject to external pressures, for instance where foreign 'experts' (or majority group experts in the case of minority language speakers) are part of the scene.

There is however a distinct risk that such a well-intentioned and informed language planning model might reflect western conceptions and be fundamentally inappropriate in multilingual underdeveloped countries. In India there has been a fruitful dialogue for many years between indigenous and international language planning experts. Language planning has been immensely complex in India, because of the extremely diverse starting points, an uneasy coalition between federal and state interests, and language serving as a mobilizing factor in social conflict. Pattanayak notes that in India fifteen languages have constitutionally guaranteed privileges and that those dominated minority languages which have succeeded in being 'recognized as associate administrative languages or even as media of primary education . . . have been so recognized only after such groups generated sufficient pressure and not as a result of a priori policy planning' (Pattanayak 1986b: 25). This empirical reality applies equally to non-official languages in the west, but in addition he distinguishes the predominantly monolingual ethos which holds in the west from the multilingual ethos of Third World societies:

From a predominantly monolingual point of view, many languages are a nuisance, as their acquisition is considered a burden. They are uneconomic and politically untenable. Even translation services are computed to be more economical than use of an additional language. In the case of multilingual countries, the reverse is the case. For them restrictions in the choice of languages are a nuisance, and one language is not only uneconomic, but it is politically untenable and socially absurd.
(Pattanayak 1986b: 22)

The use made of languages, and attitudes to language are different in the two social contexts. This means that language planning experience in each context is not necessarily of direct relevance elsewhere. Other Indian scholars also question the validity of a universal modernization norm for all languages along western lines, and reject the characterization of languages in the underdeveloped world as 'deficient' communication systems (Khubchandani 1983: 22).

Many scholars from underdeveloped countries are convinced that the attempt to copy western language planning models is theoretically untenable and has been directly harmful to dominated groups in underdeveloped countries. Even within its own frame of reference, it is not economically viable:

The amount of resources spent to produce the four per cent of English-knowing persons in India over the past two hundred years proves the absurdity of efforts to replace many languages by one under democratic planning. The cultural deprivation and sociopolitical inequality introduced by the approach of monolingual control of a multilingual policy make nonsense of any talk of economic benefit.
(Pattanayak 1986b: 22)

Pattanayak's reference to replacement and monolingualism does not imply that individuals are monolingual, nor that the declared planning goal is monolingualism (India has officially followed a 'Three Language Formula' since 1956), but rather to the promotion of the exclusive use of English in certain key high-status domains, and the linguicist structure and ideology that support this. Similarly, the social, economic, and political costs of the monolingually-inspired miseducation of minority children in the west itself are enormous, and are a direct consequence of linguicism (see Skutnabb-Kangas 1984a, 1988). Awareness of such social realities and of the limitations of available theories makes the task of informed language planning more urgent in education, and particularly in multilingual situations in which English tends to be a dominant language.

Three further points need to be made in relation to language planning. The first is that the relative status and power of languages may evolve in directions not foreseen by the planners. Thus in India there is a discord between policy and practice:

> The English language is accepted in practice as the cultural language for the modern values and aspirations, but is rejected in policy as the language of cultural domination and distortion. Given the market forces, the fear is that it is a policy of unequal bilingualism with the Indian languages being poor cousins . . . its (that of English) current position was unplanned by the policy makers.
> (Annamalai 1988: 14–15)

It is essential therefore to identify the market forces, internal and external, which determine the outcomes. The market forces include discordant hegemonic practices and beliefs. The realities of English linguistic hegemony in India are stronger than the protestations of political leaders in favour of Hindi or other dominant Indian languages.

Secondly, language planning is something that all states engage in, whether they have official agencies for the purpose or not. A very large number of policies and decisions involve language planning: educational policy for indigenous and immigrant minorities, in particular the attention accorded to their languages (status planning); policy for which foreign languages should be learnt in school (acquisition planning, which has implications for status planning); bodies set up to monitor the purity of a language or establish a common core curriculum in the dominant language, such as the Kingman and Cox Reports in Britain; a decision by an underdeveloped country to conduct education in a different language, for instance to open an English-medium university (acquisition and status planning), etc.

Thirdly, language planning also takes place at the supra-national level. As one dimension of the Europeanization process, multilingualism is increasing in Western Europe. One wonders, though, how long the EEC will survive as a multilingual organization which in principle accords equal rights to the nine official languages of the twelve member states. Running a translation service at a cost of over 11 billion dollars a year constitutes 40 per cent of the EEC's administrative budget (Henriksen 1990). Will economic pressures lead to curbing the rights of less powerful languages? And if English and French become official working languages, what factors other than economic ones will trigger off such a decision, and what consequences will follow for other languages? Such supranational language planning has major implications at the national level, as indeed do a range of EEC decrees and practices, even if education, culture, and language were deliberately excluded from the Treaty of Rome.

> The EEC treaty aims at guaranteeing free and unhindered economic activity across intra-Community borders. As language is the medium of all economic activity, the rules of the EEC treaty also, implicitly, establish the principle of free language use in transnational economic activity. As this linguistic freedom is often limited by national rules on language use, a conflict may arise, which, due to the principle of the supremacy of Community law, is to be decided in favour of the EEC rules.
> (de Witte 1991)

Choice of language has been contentious in such matters as the right to employment in a given country, transfrontier television, and product labelling. There have been cases at the European Court of Justice which have established that this Court has the right to decide on matters of language use (ibid.).

Theoretical models of language teaching and learning

Theoretical models of language teaching and learning do not totally ignore the social and political context in which such activity takes place. For instance, Strevens's 'theoretical model of the language learning/teaching process' distinguishes twelve essential elements, one of which is 'policy and aims' (Strevens 1976: 131). The others relate to administration, teacher training, the syllabus, the learner, etc. The elements represent a kind of flowchart of the teaching/learning process. Policy and aims reflect 'the public will, the social sanction for the organized provision of language instruction, the response to the linguistic needs of the community . . . This element is where the sociolinguistic facts of a community . . . find their general expression, and where this general expression is to some extent refined into opinions about how many of the population should be encouraged to reach what kind and level of proficiency in which languages' (ibid.: 131). Like earlier models (Mackey 1970) and Spolsky's recent (1989) synthesis of second language learning theories, there is explicit recognition that language policy and educational policy reflect social pressures and government decisions. However the nature of these pressures and decisions is not pursued, nor is the question of what international or national factors influence the public will. The policy and aims element seems to reflect national consensus, as though there are no conflicting sources trying to influence it, and is regarded more as a backdrop which is not of central concern to language pedagogy. It is seen as a 'given' which language pedagogy should not seek to influence.

A good example of a textbook on foreign language pedagogy conceived within such a paradigm is Færch, Haastrup, and Phillipson (1984). The book makes a break with more traditional approaches to language study and the organization of learning, by adopting a learner-centred approach, the goal being to develop the theory and practice of language pedagogy so as to facilitate the teaching and learning of English in a more efficient way. Theories of language learning and teaching principles, from the identification of objectives to classroom activities, are explicitly placed within a political and educational framework, but the relationship between the various components is not analysed, and the overarching political and educational framework is of peripheral concern. It remains a backdrop.

A substantial amount of empirical research work into foreign and second language learning currently takes place, the general purpose being to analyse what happens and why, and to contribute to improved teaching and learning. However, several contributors to a state-of-the-art survey of interlanguage studies (Davies, Criper, and Howatt (eds.) 1984) point out that much research is limited by an exclusive dependence on the methods of linguistics, sociolinguistics, neurolinguistics, or psychology. McLaughlin (1987) analyses theories of second language learning in an analogous way and concludes that each approach ignores many variables. Lightbown (1987) suggests that adequate theories of language acquisition must draw not only on linguistics, psychology, and neurology, but also on sociology. This is evidently not yet the case in much research into foreign/second language learning either in schools or among adult immigrants, although one can envisage that it is particularly in connection with immigrant language learning that more coherent multi-disciplinary theories might emerge.

There is a move now to expand the range of variables which are considered important conditions for successful second and foreign language learning within a framework of curriculum rather than merely syllabus development (Johnson 1989). Rodgers notes that educational innovation has a low success rate, and that this may be in part explained by language pedagogy tending to ignore work in education and 'political concerns, in the largest sense'. He suggests a concentration on 'polity determination' in the sense of '1) the analysis of the existing socio-political context into which a new educational program is to fit as well as, 2) the development of strategies to optimize the probable success and effectiveness of the program in such a political context', and exemplifies how such a scheme can be operationalized (1989: 29–34). He refers to several ELT projects which list a large number of constraints that influence curriculum development, and proposes a framework for integrating the variables (knowledge factors, learner factors, instructional factors, and management factors) into a dynamic planning process. There is certainly, as we shall see later, a good deal of creative thinking along similar lines in the ELT profession, propelled, as is Rodgers, by dissatisfaction with the 'conventional' paradigms in this area. What we shall be concerned with in the first place is uncovering why the dominant paradigm took the form it did.

More attention is paid to the policy dimension in Stern's 'general model for second language teaching' (Stern 1983: 44), which is described as a general conceptual framework for language teaching, designed to make it possible to identify, develop, or evaluate commonly held theories, views, or philo-sophies on the teaching of languages, and cull insight from scientific disciplines (linguistics; sociology, sociolinguistics, and anthropology; psychology and psycholinguistics; educational theory) (ibid.: 45). Stern's model is more comprehensive and multidisciplinary than that of Strevens (it is in fact the skeleton which an entire book fleshes out), and posits a dialectical relationship between theory and practice and between the various elements in his model. Contextual factors are grouped into six sets: linguistic, socio-cultural, historical/political, educational, economic/technological, and geographic (ibid.: 274), all of which impinge on educational language planning. When the effectiveness of a foreign language or bilingual education programme is evaluated, the relative influence of each factor can be assessed. This model does not relegate contextual factors to the background, but it cannot account in detail for processes of international language spread, or for structures of domination and inequality between languages, or for professionalism as an ideology with structural implications.

Linguistic human rights

One way of campaigning for greater justice for speakers of dominated languages is to mobilize supranational human rights covenants in their favour. Human rights have a pedigree going back several centuries, to the transition from absolutism to more democratic social structures in Western societies. The treaties signed at the conclusion of the 1914–1918 war attempted to ensure international recognition of the rights of many minorities in central and eastern Europe. Since 1945, a substantial effort has gone into codifying and extending 'universal' declarations, with the aim of establishing generally agreed minimal conditions necessary for a just and humane social order. The primary goal of all declarations of human rights, whether national or international, is to protect the individual against arbitrary or unjust treatment. Human rights declarations have progressed through various phases: the first generation related to personal freedoms, civil and political rights (extended in the decolonization phase from the rights of individuals to the right of oppressed peoples to self-determination); the second generation related to economic, social, and cultural rights; and the third generation covers 'solidarity' rights (peace, development, an unspoilt environment). A corollary to the notion of a 'right' is the obligation of some other party, generally the state, to refrain from unjust treatment, or to provide conditions which permit the enjoyment of rights. Universal rights represent a normative standard, an inherent right which the state cannot be justified in restricting. In this sense they do not need arguments to legitimate them. They are absolute or inalienable rights.

Article 27 of the International Covenant on Civil and Political Rights (1966) declares:

In those States in which ethnic, religious, or linguistic minorities exist, persons belonging to such minorities shall not be denied the right, in community with the other members of their group, to enjoy their own culture, to profess and practice their own religion, or to use their own language.

A major survey was conducted for the UN (Capotorti 1979) to analyse juridical and conceptual aspects of protection against discrimination, and to solicit information from governments worldwide so as to assess how minorities are treated *de jure* and *de facto*. Immigrant minorities were explicitly excluded from consideration. The report concluded that most minorities, not least linguistic ones, were in need of much more substantial protection. It stresses the key role of education through the medium of the mother tongue for linguistic and cultural maintenance and vitality. It also interprets article 27 as imposing an obligation on states to actively promote minority languages. This presupposes that the state provides adequate financial support for them.

There is, however, abundant evidence that groups and individuals are deprived of their linguistic human rights, and that language shift occurs as a result. Many covenants, beginning with the UN Charter, declare that discrimination should be outlawed but do not oblige states to promote minority languages. Most states in fact expect their indigenous and immigrant minorities to assimilate to the dominant culture and language. A range of national constitutions and international covenants have been analysed (Skutnabb-Kangas and Phillipson 1986a, 1989), in order to gauge to what extent these texts provide support for dominated languages. We devised a grid on which the essential dimensions of language rights can be charted. The two dimensions are degree of overtness (from covert to overt) and degree of promotion (from prohibition of a language, via toleration of it, non-discrimination prescription, permission to use it, to promotion of it). The results of our review of a number of national constitutions indicate that a few countries, such as Finland, India, and Yugoslavia provide for the promotion of some, but by no means all, minority languages. Our review of international and European conventions and decrees (*Charter of the United Nations, Universal Declaration of Human Rights, the Convention on the Rights of the Child*, etc. Skutnabb-Kangas and Phillipson 1989: 13–19) indicates that no declarations ensure the maintenance of the mother tongue, despite the many clauses condemning discrimination. A valid conclusion is therefore that the *existing international or 'universal' declarations are in no way adequate to provide support for dominated languages.* The evidence shows unmistakably that while individuals and groups are supposed to enjoy 'cultural' and 'social' rights, linguistic human rights are neither guaranteed nor protected.

Awareness of this has led to a number of concerted initiatives intended to promote minority languages. Several organizations are involved—European supra-national bodies, UN bodies, and language teachers' associations.

Several European Parliament resolutions (most recently the Kuijpers Resolution 1987) recommend that 'regional' minority languages should be taught in official curricula from nursery school to university, and that these languages should be used in the media and in dealings with public authorities. The problem is that such resolutions have no legal force in individual countries, but their value in shifting public opinion should not be underestimated.

The European Community lends cautious support to the promotion of these languages, and supports a 'European Bureau for Lesser Used Languages' for this purpose. 'Lesser used' refers to 31 of the 60–65 autochthonous European languages, the mother tongues of close to 50 million of the 320 million citizens of Member States.

The Conference on Security and Co-operation in Europe (CSCE, the Helsinki accords) also seeks to guarantee the rights of minorities in participating countries: there are, for instance, several clauses guaranteeing linguistic rights in the closing document of the Copenhagen meeting, June 1990.

But the most comprehensive and substantial document is the Council of Europe's proposed *European Charter for Regional or Minority Languages* (Resolution 192, 1988, of the Standing Conference of Local and Regional Authorities in Europe. For the history of the charter, its rationale, form and thrust, see Woehrling 1990). This has been passed by the parliamentary assembly of the Council of Europe, and is awaiting approval by the Council of Ministers. It is significant that while recommending massive support for minority languages, the charter assumes a multilingual context, and expressly states that support for minority languages in no way represents a threat to official languages.

Within the UN system, there are several interesting developments. The *Draft Universal Declaration on Indigenous Rights* (as
contained in document E/CN.4/Sub.2/1988/25) constitutes a
step in the right direction, as it establishes as fundamental
human rights that indigenous peoples should have:

9   The right to develop and promote their own languages,
    including an own literary language, and to use them for
    administrative, judicial, cultural, and other purposes.
10 The right to all forms of education, including in particular
    the right of children to have access to education in their
    own languages, and to establish, structure, conduct, and
    control their own educational systems and institutions.

Unesco is also now committed to the elaboration of a
Universal Declaration of Linguistic Human Rights. An international seminar on Human Rights and Cultural Rights held in
October 1987 in Recife, Brazil and organized by AIMAV (the
International Association for Cross-cultural Communication)
with Unesco support, elaborated an extensive rationale
expounding the need for linguistic human rights to be explicitly
protected, and recommended that steps be taken by the United
Nations to adopt and implement a *universal declaration of
linguistic rights*. A preliminary four-point Declaration was also
adopted by the Seminar.[1] Among its goals would be to ensure
the right to use the mother tongue in official situations, and to
learn well both the mother tongue and the official language (or
one of them) of the country of residence. Such a declaration
might provide some protection for immigrant minority languages, which are not covered by the European resolutions or
Charter (and which get only marginal support from an EC
Directive on their teaching).

A conference on linguistic human rights was held at Unesco
in Paris in April 1989, organized by the FIPLV (Fédération
Internationale des Professeurs de Langues Vivantes). It expanded
the Recife Declaration and endorsed the call for a Universal
Declaration of Language Rights. As a result of the conference a
document is being circulated to a substantial number of
professional associations and researchers, and the elaborate
machinery for processing such a declaration is being set in
motion. The exercise will involve a major task for the scientific
community in clarifying concepts, drawing international comparisons, and elaborating a declaration of universal relevance
and applicability.[2] Substantial co-operation between linguists

and lawyers already exists (Pupier and Woehrling 1989; Turi forthcoming).

There is a serious risk of disagreement about what the scope of such a declaration should be and what exactly a linguistic human right is. The FIPLV would like a broad definition, and are canvassing the notion of the right to learn any foreign language for purposes of 'international understanding' as a human right. Ironically, a major factor influencing them in this direction is the dominance of English in Europe and a wish to provide a counterbalance. As European barriers are progressively lowered in preparation for the integrated market in 1992, freer market forces will intensify the movement of goods, people—and languages. The attempt in 1989 to ensure that all Western European children learn two foreign languages at school was designed to promote the learning of the official EC languages, but it also reflected European concern at the dominance of English. A two-foreign-languages proposal was blocked at a meeting of EC Ministers of Education by British resistance (for analysis of the reasons given by Britain see Stubbs in press). Britain is well aware that linguicism favours English at present.

Clearly those foreign languages that can succeed in legitimating massive presence on school timetables are dominant languages. There is a curious paradox here: continental European governments allocate huge resources to the learning of a language which threatens the continued viability of their own culture and language. One means of sugaring this pill would be to ensure that more than one dominant language was learnt, which is what politicians, abetted by language teachers' associations, are aiming at. The following comes from a submission to Unesco on foreign language education up to and beyond the year 2000 by the FIPLV:

> Increasing economic pressures on governments and local authorities has produced in many national curricula the linguistic and cultural hegemony of one foreign language, which, as an albeit diluted form of outmoded imperialism, frustrates the aim of international understanding insofar as the opportunity for young learners to study other languages and cultures, or to be receptive towards them, is thus removed. Single language dominance must be avoided for, in this respect, it is not defensible on educational grounds. Moreover, it tends to favour the 'privileged' languages of the world and neglect utterly the legitimate interests of others. (FIPLV 1988: 1)

The underlying rationale of this submission seems to be that dominant international languages have a legitimate interest in their promotion in foreign education systems, but only if diversity is assured. But however laudable the goal of international understanding may be, there is a serious risk of this proposal leading to a blurring of the distinction between languages which are *necessary* for cultural maintenance and survival, and languages for personal *enrichment* and national benefit. There is thus a tension between

- the struggle of dominated indigenous and immigrant languages for basic human rights and justice
- the interest of European nation states in maintaining the integrity and vitality of their official languages by ensuring that there are some limits to the advance of English, where the hope is that this will be achieved by ensuring that European schools equip people to operate in two foreign languages.

How this tension will be resolved, at the level of professional associations (several are likely to be involved)[3] and of Unesco, is unclear at present, but there is no doubt of the commitment of scholars, politicians, and a substantial number of supra-national organizations to this cause (see Giordan 1992; Skutnabb-Kangas and Phillipson forthcoming). It also needs to be recalled that there are limitations to all such international covenants. Their precise legal status is unclear, though some states incorporate obligations undertaken under international law into their domestic law, and Europeans have the right, if they fail in a case in their national courts, to take it to the European Court of Human Rights. Litigation is, however, inevitably a lengthy, expensive, and chancy business.[4] Another weakness is that there is a tendency for covenants to be conceptually vague, allowing nation states to interpret them as they please. However, the assertion of a normative, inalienable standard is of major significance for minority groups, and can help to legitimate dominated languages and delegitimate the claims of dominant groups and languages.

Two approaches, Wardhaugh and Calvet

As a final indication of how some of the issues raised in this book have been approached, two recent books which deal with similar topics will be analysed. They are *Languages in Competition: dominance, diversity and decline* by Ronald Wardhaugh (1987), and *La guerre des langues et les politiques linguistiques* by Louis-Jean Calvet (1987). The comparison shows different theoretical standpoints, different perceptions of what is significant in the study of language dominance, and different value judgements underlying their positions. This highlights the complexity of coming to grips with this area, and also raises ethical issues in relation to professionalism.

The two books are general introductions to glottopolitics and how languages rise and fall. Both authors see languages as living organisms which emerge, grow, and prosper or die. Languages battle with each other for dominance and survival. But the biases of each author are clear from their respective titles. Wardhaugh's is a liberalistic approach to a free market of linguistic competition. For Calvet, some languages are killed, as the expansion of one language often means the disappearance of another. Linguistic warfare is for him a reality and not merely a metaphor for the politics of language and relations between languages. The title links warfare with language policy, which can influence the outcome. That is where linguists come in.

It is a source of strength that both books review a large number of linguistic situations, but when coverage is inevitably brief, the success of the venture depends crucially on the overall structure of the book, the chosen theoretical framework, and the way empirical material is handled. Theory-building is notably lacking in this field, despite the massive documentation of linguistic inequality worldwide. Hymes (1985: v) has noted the absence of a unifying theory of linguistic inequality.

Wardhaugh's first three chapters are a summary of the approaches of several disciplines to such issues as language spread, diversity, ethnicity, and nationalism. Thereafter the book is mainly geographically and historically motivated (language in Britain, France, and Spain, the promotion of English and French worldwide, sub-Saharan Africa, Canada, USA, etc.). Linking these topics is what for Wardhaugh is the core issue— the struggle for power between English and French worldwide. Competition from the original indigenous languages in Britain and France is accorded serious attention, but the same principle is not followed in analysing the Europeanized countries of the new world. In the description of the USA and Canada, the languages of Native American peoples are totally ignored, and Australian Aborigines only merit a passing reference. It is the big languages that interest Wardhaugh. As these have experienced a modest challenge from the languages of recent immigrants, the competition from them is also described. Even in Africa, the key drama is held to be the competition between the former colonial languages, though of the major local languages, Arabic in the Maghreb and Swahili in East Africa are regarded as strong enough to be considered good competition, and are therefore given substantial coverage.

Calvet's book is divided into three parts, on, respectively, the origins of linguistic conflict (covering the origins of language, religions and language, multilingualism, and doctrines of linguistic superiority); the battlefield (covering 'gregarious' and 'vehicular' languages, 'mother tongues' and the family, markets and multilingualism, language death); and headquarters (language policy and imperialism, language planning—various case studies—the war of the alphabets, the war of lexis, the defence of French as a case of trench warfare, and Esperanto as an example of the pacifist illusion).

From these panoramic synopses it can be seen that the unifying theme for Wardhaugh is the empirical facts of language competition in nation states, viewed against a background of potentially relevant theory, whereas Calvet's military theme provides a structure for an analysis of key influences on linguistic struggle and on the main actors in the field. Wardhaugh's descriptions in fact draw very little on the theoretical and conceptual tools he initially presents, whereas for Calvet the necessary theory is introduced *ad hoc* in order to explain how language relates to power, what societal processes are mediated by language, and the relationship between ideological and structural phenomena. The appealing symmetry of his book is bolstered by a coherent, multidisciplinary theoretical framework. His scientific position is explicitly stated, whereas Wardhaugh aims at presenting competing analyses, without declaring his own hand directly.

Theories of the kind reported by Wardhaugh tend to be restricted to typologies of large numbers of variables, as noted in the discussion above of language spread and the sociology of language. He writes as a professional linguist, and makes no attempt to integrate the perspectives of several disciplines into a unified theory in order to account for the evidence of his analyses. Calvet's book follows on logically from his earlier work, particularly *Linguistique et colonialisme: un petit traité de glottophagie* (1974), which analysed the history and nature of scientific paradigms and some central concepts within linguistics in order to identify the social interests served by scientific activity, and in particular the way linguists legitimated colonialism. His new book treads new ground in relation to many familiar concepts such as diglossia, lingua franca, and mother tongue, and his major contribution is to link up linguistics, and language planning in particular, with the societal and political framework within which it operates. His plea is that linguists should be aware of their own value judgements and hoist their democratic antennae whenever they work for the State, which is almost invariably the commissioning source of their work. This is necessary because there is always the risk of powerful 'experts' dispossessing people of their languages. If war is the continuation of politics by other means, then the conduct of linguistic policy is the civil form of the battle between languages, in which case the linguist needs to strive for the maximum amount of democratic control of all aspects of language policy.

Wardhaugh's study is mainly anchored in the sociology of language, even if he is a linguist. Linguists and linguistics are curiously absent, and there is relatively little sign in the book of the contribution that the linguist might make to the resolution of ongoing linguistic struggles. Here, too, Calvet differs: he frequently shows how the linguist is in a key position, both as a language planner (for instance in relation to choice of scripts, or the promotion of a particular dialect) and in sociolinguistic research. He has himself done extensive research on the role of languages in the family and the marketplace in West Africa, and the richness of his empirical observations, from Latin America to China, permeates the book.

As a linguist Wardhaugh is interested in the validation of norms for a language. Here he sees decisive differences between a monolithic French approach, with insistence on a metropolitan standard, and multipolar English (British, American, Australian, Indian, etc.) positions. He is strongly influenced by the official rhetoric surrounding French, the idea that French people believe their language is inherently superior, and the prescriptivism which this entails. This has of course been a key component of France's *mission civilisatrice*. So far as English is concerned, he believes that the language-culture equation is weaker and that 'speakers of English are much more accepting of differences in the ways in which English is spoken and used in the world' (op. cit.: 14). He assigns this difference in attitudes a causal role in accounting for the spread of English as a second/foreign language and the relative failure of French to do likewise. In this, he is on shaky ground, for two reasons. Firstly, it is an empirical fact that French now has more speakers of the language, as a first and second language, than at any time in its history (Calvet 1987: 263). This scarcely indicates decline, though it does not alter the fact that English is expanding faster in many domains (including key ones such as academic writing and international organizations) at the expense of French—in the sense that previously French was the favoured language, providing its native speakers and their culture with advantages and simultaneously excluding others. Secondly, beliefs and attitudes are integrally related to the relative power of languages, which has multiple causes, of which the most important are economic and political. While it is correct to note the importance of attitude, it cannot be seen in isolation from structural power (which neither linguicism theory nor Kachru's approach does). The British, Americans, and French have all been keen to impose their linguistic norms worldwide. The issue here is essentially one of control. Wardhaugh's theoretical framework provides no means of assessing the truth value of his assertion that attitudinal factors would be of more significance in the case of one dominant language than of another.

Wardhaugh's book is flawed by a number of errors of fact (for details, see Phillipson 1990), and also by contradictory statements. On the one hand he rightly notes that in Africa proficiency in the former colonial language is crucial for access to élite social strata. On the other he claims that language has 'not yet been tied to the spoils system' (op. cit.: 175). Similarly, he regards English as 'neutral' and divorced from cultural associations (op. cit.: 15), while at the same time it is linked with Anglo-American values, influence and 'modernity' (op. cit.: 132). These conflicting messages may in some measure derive from the way Wardhaugh has chosen to present the issues. Many analyses and interpretations are presented in terms of 'there are those who think', 'some critics/advocates claim . . . ', with no indication of their source. This is a characteristic feature of a book which is guided by a 'parliamentary theory of knowledge', and which presents the main views and then lets the reader make up his or her mind. The preface explicitly states this as a strategy. However, this stance leads to muddle and inconsistency. Thus, neo-colonialism is identified correctly as leading to 'the continuation of certain types of linguistic influence and to new pressures' (op. cit.: 12). A whole chapter is devoted to describing such activity, namely the efforts of the British, Americans, and French to promote their languages worldwide. Yet the claim is simultaneously put forward that 'The majority of states pursue a policy of linguistic and cultural assimilation of minorities within their borders while observing the convention that one state should not interfere in the internal affairs of others, at least not directly' (op. cit.: 28). Such conflicting signals are compounded by the way Wardhaugh mostly puts concepts like neo-colonialism and race in inverted commas, as a way of distancing himself from the terms rather than using them as rigorous analytical concepts.

When it comes to analysis and drawing conclusions, however, Wardhaugh almost invariably does take sides. He is partisan in according different treatment to English and French (for details, see Phillipson 1990). His approach is typical of native English-speakers who uncritically applaud the spread of English. There is a strong element of the triumphalism of apologists of dominant languages that Fishman so deplores (1988).

In general, Wardhaugh feels that it is unlikely that minority languages (Irish, Gaelic, Welsh, etc.) will survive. This is largely because his analysis of language competition is coloured and skewed by a monolingual view of the world. He has a subtractive view of bilingualism, regarding it as leading inevitably to societal and individual monolingualism. He blurs the distinction between grassroots multilingualism and bilingualism achieved through formal education (European languages in Africa can only be learnt in formal education). He is not persuaded by any of the evidence of resistance to language displacement and shift and is suspicious of the multilingualism which is the norm for many, perhaps a majority of people in the world.

Calvet begins with how languages emerge, the 'paleontology of language'. There is neurolinguistic evidence that specialization of the brain for communication functions was directly related to humans becoming bipeds and starting to use tools, which indicates that these evolutionary processes were closely linked. Verbal communication evolved to meet specific social needs, when gesture and grunts were no longer adequate. Language emerged therefore polygenetically, and humankind is multilingual. The socio-historical and biological evidence thus conflicts with the Biblical myth of a single language and with multilingualism as the curse of Babel. Language evolved as a result of social pressures, including the pressures of language contact. Its origin is inescapably linked to relations of force, to power and its negotiation. Calvet concludes that humanity is thus in a constant state of semiological conflict.

Calvet expands the concept of diglossia so as to anchor it more firmly in societal power and permit analysis of nested multiglossic situations (Pride 1982 also refers to triglossic situations), such as in Tanzania. Calvet then presents a typology of diglossic situations, exemplified in relation to countries in which French is spoken. His types are: multilingualism with a single dominant language (France); multilingualism with minority dominant languages (the Maghreb, with 'official' Arabic sharing cultural dominance with French and monopolizing socio-political dominance); multilingualism with a single minority language dominant (francophone Africa); multilingualism with an alternative dominant language (creole countries in the Caribbean); and multilingualism with dominant regional languages (Switzerland, Belgium).

Calvet's 'linguistic racism' has similarities with linguicism, the most obvious example being the ideology of linguistic superiority associated with dominant languages. This can be traced back to the Greeks. The French later harnessed it to a linguicidal policy at home and abroad. The eighteenth-century idea of the 'universality' of French, at a time when only a minority of citizens of France spoke the language, was due to French being the international language of the European ruling groups. In addition to functional arguments, a fundamentally racist ideology of superiority (elegance, clarity, the 'natural' order of its syntax) was propagated: those languages which did not have the same syntax as French were not 'logical' and were therefore inferior. This ideology was used to legitimate an unequal distribution of power and resources to the dominant language.

Central theoretical constructs for Calvet in categorizing the vast diversity of language functions are two poles, the 'vehicular' and the 'gregarious'. Gregarious language serves purposes of social intimacy, shared identity, the small group. Vehicular language by contrast serves the purpose of wider communication, an extreme type being pidgin. Calvet's use of vehicular corresponds to what Anglo-Saxons generally refer to as lingua francas (see Chapter 3), but is broader and permits a link-up to official languages. Social mobility necessitates the use of a vehicular language (the gregarious language with power), and linguistic shift may mark the demise of gregarious languages.

Calvet shows that language survival depends crucially on the language(s) of primary socialization in the family, a point also made by Fishman (1990) in his typology of factors necessary for reversing language shift. The family is thus a microcosm of the linguistic conflicts of the wider community. Calvet exemplifies the pecking order of languages and their establishment by presenting empirical data on language use in markets in Canton (China), Brazzaville (Congo), and Niamey (Niger). Despite multilingual diversity, languages achieve necessary social purposes, and language use is a mirror of the societal power of the languages in question. The market is a catalyst for the emergence of vehicular languages. Presumably the same applies in the global marketplace, with linguicism operating to concentrate the power of the dominant languages.

Calvet anchors language policy clearly to the interests of the state. As language planning is one aspect of national planning, and as intervention can change both the corpus of a language and relationships between languages, this casts linguists in a new role. They are no longer merely observing and identifying rules, they are now making the rules. If one includes acquisition planning within language planning, this would mean that applied linguists involved in planning language education are also 'making the rules'.

Several case studies are presented in some detail: the consolidation of Pu tong hua in China and Hindi in India, and the use of local languages as the medium of education in Guinea. Calvet's conclusion (op. cit.: 180) is that in each of the three cases there is a State thrust towards monolingualism, to boost the idea of a single language, nation, and State.[5]

Calvet presents one case study of successful resistance to linguistic imperialism. The Jivaros of Ecuador, or 'Shuars' as they call themselves, are, according to Calvet, the only indigenous Latin American group who have succeeded in integrating their own language and culture into education and in educating their people bilingually in Shuar and Spanish. (Similar moves are apparently gaining strength in Mexico, Hamel 1990.) Shuar schools operate independently of State control, make extensive use of radio and TV, and demonstrate that a peripheral dominated group can liberate itself from the linguistic and educational norms of the centre, and can, through its own efforts, upgrade its gregarious language, and ensure its transmission from one generation to the next.

The 'defence' of French is traced back to the establishment of the Alliance Française in 1883. Only a language which is in decline needs 'defending'—though much of the rhetoric of declining standards and linguistic sloppiness is also heard in relation to expansionist English. One embarrassing parallel for the combatants for French purity is that the legal measures enacted to buttress French closely parallel those of Fascist regimes (Italy, Germany, Spain): intolerance of dialects and minority languages within national borders, xenophobic national linguistic purity, and an expansionist urge externally. Calvet is critical of French efforts to protect the intrinsic structure of French, mainly on two counts: they are doomed to be ineffective, and they ignore the root cause of the problems of French, which has nothing to do with French at all but is, in fact, English. This is an external factor, rooted in politics and economics rather than language.

On the global diffusion of American culture, Calvet has little to say, apart from a rather limited study of the Summer Institute of Linguistics (SIL). Calvet reports some of the criticism of this missionary body—that it has been accused of CIA activity—and of furthering commercial interests, and in general of serving the interests of the West and the central governments that permit them to operate, rather than the indigenous people they are purportedly 'helping' (via alphabetization and evangelism) on the road to western 'development'. There is abundant evidence that the SIL is patronizing, holds up the USA as a model, stigmatizes indigenous cultures, and that their influence is disastrous for indigenous people. Even if the missionaries themselves have the best of intentions, and have been instrumental in alphabetizing some threatened languages, structurally they are cultural imperialists. There is no analysis of how language policy and language pedagogy have served American interests worldwide.

Some of Calvet's theoretical principles are stated more explicitly in his study of linguistics and colonialism (1974). The thrust towards monolingualism, both in France and in the French empire, involved the dominant language 'eating up' the dominated ones (glottophagie = linguistic cannibalism). The linguistic division of labour was an integral part of the exclusionary practices of colonial racism. Calvet uses the term 'linguistic superstructure' to refer to the 'linguistic status which characterizes certain power relationships (not only in the colonial situation), bilingualism with opposition between the dominant and the dominated language, the crushing of one or more languages by another, exclusive language, etc.' (1974: 65). This definition manifestly has affinities with the definition of linguicism, has some elements of structure in it, and also covers the consequences of this 'linguistic superstructure'.[6]

Calvet's analysis of dominant and dominated languages, and the way linguistics serves to legitimate such inequality leads him to conclude that in underdeveloped countries ' . . . any nominal liberation which is not accompanied by an overthrow of the linguistic superstructure is not a liberation of the people, who speak the dominated language, but a liberation of the social class which spoke and continues to speak the dominant language' (ibid.: 137). 'There cannot be economic and political decolonization without in the course of this process, there being a linguistic decolonization' (ibid.: 152). It is time now to look in more depth at colonial linguistic policies and their legacy in the contemporary world.

Notes

1   The Recife declaration was almost identical with a proposal put forward by Tove Skutnabb-Kangas (1984). The four points were:
    (a) Every social group has the right to positively identify with one or more languages and to have such identification accepted and respected by others.
    (b) Every child has the right to learn the language(s) of his/her group fully.
    (c) Every person has the right to use the language of his/her group in any official situation.
    (d) Every person has the right to learn fully at least one of the official languages in the country where s/he is resident, according to her/his own choice.
2   Debate about whether rights are individual or collective tends to be somewhat sterile, as the one is frequently meaningless without the other. Likewise, whether rights can inhere in a language (which the proposed European Charter

opts for) or only in its speakers also seems something of a chicken or egg discussion.

3   AILA, the Association Internationale de Linguistique Appliquée, is already involved.

4   The standard textbook on human rights conventions and case law is Sieghart 1983. A case of extreme interest for minorities is currently being heard in the Norwegian courts (Skutnabb-Kangas and Phillipson 1989, Chapter 11). A Sami is suing the state for compensation on the grounds that it failed to provide him with the education he was entitled to, and that his life chances were adversely affected. He arrived at school speaking no Norwegian, and the teachers spoke no Sami.

5   So far as India is concerned, there is substantial counter-evidence to a monolingualism hypothesis: constitutional protection for linguistic minorities, élite multilingualism via schooling, the three-language formula, etc., quite apart from the reality of grassroots multilingualism.

6   Calvet's terminology here is drawn from Marxist theory. He relates his framework explicitly to Stalin's comments on language not being a superstructural phenomenon (see also Goodman 1968). He is critical of Stalin for ignoring multilingualism and the way different classes use different forms of a language, or, in a diglossic division of linguistic labour, different languages. For Calvet, Stalin's concern, whether language belongs to the superstructure or to the base or both, is a false way of conceptualizing the issue. It is not a language that is a superstructural phenomenon but 'social linguistic organisation'.

5 The colonial linguistic inheritance

Their masters' language

> I was greatly delighted with my new companion, and made it
> my business to teach him everything that was proper to make
> him useful, handy, and helpful; but especially to make him
> speak, and understand me when I spake, and he was the aptest
> schollar that ever was.
> (Defoe 1719; 1965: 213)

Robinson Crusoe's version of how and why he taught Man
Friday English is one of the first published descriptions of
English teaching. The motivation for a shared language was
obvious, the power relationship between the two people in
Defoe's fantasy clear-cut, faithfully reflecting the racial structure
of western society at the heyday of slavery. Crusoe sought
adventure and fortune overseas, like so many of his compatriots.
Wherever the British have settled, they have taken their language
with them. It has been suggested (frivolously, but in an academic
setting) that Robinson Crusoe is the unacknowledged founder of
the British Council (Politi 1985: 195).

It is not frivolous to regard Defoe's book as having a
significant and widespread impact. In the words of an expert on
eighteenth-century European literature, *Robinson Crusoe* 'began
to set a style and dominate a reading public on the continent . . .
It was much wider in its influence than had been any single
English book up to that time' (Stone 1959: 17). Defoe's classic
adventure story has followed the British round the world. When
simplified readers were first produced by a British publisher so as
to assist colonized subjects in acquiring English as a foreign
language, the first title published was none other than *Robinson
Crusoe* (the Longman New Method series, 1926). Presumably
the subject matter was regarded as pre-eminently suitable for the
colonial context.

Proficiency in English was essential for functioning in colonial
periphery-English societies, at least for those who had dealings

with the colonizers. This was true in lands which were being Europeanized by settlers, from North America to Australia, and which now have the status of core-English countries. It was equally true in all parts of the periphery-English world where the British flag once flew.

Colonial educational language policy and practice

The significance of language was understood from the early expansionist phase of imperialism. In India, the English language was regarded as a force for the 'modernizing' of the country, the purpose being to educate a class of Indians who could function as interpreters between the British colonial power and the millions of Indians they governed, 'a class of persons Indian in blood and colour, but English in taste, in opinions, in morals, and in intellect', to cite Lord Macaulay's dictum of 1834 (quoted in Khubchandani 1983: 120; see also Pattanayak 1981: 174 ff.). Macaulay was chairman of the Governor-General's Committee on Public Instruction.

Macaulay's formulation of the goals of British educational policy ended a protracted controversy which had excercised planners both in India and in the East India Company in London. Education in 'orientalist' traditions, through Sanskrit, Arabic, or Persian, was weighed up against a scientifically-oriented 'anglicist' approach. When Macaulay one-sidely favoured the British model, he doubtless quite genuinely believed that English could do for India what Greek and Latin were assumed to have done for western Europe. The same argument was still in use in the 1950s (Nuffield Foundation and Colonial Office 1953: 82). The decision to promote English language and thought needs to be seen in conjunction with accompanying political, economic, and social pressures, and not least the role assigned to indigenous education. The administrative decree effectuating Macaulay's policy in 1835 is unambiguous on this: 'the great object of the British Government ought to be the promotion of European literature and science among the natives of India; and that all the funds appropriated for the purpose of education would be best employed on English education alone' (Khubchandani 1983: 120). This decision on funding firmly slammed the door on indigenous traditions of learning. The power of English was further strengthened by a decision in 1837 to replace Persian as the official language of the law courts with

English. By 1844, when results of the educational policy were beginning to show, it was decreed that when Indians were recruited to posts under the government, preference would be given to those who had received an English education.

The result of this policy was that throughout the Indian subcontinent 'English became the sole medium of education, administration, trade, and commerce, in short of all formal domains of a society's functioning. Proficiency in English became the gateway to all social and material benefits' (Misra 1982: 150). This was one of the main achievements of nearly two centuries of British rule, and one of the most durable legacies.

Macaulay had a seminal influence on language policy throughout the British Empire. His strategy was endorsed at the Imperial Conferences of 1913 and 1923. In the words of the head of the British Council's English teaching operations for many years, Macaulay 'determined what we should do, quite literally, from Hong Kong to the Gambia'[1] (King 1961: 23). English was the master language of the empire. The job of education was to produce people with mastery of English.[2] 'Education' was of course conceived very differently then, as it was intended for a limited proportion of the subjects of the empire. Linguicist beliefs about the superiority of one language were embedded in an educational structure which gave preference to this language.

It is widely believed that a *comparison between the British and French empires* reveals a fundamental difference in their language policies. The justification for this contention seems to be that the French were more singleminded in the prosecution of their language, more conscious of a 'civilizing mission', more intolerant of the use of indigenous languages at any stage in education, and more effective in educating black men (and far fewer women) to speak the metropolitan language beautifully. However, this is a very selective over-simplification of the issues involved. While it is true that in the Arab world and sub-Saharan Africa virtually no teaching was permitted in local languages, in Indo-China the French departed from their French-only policy and allowed education in local languages. British policy in India followed Macaulay in excluding Indian languages for many years, but shifted to a linguistically stratified system by the end of the nineteenth century. The British policy of 'indirect rule' was to be effectuated by educating the élite exclusively through the medium of English; primary education could for others be in the vernacular, and for the few who continued into secondary education, a switch to English was made (Khubchandani 1983: 121). In British colonies in Africa, African languages generally served as the medium of education for the first few years of the primary school. But instruction through a local language was invariably seen as a transitional phase prior to instruction in English. Local languages were never accorded high status in any colonial society.

The overall goals of the colonial powers were conceived differently, the French aiming at *la France outre-mer* and ultimate union with metropolitan France, the British accepting the principle of trusteeship, leading ultimately to self-government and independence. Whether these variants were experienced differently by colonial subjects, or have had different major long-term effects of a structural or ideological kind is doubtful. Education served the interests of the colonizing power, and large areas of social life were unaffected by colonial education or linguistic policies. Even if the French organized education exclusively through the medium of French in Africa, the proportion of the population involved was minute, and only slightly larger in British Africa. A few examples will illustrate this.

– According to French government sources, when the French arrived to 'civilize' Algeria, the literacy rate in urban Algeria was 40 per cent—far higher than in France at the time. When the French left after 130 years of colonization, the literacy rate among Algerians was, according to an optimistic reckoning, 10–15 per cent (Colonna 1975).

– Figures for French Equatorial Africa for 1938 and 1955 indicate that, even when accorded the most favourable interpretation, less than 1 per cent of children attended school (Calvet 1979: 132). In (British) Tanganyika and the Belgian Congo by comparison, roughly 4 per cent attended school in the same period (ibid.: 145). However, such figures are themselves misleading, because of the annual attrition: in Tanganyika in 1950, 58,144 pupils attended the first year of the primary school, 40,201 the second, 30,464 the third, and 23,142 the fourth. The same pattern was true elsewhere in British tropical Africa (Nuffield Foundation and Colonial Office 1953: 77). The study group which compiled these figures estimated that for children who completed less than four years of schooling, no lasting literacy benefits material-

ized and the experience of school could well have been psychologically damaging (ibid.: 77).
– The big expansion of secondary education dates from the 1950s, following the recognition that some form of independence for colonies was much more imminent than had been appreciated earlier, but the educational pyramid was still steep: for instance in Central Africa the number of children completing the fourth class, as a proportion of the children in any one year of school age, ranged from 10 per cent in Nyasaland to 39 per cent in Northern Rhodesia (now Zambia). But by the eighth class the figure was under 3 per cent in both countries, and by the end of the twelfth class the figure was 0.05 per cent. Expansion took place rapidly. For instance in Nigeria the number of secondary pupils increased from 9,908 in 1947 to 134,799 in 1959 (Spencer 1971: 539).[3]

These figures relate only to schooling run by the European colonial power and ignore traditional African methods of upbringing and training for adult responsibilities. They conceal the fact that in some African countries there was widespread literacy in Arabic for secular as well as religious purposes. Such schooling was not considered 'educational' by the French (ibid.: 543). The French and the British were in concert in stigmatizing or simply *ignoring local traditions in educational practice*.

Although the imperial powers had slightly different ultimate goals and education policies, and considerable autonomy was allowed to the many Christian missions who bore the brunt of teaching, the goals tended to be formulated in identical terms. The French 'civilizing' mission was an explicit policy, and was based on the myth of Reason as an ideology for all citizens, which the French language ensured access to (Achard 1986: 18). The reformist French Third Republic set out on a programme of democratizing education in France after 1870 and incorporating social classes hitherto regarded as inferior and not worth educating. The overseas possessions were under the direct jurisdiction of Paris, and the same educational laws were put into effect throughout the French empire. The purpose and historical mission of education in the French empire was outlined by Rambaud, the Minister of Public Education in 1897, in relation to Algeria:

> The first conquest of Algeria was accomplished militarily and was completed in 1871 when Kabylia was disarmed. The second conquest has consisted of making the natives accept

our administrative and judicial systems. The third conquest will be by the School: this should ensure the predominance of our language over the various local idioms, inculcate in the muslims our own idea of what France is and of its role in the world, and replace ignorance and fanatical prejudices by the simple but precise notions of European science.
(quoted in Colonna 1975: 40)

The French attitude was expounded by a senior inspector with responsibility for overseas education in 1910 as follows:

. . . to attach them to the Metropole by a very solid psychological bond, against the day when their progressive emancipation ends in a form of federation, as is probable . . . that they be, and they remain, French in language, thought, and spirit.
(Foncin, quoted in Ashby 1966: 365)

School had a specific role in achieving this transformation.

To transform the primitive peoples in our colonies, to render them as devoted as possible to our cause and useful to our commerce . . . the safest method is to take the native in childhood, bring him into assiduous contact with us and subject him to our intellectual and moral habits for many years in succession, in a word to open schools for him where his mind can be shaped at our will.
(Hardy 1917, quoted in Taleb Ibrahimi 1973: 12)

Macaulay's statement of British goals in India has already been quoted, and is in the same vein as the French policy statements. That period saw similar British pronouncements, with a rather more explicitly Christian bias, for South-East Asia and Ceylon (now Sri Lanka) (see the examples in Kachru 1986).[4] British involvement in education in Africa also dates from the beginning of the nineteenth century, in the first place on the initiative of missions. Whereas in India there was controversy over the relative merits of competing systems of education, in Africa the decision to introduce education of a British kind was taken 'instinctively, on the assumption that no other course was open' (Ashby 1966: 148). The first schools were modelled on the charity schools in Britain, and taught basic literacy and numeracy skills but concentrated on religious instruction.

There was considerable diversity in educational practice in the colonies of the British empire:

Education in each colony tended to be greatly influenced by individuals—governors, directors of education, and particularly by heads of schools or institutions. Colonial educators and administrators were very wary indeed about the relevance of Indian examples and experience, and Macaulay had little influence . . . The Colonial Office published reports by its advisory committees, often composed of those with direct experience in various colonies, but did not lay down rules, only principles. In practice there were great differences between the various colonies.
(Perren, ms)

For much of the nineteenth century Sierra Leone was the only British colony in West Africa, the Gold Coast being added in 1874, and Nigeria not being unified under one governor until 1914. Meanwhile the missions, who provided most of the (European) education available, and who were by no means all British, had a fairly free hand. The goal in any case was limited:

When modern education was first introduced into Africa there was little expectation that its purpose would be more than to provide a limited number of craftsmen, catechists, teachers, clerks or minor functionaries for the service of missions or the colonial administration.
(Perren 1969: 198)

A plan presented to the Colonial Office in 1847 recommended a practically-oriented curriculum, to be devised after careful study of local customs and needs. This in many ways enlightened document however reflects faithfully the thought of the time when it proclaims that a grammatical knowledge of the English language was 'the most important agent of civilization for the coloured population of the colonies' (quoted in Ashby 1966: 150).

The hegemony of the dominant colonial languages was buttressed by a linguicist ideology in both empires. Whereas the French more actively propagated a discourse of linguistic supremacy, the British, though apparently more pragmatic and *laissez-faire*, had a fundamentally similar attitude to the virtues of English and failings of other languages.

There was genuine uncertainty about what the essential content of primary education should be in British Africa, reflecting the duality of an evangelizing, transforming cause and the need for sensitivity to local acceptability. However a visit to

Sierra Leone in 1867 by an Inspector from London was decisive in consolidating the transfer of a strictly British educational model. This had far-reaching consequences, because Sierra Leone was unlike all the other British colonies in Africa. Sierra Leone was founded as a home for freed slaves and had therefore an untypical ethnic and linguistic composition. The first Inspector for West Africa, the Reverend Metcalfe Sunter, who held office for a decade from 1873, was an inflexible ethnocentric: he felt that the Africans had no history of their own, and was staunchly opposed to the study of indigenous languages. His utilitarian arguments in favour of English and against the use of local languages have a curiously contemporary ring about them: the local languages were still imperfectly reduced to written form, the dialects were no more than locally useful, England was a country 'of which they ought to know something', and English was the language of commerce and the ruling power (ibid.: 154).

> His main achievement was the administrative one of having brought all British West Africa under the effective operation of the educational system inaugurated at Sierra Leone. He had thus helped to fix the missionary approach in an essentially English image of education, which took little account of the practical needs of the African and almost none of his cultural susceptibilities.
>
> (quoted in Ashby 1966: 155)

This verdict seems to apply as much when missions learnt local languages and used these as the medium of education as when English was used.

In ignoring the African past, the Rev. Sunter faithfully mirrored imperialist ideology. Even in academic fields such as ethnography a similar blindness to African cultures prevailed until the 1950s (Davidson 1982: 445). The eurocentric bias of such social sciences as economics, psychology, and social anthropology has impoverished these disciplines by making them unaware of alternative sources of knowledge (Joseph, Reddy, and Searle-Chatterjee 1990). The functionalist anthropology school which dominated the field in the 1920s and 1930s was committed to studying contemporary African societies in order to make colonial administration more effective or functional (Fisher 1982: 249). Their work was largely financed by the Rockefeller Foundation, which had such a pervasive influence that, to a great extent, it 'determined not only "what" should be studied in the social sciences but also "how" these studies were conducted' (ibid.: 233). The best known of these applied anthropologists was Malinowski, whose efforts were motivated by a wish to assist colonial control. His advice on the curriculum was that it should not develop in the African 'the hope that through education he can become the white man's "brother" and his economic and political equal' (Malinowski 1936: 504). Malinowski's position was in fact ambivalent. In much of his writing he attempted to educate policy-makers into much greater awareness of the complexity and strengths of the indigenous cultures of Africa. For instance his Introduction to Kenyatta's analysis of Gikuyu culture (1938) praises it as competent scholarship, warns against the folly of ignoring African intellectuals or treating them contemptuously as 'agitators', and points out that western culture in the 1930s (fascism, Stalinism, complicity in Italian aggression in Abyssinia, religious sectarianism) was riddled with the kind of superstition that 'primitive tribes' are accused of, and was, indeed, scarcely 'civilized'.[5]

Although colonial educational policy was fundamentally racist (there was still separate education for Europeans, Asians, and Africans in Kenya in the 1950s) and linguicist, there is no doubt that many of the policy-makers and the workers in the field were well-intentioned and genuinely wished not only to export what was best in British education to the colonies but also to adapt the education to perceived local needs. In Africa serious attention was given to the question of standards, not least because the Africans themselves did not want to be fobbed off with anything second-class or to be confined to vocational training. In India in the second half of the nineteenth century there was debate about whether the emphasis on literature should be changed towards more technical subjects (Bolt 1971). Literature was taught in Britain through a canon of 'difficult' set books, and this tradition was exported overseas, via examination boards and British personnel: 'British-trained teachers and inspectors have, often without question, assumed that what was believed right for Britain (especially anything concerned with the English language) would also be valuable overseas' (Perren 1963: 113).

There was a call for the creation of a university in West Africa as early as 1872 (Ashby 1966: 163). Some colonial governors in the nineteenth century could see the advantages of creating

thriving local institutions, and it appeared then that by analogy
with Western Europe after the reformation, flourishing universities could come into existence even when secondary schooling
was embryonic. However the Colonial Office was cautious, and
keen to learn from developments in university education in
Europe, North America, and India. It was only after the Second
World War that the prospect of independence for many colonies
was seriously envisaged. From that point education was expanded dramatically at all levels.

Policy reports on various aspects of colonial education were
produced at regular intervals throughout the first half of this
century.[6] The first thorough investigation of colonial education
was undertaken by representatives of an American philanthropic
trust, the Phelps-Stokes Fund, at the request of the Foreign
Missions Conference of North America. They visited West,
South, and Equatorial Africa in 1920–1 and East, Central, and
South Africa in 1924, with the blessing of the colonial
authorities. The Phelps–Stokes Reports criticize the education
then offered to Africans, at all levels, for being too divorced from
life outside the classroom and not being adapted to African
conditions (Jones 1922, 1925).[7] The reports stress that the
mother tongue of the learners should be used in the early stages
of education. There is a clear analysis of relevant factors to be
considered when forming policy for education in multilingual
settings. Many of their proposals, for instance on the use of the
mother tongues and avoiding the creation of a class of Africans
who would be estranged from the masses who had not had a
European-style education, were incorporated into a Colonial
Office policy statement, a *Memorandum on Education Policy in
British Tropical Africa* in 1925. This lays down thirteen 'broad
principles', among them a focus on African languages, the
provision of appropriate textbooks, the education of women and
girls, a principle that 'education should be adapted to the
mentality, aptitudes, occupations, and traditions of the various
peoples, conserving as far as possible all sound and healthy
elements in the fabric of their social life' and the fostering and
educational use of African arts and culture so as to 'narrow the
hiatus between the educated class and the rest of the community,
whether chiefs or peasantry' (from the summary in Nuffield
Foundation and Colonial Office 1953: 3).

The key investigator for the Phelps-Stokes Fund was Thomas
Jesse Jones, a Welsh American who was closely associated with

the policy of separate education for the blacks of the USA. The philosophy behind the policy of providing appropriate education for the blacks was formulated clearly at the turn of the century: 'the white people are to be the leaders . . . the Caucasion will rule . . . in the negro is the opportunity of the South. Time has proven that he is best fitted to perform the heavy labour in the Southern states . . . He will willingly fill the more menial positions, and do the heavy work, at less wages, than the American white man or any foreign race' (quoted in Berman 1982: 180). Special education for blacks, associated with the Tuskegee Institute and the Jeanes schools, was set up with foundation money. Jones wrote a two-volume survey of Negro education in the American South in 1917, which lent an aura of intellectual respectability to what was basically a discriminatory pedagogic practice (and which was spuriously legitimated with quotations from the Bible— Blacks as 'hewers and drawers of water' for Whites, Joshua 9: 21).

British missions had been pressing the Colonial Office to provide a more coherent educational policy before the First World War, and influential missionary-educators visited Tuskegee in 1912 (Berman 1982: 185). It is not surprising that policy-makers on both sides of the Atlantic approved of the idea of a review of African education being entrusted to the Phelps-Stokes Fund, of which Jones was educational director. The first of his two reports stressed the importance of agricultural education and simple manual training, and showed clearly what literacy in the mother tongue was to be used for: 'an emphasis on vocational rather than literary education was the surest way to achieve the formation of a malleable and docile African worker' (ibid.: 187).

The Colonial Office was so enthusiastic about the first report that they prevailed upon the Phelps-Stokes Fund to despatch a second team to eastern, central, and southern Africa, where the educational problems were regarded as more intractable because of the presence of white settlers. Jones regarded the American South experience as being even more centrally relevant here, and his second report makes similar recommendations. This suited the colonial officials and settlers admirably. Kenya's colonial secretary appreciated that a restricted educational offering would ensure 'an intelligent, cheerful, self-respecting, and generally docile and willing-to-learn African native' (ibid.: 188). This was the official line in other colonies, such as Malaysia in the late nineteenth century, where education was not to 'unfit them for the duties of life and make them discontented with anything like manual labour' (Benson 1990: 20). The Governor of Northern Rhodesia wrote that Jones had urged 'very strongly that the direction of Native Education should not be in the same direction as European, and he convinced me of the correctness of that view' (ibid.: 199). The architects of apartheid education in South Africa were in close touch with Jones and with Tuskegee philosophy and practice, and hoped that education run along these lines would reduce racial friction and make the white minority in South Africa more secure (ibid.: 194).

This analysis of the background of the Phelps-Stokes reports demonstrates that educational and linguistic policy recommend-ations need to be analysed in a wider historical and social perspective. An apparently sound focus on the mother tongue as medium of education does not in itself provide a guarantee of enlightened education (Skutnabb-Kangas 1984a). The Bantu education offered to blacks in South Africa, and until 1990 in Namibia, is not redeemed by the fact that the mother tongue is the medium of education (Phillipson, Skutnabb-Kangas, and Africa 1985). Language policies are one part of educational policy, which is itself determined by the overall societal goals of the community in question. The Phelps-Stokes reports conform to a colonial vision of education and attempt to export repressive strategies from part of the English-speaking Centre, the American South, to the colonial Periphery.

The significance of the reports lies more in their impact on educational and administrative thought than on African children. Despite official endorsement of the policy, education in the colonies continued bookish and alien, and did not affect the lives of the masses of the people. It also impinged in a negative way. 'This deep belief that only European ways of thinking, of clothing themselves, of playing games, of buying and selling goods, are right, and that all things African are of inferior quality, is one of the most destructive and undermining influences in Africa' (Malinowski 1936: 490).

Kenyatta, speaking as a representative of a colonized people, complains of European educators not appreciating that they have anything to learn in Africa (1979: 125):

> The European should devote more time to the study of African language and culture before he starts teaching in Africa, for without a proper knowledge of the functions of African

institutions, the more the European tries to influence his pupils in the direction of new habits, standards of life and general Europeanisation, the more he comes up against a social background which he does not understand.

Policy on colonial education or language matters was not guided by academic research, as no scholars were giving regular ongoing attention to the problems. J. R. Firth, who held the first chair in linguistics at London University (at the School of Oriental and African Studies) and was a delegate to the Imperial Education Conference in 1923, wrote in 1930:

> It comes as something of a shock to realize that we English, largely responsible for the future of the only real world language, partners in a world Empire with hundreds of millions of Asiatics and Africans speaking hundreds of languages, representatives of the civilization of all Europe in the four quarters of the globe, have up to the present made no adequate provision for the study of the practical linguistic problems affecting educational technique, the spread of English as a second language in foreign countries, the cultural problems arising in India and Africa, and our future relations with the rest of the English-speaking world.
> (Firth 1964: 211)

Little changed during the period of the two world wars and the intervening depression (except perhaps for efforts to convert the Gold Coast into an 'advanced' colony). The results were seen in 1952 as follows: primary education produced 'the boy who knows that the Stockton and Darlington railway was opened in 1825 but has no idea what a railway is like . . . it is probably true that the African child after, say, four years in school has imbibed more factual knowledge than his English counterpart; it is certain that he has gained less understanding' (Nuffield Foundation and Colonial Office 1953: 22). This judgement comes from a major study of 'African Education: Educational Policy and Practice in British Tropical Africa', consisting of reviews of West and East African practice and comprehensive coverage of policy. A major stimulus for the study was an awareness that all was not well with education in Africa, despite official guide-lines and the dedicated efforts of those involved. The report is informed by a keen awareness of African education and indeed African society being in crisis, but does not question the colonial mandate or doubt that colonized societies are being put on the right path.

The solution to the 'moral crisis' in African colonial societies, symbolized by crime and urban rootlessness, is more religious instruction and teachers who can set a good example (ibid. 71). The report is optimistic that education will contribute substantially to the solution of Africa's economic and social problems, and a very large number of specific recommendations are put forward, on the content, organization, and methods of education at all levels, on the teaching profession, the special needs of women and girls, agriculture, adult education, etc. The report was then debated at a conference in Cambridge which brought together people from all the territories concerned. Working parties discussed organization and control, the expansion of the education system, the problem of wastage, teacher education, the curriculum, improved examinations, etc.

The report contains sensitive and constructive coverage of many pedagogic and linguistic issues, and stresses the significance of literacy in the 'vernacular' (ibid.: 80). However, when deliberations on complex issues are formulated as recommendations or summarized pithily, there is a tendency for the complexity to be blurred (perhaps inevitably) and for the discourse to focus uniquely on what is of most central concern to the dominant ideology. This can be seen in the following extract from the appropriate working group summary at the conference.

> In some areas, where there is no dominant vernacular, the choice may rest between teaching both a vernacular and English as foreign languages, or concentrating on English alone: in Muslim territories the necessity for teaching Arabic for religious reasons will mean that children must learn both Arabic and a vernacular, with perhaps English as an additional language: in other areas it may be right to aim at permanent literacy in the vernacular with a working knowledge of English in addition . . . A large majority of our group, including all our African members, feels strongly that the teaching of English should have priority, and that, in the long run, this will not prove detrimental to the development of vernacular languages large enough to evolve a literature of their own. We are unanimous in our opinion that great attention must be paid to English in the training colleges, and that the problem of teaching English as a foreign language should be studied in centres of educational research.
> (Nuffield Foundation and Colonial Office 1953: 172)

This is a clear example of the discourse of English linguistic imperialism in operation. After careful consideration of the options, the dominant ideology of the 'priority' of English is affirmed. The views of Centre and, significantly, also those of Periphery representatives are used to legitimate the allocation of material resources (jobs and time in teacher training colleges) to English rather than other languages. Anglocentricity is invoked: those languages which succeed in becoming like English, by developing large enough literatures (for which no support is offered) may at some unspecified date in the future be on a par with English, and until then must take a back seat. Arabic is to be confined to the private devotional sphere. No claims are made for the professionalism of English teaching, the dearth of which provokes a proposal for research into EFL. *English linguistic imperialism is thus asserted in the domains of teaching, teacher training, and research. A foundation is laid for the maintenance of structural and cultural inequalities between English and other languages in the post-colonial age.*

The first Commonwealth Education Conference met in Oxford in 1959 to consider how education could be boosted in periphery-English countries, and made a number of proposals for improving the teaching of English. It noted the distinction between English as a subject and English as a medium, and recorded that the topic of English as a second language was 'still a relatively unexplored field' (Commonwealth Relations Office 1959: 8). The Conference of Commonwealth experts which was called, at the suggestion of the Commonwealth Education Conference, to pursue the matter, and met at Makerere, Uganda in 1961 felt that English as a second language was 'still a field inadequately cultivated, imperfectly understood, and . . . insufficiently financed' (*Makerere Report* 1961: 3).

That the teaching of both English and African languages needed urgent attention was appreciated long before this. Two commissions on higher education (the Elliot and Asquith commissions) which reported in 1945 made wise recommendations regarding the study of linguistics and indigenous languages:

> They realized that the teaching of English as a foreign language raised problems unfamiliar to conventional English scholars, and that these problems needed special study . . . colonial universities should study the local languages and

particularly the comparative linguistics of English and vernacular languages, in order to understand the differences in
patterns of thinking between those whose native language is
English and those whose native language is (say) Ibo or
Hausa. This research, in close association with anthropological and sociological studies, 'might with advantage' (the
Asquith report says) 'be put in hand during the earliest stages
of the development of a Colonial university institution.'
(Ashby 1966: 221)

Ashby, in his history of colonial higher education (op. cit.)
reports that this advice was not followed, nor was full advantage
taken of the flexibility which the University of London offered
the West and East African colleges which were established soon
after 1945.[8] The colleges prepared undergraduates for London
University examinations. Unfortunately the concern to ensure
that degrees came up to an international standard (which in that
anglocentric world meant British standards) was given priority
over developing African institutions so as to respond to local
needs. As a result, experiment and independence were stifled.

Ashby, a Cambridge don, was himself a policy-maker in
Africa. He produced a report on higher education for Nigeria in
1960, which served as a blueprint for expansion. The local
languages are not referred to in his report—there is no mention
of Hausa, Igbo, or Yoruba (Firth 1961: 15). In this linguicist
discourse, Nigerian languages are not merely stigmatized as
'vernaculars', as in the earlier reports referred to. They are
invisible,[9] hence banished to the extreme point of an exclusionary division of linguistic labour. Nigerian languages are assumed
to be irrelevant, so that ink is not even wasted on English having
to legitimate itself. Ashby's report is a clear case of linguicism
supporting English linguistic imperialism, carefully packaged in
an ambitious plan for how the new nation could be put on its
academic feet, and doubtless with the best of intentions on the
part of its progenitor. When the linguicist ideas and plans
(immaterial resources) are converted into budgets and institutions (material resources), the linguicism acquires more
concrete forms, and the structure of dominance by English at the
expense of other languages is consolidated.

Although several official reports in the colonial period had
recommended that a School of African Languages should be
established at Makerere College (situated in Uganda but serving
Kenya and Tanganyika too), this was never put into effect.

George Perren reports (ms) that when he was involved in teacher training at Makerere in 1956, 'it was impossible to get students to take any serious interest in their languages, they seemed to think it a bit infra dig'. In the early 1960s courses on Swahili and Luganda were offered to students training as teachers of English, mainly as an aid to the diagnosis of interference in language learning (Brumfit, interview). After independence, English was the only language taught, according to Mazrui (1978a). Later Makerere (by then a university) added French and German, followed experimentally by Russian. All this occurred before any action was taken towards establishing departments for indigenous Ugandan languages or for Swahili (which is widely understood in Uganda and throughout much of eastern Africa),[10] or for Arabic (the language of the most important of Uganda's neighbours in the Nile valley) (ibid.: 336).

A principal reason why higher education in Africa so closely resembled the parent British model was that the staff were recruited from Britain by the Inter-University Council for Higher Education Overseas, a body representing all British universities, which was given the task from 1945 of building up Commonwealth universities and ensuring that standards were internationally valid (Kolinsky 1983). Higher education in French colonies in Africa was also run in close collaboration with metropolitan universities. In the more centralized French case, the entire education system was run from Paris along identical lines to those applying in France.

The *unsuitability of the education* offered to Africans is a recurrent theme in reports in the nineteenth and twentieth centuries. Report after report comments on the need to strengthen general education and the vernaculars, and expresses concern at the amount of effort being devoted to English. The Colonial Office *Memorandum on Language in African School Education*, 1943, warns that if the teaching of English was over-emphasized, both general education and vernacular teaching might suffer (Tiffen 1968: 78). The Unesco conference on 'African Languages and English in Education', held at Jos, Nigeria in 1952, warned that public demand for a greater emphasis on English in the early stages of education was misguided and conflicted with the overall aims of education and the psychology of language study; the conference saw the need to make African languages more functional, recognized that teacher attitudes are influential, and recommended that African languages should be taught right through secondary school and that consideration should be given to using them as media of education in training colleges (ibid.: 104). The Leverhulme conference on universities and the language problems of tropical Africa, held at Ibadan, Nigeria in 1961 warned against discarding the study of vernacular literature in secondary schools and foresaw the risk of creating 'millions of culturally displaced persons in Africa' (ibid.: 109).

These anxieties were expressed at a time when there was an increasing tendency to believe that the most effective way of ensuring a high standard of English at the more advanced levels of education was by using English as a medium of education from as early as possible (see Chapter 7). Unlike the French, the British had encouraged the extensive use of *local languages* in the early years of primary schooling. In 1950 there were ten 'vernacular' literature bureaux or committees in British Africa for the production of teaching and reading materials and for studying the technical, practical, and linguistic problems involved. Figures for languages actually used in education are unreliable, partly because the colonial governments themselves had an incomplete idea of how many languages were used in the mission schools in their territories. This is not altogether surprising when one realizes the staggering number of mission schools involved. In Nigeria in 1946 there were 1,910 Roman Catholic mission schools, 1,654 run by Anglican churches and the Church Missionary Society, 365 by the Methodists, 175 by the Presbyterian Church and the Church of Scotland, along with a further 25 categories of denominational missions (Nuffield Foundation and Colonial Office 1953: 46). The International African Institute estimated that nearly 400 languages were spoken in British tropical Africa, that literacy materials were available in 40 languages and that nearly one hundred languages were in use in education in British Africa (ibid.: 1 and Unesco 1953: 17). These figures probably err on the low side. Perren conducted a questionnaire survey for the Kenyan colonial education service in the mid-1950s, which revealed that in Kenyan education alone 47 languages were in use, including Arabic and eight Indian languages (Perren, interview). It is easy to understand why the idea of English replacing this patchwork of African languages must have been one that appealed to administrators and teacher trainers, initially in order to provide for a common language of instruction in 'inter-tribal' schools and training colleges.

Although English was the master language of the empire, the British colonial service was aware of the importance of local languages, perhaps to a greater extent than their successors in the education or aid field are now. It was primarily missionaries who did the pioneer work of alphabetizing African languages and writing descriptions of them, but colonial service officers could not function in English alone. They were required to learn at least one local language and to take three language examinations in the first decade of their career overseas. If they failed to do so there were financial penalties.

A major limitation on the African languages was that so few reading materials were available in most of them. In some cases there was literally nothing more to read once the primer had been completed, in others the few texts available were on the joys of Christian living and the perversity of venereal disease. The genre is still available (at least in English-language editions) in African bookshops. A second major limitation was that English was invariably the high prestige language, and reading matter in English was consequently much more sought after. Literacy in the local language was merely a stepping-stone towards literacy in the dominant language, English, for the few who succeeded in climbing the educational ladder. The political context of this education was that the British 'saw an unbridgeable cultural gap between themselves and their African subjects' (Spencer 1971: 541), and pursued a policy of racial segregation and 'separate development' which held out only the long-term prospect of a limited élite group of Africans ultimately being raised to a European level. Huge discrepancies between the salaries paid to Africans and Europeans underlied the cultural gap materially.

This *apartheid inheritance* is of great significance for African perceptions of their mother tongues and European languages. Africans in the periphery-English nations seem, with few exceptions, to feel that support for African languages is intended to confine them to an inferior position. The French policy of simply ignoring indigenous languages may have had exactly the same effect on their subjects. The tiny 'assimilated' African élite who were proficient in French were in theory as good as French, which implies a rejection of African linguistic and cultural values. Thus apparently major differences in the form of the language policies of the colonial powers may prove to be of only minor consequence or long-term significance. Education has had a similar *structural* role in both the French and the British empires, namely of producing a limited élite with Europeanized values and skills. What the French and British empires had in common was:

- the low status of dominated languages, whether these were ignored or used in education
- a very small proportion of the population in formal education, especially after the lowest classes
- local traditions and educational practice being ignored
- unsuitable education being given to Africans
- an explicit policy of 'civilizing the natives'
- the master language being attributed civilizing properties.

The continued dominance of French and English in independent African countries indicates that these countries have inherited the same type of legacy. This is a legacy of linguicism in which the colonized people have internalized the language and many of the attitudes of their masters, in particular their attitude to the dominant language and the dominated languages. This linguicist legacy was the foundation on which French and English linguistic imperialism were to build in the neo-colonial phase of imperialism.

The importance of English as a colonial inheritance

What is clear from this analysis of the history of colonial language policies is that both the dominant language of education, English, and the content of education were alien, had their origins in totally different social and economic conditions, and were of very dubious relevance. Yet naturally the successful products of the system and its progenitors were to a high degree committed to it and dependent on it. Their success was in large measure due to their proficiency in the colonial language, as a result of which they were caught up in the exciting process of building up something new in their country.

The successful learning of English was the primary goal in colonial education systems. Here it was felt that the major obstacle to a greater degree of success was that the vast majority of primary and secondary school teachers were underqualified. Blame was therefore attributed to the individual Africans, rather than to colonial policies or to misconceived educational principles. A similar policy is followed in immigrant education: the learning problems are falsely attributed to deficits in the immigrants themselves, their languages, or cultures, with the result that educational policies inspired by such attitudes, and which ignore structural factors, are doomed to failure (Skutnabb-Kangas and Leporanta-Morley 1986). Much the same applies in class-biased education and 'compensatory' programmes inspired by a deficit approach (Bernstein 1970).

The transition to formal independence for African colonies came about much more swiftly than most of those involved in education had expected.[11] The lack of preparation for the diversified challenge of a post-colonial education system may have given the possession of English an even higher value than it would otherwise have had, though the evidence from colony after colony of the supreme importance of the colonial language echoes the description of English in India quoted earlier in this chapter (Misra 1982).

Even where British rule lasted for only a relatively short period, as was the case in much of Africa, English was effectively established as the dominant language. This was so, for instance, in Tanganyika, which was transferred from Germany to British 'Trusteeship' by the League of Nations after the First World War, and became an independent nation in 1960. Here too, it was the school system which determined access to influence, and in school 'English . . . was the real key to success' (White 1980: 269).

The same was true in West Africa: 'Education to many people came to mean simply the ability to speak and write English' (from a history of Ghana, 1963, quoted in Mazrui 1968: 186). The same refrain is echoed in Kenya:

> The colonial system of education, in addition to its apartheid racial demarcation, had the structure of a pyramid: a broad primary base, a narrowing secondary middle, and an even narrower university apex. Selections from the primary into the secondary were through an examination, in my time called 'Kenya African Preliminary Examination', in which one had to pass six subjects ranging from Maths to Nature Study and Kiswaheli. All the papers were written in English. But nobody could pass the exam if he/she failed the English-language paper, no matter how brilliant the result in the other subjects. I remember one boy in my class of 1954 who had distinctions in all the other subjects but did not pass in English. He

therefore failed the entire exam and went on to become a
turnboy in a bus company.
(Ngũgĩ 1985: 115)

The key to success in secondary education in colonial times was,
in the view of a Zambian scholar, 'the ability to transpose one's
mind from the immediate environment to the European one'
(Chishimba 1981: 171).

English was equally privileged in the entrance requirements at
university level. A credit, rather than a pass in English was
required. 'Thus the most coveted place in the pyramid and in the
system was only available to holders of an English-language
credit card. English was the official vehicle and the magic
formula to colonial élitedom' (Ngũgĩ 1985: 115).

'Those who rose to the very top as Africa was emerging from
colonial rule owed a good deal of their success to the gift of the
gab in the imperial language' (Mazrui 1978b: 15). English
therefore came to play a decisive role in the consciousness-
formation of élites, whether in Africa or Asia. The way English
was defined, used, and learnt in formal education influenced
the forms of nationalism which ultimately wrested political
independence from the imperial power (Mazrui 1975). The
English in question was a replica of British English. It was
generally taught by native speakers from the secondary level
upwards. The content of secondary and higher education was
essentially the same wherever the sun set. As the education had a
strong literary bias, leading periphery-English representatives
became familiar with a literary tradition which contained
potentially subversive ideas that could be at variance with
colonial interests. However it is unlikely that the potentially
revolutionary content of literary works loomed large in the
classrooms of the colonies. An article in the journal *English
Language Teaching* in 1958 reports that first year students at
Makerere struggled with seventeenth-century English poetry,
and that final year students had trouble in understanding British
texts because of their entire lack of familiarity with English
background, exemplified by Father Christmas, cricket jargon,
and potting-sheds (Warner 1958. Warner held the chair of
English at Makerere). Even so, this sort of literature was
regarded as the prime channel for African students to acquire the
English language and the culture it emanated from. This
socialization had deep consequences.

University graduates in Africa, precisely because they were the most deeply Westernized Africans, were the most culturally dependent. They have neither been among the major cultural revivalists nor have they shown respect for indigenous belief systems, linguistic heritage, modes of entertainment, or aesthetic experience. The same institutions that have produced nationalists eager to end colonial rule and to establish African self-government have also perpetuated cultural colonialism. (Mazrui 1978a: 334)

English fulfilled simultaneously a number of conflicting roles. Revelling in the English language stressed 'what the political "intellectuals" had in common with one another regardless of tribal affiliation—but it was also to emphasize what they had in common with the imperial power from whom they had borrowed that language. The same language that helped the growth of solidarity between "natives" reduced the foreignness of the foreign power' (Mazrui 1968: 185). The Africans were intent on demonstrating that they were capable of mastering the Imperial culture. 'Competence in the English language was therefore a step towards contradicting the racialist myth of the Negro's "retarded mentality"' (ibid.: 186).

The Africans and Indians who learnt their masters' language in this way took the language to themselves. As a result, there is an immense variety in the types of English now spoken worldwide, and the domains and functions these Englishes serve (Bailey and Görlach 1982; Pride 1982; Platt, Weber, and Ho 1984). One outcome of this development is the rich flowering of creative writing in English from English-periphery countries (Thumboo 1985). Such literature, written in the language of the colonizer, and partly inspired by familiarity with liberal political and social ideas of the west, has been a vital medium for working over the colonial experience and its aftermath. These works are intended for an international English readership and the small minority in periphery-English countries who can read books in English. Successful Indian and African writers in English, whose work blends elements from centre and periphery cultures and languages, aim to 'decolonize' literature written in English (Chinweizu, Jemie, and Madubuike 1983). The choice between writing in English or in a local language has implications not only for the intended readership but also of a wider political kind. One successful English-language novelist who now chooses to write in his mother tongue, Gikuyu, is Ngũgĩ wa Thiong'o. He sees language as being at the heart of the continuing struggle for Africa:

> The choice of language and the use to which it is put are central to a people's definition of itself in relation to its natural and social environment, indeed in relation to the entire universe. Hence language has always been at the heart of the two contending social forces in the Africa of the twentieth century.
> (Ngũgĩ 1985: 109)

For Ngũgĩ, these contending forces are imperialism on the one hand, which includes the legacy of linguicism, and the struggle for liberation from imperialism on the other (Ngũgĩ 1972 and 1981). For Fanon too, the problem of language in the relations between the dominant and the dominated was of 'capital importance' (Fanon 1952: 21).

Over the past 30 years, a colossal effort has gone in periphery-English countries into promoting and improving the teaching and learning of English, the dominant language. The educational scene has been characterized by anglocentricity, and, with few exceptions such as the promotion of Swahili in Tanzania and Malay in Malaysia, other languages have been overshadowed. The professionalism of ELT has been built up and propagated. These developments are a natural extension of colonial language policies and are legitimated analogously. They also reflect an internalization on the part of many periphery-English leaders of linguicist norms which can be traced back to their socialization in pre-independence days. How and why the post-independence policies were evolved, and what the contribution of centre inter-state actors was to some periphery-English country policies, will be pursued later, but two points can be made in concluding this analysis of the colonial linguistic inheritance.

Firstly, many of the analyses and reports over the years have, with considerable insight and sensitivity, raised the relevant issues (the role of the mother tongue, integrating education into the community, getting relevant research done), but there has not been effective action thereafter. This may be a theoretical problem, in that there has been no framework for identifying and weighting the various factors which make up and account for a complex problem, or for specifying which variables can be influenced and which cannot. Some of the major tenets that have underpinned ELT, the theoretical basis that they have sprung from, and their validity in the light of current understanding of the issues, will be looked at in Chapter 7. Alternatively there may have been a lack of political will to achieve more equitable and less linguicist goals. This seems to be an inescapable conclusion to draw from the evidence of the colonial period.

Secondly, since its modest beginnings 30 years ago the intense cultivation of ELT has resulted in the educational scene in periphery-English countries continuing to be massively influenced by the core-English countries. The *British Council Annual Report* for 1960–61 has a detailed state-of-the-art summary of the English language abroad, which makes it clear that the British at least were exploring this field very actively. The British had been co-operating with the Americans since the mid-50s, and a senior British Council representative reported in 1960 that the Americans were planning a 'great offensive' to make English a world language, an 'English language campaign on a global basis' on a hitherto unprecedented scale (King 1961: 22). The underdeveloped world's 'need' for development was to be assisted by support for English teaching from the English-speaking powers. The *British Council Annual Report* for 1960–61: 16, prophetically anticipates a global melting-pot and draws analogies between the monolingualism imposed internally and English as a common world language:

> America, with its vast resources, its prestige and its great tradition of international philanthropy, no less than because it is the largest English-speaking nation, is one of the greatest English teaching forces in the world today. Teaching the world English may appear not unlike an extension of the task which America faced in establishing English as a common national language among its own immigrant population.

It is to the British and American motives in this venture that our attention should now turn.

Notes

1   Macaulay's role in the elaboration of educational policy has tended to be exaggerated and misunderstood. Detailed studies by a British Indian education administrator (Mayhew 1926) and an American historian (Clive 1973) point out that the policy which Macaulay enunciated was a *fait*

accompli by the time Macaulay reached India, and never fully implemented. The famous Minute was written only a few months after his arrival. Macaulay's contribution was the actual formulation of the Anglicist argument in a Minute in which his propensity for bombastic rhetoric led to gratuitous rudeness about Indian culture, of which he was ignorant. During his time there he made no effort to learn any Indian language. This is puzzling cultural myopia in a man whose breadth of reading in European languages was phenomenal. His major achievement in India was writing the penal code, a task which he accomplished in two years, and which would have taken lesser intellectuals a decade.

Trevelyan, Macaulay's brother-in-law, was one of the most impassioned Anglicists, seeing English as a first step towards the 'filtration' of Western ideas via an educated élite, mainly through translation into vernaculars, the ultimate goal being the Christianization and moral reform of Asiatics.

2   The male orientation of 'mastery' is appropriate in this context, as females were neglected in colonial education. An awareness of the need to counteract discrimination against women and girls in education is however not a recent phenomenon (see Nuffield Foundation and Colonial Office 1953: 107–115).

3   For basic statistics of colonial education the best source is the series of annual or triennial departmental records of each colony, available in the Colonial Office library.

4   Comparable policies were followed in 'internal colonial' situations. On the linguicist assimilation policies used against the Sami (called 'Lapps' by the dominant group) and Finns in northern Scandinavia, see Eriksen and Niemi 1981; Gaski 1986; and the analysis in Skutnabb-Kangas and Phillipson 1989.

5   For a critique of colonial anthropology, see Onogo 1979. Kenyatta's book was published within a couple of years of the more celebrated *Out of Africa* of Karen Blixen, whose African farm was in Gikuyu country. Ngũgĩ has in several articles analysed Blixen's racism.

6   The major ones are Jones 1922 and Jones 1925 (the Phelps-Stokes Fund reports), *Higher Education in East Africa* 1937, the Elliot Report 1945, the Asquith Report 1945,

and Nuffield Foundation and Colonial Office 1953; for extracts from five conference reports relating to language in education see Tiffen 1968.

7   For a summary of missionary activities in Zambia and the Phelps-Stokes Commission recommendations for improvements there, see Ohannessian 1978: 274 ff.

8   The University of Ibadan, Nigeria was founded (as a college affiliated to the University of London) in 1948, the University of Legon, Ghana, also in 1948, Makerere University College of East Africa in Uganda in 1950, and the University of Liberia in 1951. Fourah Bay College in Sierra Leone was affiliated to the University of Durham in 1876 but only achieved the status of a University College in 1961 (Yoloye 1986: 32). For detailed histories of colonial universities, see Ashby 1966 and Maxwell 1980.

9   The invisibility of Nigerian languages is comparable to the invisibility of women in male-dominated sexist language.

10   The Nuffield Foundation and Colonial Office report (1953: 84) advocates a reduction in the use of Swahili in schools, without the underlying reasons for this policy being made very clear. On the varying roles of Swahili in different East African states, see Merrit and Abdulaziz 1988. George Perren (ms) reports that in the 1950s 'Swahili was disliked Uganda because of its association with the slave trade, Islam, the army (it was the language of command of the King's African Rifles), the police (ditto) and with those Kenya settlers over the border who used it to shout at Africans in general.'

11   'The mess which we left behind in practically every colonial territory was simply because we were caught on the hop, in every case, I think, with the possible exception of Ghana, no one had quite foreseen how quickly independence was coming, and the preparation for it educationally was very small indeed' (George Perren, formerly of the Kenyan Education Service, interview).

6 British and American promotion of English

Our language . . . stands pre-eminent even among the languages of the West . . . Whoever knows that language has a ready access to all the vast intellectual wealth which all the wisest nations of the earth have created and hoarded in the course of ninety generations . . . It is likely to become the language of commerce throughout the seas of the East.
(Thomas Babington Macaulay, 1835, in Trevelyan 1881: 290)

Within a generation from now English could be a world language—that is to say, a universal second language in those countries in which it is not already the native or primary tongue.
(British Cabinet Report, Ministry of Education 1956)

We will now look at why the British and American governments have been so eager to promote English, and what sorts of professional platform were used for launching this new international crusade. The British Council has established itself as a key agency for nurturing the teaching of English worldwide, and it is therefore important to look into its origins and structure. The organization is at the centre of the promotion of English, with government, academic, and commercial interests radiating to and from it. The USA has a variety of government and private organizations exercising a corresponding range of functions, and slightly different constituencies at home and abroad. British and American efforts are to some extent co-ordinated. Why and how this is done will also be examined.

There is a great deal of source material documenting the developments of the past 50 years in this area. The main protagonist institutions have needed to justify their existence to their paymasters and have regularly advertised their wares and achievements (the British Council in its *Annual Reports*, American agencies through the *Linguistic Reporter*, the newsletter of the Center for Applied Linguistics in Washington). The British government has also subjected the British Council to repeated reviews of its activities by investigatory committees.[1] The promotion of English has sailed steadily through the ebb and flow of fluctuating budgets and definitions of Britain's foreign policy. In view of the widespread political consensus on the potential value of Britain's linguistic asset, the important issues to scrutinize are the origins and legitimacy of expertise in this area and the measures taken to invest in and capitalize on the asset. Of theoretical interest is the question of the role of the State in commissioning English linguistic imperialism, and the relationship between the legitimation of global English linguistic hegemony and the professionalism of those involved in ELT. A logical starting-point for the analysis is to look at when government first saw the need to fund the promotion of English.

The origins and structure of the British Council

The British were slow to see the need to promote their interests abroad by cultural diplomacy. Both the French and the Germans had promoted their language and established schools abroad in the nineteenth century. Funds came from public and private sources. This promotional work, for the benefit of expatriate communities and local élites, was intensified in the first decades of this century (Haigh 1974: 30). In the inter-war years, both the Soviet Union and the Fascist powers were increasingly active in cultural propaganda overseas, using methods developed by the major combatants in the First World War. Private foundations such as the Carnegie Endowment for International Peace, established in 1910, financed academic exchanges between the USA and abroad and supported the teaching of English (Ninkovitch 1981: 12). At this time it was felt that one of the sources of international conflict was linguistic misunderstandings.[2] Efforts were made on both sides of the Atlantic to devise simplified forms of English in the belief that this would facilitate international understanding (ibid.: 21).[3]

A Foreign Office investigation in 1920 into the 'position of British communities abroad' suggested an expansion of cultural propaganda activities, but failed to win Treasury approval (Nicolson 1955: 7). The Foreign Office began cultural work cautiously in 1934 as a result of prompting from the business world. A committee, designated 'The British Council for Relations with other Countries', 'assembled a body of business men and educational experts under the chairmanship of Lord

Tyrell to consider a scheme for furthering the teaching of English abroad and to promote thereby a wider knowledge and understanding of British culture generally. The scheme was to be partly financed by commercial firms and the earlier meetings of the committee were held in Shell-Mex House' (ibid.: 10). The government grant, on the Foreign Office vote, rose rapidly from £6,000 in 1935 to £386,000 in 1939, while donations from commercial firms dwindled to a few hundred pounds a year by that date, 'although substantial funds from private sources were still available for work in the Near East' (ibid.: 11), presumably a veiled reference to oil company activities. The funding of the British Council is a copybook example of the state taking over responsibility, including financial and ideological control, for an activity which initially had a mainly private, commercially sponsored budget.[4] Curiously enough, the wheel has come full circle again, as a result of the government privitization drive of the 1980s. It is particularly activities in the arts, exhibitions, theatre tours and the like, which attract sponsorship. The amount involved, £2.5 million in 1989/90, is a fraction of the Council's overall budget, £321 million.

A proximate cause for establishing the organization was the concern of the Foreign Office to combat German and Italian propaganda. The potential value of a semi-autonomous organization of this kind, and the symbiosis of linguistic promotion with political benefits was appreciated from the start. Royal patronage was soon forthcoming. At the ceremony of official inauguration in 1935, the Prince of Wales (later Edward VIII, and later still Duke of Windsor) stated:

> The basis of our work must be the English language . . . (and) we are aiming at something more profound than just a smattering of our tongue. Our object is to assist the largest number possible to appreciate fully the glories of our literature, our contribution to the arts and sciences, and our pre-eminent contribution to political practice. This can be best achieved by promoting the study of our language abroad . . .
> (White 1966)

Under the terms of a Royal Charter, granted to 'The British Council' in 1940, the purpose of the organization was 'promoting a wider knowledge of the United Kingdom of Great Britain and Northern Ireland and the English Language abroad, and developing closer cultural relations between the United Kingdom and other countries, for the purpose of benefiting the British Commonwealth of Nations' (quoted in the *Annual Report* 1940–1941: 10).

The Commonwealth then consisted only of Great Britain and the dominions—Canada, Australia, New Zealand, and South Africa. India and the colonies were dependencies and part of the British Empire, and might accede to membership of the Commonwealth on gaining independence. It is the Commonwealth in this restricted, Europeanized sense which is referred to in the Charter and in the first *British Council Annual Report*, for 1940–41, which proclaims boldly that 'British life, thought, and achievements are the life, thought, and achievements of the British Commonwealth of Nations. In spreading British culture the Council is therefore spreading a culture which is that of the whole Commonwealth . . .' (ibid.: 44).[5]

The aims of the organization were formulated thus in 1941:

> The Council's aim is to create in a country overseas a basis of friendly knowledge and understanding of the people of this country, of their philosophy and way of life, which will lead to a sympathetic appreciation of British foreign policy, whatever for the moment that policy may be and from whatever political conviction it may spring.
> (quoted in the *Annual Report* 1940–1941: 15)

> National interpretation, a happier phrase than cultural propaganda, implies the employment by the state to the national advantage of the whole cultural resources of the nation. The term 'cultural resources' may be deemed to include all achievements of the nation past and present in the spheres of intellect, art, science, government, education, and invention, and that intangible but powerful force, the national personality, as manifested in a country's past history and present way of life.
> (ibid.: 16)

This élitist, idealist notion of culture was to be disseminated by such means as 'the encouragement of English studies in foreign schools and universities . . . the encouragement throughout these institutions and elsewhere of the knowledge of the English language' (ibid.: 22) and a range of activities which necessarily used English as their medium, such as the establishment of cultural centres, anglophile societies, scholarships for study in Britain, support for British schools abroad, book donations and exhibitions, theatre performances, etc.

There is a clear awareness of the role of *language* in this work: 'It is firmly believed by the Council, and indeed would appear self-evident, that a knowledge of the English language is of major assistance in securing a proper understanding of this country. On the extension of this knowledge lies the surest method of developing permanent cultural relationships with foreign peoples' (ibid.: 27).

The term 'understanding' is still used in Council discourse, though this seems to have been played down in recent years. The *Annual Report* for 1984/85 declared on the title page that 'the aim of the British Council is to promote an enduring understanding and appreciation of Britain in other countries through cultural, educational, and technical co-operation.' The following two annual reports had pruned this down to 'The British Council is an independent body which promotes Britain abroad. It has offices in eighty-two countries.' By 1987/88 this had become a brisk 'The British Council promotes Britain abroad through educational, cultural, and technical co-operation. We have offices in eighty-two countries.' In Council discourse 'understanding' is equated with making good friends for Britain and making foreigners anglophiles (for example in the Prime Minister's letter of congratulation to the British Council on its fiftieth anniversary, quoted in the *Annual Report* 1983–84).

The *Annual Report* for 1940–41 also noted that a central but controversial issue was *methods of teaching*. The writers anticipated that a method which had the virtues of all systems and none of their defects could, after careful investigation, be achieved. The report does not contain any suggestion that the imperial venture had made Britain specially qualified in this area. Indeed, because of the limited scale of Council operations it did not have access to experience in the dominions or colonies. The Council's activities were concentrated in four main areas: Egypt and the Middle East, the Balkans, South America, and Portugal. This was where the Italians and Germans had concentrated their propaganda efforts. In other words they were areas of strategic importance. A contemporary German writer pointedly asks why, if the Council was really committed to international understanding, it had not been active in Nazi Germany where presumably the need was greatest (Thierfelder 1940: 64).

The competitive, eurocentric nature of cultural relations is apparent in the following: 'In Egypt the predominant cultural influence among the educated upper class of Egyptians was

French, following many years of well-conducted French propaganda' (*British Council Annual Report* 1940–41: 17).

Almost the entire budget for the British Council came from Parliament via the Foreign Office, 'it will be clear therefore that the Council's work must be carried on under the supervision of the Foreign Office' (ibid.: 13). This report does not claim autonomy for the Council, though its proclaimed independence from the government machine is central to the organization's identity. At the time it would have been difficult to claim independence for the organization, as its chairman for the previous four years, until his death in 1941, was Lord Lloyd, who was simultaneously Secretary of State for the Colonies in Churchill's government. The pragmatic motives for creating an independent organization are explained by the Council's first official biographer: 'It was felt that, on the analogy with the British Broadcasting Association, better results would be secured if the Council, in its administration and functioning, were to be accorded the greatest possible autonomy' (Nicolson 1955: 11). There is, significantly, no suggestion that the Council should decide its own policy.

Policy is the responsibility of the government of the day, supported by the relevant government departments (the Foreign Office, the Commonwealth Relations Office, the Colonial Office— all now superseded by the Foreign and Commonwealth Office)— and the Board of Trade). Post-war British government propaganda overseas has been the responsibility of these departments, the external services of the BBC, and the British Council. The *relative autonomy of the Council* is a complex question with several strands to it. They need to be unpicked before the historical narrative can be resumed.

So far as *funding* goes, the Council is dependent on grants from the Foreign and Commonwealth Office (FCO) and the Overseas Development Administration (ODA)[6] for the majority of its activities, is accountable to them, and necessarily works in close liaison with them. A review of this aspect of the Council's work states that too tight a control is exercised by the granting department (Seebohm 1981: 15), but it is clear that even if this supervision were relaxed, the funds are allocated for purposes which are defined by the government. The total budget for 1989/90 was £321 million, of which £110 million are a government grant via the FCO, intended for cultural diplomacy work; £157 million are from the ODA and the FCO for specific schemes ('aid', technical assistance, scholarships, etc.); and £55 million are earnings by the Council through English teaching activities, publishing, education projects, etc. (*Annual Report* 1989/90: 8).

So far as *activities* are concerned, the Council has offices in 86 countries, has 55 English teaching centres in 32 countries, maintains 116 libraries, recruits specialists for teaching and advisory posts, and organizes a vast number of exchange visits to and from Britain (for details see the *Annual Reports*). In Britain, the Council works closely with the academic world, local authorities, civil servants, publishers, and professional people of all kinds, acting as a facilitator of international exchange. Abroad it has distinct status and premises except where diplomatic protection is required, which has been the case in communist and socialist countries. It is clearly an advantage in dealing with the general public and with key professional contacts (universities, teachers, the arts world, etc.) not to be identified with government or with a diplomatic mission. The independence of the Council is therefore true at the operational level. The ideological significance of the notion of autonomy is that it serves to strengthen the myth that the Council's work is non-political.

So far as *policy-formation* is concerned, the Council's activities are under constant government and public scrutiny, and the organization has repeatedly had to prove that it gives good value for its (public) money (Donaldson 1984). Quite apart from external reviews increasing accountability and synchronizing Council activities with government priorities, the leadership structure of the Council ensures that a considerable range of interests is represented on its managing board, including nominees from government departments, the business world, and publishing. Abroad, the Council liaises closely with the British Embassy so as to maximize mutual supportiveness. The most senior officer of the Council, the Chairman of the Board, is a part-time appointee with a decisive role in representing the Council *vis-à-vis* the government and the funding departments. The present head of Britain's cultural diplomacy organization was appointed after a career in international business.[7] The Director-General, the senior executive of the Council, has generally had a government service background, and none has ever been appointed from within the Council's own ranks. The Director-General since July 1987 is Richard Francis, formerly Managing Director of BBC Radio. The Council's substantial headquarters staff is responsible for the operation of Council activities in each of its spheres of activity. It is assisted by a network of advisory committees, covering such topics as medicine, agriculture, the fine arts, and all the main areas of Council activity, including publishing, libraries, and English language teaching. These committees of eminent professionals ensure that the organization has access to key people and developments in the relevant field, but they have not played a major role in forming Council policy (Seebohm 1981).

This complex network of links permeates the strands of funding, operational activities, and policy-formation. It guarantees that the Council is sensitive to a considerable range of pressures from both government and private interests. It is relatively autonomous at the executive level, but could not function effectively unless it was attuned to the needs of government and to relevant sectors of private business. Policy for the organization is only made explicit in very general terms. The overseas representations have considerable freedom to run their activities flexibly in response to local perceptions of needs, as there is a broad consensus on what form legitimate activity takes. The ODA decides where activities funded by them are to take place. Major policy decisions, such as opening up an office in a new country, or a shift in global priorities, are decided by the FCO, in consultation, naturally, with the Council. Thus funds were made available for increased activity in Europe when Britain joined the European Economic Community in 1972.[8]

We can now resume the narrative of the evolution of the organization, prior to probing in more depth into policy-making for the promotion of English. The fate of the British Council was uncertain after 1945. During the war it had built up an enormous network of contacts in Britain, as it was responsible for the welfare and the linguistic and cultural needs of the many refugees from all over Europe who were in Britain (Haigh 1974). Uncertainty about Britain's overseas role in the post-1945 world, and extreme financial austerity meant that the Council was only given a provisional lease of life. It was not until the publication of key policy documents in the 1950s that the future of the organization and the expansion of ELT were secure. Uncertainty about priorities in foreign policy in the post-war period reflects the fact that Britain was undergoing the painful adaptation process from major world power to second-rate power. All post-war British governments have been preoccupied with fundamental problems, notably how to cope with a flagging economy, how to reduce excessive military spending to a level commensurate with reduced global influence, and how to align Britain in relation to the USA, with whom it had a 'special alliance', to the Europe of the Common Market, and to the Commonwealth. Commercial needs have become the primary concern of diplomacy, a policy confirmed in a review of overseas activities of 1969 (*Duncan Report* 1969).

Within this perspective it is possible that cultural diplomacy might to some degree compensate for the new more cramped world role. This hypothesis is put forward by a historian, in a study of diplomacy and foreign relations.

> There exists another dimension to Brtish external policy in the realm of culture and institutions. In such things as the English language, the BBC World Service, parliamentary government, legal processes, sport, university structures, intellectual and literary exchanges, it has been argued, there can be seen not only the residues of the past but also those features of political and social behaviour which are of continued and growing importance. Here, even more than in its cosmopolitan commercial connections, Britain *still* occupies a role in the world out of all proportion to its area and population.
> (Kennedy 1981: 382)

The English language is arguably the key factor, in that it is the medium for acquiring influence in all the areas enumerated here, just as it is the medium for commercial and military links.

Government policy-makers have been well aware of the significance of English. The British Council has reiterated the message constantly over the past 50 years, in case anyone was unaware of the profitability of investment in English and the way that linguistic influence dovetails with other types of influence. The Chairman has drawn these threads together very neatly and explicitly (*British Council Annual Report* 1983–84: 9):

> Of course we do not have the power we once had to impose our will but Britain's influence endures, out of all proportion to her economic and military resources. This is partly because the English language is the lingua franca of science, techno-logy, and commerce; the demand for it is insatiable and we respond either through the education systems of 'host' countries or, when the market can stand it, on a commercial basis. Our language is our greatest asset, greater than North

Sea Oil, and the supply is inexhaustible; furthermore, while we do not have a monopoly, our particular brand remains highly sought after. I am glad to say that those who guide the fortunes of this country share my conviction in the need to invest in, and exploit to the full, this invisible, God-given asset.

A rationale and plan for investment in English, and a strategy for building up a worldwide English teaching profession did not exist until the British government commissioned some key policy documents in the 1950s. These founding texts of the ELT profession need to be considered in some depth.

The British strategy for expanding ELT

The *Report of the Independent Committee of Enquiry into the Overseas Information Services*, chaired by Lord Drogheda, and published in 1954 (Drogheda Report summary 1954), is a key post-war British foreign policy statement. The *Drogheda Report* covered the projection of Britain by Embassies, the BBC, and the British Council. The committee were initially sceptical of the value of such activity and suspicious of 'this invasion by Government of a field which in the not very distant past could be left to non-official agencies' (ibid.: 4), but after a year and a half of analysis and foreign tours of inspection they could not 'avoid the conclusion that a modern Government has to concern itself with public opinion abroad and be properly equipped to deal with it' (ibid.: 4). National propaganda overseas was needed for the following purposes:

– to support our foreign policy
– to preserve and strengthen the Commonwealth and Empire
– to increase our trade and protect our investments overseas.
  (ibid.: 4)

> The aim of the Information Services must always be to achieve in the long run some definite political or commercial result. Overseas propaganda which meets a demand without producing some ultimate political or commercial benefit for this country represents so much public money wasted.
> (*Drogheda Report* 1954: 6)

At the height of the Cold War the strategic importance of investment in English was clearly appreciated. At the United

Nations 'as a Colonial Power, the United Kingdom was the target of ill-intentioned and ill-informed criticism. The evolution of the Commonwealth implied the development of new relationships between its members to be cherished and strengthened. Progressive constitutional advance in the Colonies made it more and more necessary to strengthen the bonds of understanding between the United Kingdom and the Dependencies. There was a growing need to counter communist machinations in the Colonies and to meet the increasing interest of the world in Colonial affairs . . . We need to build up our export trade and to protect our overseas investments, which are increasingly threatened by the extreme nationalism in many parts of the world. In our opinion the Information Services can help in this regard by explaining our economic situation and commercial policies; by maintaining an atmosphere of goodwill towards this country; and by increasing the use of English as the common language in the East' (ibid.: 8).

'In the very long term we have no doubt that the work of the British Council, especially in regard to the teaching of English in Asia, will be highly beneficial to our overseas trade' (ibid.: 29). Singling out Asia as the part of the underdeveloped world where the British Council could make a big impact was logical in the mid-1950s. The Council was not then active in colonial Africa.

The learning of English was seen as reaching beyond instrumental needs: 'A knowledge of English gives rise in its turn to a desire to read English books, talk to British people, and learn about British life or some aspect of it. Indeed a knowledge of English is almost essential today for the study of many branches of science and technology as also, of course, for the study of English literature, history, and British institutions' (ibid.: 32).

The British Council's various activities were seen as contributing to the single process of strengthening links with the potential leaders of political and economic development abroad. The British Council 'had a great task to do in India, Pakistan, and in the Far East and Middle East. The opportunity was provided because of the importance which English had assumed as a lingua franca and as the language of science, technology, and sociology (*sic*)' (ibid.: 33).

The British Government endorsed the *Drogheda Report* and made funds available for implementing it. Further policy statements on the 'overseas information services' followed and specified where expansion should take place (Overseas Information Services 1957 and 1959). From the mid-1950s the British Council expanded its work dramatically in the periphery-English countries and retrenched in Europe.

The British Council's expertise in English teaching at that time was mainly of two types. Firstly, the Council ran English teaching operations in a large number of anglophile associations in South America and in Institutes in major European cities. Secondly, a small number of Council officers were in influential English teaching posts (mostly in higher education) and increasingly in advisory work on syllabuses, teacher training, and methods of teaching in periphery-English countries. In the mid-1950s there were about ten such 'Education Officers'. The Council's minimal experience of the problems of education in multilingual societies was to have significant consequences for the way ELT was to develop.[9]

The Government appreciated that if English teaching worldwide was to expand, special steps would have to be taken. An *Official Committee on the Teaching of English Overseas* reported to the Cabinet in March 1956 (Ministry of Education 1956). The committee consisted of representatives of the Foreign Office, Scottish Office, Commonwealth Relations Office, Colonial Office, the Board of Trade, the Ministry of Education, the University Grants Committee, and the British Council. Their main conclusion was that 'opportunities unquestionably exist for increasing the use of English as the main second language in most parts of the non-English speaking world' (ibid.: 3). The introductory summary then states that if the opportunities are to be seized, the supply of teachers overseas, in all subjects, had to be increased and such employment made relatively secure, that more potentially influential teachers from overseas should be brought to Britain for training, that more university departments should offer training courses both for British and overseas teachers, and that BBC English by Radio should be expanded.

Under the heading 'The Opportunity', the report states: 'Within a generation from now English could be a world language—that is to say, a universal second language in those countries in which it is not already the native or primary tongue. The tide is still running in its favour, but with slackening force . . . it is important that its expansion should take place mainly under Commonwealth and United States auspices' (ibid.: 3).

The threat to English is mainly seen as coming from alternative lingua francas, Hindi, Chinese, or Arabic, which are identified with political achievements or nationalist aspirations, and from communist countries, where English is efficiently taught but 'such teaching is politically partial, and it is associated with books that misrepresent British history and institutions and often grossly distort the facts of our national life' (ibid.: 4). There is also a clear wish to monopolize the field: Britain ought not 'to stand by—to take two recent examples—while Libya is offered a German professor of English for her new university and Egypt exports Egyptian teachers of English and other subjects to Kuwait' (ibid.: 4).

There is explicit recognition of the commercial relevance of English, though their view of the spread of English is remarkably ahistorical. 'The interest of the British and American peoples in spreading their language abroad has never been narrowly political or chauvinistic. A great deal of the expansion that has already occurred has been almost accidental; but many natural forces and inducements have been at work' (ibid.: 4). One hopes that this is self-deception rather than more sinister imperialist rhetoric.

The eurocentricity of the times is apparent in blindness to indigenous languages, which do not seem to have been 'discovered': 'In Commonwealth countries, for example, English has been either a mother tongue—one of two in Canada and the Union of South Africa—or the language of government, law, trade, and secondary and higher education' (ibid.: 4). In both Canada and South Africa the cleavage is seen as being between two groups of European origin rather than between European and indigenous cultures. Nor are indigenous languages in any way seen as a threat to English in the colonies and protectorates, where the main problem in education is 'the maintenance of standards'. The report forecasts that English will survive independence not merely as a lingua franca but as a second mother tongue, even in areas where Swahili is a lingua franca or Arabic is available 'for religious purposes only' (ibid.: 4).

Part of the justification for this confidence comes from the considerable effort made by the Colonial Office to provide teachers, inspectors, and administrative staff in education in the empire. A figure of 3,500 people so employed is mentioned, with possibly almost as many employed by such private agencies as missions.[10] 'Colonial schools are a major means of spreading a knowledge of English' (ibid.: 6). This was so even though the teachers and supervisors had not been trained for this work (ibid.: 12). In higher education, the Inter-University Council for Higher Education Overseas was recruiting an increasing number of British staff for the burgeoning universities in periphery-English countries, where the medium of education was of course English. It was stated in the House of Lords in 1977 that no fewer than 10,000 academic appointments of this kind were made in the post-war period; 'in the English-speaking world this contribution dwarfs what has been done by any other country' (Lord Fulton, quoted in Kolinsky 1983: 66).[11]

The report notes the extensive use of English in science and technology. A recent Unesco estimate was that over half of all new scientific publication throughout the world was in English (ibid.: 5).

The report indicates that private funds may be available. For instance the Nuffield Foundation had agreed to finance a teacher training programme in Allahabad. The report recommends that 'to enable the Council to increase its influence' in the vital field of training facilities overseas for teachers of English, more government-financed projects should be set up (ibid.: 14).

On textbooks, the report recommends more consultation between publishers, authors, linguistic scholars (where USA is regarded as far in advance of Britain), and the British Council, so as to improve the quality of textbooks (ibid.: 16). A problem which needed a policy decision was what British Council officers were to do when they were asked to write a syllabus or teaching materials for a local, as opposed to a British, publishing house. The report recommends that the Council officer's first duty is to push British publishers' 'excellent textbooks', but that if that does not work, to press ahead with local publication. 'For if the attitude of the foreign authority is such as to offer no hope of the work being done by a British publisher, it is better that it should be done by a qualified British educationalist than that it should pass into the hands of some other foreign adviser, or even of some indifferent local author' (ibid.: 17). Clearly no role was seen for the Council in assisting local publishing to get well established, and the implication seems to be that any local author would be indifferent. The course of action recommended is paradoxical in so far as elsewhere in the report there is an admission that little professional expertise was available, that only one university department specialized in English teaching overseas, and 'very few UK teachers overseas have had any special training in teaching English as a foreign language' (ibid.:

12). Even if one concedes that professionalism may have been in short supply everywhere, this policy statement smacks of commercial opportunism and cultural imperialism.

The report also considers what should be done about countries which are unable or unwilling to buy foreign books (Brazil, Chile, Indonesia, Turkey, Israel, and Pakistan) and which receive large quantities of American books. 'The supply of books as an instrument of US influence is being backed up by teacher exchanges, subsidization of the salaries of a large number of US teachers in Pakistani universities, and various other forms of aid associated with the local currency accruing from books' (ibid.: 17). It was outside the scope of the report to propose how to counteract this threat to traditional exports from Britain, but the report states that this was a 'serious problem', and appropriate measures should be taken.

So far as university training and research facilities are concerned, the report notes that the only university in Britain involved in English as a Foreign Language was London University, but that plans for a new department in Edinburgh were advanced. This was on the initiative of the British Council, and with the backing of the Foreign Office, Commonwealth Relations Office, and the Colonial Office, and with a guarantee that the Council would detach its own staff for training there as well as sending foreigners there on scholarships. The report welcomes this development, and hopes there will be expansion elsewhere (ibid.: 13).

The American effort in support of English teaching is summarized, and the report feels that even if there may be some rivalry, the UK has 'nothing to lose and much to gain by the closest possible collaboration with the United States' (ibid.: 8).

Whereas until the 1950s British anglocentricity was the order of the day in most of the English teaching world, the report recognizes the arrival on the international scene of a rival 'English' centre. It clearly regards American cultural imperialism as a threat to traditional British markets and spheres of interest, and sees the need to resist this by increasing British activity, while aiming at a framework of friendly collaboration. The fact that linguistics was better established in universities in the USA than in Britain provided an additional spur to British university expansion. It also resulted in confirmation of the widespread belief of the time that what language teaching and materials production needed most was linguistics, a focus that was a mixed blessing for ELT (see Chapter 7).

Cabinet approval of this report, and the measures instigated to put its recommendations into effect, ensured financial support for the massive expansion of the ELT field. The creation of university departments for teaching and research, the provision of ELT training in Britain and more attractive conditions of employment abroad for British teachers of English (as well as other subjects), training in Britain for key ELT people from abroad, co-ordination with British publishers, support for British books overseas—all these were to be promoted in order to provide professional and logistic backing for the effort to make English a world language, an undisputed 'universal second language'.

The declared motivation for this investment was purely British self-interest, the ultimate purpose being to achieve the foreign policy goals set out in the Drogheda report. The sections of the report which whitewash English linguistic imperialism and tar Hindi, Arabic, and Chinese with 'nationalism' or 'political achievements' are clear instances of cultural racism, whereas the goals and methods of the rival imperialist power, the USA, are clearly understood and not misrepresented. In the context of a restricted policy document intended only for the eyes of the British cabinet, little effort is made to legitimate the expansion of English in terms of anything other than British self-interest.

The reports looked at in detail in this chapter provide very clear evidence of the integration of the British Council into the government machine, and of the interdependence of cultural diplomacy with economic, political and, by implication, also military diplomacy. It may also prove something of a shock to members of the ELT profession, who regard themselves as being concerned exclusively with cultural, intellectual, liberal or non-political pursuits, to realize that the foundations of the academic and professional world in which they operate were laid by a Conservative British Cabinet which was preoccupied with the Cold War and the security of worldwide British investments.

Such a realization should not lead us to conclude that here we have evidence which supports a simplistic conspiracy theory according to which cigar-smoking leaders manipulate ELT and all its works. What it does mean is that when State backing was put into boosting ELT, the motives were various but that national political and economic interests were paramount. ELT was seen as a means of strengthening Britain by influencing the parameters of education in other 'independent' states. ELT was seen as a means towards political and economic goals, a means of securing ties of all kinds with the leaders of 'developing countries'. The global linguistic scene could be influenced by active engagement in consolidating English as a world second language, and this would help the capitalist system to adapt to and dominate a changing world. The evidence thus far, from looking at the evolution of ELT in a broad historical perspective, is therefore that ELT is unquestionably neo-colonialist and operates within a framework of imperialism. Whether one can conclude that English linguistic imperialism has in fact taken place will depend on more detailed analysis of specific structures and professional ideologies. Before going on to these issues, let us first look at what the Americans were doing in order to promote English and at Anglo-American co-ordination in this field.

American promotion of English

The British Cabinet committee report of 1956 on the teaching of English overseas was anxious that the expansion of English globally should occur 'mainly under Commonwealth and United States auspices' (Ministry of Education 1956: 3). The report noted that although the Americans had extensive experience of teaching English to immigrants and members of allied armed forces, there had as yet been little promotion abroad (ibid.: 8). It also stated that the British Council had already started co-ordinating strategy with their American counterparts. In fact by this stage the British Council and the State Department had issued identical circulars to their overseas offices endorsing co-operation between the British and the Americans in the field.

What the Cabinet report does not refer to is the fact that the USA also had experience of imposing the English language as a colonial power. For instance, from the beginning of the century the Americans introduced English in the Philippines as the primary medium of instruction. 'With American textbooks, Filipinos started learning not only a new language but also a new way of life. Mastery of English was passed off as the mark of the educated man . . . The colonial relationship between the US and the Philippines demonstrates that language is power. With the imposition of the English language, the country became dependent on a borrowed language that carries with it the dominant ideology and political-economic interest of the US. With the dependence of the country on a borrowed language, it became dependent too on foreign theories and methods underlying the borrowed language, thus resulting in a borrowed consciousness. The people's values were then more easily modified so that they equate foreign interest with national interest. Thus it became easier for the US to further subjugate the Filipino people and impose its will on them' (Enriquez and Marcelino 1984: 3).

The Philippines became officially independent in 1946, but the structures and attitudes imposed by the Americans have largely remained in force since. In the quest to legitimate local cultural norms and languages, a few scholars have made strenuous efforts to decolonize and de-anglicize such university subjects as psychology. There has been debate about the appropriate medium of education in schools, but there is extreme resistance to any switch away from English as the medium of instruction. In recent years the World Bank and the International Monetary Fund have been pressing for a renewed emphasis on English in order to further the 'goals of national development' (ibid.: 4).

Other US possessions in the Pacific have suffered a similar fate. In an article entitled 'ESL: a factor in linguistic genocide' (Day 1980), the experience of Guam is described. In 1906, eight years after the island was ceded to the US, an English-only policy in court proceedings, land registration, government offices, etc. was introduced. In 1922, the indigenous language, Chamorro, was prohibited on school grounds and Chamorro dictionaries were collected and burned. Even though Chamorro was declared an official language in 1974, the linguicist attitudes of earlier times prevail: English is regarded as the key to economic success, and Chamorro is felt to be inadequate. Day expresses the fear that current ESL programmes are reinforcing such prejudices by focusing on the limited English proficiency of learners and stressing the learning of English, rather than bilingual competence. On English in the South Pacific, see the thematic number of *World Englishes*, 8/1, Spring 1989.

By the mid-1950s all American foreign policy activities were subordinated to the strategic needs of the Cold War. Prior to the Second World War, Washington had been reluctant to take on responsibility for work that was done effectively by private agencies, particularly the philanthropic foundations. It was not until 1938 that the State Department acquired a Cultural

Relations Division. It was then expected that most activity would continue to take place on private initiative. It was hoped that the foundations would continue to fund the international activities of such bodies as the American Council of Learned Societies and the American Library Association, with the State Department playing a co-ordinating role. In any case the same individuals who dominated politics and business were also trustees of the Carnegie, Rockefeller, and Ford foundations, representing a microcosm of the American power élite (Berman 1982b: 204), so it was unlikely that divergent goals would be pursued.

During the war a much more active foreign cultural policy was pursued, mostly in Latin America, the chief goal being to combat the propaganda of the Fascist states. During the immediate post-war years, outwardly an initial policy of internationalism was pursued. The Americans were very active in the creation of Unesco, and determined to ensure that the organization would serve American purposes (Ninkovich 1981).[12]

It goes without saying that foreign cultural policy serves overall *foreign policy goals*. What is not so immediately obvious is that in core English-speaking states foreign policy goals are decided by those who determine domestic policy goals. This can be seen clearly in American policy-making, as Chomsky's analysis shows:

> On foreign policy since the Second World War a principal source is the memoranda of the War and Peace Studies of the Council on Foreign Relations during the war. Participants included top government planners and a fair sample of the 'foreign policy élite', with close links to government, major corporations, and private foundations. These memoranda deal with the 'requirements' of the United States in a world in which it proposes to hold unquestioned power, foremost among them being 'the rapid fulfillment of a program of complete re-armament' . . . The areas which are to serve the prosperity of the US include the Western Hemisphere, the British Empire and the Far East, described as a natural integrated economic unity in the geopolitical analysis of the planners. The major threat to US hegemony in the non-German world was posed by the aspirations of the British. The contingencies of the war served to restrict these, and the American government exploited Britain's travail to help the process along. Lend-lease aid was kept within strict bounds,

enough to keep Britain in the war but not enough to permit it to maintain its privileged imperial position . . . In this conflict within the alliance, American interests succeeded in taking over traditional British markets in Latin America and in partially displacing Britain in the Middle East, particularly Saudi Arabia.
(Chomsky 1982: 95)

The war was effectively turning Britain into an economic satellite of the USA, a process which has accelerated since the war and come out into the open in the 1980s (for instance in the rift in the Thatcher government over the sale of Westland Helicopters and part of British Leyland to American corporations). In the circumstances it seems highly unlikely that Anglo-American collaboration on English teaching would be uninfluenced by this inter-ally struggle. At the same time each nation subscribed in principle to similar democratic goals. The promotion of their common language could be of benefit to both powers. The Americans were as aware as the British of the indivisibility of economic and cultural policy, and developed their own version of a civilizing mission to legitimate the spread of American influence. The meshing of economic-political strategies with legitimation of such goals is a logical expression of corporate self-interest in our times. This is well documented by Chomsky:

> In modern state capitalist societies such as our own, domestic decision-making is dominated by the private business sector in the political as well as the strictly economic arena . . . Those who have a dominant position in the domestic economy command substantial means to influence public opinion. It would be surprising indeed if this power were not reflected in the mass medias, themselves major corporations—and the school and universities: if it did not, in short, shape the prevailing ideology to a considerable extent. What we should expect to find is 1) that foreign policy is guided by the primary commitment to improving the climate for business operations in a global system that is open to exploitation of human and material resources by those who dominate the domestic economy, and 2) that this commitment is portrayed as guided by the highest ideals and by deep concern for human welfare.
> (Chomsky 1982: 5)

An example of this legitimation rhetoric is found in a National

Security Council report of April 1950 on a strategy for world hegemony, written when the cold war had frozen and it was essential to persuade the general public that it was a real war. 'The Americans should undertake "the responsibility of world leadership", "foster a world environment in which the American system can survive and flourish". This should not be difficult, in the light of our moral ascendency, the essential tolerance of our world outlook, our generous and constructive impulses, and the absence of covetousness in our international relations' (cited ibid.: 22).

This imperialist rhetoric did not dupe the British Colonial Office, which had earlier been suspicious of the American attempt to dismantle the British imperial preference system. 'The Americans are quite willing to make their dependencies politic-ally "independent" while economically bound to them and see no inconsistency in this' (quoted from Colonial Office sources in Chomsky 1982: 8). What is perhaps most revealing about this quotation is that it demonstrates that a spokesperson for one imperialist power was perfectly conscious of the nature of imperialism. It somehow always seems to be easier to credit one's competitors with self-interested motives than to acknow-ledge them in relation to oneself.

Language promotion forms part of the American global strategy. Some measures had been singled out for attention as far back as during the war, among them book promotion and an increase in the number of foreign students in the USA. Independently of each other, British and American publishers were preparing for the post-war world. The Americans were investigating how to break the European dominance of the Latin American market and were exploring the possibility of a state subsidy for the purpose. The British were plotting how to keep their preferential position in the British Empire, and to perpetuate what the American Embassy saw as the maxim 'trade follows the book' (Ninkovich 1982: 90). As the British domestic market was relatively small, the proportion of books exported was an important factor in British book prices. Exports of American books amounted to 5.5 million volumes per year, or 2.5 per cent of total book sales, whereas British publishers exported 48 million volumes per year, roughly 30–35 per cent of their gross annual output (ibid.: 90). A cartel for American exports was established in 1945, but it was wound up after two years because the buyers were still too impoverished, and little government funding for cultural diplomacy was available then. Within a few years such funds were forthcoming on a massive scale.

A second ingredient was the education of foreign students in the USA. Numbers rose from 7,000 in 1943 to 26,000 in 1949 (ibid.: 139). Here, too, there was a problem of finance, but this was solved by the simple device of transforming funds owed abroad to the USA in non-convertible currencies into Fulbright awards, so named after the senator who moved the relevant legislation. The number of foreign students in the USA rose to 140,000 by 1971, as compared with 27,000 in Britain (Unesco 1974). Of those in the USA in order to learn English, prior to technical training or study of some kind, the largest sector is military (Coombs 1964). The military have been extensively involved in foreign language learning since the Second World War, and have had a decisive influence on the evolution of American ELT methods.

American government funding for all types of educational and cultural work throughout the world became increasingly available in the 1950s. By 1964 at least 40 governmental agencies were involved, between them spending 200 million dollars per annum (Coombs 1964). Large though this figure was, it represented less than 1 per cent of the military budget. Coombs, appointed by Kennedy to provide for more coherent administration and policy-formation in this area, dubbed education and culture the 'fourth component' of foreign policy, in addition to economic, political, and military components. He was convinced that the area was under-financed because of the ignorance of politicians of its value. While this may be correct, the argument appears a trifle disingenuous when one recalls that the foundations were disbursing vast funds for educational and cultural work (see Arnove 1982: 6).

While the meshing of cultural diplomacy with political and economic interests is assumed on both sides of the Atlantic, it is a proclaimed principle of American aid that economic and military goals are indivisible. A recent policy review (Commission on Security and Economic Assistance 1983) states unambiguously that 'the instrumentalities of foreign assistance are potent and essential tools that advance our interests . . . The keystone to our recommendations is the conclusion that economic and military assistance must be closely integrated' (ibid.: 2). There is no pretence that foreign aid is disinterested: 'a judicious use of foreign assistance tools can optimize US influence and contribute importantly to the success of American foreign policy' (ibid.: 38).

American goals for cultural diplomacy are stated in the *Fulbright-Hayes Act* of 1961: 'to increase mutual understanding between the people of the United States and the people of other countries . . . to promote international co-operation for educational and cultural advancement; and thus to assist in the development of friendly, sympathetic, and peaceful relations between the United States and other countries in the world' (quoted in Coombs 1964: 51). No fewer than six government agencies were involved in English-teaching activities: 'the Department of State through the Fulbright program; the Agency for International Development; the US Office of Education, through the International Teacher Exchange Program; the Department of Defense; the Peace Corps; and the Department of the Interior, which has the responsibility for English instruction in the Indian schools in this country and the Trust Territories overseas' (Marckwardt 1967: 2). There are also many private organizations which sponsor activities with similar goals of promoting understanding of the language and culture of the USA, for instance school exchange programmes. The main government agencies can be described briefly.

The *United States Information Agency* has the mission, in the words of its former director in 1963, to 'further the achievement of US foreign policy objectives . . . by influencing public attitudes abroad in support of these objectives . . . through personal contact, radio broadcasting, libraries, television, exhibits, English language instruction, and others' (Coombs 1964: 60). Abroad, USIA has equivalent operational functions to those of both the British Council and the British Embassy's Information Departments. USIA forms part of the American Embassy and is more closely geared towards pursuing short-term foreign policy goals than the British Council. Although the English language was described in the 1960s as USIA's most 'booming item', far fewer specialists in ELT are employed specifically for work in this area than by the British Council. In USIA-supported 'bilateral/bicultural' teaching centres, 381,500 people attend English-language classes annually (United States Advisory Commission on Public Diplomacy 1986 Report: 39).

Substantial numbers of young volunteers have been sent all over the world under the aegis of the *Peace Corps*, comparable to the British Voluntary Service Overseas (VSO) scheme. A figure of 7,000 is quoted for those involved, formally or informally, in the teaching of English in 1964 (Center for Applied Linguistics 1964: 21). Those participating in other types of 'aid' work (in health care, technical tasks, etc.) operated through the medium of English, though they were also given some proficiency training in a local language. The official aims of the Peace Corps are to meet the need for trained personnel, to promote a better understanding of Americans among the people served, and to promote a better understanding of people of other countries among the American people (Development Issues 1985: 133). Over 100,000 Americans have participated in the scheme.

The *Agency for International Development* has a substantial budget for training non-Americans in the USA and posting Americans abroad. As an example of the beneficial results of such collaboration Coombs cites relations between India and the USA. These have been cemented by a massive American presence in Indian universities and ministries and a huge training programme for Indians in the USA (Coombs 1964: 105). Coombs is also optimistic that the groundwork had been laid for a 'common political and economic interest' with African countries as a result of the establishment of educational and social ties. 'Tomorrow's historians are likely to label education as America's most strategic investment in the new Africa of the 1960s' (ibid.: 110).

Coombs's book is a revealing sample of American cultural 'aid' ideology of the early 1960s. He regards the four components of foreign policy as inextricably related. He also appreciates that the flow of ideas and influence is not exclusively unidirectional. However, even if he recognizes that educational aid involves a bilateral learning experience, he refers frequently to American 'leadership' and sees no reason to legitimate the right of Americans to 'lead'.

Coombs moved from Washington to become Director of the Unesco International Institute for Educational Planning. This Institute conducted research in English-speaking and French-speaking African countries in the mid-1960s in order to contribute to the solution of 'important problems confronting educational planners in virtually all developing countries' (Unesco 1969: 5). The 'development' paradigm favoured by Unesco in this work was scarcely likely to be uninfluenced by American ways of thinking.

The American foreign policy élite still consider that they not only represent the interests of the American state but those of the entire world. 'The US leadership role requires that it take an active interest in the support of the institutions of the world order *per se*. As distinguished from most other powers, the impact of US action is global' (Commission on Security and Economic Assistance 1983: 38). The world order issues covered in this particular report are global economic conditions, assistance to developing countries and the long-term national interest (such matters as that 40 per cent of US exports go to developing countries, and 25 per cent of US investments have been placed there and give a rate of return which is nearly 40 per cent higher than for investments in the developed world, ibid.: 41), and conflict with the developing countries (conflagration points and the Soviet threat). It is within this framework that America reserves the right to intervene in the affairs of foreign countries if it assesses that human and ethical ideals as understood in American ruling circles are at risk. 'The United States—founded on principles of freedom, democracy, and humanitarianism—cannot be indifferent to the international neglect of these same principles without imperilling its own future' (ibid.: 42).

Such a policy statement is a blueprint for imperialism in all domains. Not only is the fusion of economic and military aid a declared principle of American hegemony, but ideological conformity is also required of the recipients. Not surprisingly, such official discourse from the early 1980s, on the pre-Gorbachev cold war front, does not refer at all to such relatively subtle concerns as cultural diplomacy or the role of English internationally.

The Reagan administration, unlike that of its predecessor, has chosen to base its human rights policies not on the principles of international covenants such as the *Universal Declaration of Human Rights* but rather on exclusively American tradition and documents, a tradition which defines post-war human rights issues as a competition between East and West. A study of the aid policies of the Carter and Reagan administrations however shows that they were broadly similar, despite a change in rhetoric, that political-military considerations are paramount, that economic interests play a significant role, and that it is false to separate out 'development' and 'security' assistance programmes (Lebovic 1988).

The *foundations* played a decisive role in establishing ESL as an academic discipline. This was one component of a general strategy to link the education systems of periphery-English countries to the values, institutions, and ways of work of the United States. The strategy of the foundations 'led to (1) the creation of lead universities located in areas considered of geostrategic interest and/or economic importance to the US; (2) an emphasis within these institutions on social science research and related manpower planning programs; (3) programs to train public administrators; (4) teacher training and curriculum development projects; and (5) training programs which shuttled African nationals to select universities in the US for advanced training and returned them home to assume positions of leadership within local universities, teacher training institutions, or ministries of education' (Berman 1982: 208). A corollary of this was training Americans to function as experts overseas. This 'aid' has had a considerable and durable impact.

The specific impact on the growth of ELT can be seen from the following examples. From 1952 onwards the Ford Foundation provided grants to develop resources in English teaching abroad. By the mid-1960s it had projects in 38 countries (Fox 1979: 4).[13] Ford also provided grants to American universities for the establishment of training programmes for teachers of ESL. According to Alan Davies of the University of Edinburgh, the Ford Foundation was also involved, along with the British Council, in the original planning of the establishment of the School of Applied Linguistics in Edinburgh in 1957 (Davies 1991). The Rockefeller Foundation supported several projects overseas, including a major one in the Philippines in co-operation with the University of California at Los Angeles. Ford Foundation funds have been decisive for the establishment and continued existence of the Center for Applied Linguistics (CAL) in Washington. One of its chief functions is to promote improved ESL teaching by stimulating research and the production of teaching materials, and by serving as an information centre. CAL has focused more on ESL in bilingual education in the United States than on ELT worldwide.[14]

Among the reasons given for the establishment of the Center was that the Fulbright programme for the export of American academics worldwide was in short supply of qualified ESL teachers and wanted some to be produced fast. Another goal was to stimulate foreign language teaching in the United States. More competence in foreign languages was needed, partly to equip

America to recover from the 'Sputnik shock', partly in order to qualify people for aid work (Center for Applied Linguistics 1959).[15]

There has always been relatively closer collaboration between the modern language teaching profession and ESL in the US than in Britain.[16] The Center for Applied Linguistics was for the first six years of its life a unit of the Modern Language Association of America (which had always included English among its philological and literary research interests). The first director, Ferguson, regarded the affiliation of CAL to the MLA as a guarantee of its academic respectability and some defence against too much direct influence by government agencies or particular foundations like Ford (Perren, ms). Ferguson remained an active scholar in linguistics throughout his time at CAL.

ESL (and CAL that was set up to nurture it) has tended to be dominated by linguistics rather than educationalists. The major influence on training, professional identity, and teaching methods has come from the dominant linguistics tradition of the time, structuralism, and its kindred ally in psychology, behaviourism. The major pedagogical experience drawn on was the intensive teaching of foreign languages to service personnel in the war. The methodology elaborated here tended to be transferred uncritically to other learning situations. The first English teaching projects that Americans were involved in were in countries like Indonesia, where English was needed by adults for professional purposes. The experience of the American linguists involved there came to set the tone for future work, even when the learning problems were quite different, in particular in contexts where English is learnt as a medium of education in schools.

The ELT profession acquired solid institutional foundations on both sides of the Atlantic by the 1950s. It emerged as an 'autonomous profession' (Howatt 1984: 212), straddling government bodies for the promotion of English, academic institutions for research, teaching and information, and private sector interests, in particular language schools and the foundations. The USIA was keen to forge a shared identity for this far-flung profession: their policy was that 'nothing was more important to the world today than to have solidarity among the English teachers' (Center for Applied Linguistics 1959: 195). Attractive career prospects were a necessary part of this, appealing to many motives, including the idealistic one of wishing to lift a little of the white man's burden off the backs of 'Third World' people. The rationale for teaching English overseas is explicitly formulated in the principal article of the British Council's *Annual Report* for 1961–62, entitled 'Teaching Overseas'. The same argumentation was used by American recruiting agencies.

> For many years there is likely to be a massive, worldwide demand for British teachers, which is already presenting this country with both a challenge and an opportunity. Those who meet the challenge will have the satisfaction of serving their own country as well as the other country, and of making some contribution to international understanding.
> (British Council 1962: 18)

English teaching is legitimated as being in the national and international interest. Such interests are not specified, but are assumed to be generally valid. 'A typical thesis of the propaganda system is that the nation is an agent in international affairs, not special groups within it, and that the nation is guided by certain ideals and principles, all of them noble' (Chomsky 1982: 87). 'In the United States, the prevailing version of "the white man's burden" has been the doctrine, carefully nurtured by the intelligentsia, that the US, alone among powers of modern history, is not guided in its international affairs by the perceived material interests of those with domestic power, but rather wanders aimlessly, merely reacting to the initiatives of others, while pursuing abstract moral principles: the Wilsonian principles of freedom and self-determination, democracy, equality, and so on' (ibid.: 73). This myth of American benevolence is the contemporary version of the 'civilizing mission' (ibid.: 74).

In the ELT world the myth of 'academic freedom' combined with the myth of the non-political nature of the language teaching business. The profession acquired slightly different agendas on each side of the Atlantic, but each was explicit on the technical concerns of ELT and relatively silent on the foreign policy element of their work. With both the British and the Americans rapidly expanding their international English teaching effort, there was an obvious need for co-ordination. The British and the American civilizing missions needed harmonizing, so as to ensure that the gospels were complementary rather than competing.

Anglo-American collaboration

It was clear by the mid-1950s that the leading ELT figures in Britain and the USA needed to learn from each other, as well as to compare notes on strategy, means, and goals. The British Council organized a conference for its own specialist ELT staff in July 1955 in Oxford, to which members of the USIA were invited to send delegates. Any reports of this conference at the British end have been destroyed, consigned to the shredding machine in a later purge of files not thought to be of any permanent interest.

In May 1959, USIA, in collaboration with the Center for Applied Linguistics, and with Ford Foundation funding, organized a conference on 'Teaching English Overseas' in Washington to which the British Council sent five participants. The delegates were academics and cultural diplomacy bureaucrats from head office and the field. The proceedings of this conference were published verbatim (Center for Applied Linguistics 1959).

The conference report contains detailed descriptions of all the main activities in English teaching abroad undertaken by the British and the Americans. There is description and evaluation of experience in key countries, of teacher training, methods and materials, examinations, audio-visual aids, bibliographies, etc. Although the report is predominantly about technical practicalities of this kind, ideological anxieties also come to the fore. One American delegate's concern that books produced in communist countries are explicitly anti-imperialist is compounded by the fact that the cultural content of American-produced teaching materials was 'more nearly a vacuum than you would think possible' (ibid.: 46). The British proclaimed less worry on this score because there was close liaison between the British Council and publishers, meaning that any available expertise was being used (ibid.: 106). The orthodox British view was in any case that the teacher made more impact than the book (ibid.: 68).

The report indicates that there was a consensus among delegates that they were in the business of fighting communism, but the language experts seem to regard their work as untainted by political motives. A British Council delegate stated: ' . . . we have an autonomy of our own. We have our Royal Charter under which we operate and so we are not bound by any dictates of foreign political policy' (ibid.: 108). The Director of the fledgling Center for Applied Linguistics, Ferguson, seems to wish to avoid political contamination in a similar way: 'policy decisions have to be made by government agencies and so on, and I think we're going to play a zero role here, a small one anyway' (ibid.: 182). These declarations are clear examples of the myth of non-political ELT. They show little awareness of the contribution of professionalism to the constitution and affirmation of hegemonic ideas. The experts are probably intuitively aware that central professional practices, procedures, and norms represent a paradigm that is being exported, directly or indirectly, to periphery-English countries, yet this is not regarded as educational or cultural imperialism, let alone political in any sense. Their narrow interpretation of this implicitly identifies the 'political' as the discourse of professional politicians or diplomats. They are also inconsistent, since they can immediately identify the political motivations of communist textbooks, yet want their own to project Western values. Their protestations ring somewhat hollow, when their work is explicitly intended to benefit the State they represent.

Despite an ideology of political purity, the delegates gave serious consideration to the question of a papal line of demarcation for British and American spheres of ELT influence in the world. This idea was rejected in favour of collaboration globally, including the joint staffing of teachers' courses, regular liaison, and comprehensive exchange of information. The importance assigned to such work is apparent from the fact that the next Anglo-American conference was held only two years later.

One further conference report from this period sheds light on the ideology of the founding fathers (*sic*: they were all male) of ELT. In June 1961 an 'Anglo-American Conference on English Teaching Abroad' was held in Cambridge, organized by the British Council, with a strong American presence. As before, the delegates consisted of trusted academics and the professional ELT bureaucrats and field staff.[17] The conference report quoted below (*Anglo-American Conference Report*, 1961) was published by the British Council for internal circulation.

The topics covered at the conference included the state of the art in teacher training, the use of educational aids, existing cooperation, research needs, etc. The delegates also decided to try to go beyond practicalities and pious rhetoric. They therefore chose to reaffirm some 'fundamental propositions'. The first of these indicates that they were well aware that the 'development' process that English represented for Third World countries was revolutionary:

> The teaching of English to non-native speakers may permanently transform the students' whole world. Such teaching should be within the total linguistic and educational requirements for the economic, social, and human development of the host country.
> (*Anglo-American Conference Report* 1961: 7)

This seems to be a reformulation of a point made by Professor I. A. Richards in his opening address:

> If and when a new language becomes really operant in an undeveloped country, the students' world becomes restructured.
> (*Anglo-American Conference Report* 1961: 2)

This process has close parallels with the imposition of a standard language within a nation, and is as fundamental in its repercussions, as the French sociologist, Bourdieu, explains:

> The conflict between the French of the revolutionary intelligentsia and the dialects or patois is a conflict about symbolic power where what is at stake is the *creation* and *re-creation* of mental structures. In short it is not only a question of communicating but of ensuring the acceptance of a new discourse of authority, with its new political language, its terms of address and reference, its metaphors, its euphemisms, and the representation of the social world that it expresses, and which, because it is linked to the new interests of new groups, is not expressible in local tongues shaped by usage linked to the specific interests of peasant groups.
> (Bourdieu 1982: 31)

What is at stake when English spreads is not merely the substitution or displacement of one language by another but the imposition of new 'mental structures' through English. This is in fact an intrinsic part of 'modernization' and 'nation-building', a logical consequence of ELT. Yet the implications of this have scarcely penetrated into ELT research or teaching methodology. Cross-cultural studies have never formed part of the core of ELT as an academic discipline, nor even any principled consideration of what educational implications might follow from an awareness of this aspect of English linguistic imperialism.

The second proposition formulated by delegates to this Anglo-American conference is that 'increasing self-sufficiency of the host country in English teaching is the objective. This can best be furthered by the closest collaboration between resource and host countries' (ibid.: 7). It was felt that the 'resource' countries—Britain and the USA and some Commonwealth countries—should respond to host countries' needs, but that although the host countries must decide policy for themselves, they need firm guidance so that they appreciate what is good for them. What this means in practice is brought out in I. A. Richards's summary 'impression' of the conference, published as an appendix to the report.

> This recognition of national independence went along with a realization that nationalistic spirit could wreck all hopes for English as a second language. Resource countries—those which have potential teaching services to offer along with what is needed to supply it—must do all they can in the interests, first and foremost, of their hosts. That was heartily agreed on. It had to be reconciled somehow with awareness that a Ministry of Education—under nationalistic pressures—may not be a good judge of a country's interests. And reconciled, further, with the remembrance that, insofar as a second language becomes truly operative, the view that the mind takes will change. Firm words were said on this and on the dangers of propaganda to host and resource country as well. An important consideration here is that English, through its assimilations, has become not only the representative of contemporary English-speaking thought and feeling but a vehicle of the entire developing human tradition: the best (and worst) that has been thought and felt by man in all places and in all recorded times. It is equally the key to the prodigious mysteries the swift oncoming years will bring upon us.
> (Richards 1961: 19)

This is an apologia for English at all costs. The language is all that any human can need so as to understand the past or face the future. If Ministries of Education fail to appreciate this universal truth, because they are blinkered by 'nationalism', it is the duty of the core English-speaking representatives to override them. When the imposition of English thought processes has been effectuated, these hindrances to the 'hopes for English as a second language' will no longer exist.

Richards's ideas are a direct echo of Matthew Arnold's

doctrine that the educated élite, as men of culture, were 'true apostles of equality' whose duty it was to 'make the best that has been thought and known in the world current everywhere' (from *Culture and Anarchy*, 1868/9, quoted in Sutherland, 1973: 183). Arnold was an educationalist, and was quoted in Chapter 2 for his linguicidal view of how the Welsh language could be extirpated. The Anglo-American gathering appears to be continuing along the same linguicist line, casting ELT in a traditional classist mould, in which education implied alertness to '*real* thought and *real* beauty', and with ELT missionaries as the twentieth century version of the great men of culture, who are 'those who have had a passion for diffusing, for making prevail, for carrying from one end of society to the other, the best knowledge, the best ideas of their time' (ibid.).

To describe English as a 'second' language in such contexts is a gross misnomer, at least if it contains a notion of 'secondary'. The whole thrust of Richards's argument is that English should become the dominant language, replacing other languages and world views. The mother tongue will be learned chronologically first, but English is the language that by virtue of its use and functions becomes the primary language. The issue of how to categorize English in various contexts (second, foreign, etc.), particularly in relation to societal bilingualism and language teaching, will be discussed in Chapter 8.

The report analysed here was written for British Council internal purposes, and consequently has a different tenor from equivalent papers intended for open circulation. It provides telling insight into the dominant ideology and what lies behind the public rhetoric of 'international understanding'. It shows language experts stepping outside their field of specialization and pronouncing on what is good for other, dependent societies. It advocates English linguistic hegemony, the saturation of the Periphery with Centre ideas to the point where there is consent to Centre policies. The Centre's right to 'leadership' is taken for granted. The report proclaims that the Centre has a monopoly of language, culture, and expertise, and should not tolerate resistance to the rule of English.

By the early 1960s the governments in Britain and the USA had created an ELT professional base from which ELT activities could operate. The French had embarked on a similar, and even more ambitious operation (Coste 1984), imbued with the conviction that 'where they speak French, they buy French' (ibid.: 33) and France as an intellectual and cultural leader. The five-year plan formed in 1957 explicitly states the goals of foreign cultural policy, and unlike the covert British operation, these were published and discussed in the media. They were fully implemented in a 'spirit of mission' (ibid.: 30). The British (FCO, British Council) and the Americans (State Department/USIA) have maintained regular contact, but at a fairly low-key level.[18] There were divergences between the views and approaches of the British and the Americans on the methods and means of ELT. Each had a fairly narrow but open-ended professional ortho- doxy that the major 'aid' tasks that lay ahead could build on, with various academic interests better positioned than others to fill the obvious gaps. Little separated the British and Americans as regards goals, either for the ELT task *per se* or for the more general political task of promoting national and Western interests. Manifestly, English linguistic imperialism both facili- tated global imperialism and was a consequence of it. The dominant professional discourse was technical, and awaited the day when scholarship would make it more scientific.

Notes

1 For a detailed narrative, with a main focus on Whitehall drama, see the semi-official biography of the British Council, Donaldson 1984.

2 This argument is not often canvassed, but it reappeared when there was speculation that the Gulf crisis of 1990 was triggered off by a misunderstanding between the American Ambassador to Iraq and President Saddam Hussein at a meeting just before Iraq invaded Kuwait.

3 Basic English was the most celebrated of these. It became politically significant when Winston Churchill returned from a visit to the United States during the Second World War convinced that Basic English should be promoted widely by Britain as an 'international auxiliary language'. *Basic* stands for 'British American Scientific International Commercial' and is a compressed selection of the vocabulary and grammar of English, and unsuitable to serve as a medium for social interaction (Howatt 1984: 250). The British Council was given responsibility for its promotion, a task which it undertook with so little enthusiasm that interest for the construct died out rapidly. The official explanation for this

was that the British Council did not partisanly support any one method for learning English (White 1965: 47).

Verschueren (1990) raises the issue of the ubiquity of English blinding us to the fact that the huge variety of forms of English does not ensure communicative efficiency. On the contrary, different cultural starting-points are bound to lead to misunderstandings.

4 The same pattern holds for university institutions which would never have come into existence but for a foundation grant. This was the case, for instance, of several higher education institutions in India, set up with Ford Foundation money and which the Indian government provided capital and running expenditure for and for which it is now solely responsible (Sancheti 1984: 10). The extension of the State's range of activities is of course a general feature of the twentieth century (see Chapter 2). How business interests commissioned academic work of considerable social and political importance, nationally and internationally, through the creation and management of the Institute of Race Relations, has been studied in Mullard 1985, which also describes how a palace revolution evicted the business interests.

5 The present-day Commonwealth by contrast is committed to such goals as the promotion of peace and individual liberty, the abolition of colonial and racial oppression and of the wide disparities existing between different sections of mankind, Commonwealth Secretariat 1982.

6 The ODA is now a department of the FCO, but has been a separate ministry in earlier administrations. A substantial proportion of its staff worked originally for the Colonial Office.

7 The present Chairman, Sir David Orr, had a career with Unilever, ending up as chairman. He lists his interests in *Who's Who* as golf, rugby, and travel. His predecessor, Sir Charles Troughton, who now has the honorary appointment of President, was chairman of W. H. Smith Limited, and has held directorships in several multinational concerns, including Barclays Bank International and William Collins.

8 President Pompidou's worries about the French language being eclipsed by English were fully justified. Pompidou stated on British television on 17 May 1971 that French was the natural language of the peoples of Europe, English that of America (Haigh 1974: 33).

9   George Perren (ms) notes that in the late 1950s and early
    1960s the Colonial Office was reluctant to accept the
    British Council's claims to educational expertise. The same
    applied to the Ministry of Education, which claimed
    exclusive competence in the area of the learning of English
    in British schools.

10 The figure of 3,500 may be a modest one for the territories
    covered by the Colonial Office, including Malaya, the West
    Indies, Ceylon, and the African dependencies. Very few
    British Local Education Authorities were willing to co-
    operate in secondment schemes. The French were able to
    post teachers overseas for a tour of duty as part of their
    ordinary service, and did so on a massive scale (Perren, ms).

11 Figures for Inter-University Council for Higher Education
    recruitment are given in Kolinsky 1983: 56. In the 1970s
    the Ministry of Overseas Development reduced funds for
    subsidizing the appointment of British academics to peri-
    phery-English universities, preferring to aim aid at less
    privileged sectors of Third World societies. The IUC was
    assimilated into the British Council in 1981.

12 A conference of Ministers of Education, an embryonic
    Unesco, was started among the many governments in exile
    in London during the war. The Americans were quick to join
    this and to influence plans for what became Unesco.

13 For a review of Ford Foundation funded activities in
    language and development see Fox 1975.

14 For a survey of CAL's activities, see the 20th anniversary
    commemoration issue of *The Linguistic Reporter*, 21/7,
    1979. For an evaluation of its international impact see
    Cawston 1975.

15 In Britain the two wings of the language teaching profession
    (ESL and foreign languages) have in recent years experienced
    a rapprochement in the policy co-ordination work of the
    National Congress for Languages in Education. It is ironical
    that in both countries, while ESL has become a flourishing
    profession, foreign languages remain a low educational
    priority. In the US the need to train a more substantial
    number of American speakers of foreign languages has been
    reiterated officially at regular intervals, while the languages of
    America's ethnic minorities have not generally been regarded
    as a useful resource. For a nation aspiring to world leadership,
    American incompetence in foreign languages is dysfunctional.
    'Effective leadership in international affairs, both in govern-

ment and in the private sector, requires well-trained and experienced experts. And in a democratic society such as ours, leadership is paralyzed without a well-informed public that embraces all our citizens. But the hard and brutal fact is that our programs and institutions for education and training for foreign languages and international understanding are both currently inadequate and actually falling further behind' (Report to the President from the President's commission on foreign language and international studies 1979: 4). Things are no better on the British side of the Atlantic. The Department of Education and Science noted in a consultative paper the abysmal record of traditional modern language teaching in Britain (Department of Education and Science 1983).

16 Ferguson's main assistant, Sirapi Ohannessian, was an educationist by training and experience, with no illusions about the limitations of American applied linguistics or British ELT. Perren's assessment (ms) of CAL in the early 1960s is that it was 'remarkably free from political, national, or indeed academic bullshit, more so than any comparable organization.'

17 Perren (interview), who was closely involved in the organization of these gatherings and the joint Anglo-American-French meetings of this period on the British side comments: 'CAL convened the meetings, and they also involved USIA and AID, and selected academics, these were very carefully chosen, because they were reckoned to be the sort of chaps who would say the right sort of thing. It wasn't a free academic discourse at all.'

18 Biennial meetings between the British Council and the USIA/ State Department are still held. Small numbers of senior staff are concerned, and the meetings are an exchange of views rather than more ambitious attempts at co-ordinating strategy. Throughout the 1960s regular conferences on second language problems were organized by the Center for Applied Linguistics, the British Council's English-Teaching Information Centre, and the French Bureau pour l'Enseignement de la Langue et de la Civilisation Françaises à l'Étranger (BELC). Details of these can be found in *The Linguistic Reporter*. The need for such academic gatherings is presumably now met by the triennial conferences of such professional associations as AILA, the Association International de Linguistique Appliquée, the creation of which was encouraged by the national institutions named above.

7 Creating a profession: the structure and tenets of ELT

What was the professional base on which ELT expanded when the political will to promote English had created the prospect of increased funding for the new profession? Where was the expertise to be found? Who took the initiative in laying down the academic foundations of ELT in Britain? What was the source of the legitimacy of ELT, and whose interests was it likely to serve? I shall attempt to answer these questions and analyse, in particular, some of the key tenets that were to guide ELT work in the major expansion of the 1960s, look at their genesis, relate them to the state of academic knowledge at the time (and to some extent also at the present), and consider the structural and ideological consequences that follow from them.

Creating a British academic base for ELT

The two main pillars on which ELT could build were the widespread but largely unanalysed *experience* of teaching English as a foreign language on the one hand, and the *theoretical disciplines* which were thought to be of relevance to language teaching on the other. These two pillars are complementary and interdependent. In the 1950s, theoretical expertise in ELT was in very short supply on both sides of the Atlantic, which meant that the field was to some extent open to opportunistic initiative.

In Britain, the Institute of Education at the University of London offered teacher training for ELT, and had experience going back to the 1920s, but little attempt was made there to pursue ELT in a theoretically explicit way.[1] The University of London also had a strong phonetics tradition, founded by Daniel Jones, and a strong linguistics department at the School of Oriental and African Studies, spearheaded by J. R. Firth. As the name of the school implies, the primary concern was with foreign languages, essentially those of the British empire, rather than with English. Said (1978: 214) describes the genesis of the school. Lord Curzon, formerly the Viceroy of India, argued in 1914 that it was an 'Imperial obligation' and 'patriotic duty' to establish a School of Oriental and African Studies, so that the 'genius of the East' could be properly understood, and he solicited financial support from the City for the purpose (ibid.). Its establishment reflected the utilitarianism combined with liberalism and evangelicalism which characterized British rule in the East. This departure from the Macaulay doctrine was motivated by an urge to consolidate British interests in India. Firth was quoted in Chapter 5 as lamenting that the imperial remit had not resulted in any research on language planning or the teaching of English worldwide.

As a result of the shortcomings of the available theories and reference works for ELT (see below), it drew in its early years on fragmentary principles for describing language, and inadequate descriptions of English. Although the considerable ELT experience of nearly a century had produced several books on language learning and considerable refinements in materials development (see the review in Howatt 1984), until the late 1950s nowhere in Britain was there an institutional base for the scientific study of language learning and teaching, either for foreign languages or ELT. Research into ELT was mostly small-scale development projects (Wingard 1959, at Makerere in Uganda).[2] There were few channels for exchanging experience with colleagues on the continent or further afield.[3]

This situation changed with the establishment of the School of Applied Linguistics at Edinburgh University in 1957. The school was set up at the initiative of the British Council, which guaranteed to supply the new post-graduate courses with students. These would be the British Council's own career ELT staff,[4] and foreigners on scholarships. The university could draw on expertise in the departments of Phonetics, English Language and General Linguistics, English Literature, and Education. The new School succeeded in attracting people with extensive experience of ELT, as staff and students. The overall goal of the school is stated in its prospectus (quoted in *Center for Applied Linguistics* 1959: 148): 'The primary aim of the school is to provide a theoretical basis for the teaching of English as a foreign language within the wider framework of language teaching in general, which in turn is treated as a branch of Applied Linguistics.'[5]

The name of the Edinburgh department is slightly surprising.

Why does it highlight linguistics and none of the other disciplines which contribute to an understanding of language learning and teaching? Was the department only concerned with applying linguistics? Why is there no reference to English as a foreign/ second/ world language in it, if English was the *raison d'être* of the institution? What does the term 'applied linguistics' connote, and why was it chosen as a designation for the new department?

The term has a long pedigree going back at least to the Danish linguist, Rasmus Rask (one of the three founding fathers of comparative philology, with Grimm and Bopp) in 1814. He distinguished between theoretical linguistics, the study of the principles governing language form and use, and applied linguistics, the preparation of useful, informative reference works such as grammars and dictionaries (quoted in Gregersen 1991). The Polish-Russian linguist Jan Baudouin de Courtenay in 1871 distinguished between the more scholarly pursuits of applied linguistics and more practical ones (Catford 1981: 13), a distinction which still characterizes the activities which go under the name of 'applied linguistics'. The American journal *Language Learning*, subtitled *The Journal of Applied Linguistics*, has appeared since 1948.

The theoretical/applied dichotomy is of course a familiar one (in mathematics and the natural sciences, in OECD reports, etc.), but there are problems in using the label 'applied linguistics' for the theoretically supported study of language learning and teaching. There has also been considerable confusion within the ELT profession as to what applied linguistics is and what language teachers can expect from it. If 'applied' points only to practical implementation in a language teaching situation, theoretical pursuits seem to be a secondary consideration. Whereas if applied linguistics means the theoretically explicit exploration of scientific questions about language learning, it cannot be immediately concerned with the solution of problems in language pedagogy and should perhaps be called 'theoretical applied linguistics'.

Why, though, is linguistics alone singled out? While it is true that linguistics can be drawn on in many applied activities, as is shown in the range of activities engaged in by members of the national affiliates of the Association International de Linguistique Appliquée (AILA), the theoretical study of ELT requires the application of other disciplines as well as linguistics (cognitive and educational psychology, sociology, anthropology, etc.).

A further problem is that of the epistemological status of the activity, where there are two main positions. In one, applied linguistics takes over theories and methods from other areas of scientific study, which then have the status of feeder disciplines, in the other, it is an autonomous scientific activity requiring the elaboration of its own theoretical base in relation to its intended applications. When all these ambiguities in the term exist, it is not surprising that there is uncertainty about what 'applied linguistics' stands for.

The name of the Edinburgh department also seems restrictive as a designation for the theoretical study of language learning and teaching when one looks at the very broad course content that students were exposed to in the early days at Edinburgh. This embraced psychology and education as well as linguistics, in a broad social perspective. 'First of all they have to know something about the theory of bilingualism, of languages in contact and of the problems that arise in language contact situations . . . They have to be able to cope with the analysis and evaluation of the wider setting of language teaching operations; of geographical, political, educational, and linguistic conditions in the country where the teaching is going on, and the relation of these factors to the design of syllabuses and so on' (Catford 1961: 35).

Such concerns have in practice seldom loomed large in ELT or applied linguistics as they have evolved. For that to have happened would have involved bringing in sociologists, economists, political scientists, anthropologists, and comparative educationists from the start. One might then have seen ELT develop along comparable lines to the sociology of language or language planning, or, a rather closer parallel, minority education and bilingualism (see, for instance Skutnabb-Kangas and Cummins 1988). In fact it was linguistics which dominated theory-building in the first phase of ELT expansion, on both sides of the Atlantic, even at the expense of education. The name of the Edinburgh department correctly reflects this bias.[6] The reasons for omitting 'English' from the name of the department can only be guessed at. They possibly reflected a wish on the part of those concerned to stress that a theoretical approach was needed.

In Britain in 1960 the *output of trained British postgraduates* in ELT was modest in the exteme. The average was 20 a year, the majority from Edinburgh, and a few from London (Wayment 1961: 59). Whereas the Edinburgh course was intended for experienced teachers, the London course was for initial training in EFL. (The number trained at European universities as teachers of EFL was astronomical by comparison, but somehow never entered into the calculations of ELT planners in Britain or the USA.) British people were in a minority on the London course, but their proportion increased as career prospects abroad began to open up. From 1959, the British Council offered 14 studentships a year to young graduates for the duration of the course, to attract recruits (White 1965: 113). In the USA at this time, more foreigners than US nationals graduated from ELT programmes, and the balance only swung over to a much higher proportion of Americans during the 1960s when ESL work in the USA expanded.

In 1960, in order to identify ELT expertise at British universities, and elaborate a blueprint for university expansion, and at the suggestion of the Committee of Vice-Chancellors and Principals of United Kingdom Universities, the British Council called a conference on University Training and Research in the Teaching of English as a Second/Foreign Language (the Nutford House conference, reported in Wayment 1961).[7] The list of participants contains few names of people with first-hand experience of ELT. The gathering essentially consisted of academics whose departments (linguistics, English literature, education, etc.) could potentially contribute to the expansion in ELT and benefit from it. The participants discussed the pertinence of their own academic patch, identified a range of research needs, and made a set of recommendations which could legitimate increased funding from the University Grants Committee.

The British cabinet had decided in 1956 to make teaching overseas more secure and attractive. The Nutford House conference of British academics expressed its approval of this prospect and made recommendations which were designed to ensure that British universities could train the recruits to the profession appropriately. Their main recommendations covered support for overseas and British institutions, a worldwide career service for ELT experts, and an expansion of training facilities for British and foreign ELT people in Britain. Financial support for overseas institutions was not specifically intended to build up periphery-English country expertise, but was earmarked for the appointment of British staff to work in them. Subsidizing British people abroad was seen as 'a pre-condition for the further development in the United Kingdom of properly planned and effective training in the teaching of English as a foreign or second language' (ibid.: 58). The career service recommendation is likewise seen purely in terms of the benefits that would accrue to the Centre, and only indirectly (and this is not spelt out) to the Periphery. 'A worldwide career service for key British experts in English teaching must be created not only to encourage a flow of suitable recruits, but to ensure that British universities can establish and correlate training within a proper academic framework of the necessary disciplines' (ibid.: 59).

Even granted that the report may have been mainly written to impress and extract funding from the University Grants Committee, this seems an ethnocentric perspective.[8] There is frank admission that British ELT has an inadequate academic base and that one needs to be built up. It does not appear, however, that British academics in 1960 thought in terms of partnership or reciprocity in establishing a worldwide corps of English-teaching experts, nor that they appreciated that Periphery countries should have a decisive influence on what was required there. The view from the Centre was that professionalism could only be developed in the Centre, along with a considerable Centre presence in the Periphery. All the recommendations are designed to strengthen the ELT base in Britain so as to qualify English people to meet the need for English teaching abroad. The ideology of English linguistic imperialism is thus implicit in the suggestions made by the conference, and the structure is asymmetrical. The recommendations are deeply imbued with anglocentricity, which was defined earlier as taking the forms and functions of English as it is used in the core English-speaking countries and the promise of what English represents as the norm by which all language activity or use should be measured. Implementation of the recommendations would lead to a strengthening of the structure of English linguistic imperialism.

The eurocentricity of the approach can be seen in the fact that the Centre arrogated to itself the right to decide what 'needs' the Periphery had and how they should be met. One paper to the conference pointed out that there was no simple relationship between the *use* of English for various purposes in periphery-English countries, the *needs* that arise in order to equip people to use English, and the *demand* for English teaching as an expression of these needs (King 1961: 24). Needs are in fact notoriously difficult to specify, the more so when instrumental language use merges with general educational goals. Needs also tend to be defined top-down, whereas a human rights perspective would tend to favour a bottom-up approach with the learner empowered with rights (see Gomes de Matos 1985). At the Nutford House conference it was the Centre's perception of the Periphery's needs that served as the justification for the expansion of ELT. The possible benefits for Britain are not mentioned, and it is not thought necessary in the report to legitimate why Britain should play a prominent role.[9] The preamble to the recommendations refers to unspecified 'responsibilities' which are part of the justification for the British to step up their efforts: 'There exists an increasingly urgent demand for more English teaching overseas. It is believed that this overt *demand* is but the visible aspect of a still greater and as yet incompletely assessed *need* for wider and more specialized English teaching, and indeed for teaching in English, not only within the Commonwealth but throughout the world . . . This conference believes that Britain and British teachers have special responsibilities for securing both more and better English teaching abroad' (Wayment 1961: 58). The white man's burden had been metamorphosed into the British native-speaking teacher's burden.

The architects of ELT considered the whole world as their laboratory. Linguistic imperialism thus paralleled economic, political, and military imperialism. The structure of scientific and educational imperialism ensured that it was mainly in the Centre that expertise and theory-building would accumulate (assisted by the brain drain, which sucked Periphery scholars to the Centre). The structural relations between Centre and Periphery ensured that all the beneficial spin-offs would accrue to the Centre, as it built up its research and training capacity. Galtung sees close parallels between the extraction of raw materials and the extraction of ideas in the Periphery: in the 'skill and education' field, not much is needed 'beyond a hole in the ground' (Galtung 1980: 114). The international division of labour means that the Periphery supplies the raw materials, the Centre the finished products, whether manufactured goods, books, or theories.

This process can be seen in relation to expertise in the description of English, and the way this is built up in schools and universities. The participants at the conference agreed that one of the fields where scholarship was lacking was in the description of the contemporary English language. 'There is an acute shortage of specialists in contemporary English who have a thorough training in linguistics and phonetics' (Wayment 1961: 61). Quirk's contribution to the conference also points out that until 1960 it had been extremely difficult to obtain funds for basic research into the structure of the English language. University departments of English were dominated by literary concerns, which matched up with the teaching of English in schools, where literature dominated at the upper levels. This practice had been exported to the periphery English-speaking countries (Press 1963; on Nigeria and Pakistan, Wayment 1961: 13; on India, Kachru 1975; on West and East Africa, Neville Grant, interview), where it reportedly still dominates.

English people going abroad to teach English were unlikely to have studied their mother tongue much beyond 'O' level. 'Hundreds of British graduates who are not specially trained go overseas to teach every year, but they are by no means qualified for the responsibilities which may fall to their lot, nor does their undirected experience necessarily generate the expertise required' (from the Nutford House conference recommendations, in Wayment 1961: 59).

The conference appreciated that the growth of ELT could have a useful influence on the teaching of English in Britain. 'The conference believes that English language teaching in schools in Britain should be extended in the upper forms beyond the customary 'O' level, and that it could well be related more closely to the study of contemporary English; the kind of training in general linguistics and contemporary English envisaged by this conference could make a valuable contribution to the teaching of English as a mother tongue, both in universities and schools' (ibid.: 63). Even if the dominance of literature has been only partially checked since 1960, the vastly increased prominence of English language study in higher education in the core English-speaking countries, as a result of the boom in linguistics, ELT, and other 'applied' linguistic concerns, is in no small measure due to the impetus generated by the increased visibility of the 'needs' of the periphery-English countries.

The picture that emerges is one of state and academic interests dovetailing. It would be naïve to assume that the state, via the good offices of the British Council, was manipulating the university world into taking on a production line of loyal inter-state actors. The universities had their own axes to grind, personal empires to be built, and certain ideas of liberal research and teaching to defend. At the same time, ELT meant money, students, departments, stimulus, and growth. The meshing of state and university interests permitted the university departments that evolved, with ELT as a principal legitimatory motor, each to have its own stamp. This seems to indicate a combination of external and internal definitions (in the sense presented in Chapter 3) for the new academic field, but with a relatively high degree of external definition, in view of the state's interest in harnessing the expertise generated by ELT. The Edinburgh School of Applied Linguistics was set up specifically to service ELT, as indicated above. This the school has done, very probably in a more distinguished way than any other university in Britain (Davies 1991). It has simultaneously been influential in creating applied linguistics as a theoretically coherent discipline, of relevance to all language teaching rather than ELT alone (with some uncertainty as to how directly relevant it is to language teaching, and with linguistics still as the dominant influence). Other universities have played the ELT card in order to create other academic empires. For instance ELT at Leeds has had a strong bias towards linguistics rather than pedagogy: in the 1960s ELT cohabited uneasily with the School of English, which was primarily a literature department and which it forsook for linguistics when the university established a distinct department of linguistics, in a merger with phonetics.

One consequence of the callowness of the ELT academic base in the 1960s was that the courses offered reflected local, often fumbling attempts to evolve appropriate content. A more fundamental problem was that although the entire exercise was an attempt to build Centre-Periphery bridges, it was firmly anchored in Centre perceptions and structures.

ELT and educational language planning for under-developed countries

While ELT was planting academic institutional roots, the British were simultaneously involved in a great deal of educational planning for underdeveloped countries. Unfortunately this was not co-ordinated with the efforts to build up a qualified ELT profession. Nor did language occupy a prominent place in much of the international activity of the period in the field of

education. 'The first conference of African Ministers of Education, called by Unesco in Addis Ababa in 1960, makes no
mention of language at all in the main body of the report. Its
main concern is to set a target for attaining universal literacy: the
language in which literacy is to be achieved is not considered'
(Cawson 1975:413). One might have expected that leading
educationalists from countries under British dominion, where
language had been a controversial policy issue, would appreciate
the importance of language. However this is not apparent from
the policy documents of the time.

> Education commissions sat in most African countries at about
> the time of independence. The normal pattern was for a
> majority of Africans to be chaired by British university men
> unassociated with the colonial period. Their reports either
> ignored the language situation altogether or made a few
> routine references to improving the teaching of English. The
> Malawi report of 1960 gives 3 ½ out of 360 pages to language
> (ways of improving English teaching); the Kenya report of
> 1964 gives 5 paragraphs out of 531. It isolates for special
> study 16 problems facing Kenya; language is not one of them.
> The improving of English is likewise the only matter con-
> sidered in the Uganda report of 1963, in 3 pages out of 83; in
> the Ghana report of 1967 in one page out of 160; and in the
> Nigerian report of 1960, in five lines out of 8,000.
> (Cawson 1975:412)

This linguicism is perhaps comprehensible so far as the British
report-writers are concerned, though it reveals inexcusable
ignorance of African realities (and of their predecessors' work),
and demonstrates anglocentricity of an insensitive kind. It is only
comprehensible, so far as the Africans are concerned, if one
recalls that political power was transferred in such countries to
leaders who were themselves the products of colonial education.
They seem to have internalized the colonialist mythology of the
inadequacy and divisiveness of African languages, which is what
the description of colonial educational language policy (see
Chapter 5) leads one to expect.

There is no doubt that there were major constraints when
attempts were made immediately before and after independence
to expand education simultaneously at all levels. There was in
fact an educational vicious circle: to provide the new universities
and technical colleges with the necessary students there had to be

more secondary schools, these need qualified African teachers, which only post-secondary education could supply (Perren, ms). What many of the African élites were familiar with was a highly selective system, with one or two schools in each colony modelled on British élite schools. Educational planning efforts tended to go into providing more of this, rather than revising educational aims. There was a focus on increasing the number of schools and teachers, rather than on potentially controversial matters like language policy.

The effect of such planning documents was to clear the way for Centre 'aid' in teacher training to be conducted through the medium of English and to focus on English, to the exclusion of other languages. Language teaching was inspired by the new professionalism of applied linguistics, and relatively unencumbered by experience of multilingual countries elsewhere in the English-speaking Periphery such as India. It was even less likely to draw on the experience of multilingual non-English-speaking countries such as the USSR, Yugoslavia, or Switzerland, or bilingual countries like Finland and Belgium.

The key conference which decided on priorities for ELT in the newly independent countries was the Commonwealth Conference on the Teaching of English as a Second Language, held at Makerere, Uganda in 1961. It was a direct outcome of a proposal of the first Commonwealth Education Conference, held at Oxford in 1959. The conference brought together representatives of 23 countries who were assumed to have ELT aid needs, and expected support from Britain. The British ELT world was well represented, with, among others, J. C. Catford, Director of the School of Applied Linguistics at Edinburgh University, Bruce Pattison, the Professor with responsibility for ELT at the Institute of Education, University of London, Terence Mitchell, later responsible for ELT courses at Leeds University, and Arthur King, head of the British Council's ELT operations. There was also a strong American team of 'observers' (three linguists, Marckwardt, Prator, and Ferguson—the latter, director of CAL—and representatives of USIA and the International Cooperation Agency). Missionaries with first-hand teaching experience in underdeveloped countries were underrepresented. The purposes of the conference were to 'provide opportunity for the exchange of ideas and experience among people from different parts of the world who may not be aware of developments elsewhere; and to discuss ways and means of increasing the efficiency of teaching English as a second language, particularly in the difficult initial stages, and in accordance with the needs and wishes of the countries concerned' (*Makerere Report* 1961: 2).

The deliberations of the conference focused on principles for teaching English to beginners, teacher training, literature, English for Special Purposes, tests, and research needs. Among the many recommendations made, the first was for a massive increase in the training of teachers of English for all levels. The second covered the shortage of teachers and contains a rationale for stop-gap aid. 'Our aim is to provide at all levels qualified teachers who are indigenous to the country in which the teaching takes place. However, in view of the present scarcity of qualified staff, the services of teachers from countries where the mother tongue is English will be required in other countries as well as their own, either in teaching posts or at seminars and special courses dealing with the teaching of English as a second language. Expatriate teachers from the English-speaking countries will be needed for many years to come; they should be employed increasingly as teacher trainers or university lecturers rather than as teachers in schools, since the world demand is so great that the so-called "resource countries" may not be able much longer to provide a substantial supply of school teachers' (ibid.: 6).

This paragraph succinctly formulates the Centre-Periphery relationship in ELT. The laudable goal of Periphery countries becoming self-sufficient is made dependent on the authority and example of the Centre, whose agents are to occupy multiplier positions so that their impact is maximized. The Centre's inter-state actors may not be well qualified, they are almost certain not to have insight into the cultural and linguistic backgrounds of the learners they are to take charge of, but their language and their example is what the Periphery needs.

The doctrine that was to underlie ELT work was enshrined at Makerere in a number of tenets. The tenets are not codified in any coherent way in the report, but they underlie many of the methodological principles enunciated there. They represent influential beliefs in the ELT profession, which were given a stamp of approval at Makerere and which have had a decisive influence on the nature and content of ELT aid activity in periphery-English countries. Their influence has also been substantial in core English-speaking countries, as the same tenets were initially adopted in the teaching of the dominant language to immigrants. The tenets represent a pre-theoretical distillation of the worldwide grassroots ELT teaching experience that was assembled at Makerere. They are not so rigid as to preclude flexibility in a profession that was finding its academic and pragmatic feet, but there was a risk that their status would lead to them being accepted as unchallenged dogma.

The key tenets can be formulated as follows:

- English is best taught monolingually.
- The ideal teacher of English is a native speaker.
- The earlier English is taught, the better the results.
- The more English is taught, the better the results.
- If other languages are used much, standards of English will drop.

These tenets will now be scrutinized individually, in relation to available evidence and theory at the time, and to some extent retrospectively in the light of current theory and knowledge. A working hypothesis is that each tenet is false, and that each can be redesignated as a fallacy:

- the monolingual fallacy
- the native speaker fallacy
- the early start fallacy
- the maximum exposure fallacy
- the subtractive fallacy.

The evidence for tenet or fallacy needs examination.

Tenet one: English is best taught monolingually

The monolingual tenet holds that the teaching of English as a foreign or second language should be entirely through the medium of English. The only language permitted in the English classroom is English. Gatenby, one of the founding fathers of ELT, formulated the tenet in 1950, in an article summarizing principles of language learning, as follows: 'What is essential is that the language being studied should be as far as possible the sole medium of communication in any given environment' (Gatenby 1965: 14). Implicit in the monolingual tenet is the belief that an exclusive focus on English will maximize the learning of the language, irrespective of whatever other languages the learner may know.

The monolingual tenet implicitly underpins many of the proposals in the Makerere report. Quite detailed recommendations are made for the teaching of pronunciation, structure, and vocabulary in the early stages of learning, the guiding principle being that the language units should be presented in comprehensible situations. Reference to the mother tongue should only be made *in extremis* and only as a check on comprehension (*Makerere Report*: 13; these sections, as well as the chapter on tests and examinations are reproduced in Allen 1965). On literature, the report sensibly proposes that the material to be read should be within the linguistic and cultural grasp of the children (ibid.: 14–19), but the encouragement of reading in any other language than English does not appear to have occurred to the report-writers. The focus of the conference was on the teaching of English rather than on broad educational objectives (a focus which is largely true of ELT to this day). This meant that only reading in English is covered, and no attention is paid in the report to reading in its own right. It is legitimate for English teaching to focus on reading in English, but this is a very special situation if there is no reading in any other language, and when the cultural universe expressed through English differs so radically from that of the learners' first language. Pattanayak (1986c) reports that this mismatch between the language of experience and the foreign medium of schooling imposes 'cultural perception blindspots'.

The monolingual tenet evolved as a result of experience in several language teaching traditions. Its origins go back to the colonial language teaching experience and the spoken language teaching methods which evolved as a result of the 'Reform' movement in foreign language teaching associated with the discovery of phonetics and such names as Sweet, Jespersen, Palmer, and Hornby. The theme linking these thinkers is a concentration on classroom methodology and the promotion of good spoken language learning habits and activities. Palmer was the first to provide a coherent rationale for active oral language teaching (Palmer 1922, republished 1964). His influence on ELT was immense (Howatt 1984).

We can consider first the impact of the colonial tradition on the evolution of the monolingual tenet. The banishment of other languages from the classroom has a long tradition in periphery-English countries. A Church Missionary Society report on primary education in Sierra Leone in 1808 states:

The great object which the parents of the children had in
sending them to school was their acquirement of the English
language. Therefore, according to their strict instruction, not a
word of Susu was allowed to be spoken in the school.
(quoted in Tiffen 1968: 71)

It is unlikely that the pedagogy advocated here, despite credit-
able deference to parental wishes, was ideal for learning a
language to which there was so little exposure in the environment. The ban on other languages reflects a belief that other
languages, including the mother tongue, are a hindrance in
foreign language learning, an issue taken up below. The ban also
reflects the status of languages other than English under
colonialism. Monolingualism in English teaching was the natural
expression of power relations in the colonial period. Other
languages were functionally restricted, for instance for communication with servants, or initial literacy for missionary
purposes. Other languages were transitional, merely a means of
access to English. Colonial education systems attempted to
reproduce the monolinguialism imposed in the core English-
speaking countries. In countries under American dominion
(Puerto Rico, the Philippines), 'we ignored the fact that English
was neither the first language nor the home language of the
children and that they were growing up as the products of a
totally different culture . . . Nor were British practices much of
an improvement over ours. I have seen elementary readers used
in the schools in Jamaica which had been designed for England,
perversely unresponsive, one might almost say, to the real needs
of the children' (Marckwardt 1965).

Monolingualism was supported, in the Centre and the
Periphery, by physical and psychological sanctions. Those
caught using the mother tongue risked corporal punishment or
were identified as having done something shameful, whether in
Wales (Jones 1973), or Kenya (see Ngũgĩ 1985: 114), or France
and its colonies (Calvet 1974). For examples showing how
widespread this practice has been worldwide, as a denial of
linguistic human rights, tracing the historical progression from
cruder, more brutal forms of oppression to more subtle but
equally effective forms, see Skutnabb-Kangas and Phillipson
1986a and 1989: 21–37. A monolingual methodology is organically linked with linguicist disregard of dominated languages,
concepts, and ways of thinking. It is highly functional in
inducing a colonized consciousness.

The monolingual approach was adopted in both sectors of the ELT profession, in the colonial wing and in the EFL sector, which essentially serves the adult education market (Howatt 1984). Most of the initial experience was gained in Europe, but some of the most creative work was done in Japan (Palmer and Hornby). Monolingualism was the 'hallmark which set ELT apart from foreign language teaching in Britain' (Howatt 1984: 212), the other teaching tradition that recruits to ELT might be tempted to draw on. Foreign language teaching was closely geared to translation and literary texts, and was firmly anchored in a bilingual tradition in the sense that the teachers of the foreign language were themselves people who had learnt the language as a foreign language to a high degree of proficiency, and shared the mother tongue of the learners. Implicit in the foreign language approach was a detailed familiarity with the differences between the two languages, and respect for the parity of each. The tradition was less obviously transferable to the ELT context, as it tended to underplay the development of oral proficiency, and in any case it would have required familiarity with the mother tongues of the learners, and this was extremely rare. Quite apart from that, the learning of foreign languages was always a fringe interest among the dominant group in the core English-speaking countries, where monolingualism was regarded as the societal norm.

Some of the architects of the monolingual approach were also fully aware of the influence of the mother tongue in foreign language learning, though the emphasis then differed from present-day psycholinguistic thinking. Palmer's approach was implicitly contrastive, at the phonetic, syntactic, and semantic levels (Palmer 1964: 30–1 and 58). He therefore assumes familiarity on the part of the teacher with the mother tongue of the learners. Much American audiolingual work presupposed a contrastive analysis of the source and target languages and even recommended contrastive cultural analysis (Lado 1957; Marck-wardt 1965). However the dominant paradigm in American ESL in the 1960s and 1970s turned its back on such principles, until the pendulum swung back to a more theoretical interest in mother tongue transfer in the 1980s (Gass and Selinker 1983; Selinker 1991). The *Makerere Report*, in permitting recourse to the mother tongue in order to check comprehension, also assumes that teachers know the mother tongues of their learners. Here the report is probably thinking of local teachers of English rather than native speakers of English. One can ask then why, if the Report assumes some sort of contrastive readiness on the part of teachers, there should be any reason to regard the monolingual tenet as false and potentially harmful?

The first reason has already been mentioned, namely colonial attitudes to local languages and the linguicist favouring of English in teacher training and syllabuses in colonial and post-colonial education systems. In fact, the evidence of the past thirty years is that the structural inequalities between languages remain in place.

> Years after the attainment of political independence, the majority of African independent states have continued to practice linguistic policies inherited at the time of independence, where, on the whole, foreign colonial languages are more favoured than the languages indigenous to the African continent. Indeed, in some cases, it may be possible to demonstrate that the linguistic policies being followed today in certain African independent states are still as colonial in outlook as they were during the period prior to the attainment of political independence.
> (Organization for African Unity, Inter-African Bureau of Languages 1985: 7)

A eurocentric monolingual approach contributes to the failure of the majority in school and to their exclusion from technical and scientific knowledge (ibid.: 11). Monolingualism in education, and in particular the content and ideology of English when taught and used as the medium of education, is at the heart of this cultural dislocation. The ethos of monolingualism implies the rejection of the experience of other languages, meaning the exclusion of the child's most intense existential experience. This is a direct consequence of linguicist educational policies.

The second reason is a related one, which can be more specifically traced to shortcomings in scientific knowledge, in particular in beliefs about *bilingualism*. Grassroots bilingualism or multilingualism is an essential feature of periphery-English Third World countries. Monolingualism cuts across this social reality and attempts to impose a single lens on the world. Monolingual beliefs drew sustenance from the prevailing views on bilingualism in the first half of this century, which were mainly negative. Bilingualism used to be and still is often associated with poverty, powerlessness, and subordinate social

positions (Skutnabb-Kangas 1984a: 67). The myths about bilinguals being lazy, stupid, left-handed, unreliable, morally de-
praved, subject to an inner split, etc., have been demolished by
research (see the refutation in Weinreich 1963: 116–121, and
Hakuta 1986), but ignorance of bilingualism is still widespread
in 'monolingual' western societies.[10]

Bilingualism was never studied in depth in relation to ELT,
except perhaps by Michael West, another of the founding fathers
of ELT, in Bengal in the 1920s (Howatt 1984: 245). An article
by West in the journal *English Language Teaching* in 1958 is
probably not untypical of the attitudes of the period. He
describes bilingualism as an 'inevitable disadvantage' at both the
individual and the societal levels: lack of a written literary
tradition in the home language can lead to people becoming
'emotionally warped or sterilized'. When the 'substandard child'
(*sic*) is compelled to learn at school through the medium of a
different language than the home language, their studies are 'a
dead loss'; gifted pupils who lack language-learning ability are
lost to higher education (West 1958: 96). This article conveys
false information about bilingualism, but it at least has the merit
of acknowledging that bilinguals have other types of needs than
monolinguals. In addition it recognizes the impact of social
conditions on bilingualism, instead of seeing the bilingual child
as inherently deficient (for an analysis of misuse of such
'deficiency' concepts in minority language education see Churchill 1984, and Skutnabb-Kangas 1988). However, the effect of
West's article is to reinforce a monolingual orientation.

The article provoked a riposte by two correspondents, one
advocating bilingualism and biculturalism (Christophersen 1958:
151, interestingly enough a Dane with a distinguished career in
ELT), and one describing bilingualism in Kenya as a necessity,
the crucial issue being how to achieve it effectively (Perren 1959:
18). Paradoxically, Perren's approach involves a total neglect of
any languages other than English in the school: English is a
'replacement language', replacing the many vernaculars for
educational, social, economic, and political purposes (ibid.: 21).
In other words, orthodox ELT reproduced a diglossic linguistic
hierarchy and regarded bilingualism as a matter for the
individual rather than the school.

A further reason for questioning the validity of the monolingual tenet is that it is psycholinguistically naïve. Even when
linguistics began to make an impact on ELT, the monolingual

tenet was little queried. The linguistic dogma of the primacy of speech was used as a prop for pedagogical practice: it was assumed that in order to learn the spoken language, the learner should retrace the steps of a child learning the language in natural communication situations. This also fitted with another linguistic dogma, namely that each language is a system of internally consistent contrasts and relations. This lent theoretical support to the two-code theory, the belief that learners were operating two distinct systems which needed to be kept separate, and that the best way of eliminating interference and errors was to learn monolingually.

That this view of the relationship between the mother tongue (L1) and second or foreign languages (L2) is psycholinguistically inadequate has become apparent from a wealth of psychological, psycholinguistic, and educational research. Research in bilingualism and minority education has highlighted the significance of cognitive development in L1 for effective L2 learning, and the interdependence of proficiency in each language (Skutnabb-Kangas and Toukomaa 1976; Toukomaa and Skutnabb-Kangas 1977; Cummins 1979 and 1984). Failure to provide educational conditions for the development of cognitive-academic proficiency in L1 as well as initial literacy in the L1 may invalidate efforts to build up such skills in L2. The common underlying cognitive proficiency is neglected in a monolingual approach. Studies of the pragmatic competence of L2 users (Kasper 1981), of communication strategies (Færch and Kasper 1983), transfer (Gass and Selinker 1983) and introspection (Færch and Kasper 1987) all point to the substantial contribution of L1 to L2 language use and learning.

In fact the well-known Unesco monograph on the use of vernacular languages in education (Unesco 1953) had already stressed the interdependence of L1 and L2 development, and the mutual benefits that can accrue to both languages when L1 is consolidated initially and L2 is taught efficiently later as a subject (ibid.: 58). However, the implications of this were lost on ELT, except at the modest level of the policy of initial literacy in the mother tongue or a related language. Appropriate bilingual or multilingual strategies throughout schooling were never contemplated. The monolingual tenet symbolizes the focus on English as the only really important language in education.

A further reason for querying the monolingual tenet is that it is impractical. The overwhelming majority of teachers of English are non-native speakers, but, as the *Makerere Report* indicates, local teachers are to follow the example of native speaking teachers of English. These are the experts on language teaching, serving as models for the local teachers, yet the monolingual tenet exonerates the native speaker of English from needing to learn the languages that the learners bring with them to the classroom. This is compounded by two additional shortcomings. The teacher training of local teachers neglects their mother tongues and does not prepare them to analyse or teach these languages adequately, or contrast them with English (Afolayan 1976; Chishimba 1981; Williamson 1976). Secondly, the vast majority of teachers have a poor command of English. Afolayan comments on the Nigerian scene (1976: 118): 'what really defeats all the efforts being made to improve the standard of English teaching is the tacit assumption underlying the present policy concerning the teaching and use of the English language in schools—that every primary school teacher can be an efficient English language teacher and user.' The monolingual approach is utterly inappropriate for teachers who have not been given the chance to bring their English up to a satisfactory level.

In practice, the monolingual approach is probably seldom carried through, but its very existence puts the teacher in a false position. Departures from monolingual orthodoxy are illegitimate. For instance, in Zambia, which has a policy of English-medium education from the first class, it was common knowledge that recourse was made to Zambian languages in order to promote comprehension. The revised regulations of 1976 accept this state of affairs and legalize it, but purely as a means of facilitating the use of English. Zambian languages have not been significantly upgraded.[11] The regulations have been revised in the direction of pedagogic realities. The structural inequalities between English and Zambian languages remain.

The tenets of ELT have *ideological and structural consequences*. They serve to strengthen the hold of the Centre over the Periphery. The monolingual tenet has the effect of strengthening the case for Centre pedagogy and norms for the language. It paves the way for the second tenet, which posits that the ideal teacher of English is a native speaker. The monolingual tenet also has economic consequences. It legitimates the idea of a worldwide cadre of English teachers whose professionalism is in principle equally relevant and acceptable everywhere. It creates jobs for the Centre, and for those in the Periphery who have acquired credentials verifying proficiency in the language of the Centre. This professional structure also links up with economic imperialism: it permits the marketing worldwide of monolingual textbooks emanating from the Centre, which in turn reinforces anglocentricity and the hold of ELT professionalism.

If familiarity with the language and culture of the learners was made a requirement for expert status, Centre inter-state actors would be immediately disqualified. If the same demands were made on textbooks, monolingual books could no longer be sold globally.

A debate on monolingualism has started in the parallel field of German as a foreign language. The Goethe Institut has also followed a monolingual methodology in teaching German around the world, but a recent review of their policy suggests that when the mother tongue is banned from the classroom, the teaching leads to the alienation of the learners, deprives them of their cultural identity, and leads to acculturation rather than increased intercultural communicative competence. A strategy for reorienting the teaching of German as a foreign language is therefore needed (Sternagel 1984: 20).

If there are these objections to the teaching of German as a foreign language to adult learners, whose cultural identity is presumably fairly secure, it is clear that the effect of monolingual teaching on impressionable children can be devastating. This is of course precisely what the architects of colonial education understood, and was a main reason for 'getting them young' (see Chapter 5). Those who created the ideology of ELT seem to have been fully aware of what they were doing. The Anglo-American conference at which the doctrine of English 're-structuring the students' whole world' was propounded (see Chapter 6) was held a few months after the Makerere conference. The linguicist assumption of monolingualism is that English is in a class of its own, is not comparable with other languages. If that premiss is accepted, it goes without saying that a bilingual or bicultural approach is unthinkable and that the language should be taught monolingually.

Tenet two: the ideal teacher of English is a native speaker

The second tenet holds that the ideal teacher is a native speaker, somebody with native speaker proficiency in English who can serve as a model for the pupils. 'At the outset it was the native speaker who was taken for granted as the automatic best teacher, and all other teachers looked up to the native speaker. Now that's no longer the case' (Strevens, interview). When the *Makerere Report* describes the teaching of the 'sounds of English', there is not the slightest doubt that this refers to the sounds of a native speaker, preferably with an RP accent. When the limited supply of native speakers is to be channelled towards posts in teacher training, where the multiplier effect is greatest, the purpose is to permit the largest number of non-natives to be exposed to the target of native speaker competence in the language. It was such non-natives whom virtually all African learners would be taught by initially. The native speaker serves as the model who can personify the native speaker abstracted and reified in works on standard grammar and vocabulary and in 'received pronunciation', and which teaching materials and sound-recordings seek to reanimate. The teacher who is a native speaker is the best embodiment of the target and norm for learners.

As other core English-speaking Commonwealth countries and the USA were represented at Makerere, there must have been some appreciation of the fact that other targets and norms could apply—American English, Australian English, etc. What apparently was uncontested at the time was the notion that native speaker competence in the teacher, with all its cultural associations, was the ideal.

Why should the native speaker be intrinsically better qualified than the non-native? The tenet would hold that this is the case because of greater facility in demonstrating fluent, idiomatically appropriate language, in appreciating the cultural connotations of the language, and (somewhat in the Chomskyan sense, though in this domain, too, the native speaker is no longer uncontested king, see Coulmas 1981; Rampton 1990) in being the final arbiter of the acceptability of any given samples of the language.

None of these virtues is impossible to instil through teacher training.[12] Nor is any of them something that well-trained non-natives cannot acquire. Teachers, whatever popular adages say, are made rather than born, many of them doubtless self-made, whether they are natives or non-natives.[13] The insight that teachers have into language learning processes, into the structure and usage of a language, and their capacity to analyse and explain language, these definitely have to be learnt—which is not the same as saying that they have to be taught, though hopefully teaching can facilitate and foster these qualities. The untrained or unqualified native speaker is potentially a menace— apparently many of the products of the British education system recruited currently into ELT do not know much about their own language.[14]

The literature contains warnings against over-reliance on the native speaker. 'A teacher is not adequately qualified to teach a language merely because it is his (*sic*) mother tongue' warns the Unesco monograph on the use of the vernacular languages in education (Unesco 1953: 69). This report was compiled by experts in bilingualism and foreign language teaching. In the European foreign language teaching tradition (teachers of French in Britain, of English in Scandinavia, etc.), the ideal teacher has near-native-speaker proficiency in the foreign language, and comes from the same linguistic and cultural background as the learners. It is therefore arguable, as a general principle, that non-native teachers may in fact be better qualified than native speakers, if they have gone through the laborious process of acquiring English as a second language and if they have insight into the linguistic and cultural needs of their learners. Success in learning a foreign language, particularly in learning to speak it well, may correlate highly with success in teaching (Britten 1985: 116). This being so, it would seem to be a minimal requirement of teachers of English as a second or foreign language that they should have proven experience of and success in foreign language learning, and that they should have a detailed acquaintance with the language and culture of the learners they are responsible for. The very idea of claiming that the ideal teacher of English is a native speaker is ludicrous as soon as one starts identifying the good qualities of a teacher of English. The tenet has no scientific validity.

The native speaker fallacy dates from a time when language teaching was indistinguishable from culture teaching, and when all learners of English were assumed to be familiarizing themselves with the culture that English originates from and for contact with that culture.[15] It also predates tape-recordings and other technical resources which now permit learners to be exposed to a wide range of native speaker models. It equally predates any realization of the consequences of what Kachru (1986a) refers to as 'nativization', the process by which English has indigenized in different parts of the world, and developed distinct and secure local forms determined by local norms as opposed to those of the native speaker in the Centre. In underdeveloped countries the native speaker tenet has already been overtaken by events, at least outside the classroom. Nativization should not be confused with the native speaker concept, and is invariably associated with bilingualism or multilingualism.

The tenet is however still widely accepted in ELT, even though erosion of it began soon after the Makerere conference. A paper on 'Language and Communication in the Commonwealth', prepared for the third Commonwealth Education Conference, Ottawa, 1964, notes that in the African context 'English must be seen as an African language—albeit an acquired one—and must be ready to serve as the vehicle for distinctively African cultural values' (Perren and Holliday 1965: 20). Also in 1964, Halliday, McIntosh, and Strevens suggested a new realism in norms, when they described the emergence of such nativized variants of English as 'educated West African English' and 'Indian English', labels which refer to a great number of varieties of English. They suggested that these could serve as acceptable local models, provided international intelligibility was maintained (1964: 296). This abandonment of a single, global norm was dubbed the 'British heresy in TESL' by Prator (1968), whose arguments were unmasked as being ethnocentric and unscientific by Kachru (in 1976, republished in Kachru 1986a). Kachru describes the genesis and significance of these second-language varieties of English: 'The institutionalized second-language varieties have a long history of acculturation in new cultural and geographical contexts; they have a large range of functions in the local educational, administrative, and legal systems. The result of such uses is that such varieties have developed nativized discourse and style types and functionally determined sublanguages (registers), and are used as a linguistic vehicle for creative writing in various genres' (Kachru 1986a: 19).

Sridhar and Sridhar (1986) show that the Second Language Acquisition paradigm which dominates theory-building in applied linguistics in much of the West is irrelevant for analysing at least one major group of second language learners, namely those learning English for functional purposes in a multilingual community, such as learners of English in India or most African countries, where English has evolved organically in the communities involved. Transfer has a totally different significance in a western community where the learner may be aiming at a native speaker norm and native tongue interference may be negatively evaluated, and in the context of an indigenized variety of English in which it is inappropriate to evaluate second-language learning with reference to transfer-free norms.

The implication of worldwide nativization of this kind is that we are no longer dealing with one English language, an abstraction from certain canonized uses of it, but with several 'Englishes'. In the case of the language of a speech community defined in terms of national borders, the standard language is an abstraction reflecting the result of the historical process of the consolidation of the most powerful group. The standard language is acquired, with difficulty, in formal education, and the proportion of the population speaking the prestige accent has always been small. 'The standard language is inevitably the prerogative of a rather special minority' (Quirk 1985: 4). Purism in language has therefore always been a sensitive topic, as it touches existential nerves (as George Bernard Shaw put it, the Englishman is 'branded on the tongue' and cannot open his mouth without making some other Englishman despise him). With English taking root in parts of the world to which it has been transplanted, the variation within the language increases enormously. Some of this variety has been described (Africa 1983; Bailey and Görlach 1982; Pride 1982; Kachru 1983a and b, 1985, and 1986a; Platt, Weber, and Ho 1984; the journals *English World-Wide, World Englishes*, and *English Today*).

Awareness of this variation immediately raises the question of norms. Should periphery-English speakers, in particular those ensconced in education systems, aim at an idealized exo-normative model (derived from standard British or American English), or an institutionalized endo-normative model (based on an educated indigenous variant)? This is a complex issue involving attitudes to the competing varieties of English, the extent to which they are codified, their status and functional roles in the communities in question, intelligibility (an under-researched topic, despite the attention drawn to it since the early 1960s,[16] and the identification of realistic educational goals. The most active protagonist of an exo-normative model is Quirk, who clings to the native speaker tenet, is convinced that the world's English learning problems are best handled by native speaker teachers (1990: 7) and that it is the 'leading English-speaking countries' which know best how English should be taught (ibid.: 8). The most articulate champion of an endo-normative model is Kachru (1991), who draws on linguistic, sociolinguistic, and educational arguments to support his case and to unmask the unstated value judgements underpinning Quirk's position.

There is an exactly parallel conflict of interests in the teaching of *French* as a foreign/second language. In francophone Africa, the central issue for control over French is whether the norm is Parisian French or educated African French (Tadadjeu 1980: 44). Ultimately what lies behind the question of norms and models, which is implicit in the native speaker tenet, is the issue of power and control.

Kachru's conclusion, on the basis of extensive research into the forms and functions of Indian English, and attitudes to competing norms, as well as evidence from other parts of the periphery-English speaking world, is that the gradual shift in recent decades has resulted in a definitive break with universal core English-speaking norms (Kachru 1986a). The established periphery varieties of English are anchored in the local culture; they are systemic variants rather than deficient imitations of the core norms; within the speech fellowship there is a cline of intelligibility comparable to that in core English-speaking countries. The shift is therefore towards both linguistic and cultural emancipation, and signifies the end of the era with the British and the Americans as guardians of a monopolistic global norm. Strevens (interview) agrees with this position, and sees the educated local teacher as the ideal teacher of English.

Universal norms for English teaching can therefore no longer apply. Along with this, there should be a reconsideration of 'claims for the universal applicability of particular methods and approaches for teaching and learning English' (Kachru 1985: 23). International intelligibility is needed by those learners who need the language for international purposes. For most people and most purposes, national or local intelligibility should be the target (Kachru 1986a: Chapter 7). Those Nigerians or Pakistanis who need English at the top of the cline of international intelligibility are an extremely small section of the population. Their needs should not influence multilingual educational language planning for the country as a whole, for whom English is endo-normative. It should be possible to organize education in accordance with the principles of language planning which explicitly clarify socio-economic premises, aim at democratiz-ation, and are in harmony with the principles of linguistic human rights. This cannot happen if native speaker language, and the prescriptivism and cultural specificity associated with it, is taken as the norm.

It is highly likely that the native speaker fallacy has served the interests of the Centre, while blinding both its representatives and their collaborators in the Periphery to its ideological and structural consequences. It has diverted attention away from the solution of urgent pedagogical questions, and prevented the flourishing of local pedagogical initiative which could build on local strengths and linguistic realities. The effect of the tenet has been to maintain relations of dominance by the Centre. In a similar way to the monolingual tenet, the native speaker tenet reinforces the linguistic norms of the Centre, creating an ideological dependence. The dependence is also structural, with economic consequences, as the presence of native speakers and books from the Centre, and all that they signify, is necessary to implement the native speaker tenet.

The recognition of variety in English in the Periphery raises a great many pedagogical questions. The sociolinguistic realism exemplified by Kachru is unlikely as yet to be matched by attitudinal and educational realism, among either ELT experts from the Centre or the guardians of the norm in the Periphery. So far as the second group is concerned, it appears that native speaker norms have been internalized as the only right and proper thing, and shifting to a more realistic norm will take time. The tenet of the ideal teacher being a native speaker has bequeathed a substantial legacy in the orientation of English teaching in periphery-English countries, and basically reflects the prescriptive concerns of the Centre. For instance, West African syllabuses are closely attuned to the ideal of native speaker competence, they specify obscure lexical minutiae, and there is a resistance to Ghanaian or Nigerian voices being used as a model on tapes accompanying textbooks used widely in junior secondary schools (Grant, interview). So far as the Centre ELT experts are concerned, what is at stake is the relevance of their professional skills. This should be a poignant issue for the ELT profession in the Centre.

Tenet three: the earlier English is taught the better the results

The notion that the capacity young children have to learn foreign languages informally could be tapped in formal school foreign language learning has been an influential one in the post-war period. It led to major educational experiments in North America (the FLES movement, Foreign Languages in the Elementary School) and Europe. It is currently in vogue again, with several European countries experimenting with starting English as a foreign language early in the primary school. In ELT the notion of an early start has a considerable academic pedigree. Gatenby was in no doubt. 'In general the earlier the child began to learn his second language the better. The ideal method would be for a child to learn his second language as he learned his mother tongue. That was in general impossible however. If English as a second language could not be begun at the primary stage then it should be begun as early as possible at the secondary school level' (British Council, India, 1950: 4). He regarded the age period from birth to 10+ as ideal for language learning; from 10+ to 16–17+ 'children were too old for the natural process and too young for the intellectual one, incentive was also lacking'; while from 17 onwards reduced aural, memory, and imitative skills were counter-balanced by reasoning and determination (ibid.: 5). Gatenby's analysis has the merit of recognizing different physiological and intellectual maturational phases, but his endorsement of an early start for foreign language learning is too broad unless it is linked to the organizational factors relevant in educational decision-making.

The Makerere conference report explicitly enshrines the tenet for any countries which use English as a *medium of education*. One of the 16 recommendations of the conference reads:

> Where the decision has been taken to introduce English as a medium the guiding principle regarding the age at which the language can be introduced should, subject to various limitations, be 'the earlier the better'.
> (*Makerere Report*: 7)

The limitations referred to are brought together in a later chapter under the general heading 'Factors determining the age at which teaching is introduced'. The factors are grouped into sets labelled as administrative, linguistic, psychological, social, and cultural. It is stated that the relative importance of these factors will vary from area to area. They cover such matters as the quality of the teachers, the existence of languages which could be alternatives to English as a medium, the extent to which English is used in the community, and attitudes to English.

Absent from the list is any reference to the cognitive development of the child in the mother tongue, but educational thinking
was then dominated by a mechanistic view of intelligence and
aptitude as innate constants. The factors in the *Makerere Report*
represent no more than a checklist. None the less an unambiguous conclusion is drawn:

> In countries where English is recognized as a second language,
> its teaching should be based on its direct use as a spoken
> language, and it should be introduced as early as possible in
> the child's school life when this is of advantage to the child
> (e.g. when English is used as a teaching language at an early
> stage in the school programme).
> (*Makerere Report*: 8)

The reasoning here is circular, but the general thrust is
unmistakably that the earlier English is taught the better. A
rationale is also provided for English being introduced as early
as possible. The report assumes that English will be a medium
for education for all children at some point, and instrumental
arguments in favour of English are given—the demands of future
employment, success in later examinations, ultimate profit from
later opportunities for educational advance (ibid.: 21). It is also
claimed that English is the principal means of providing equality
of opportunity, granting access to 'what a wider international
society has to offer' (ibid.: 21). The legitimacy of such arguments
and the source of their power is examined in Chapter 9.

The Makerere conference was held when the African colonies
had generated the winds of change which would blow them to
political independence. We saw in the analysis of colonial
educational practice that western education never catered for
more than a small minority of the population. The notion of
providing universal primary education in the imperial language
would have been ridiculed by colonial educationalists (Perren,
interview). The conference recommendations seem to assume
that English can be converted from an élite language to a
democratic one which will automatically propel the masses on to
the international scene. It seems probable that the delegates were
in fact concentrating on the needs of the élite, even though the
policy was pronounced as a general one which applied to all. So
far as the choice of the medium of education was concerned, the
policy-makers quite probably suffered from the liberal delusion
(also widespread in francophone African countries (Treffgarne

1986: 146), and in South Asia) that by putting all children at the equal disadvantage of being educated through a foreign language, they were giving all children an equal chance of doing well.

The report states that policy on when to introduce English as a medium needs to take into account the administrative and motivational factors already mentioned, but that these are not the decisive factors:

> By far the most important consideration lies outside the realm of education. Linguistic policy in the school is only part of a broad governmental decision. Where a community has decided to participate as speedily as possible in the technological and other advantages of a wider society, a decision to use English as a medium is likely to be inevitable, and the pressure to introduce it fairly early may well be heavy. A society which lays more stress on the preservation of a traditional way of life will not introduce English as a medium until later in the school life of the child.
>
> Although the young child will best find the stable environment and sense of security that he needs in the language of his home, in certain circumstances the languages used at school (where this is different from the home language) will have a greater influence on his development, e.g. where the school intake is multilingual or where educational advancement can only be obtained through a second language. Then, if English is likely in any case to be introduced fairly early, it may be advisable to introduce it right from the beginning.
> (*Makerere Report*: 21)

This recommendation is difficult to reconcile with the claim that the entire gathering was non-political in nature (the function of such claims was analysed in Chapter 3). The text places educational language policy explicitly in a wider 'governmental' policy context. It then postulates a simple correlation between English and technologically based progress on the one hand, and other languages and traditionalism on the other. This is then used as a legitimation for introducing English as the medium of education as early as possible, which is by no means a logical conclusion. Multilingualism is implicitly tarred with traditionalism and lack of advancement. The conference does not seem to have countenanced the possibility that pupils with a solid grounding in their mother tongue or a related language, who have learnt to use this language as an instrument for analytical thought, may be better at learning English at a later stage. There is in fact no causal link between the societal claims, which are themselves ethnocentric and debatable, and the age at which English should be introduced.

It is not entirely clear whether the final statement refers to the introduction of English as a medium rather than as a subject, but judging from the context it appears to refer to English as a medium. If so, it indicates that English linguistic imperialism was being pursued even more vigorously than in colonial times. Then the widespread practice of establishing literacy in the mother tongue or a related lingua franca and later making a gradual progression to using English as a medium gave the child, in principle at least, more chance of coping with scholastic work. In the *Makerere Report* the needs of other languages are not covered; this represents an intensification of the linguicist policy of colonial times.

The confidence with which this policy is pronounced is at variance with the admission, in annex 5 of the conference report (ibid.: 54), that research is needed into the age of introduction of English as a subject and as a learning-language, the psychological effects of a second-language medium, the influence of the English medium on the failure rate of students in subjects other than English, and many related topics in multilingual communities.

The policy is also flatly in defiance of Unesco's recommendations, which were based on a global survey of multilingualism and bilingual education. 'On educational grounds we recommend that the use of the mother tongue be extended to as late a stage in education as possible. In particular, pupils should begin their schooling through the medium of the mother tongue, because they understand it best and because to begin their school life in the mother tongue will make the break between home and school as small as possible' (Unesco 1953: 47).[17]

The thrust of an earlier-the-better English policy would not have been so clear-cut without there being some experience along these lines. In fact a policy of this kind had been recommended in a succession of reports in colonial Kenya in the 1940s and 1950s (reported in Abdulaziz 1982: 98).[18] In Ghana there was an Accelerated Development Plan in Education in the 1950s which advocated the use of English as a medium of instruction from the first year in school. The policy of using

Ghanaian languages as the medium of instruction only in the first year of school and making the transition to English as the medium of instruction in the second year was introduced in 1958 (Chinebuah 1981: 19). Since then policy in Ghana on this issue has fluctuated, but the Makerere conference might have benefited from an assessment written a decade later. The earlier-the-better policy in Ghana 'failed because of the unrealistic nature of the proposals. If time and resources had been spent on a carefully planned survey of the linguistic competence of both the pupils and the teachers and the attitudes of parents to this recommendation, the educational system of that country would have been spared some of the resulting deficiencies in the pupils' command of both English and Ghanaian languages' (Ohanness-ian and Ansre 1975: 63).

Calvet has a very similar analysis (1987) of the failure to implement the use of Guinean languages, initially 8 of the major indigenous languages, later 6, as the medium of education in Guinean schools. From this one can conclude that the policy and practice may be misconceived, whether the language being promoted is the dominant, (former) colonial one or an indigenous language which is at an intermediate position in the linguistic hierarchy, dominated by the European language, dominant *vis-à-vis* other local languages.

Some research was conducted at Makerere College in the late 1950s (funded by the Nuffield Foundation) on the transfer from vernacular medium to English medium teaching (in the Ugandan context the transfer was made in the 5th to 6th year of schooling), but this was on a small scale and does not seem to have been widely publicized. The project reports reveal considerable sensitivity to the complexity of the issues involved (and assume a contrastive linguistic background for the teachers, at least for phonetics), but the trend towards regarding an early start to English as a medium as the solution to African education problems is clear. 'The dangers of beginning to use English as a medium too early are all too apparent in the present parrot-learning, mental confusion and lack of real understanding, and inability to apply knowledge, which are found on every side. On the other hand, a great accumulation of evidence from many sources points inescapably to the conclusion that the sooner English is actually used as a medium, the better it will be learned' (Wingard 1959).

The most influential evidence was the work done at the Special

Centre in Nairobi. Here an experiment with introducing English as the medium from the first class was followed from the mid-1950s. Initially the project covered 2,000 Asian pupils, taught by Kenyan Asian teachers. The project was motivated by an urge to reform primary school pedagogy. It was a means of 'making a clean break with the thoroughly unsuitable and out-of-date classroom methods which had become almost indissolubly associated with the use of Asian languages in lower primary classes' (Perren 1968: 172). An integral part of the scheme was therefore teacher upgrading, as regards both their familiarity with active primary teaching methods and their own proficiency in English. In presenting a rationale for an early English-medium scheme, educational arguments were invoked to buttress a language planning cause which had political implications, even if, in one of the descriptions of the project,[19] it was felt at the time in Kenya that the issue was a technical rather than a policy matter:

> Educationally there are potent arguments for putting this stage as early as possible in school life, not the least being that it seems best to switch to a new medium before children have to learn subjects with a heavy content-load. The psychological tensions arising from a realization of the need to know English are perhaps more easily resolved if pupils begin to learn *in* English long before secondary school examinations bulk large on the horizon . . . Since all must use English, it is best for children to begin at an age when it is easiest, when there is no pronounced language-learning differential (apart from those imposed by general intelligence variations). This seems to be as soon as possible. Because English is to become a common means of social behaviour for different races and communities, it should *not* be specialized in its function and should include the widest possible interests—including the home.
> (Perren 1958: 20)

Again the exclusive focus on English is linguicist. Bringing the home into the classroom, activating the children so that they were learning-by-doing with familiar domestic objects, which is good infant school learning practice, has the indirect and unintended consequence that English linguistic imperialism is extended into the home.

The historical context of the Nairobi scheme needs to be remembered. Education in colonial Kenya was organized on racially segregated lines. Kenya was in a state of emergency because of the freedom struggle of Kenyans (the 'Mau-Mau' uprising among the Gikuyu), and was edging towards independence. It was not only the languages but the entire future of the different communities which were at risk. Asians and Africans could see the instrumental value of English. This might have intensified the pressure for access to English, the language of power. Sociolinguistic research into language maintenance and language shift in Nairobi in 1962 revealed extensive bilingualism within Asian families in the home as well as outside it, with English as the language gaining ground (Lieberson and McCabe 1982). Such developments outside school would strongly influence the outcome of the Special Centre project.

This project set a pattern for independent Kenya, where English is the medium of education from the first class in many urban schools, and schooling is organized around formidable terminal examinations. The scheme was extended to Africans, probably without the vital element of in-service training figuring so prominently, and without many of the implications of such a policy being appreciated. This makes it even more important for children to choose their parents carefully than in western countries. 'Wealthier, educated parents who purchase books and educational toys, who speak English in the home, who utilize private nursery schools, and who otherwise deploy resources in a manner creating pre-school conditions conducive to successful school performance provide initial advantages which are difficult to match in the poor, uneducated, and rural family' (Prewitt 1974: 206). Recent research on science education in primary schools in Kenya shows that restricting the use of learners' mother tongues or Swahili in teaching deprives learners of valid contextualization and cognitive input and intensifies the learning burden: a school which used Luo freely to increase comprehension of scientific content did better than a school where English was used exclusively, despite better material conditions and a better trained teacher in the latter (Cleghorn, Merritt, and Abagi 1989).

The extension of English in this way was not anticipated by colonial educators like Perren. 'Like every other educationalist in East Africa, I could not see any future for English as a medium for universal education, quite impossible, you couldn't find the teachers, and in some senses it would be unnatural' (Perren, interview). Yet this is precisely what was recommended at the

Makerere conference, which was attended by a considerable number of colonial educationalists, though Perren was not among them.

The earlier-the-better tenet was not seriously challenged in the 1960s. In one review of language in education in Africa, by a British Council officer, it was endorsed without reservation. (Tiffen 1968). He was aware that such a policy had implications for local languages, but did not see that strengthening English had linguicist consequences, ideologically and structurally. 'Provided we accept the premise that English *must* be taught at some stage in the primary school in order that secondary education can be carried on in it, the Kenya system could well be introduced in other parts of Commonwealth Africa . . . Such a system should not kill the vernacular. The Nairobi course provides for the vernacular to be taught at the end of each morning' (ibid.: 87). This attempt to ensure development for the vernacular is totally unrealistic. Functional literacy in a low status language cannot be achieved in one hour a day. Like the 'home language teaching' organized for immigrant children in much of Western Europe, such teaching is sheer tokenism. A timetabling structure of this kind reinforces the stigmatized role of the dominated languages.

The results have also been damaging for them. 'In all the countries of East Africa, except Tanzania, local languages are treated as peripheral to the central concerns of education' (Chishimba 1981: 179). The teachers are unlikely to be competent to teach the languages, and there is very little interest in the languages among the teachers themselves (ibid.: 180). Research among the Ibo in Nigeria, where educational failure is widespread, indicates that attitudes of both pupils and their parents are vastly more favourable to English than to Ibo (Okonkwo 1983).

The tenet is also given support in one of the first and most influential presentations of the burgeoning field of applied linguistics, Halliday, McIntosh, and Strevens 1964, published three years after the Makerere conference (at which none of these scholars was present). They recommend: 'one of the biggest single contributions to the teaching of English as a foreign language in many countries would be to lower the starting age and let the pupils learn by experiencing the language in use' (ibid.: 297). The claim is put forward as a general proposition, one which by inference is also applicable to underdeveloped countries. The recommendation is exemplified by English being used as the medium for mathematics teaching.

The problem with such a recommendation is that *age* cannot be isolated from a mass of other relevant factors. The authors would probably not wish to do so, but the proposition as it stands looks like a blanket endorsement, from a reputable academic source, of the tenet 'the earlier the better'. And scientifically the statement is false. Extensive research into foreign language learning, both as a medium and as a subject, in western countries in the 1960s and 1970s indicates that a great many conditions need to be fulfilled for any conclusions about age to hold. For instance, foreign language learning from the beginning of primary school is highly successful in the Canadian immersion programmes (Swain and Lapkin 1982), where the learners' mother tongue is not at risk, qualified bilingual teachers are available, alternative programmes exist, and societal motivation transmitted via the parents is strong. By contrast many of the programmes for the education of immigrants through the medium of a second language are inappropriate because they aim at monolingualism and ignore the cultural and linguistic needs of the children in question (Skutnabb-Kangas 1984a, 1988). A scheme for starting English as a foreign language subject two years earlier than usual in Swedish schools did not produce better results (Holmstrand 1980).

The different outcomes of such programmes indicate that a substantial number of factors are involved in any decision to start foreign/second languages earlier in school. They can be grouped in a typology with sets of factors covering the organization of learning, learner-related affective factors, and linguistic, cognitive, pedagogical, and social factors in relation to both the L1 and the L2 (Skutnabb-Kangas 1984a: 244; Phillipson, Skutnabb-Kangas, and Africa 1985). Education can lead to successful outcomes with either L1 or L2 as the medium of education, but success depends on the linguistic and societal goals in question, and the status of the learners and the relevant languages, as well as attention to all the factors listed in the typology. The failures of educational policy in Ghana (early English) and Guinea (indigenous languages) already referred to were due to inadequate attention being paid to the full range of these factors, and a false emphasis on such factors as age and the medium of education. Prosperous West European countries, which are currently lowering the starting age for English in schools (with encouragement from the Council of Europe), are in a better position to create successful learning conditions, but it is doubtful whether the educational and socio-political implications of this policy have been thought through. Another relevant issue is the question of the diverse factors that can influence the outcome of innovation in education (Rodgers 1989; Wagner 1991).

In underdeveloped countries which have opted for English from early on in the primary system, either as a medium (Zambia, see Chishimba 1971; Ohannessian and Kashoki 1978; Wigzell 1983) or as a subject (Tanzania, see Polomé and Hill 1980; Rubagumya 1990), many of the desiderata have not been met. Results have in consequence been disappointing. Pattanayak writes that in India it is élite vested interests which press for the introduction of English as early as possible in the child's school life (1981: 168). In India the arguments marshalled in favour of an early start for English are exactly those given official sanction at Makerere, and the conference report itself is invoked in support of this stance (ironically and graciously referred to as presenting 'clever conclusions', by Pattanayak, ibid.).

The effect of the application of this tenet has been to consolidate English at the expense of other languages, to perpetuate dependence on aid and expertise from the core English-speaking countries, and to raise an insuperable language barrier for the mass of primary learners. There are economic consequences too: advancing the starting age for English learning creates more jobs for teachers of English, and fewer for those who might specialize in other languages. The ideological consequences inherent in according higher status to English are already a familiar refrain.

Tenet four: the more English is taught, the better the results

This tenet holds that the more English is taught, the better the results. It is implicitly supported at Makerere, when it is assumed that if English is started earlier, schooling at a later stage will benefit. Clearly there is a sense in which quantity is important for successful foreign or second language learning, but, as with the previous tenet, certain conditions need to be fulfilled for the desired outcomes to appear.

Adherence to the tenet does, however, seem to have been widespread in ELT. Trappes-Lomax (quoted in Hill 1980: 375) refers to the slogan 'longer means better', in which the tenet is embodied in Tanzania, and points out how little basis it has in reality (he also denounces another slogan, 'earlier means better', which relates to none other than the third tenet). In India the tenet seems to have been actively propagated. 'There is an erroneous view prevalent in the country that if a language is taught for a longer period, it is learned well. Trained teachers, well written textual material and improved methods of teaching are more important than the length of time for which it is taught. In the near absence of all three the introduction of English at lower stages has resulted in wastage both in terms of teaching and learning time and financial input. If mother tongue teaching is streamlined, then the introduction of English at a higher stage is likely to yield better results than at present' (Pattanayak 1981: 169). Similar conclusions are drawn by Hill in relation to Tanzania, for a combination of practical and theoretical reasons (Hill 1980: 376).

The tenet assumes that for students who are weak in English, the more exposure to the teaching of the language, the better the results. This is intuitively commonsensical, but ignores the organizational factors referred to by Pattanayak, and, more fundamentally, the nature of the linguistic input to the child. The tenet ignores the fact that the quantity of the input is less important than its appropriacy and comprehensibility (Krashen 1981), and that for language learning to take place the input must activate the learner's hypothesis formation and hypothesis testing processes (see Færch, Haastrup, and Phillipson 1984: Chapter 11). An equally serious objection to the tenet is that it fails to consider the overall academic-cognitive development of the child, whether in L1 or L2 (Cummins 1984). Pattanayak's point is that a well developed academic proficiency in the mother tongue will facilitate the learning of another language. It seems surprising that it is necessary in many educational contexts to articulate this principle, as members of the dominant group in western societies take the principle for granted in relation to the learning of their own L1 and, thereafter, other languages.

The same quantitative argument is frequently used in contentions about the education that second language learners need in order to develop proficiency in the language of the 'host' country. In the bilingual education field, extensive research into cognitive development and educational success has proved conclusively that a *maximum exposure* assumption is a *fallacy* (Cummins 1984: 109). Such research shows that there is no correlation between quantity of L2 input, in an environment where the learners are exposed to L2 in the community, and academic success. 'Students taught through a minority language for all or part of the school day perform at least as well (and in many cases better) in majority language academic skills as equivalent students taught through the majority language for all or most of the school day' (ibid.: 110). Cummins concludes that reference to this fallacy in policy discussions indicates how great the disjunction is between policy and research, and that policy ignores theory.

Language learning theory and the psychology of language learning were relatively undeveloped in relation to foreign or second language learning at the time of the Makerere conference. ELT tended to function without any explicit psycholinguistic theory, though with a strong focus on methodology. American practice was heavily influenced by behaviourism, often with a direct carry-over from structural linguistics. British practice was also behaviouristic and atomistic, with a concentration on drilling isolated aspects of the structure of the language (see for instance the *Makerere Report*, 1961: 9–13). This was combined with a tendency to eschew explicit grammatical or metacommunicative analysis, possibly a reaction to the somewhat sterile grammar teaching native speakers associated with the mother tongue teaching they had experienced.

Since that time language learning theories have flourished, with different species evolving on different continents. There is in general in professional circles an increased awareness of the components of communicative competence and of the psycholinguistic processes involved in foreign language learning (see McDonough 1981; Brumfit 1984; Færch, Haastrup, and Phillipson 1984), though it is arguable that mainstream Anglo-American ELT has not yet absorbed theories of bilingual language development. Theories of language learning in many underdeveloped countries are heavily influenced by theories elaborated in the West, a reflection of cultural and scientific imperialism, and of the educational imperialism that the Makerere conference played a key role in. Many researchers from underdeveloped countries now stress the need for educational language planning to aim at bilingualism or multilingualism

(Afolayan 1984; Bokamba and Tlou 1980; Mateene 1980a and b; Tadadjeu 1980). Language learning theory that aims to promote the language learning of dominated groups, and documents success in so doing (Skutnabb-Kangas and Touko-maa 1976; Cummins 1984) has been regarded as directly relevant to such African researchers as Africa (1980) and Mateene (1980b).

The ideological consequences of following the more-the-better tenet are similar to those of the other tenets. An economic consequence of it is likewise jobs for teachers of English. Ironically, dropping the tenet might result in improved standards of English. This is because less English, taught by better qualified teachers, to learners who have already developed high cognitive-academc proficiency in their mother tongue, may provide better conditions for learning English. Conversely, any efforts to maximize the time allocated to English in the first six or so years of schooling are likely to be linguicist, as well as being theoretically and pedagogically questionable. An exclusive focus on English, and on language learning theory in relation to English, is unlikely to be helpful in periphery-English contexts. It is likely to be a continuation in a new guise of the maximum exposure fallacy.

Tenet five: if other languages are used much, standards of English will drop

The notion that standards in education are dropping is not unique to ELT. The notion that standards of English are bound to drop if other languages are used much is a variant which has been used to legitimate a continued British presence in former dependencies. The idea of keeping up standards is a leitmotiv in British planning for the post-colonial era:

- In the *Drogheda Report*, which sought to strengthen bonds between Britain and former dependencies, the aid effort in English teaching was seen as an attempt to 'improve standards' (*Drogheda Report summary* 1954: 33; see Chapter 5).
- In the Cabinet paper which set out plans for establishing English as a world second language, the main problem in the British colonies and protectorates was seen as the 'mainten-ance of standards' (Ministry of Education 1956: 4; see Chapter 5).

- A similar concern for standards was declared in India soon after it became independent. A British Council conference on the Teaching of English as a Foreign Language was held at Mahableshwar in 1950. The first paragraph of the introduction to the report declares: 'The object of the course, the discussion of the most modern methods of teaching English as a foreign language, was thought to be particularly relevant at a time in India when the elevation of Hindi as a first national language might lead, in spite of efforts to the contrary, to the serious deterioration of the standard of English over the next few years' (British Council, India, 1950: 1).
- The introduction to the Makerere conference report refers to 'the difficulties of maintaining reasonable standards of spoken and written English in view of the serious and widespread shortage of teachers' with appropriate training and local insight (*Makerere Report* 1961: 1).

One problem with this tenet is that what is being compared is two different situations: on the one hand, standards in an élite system, following a syllabus prescribed in the Centre, and mostly with Centre inter-state actors as teachers, a system which is effective for ensuring a hierarchy and control; on the other, standards in an independent Periphery country which is often in principle attempting to democratize education and change the ideological content and goals of education. The same yardstick cannot be used for both.

A second problem is that the tenet is based on purely subjective impressions of what standards used to be and are now. Standards easily become rosy in the memory. In fact complaints about standards falling and the sloppiness of the younger generation have been heard at least since Roman times.

More fundamentally, what the tenet is probably underpinned by is concern that the role of English is to diminish, or that there are significant changes in the functions that English will be called upon to perform. This factor is likely to be inextricably tied up with the question of standards. In fact the connection is even made explicit in the tenet, which links standards of English to the use of other languages. Implicitly what the tenet argues for is the continued use of English in periphery-English countries to at least the same extent as in colonial days.

These serious objections to the tenet are, however, compatible with a recognition that in some periphery-English countries standards of English at certain levels of the school system may be on the decline. Disappearance of a language from the timetable can result in a drop in standards, as was probably the case with English in Malaysia for a time. In reality, though, the amount of time spent on English or on education through the medium of English has been reduced in this way in few countries. For instance English has been retained as a subject throughout primary education in Tanzania. Much-needed educational reform in Zambia has been blocked by politicians who cling to the 'maintenance of standards' (Chileshe 1982). In India 'the number of students learning English has greatly increased, but their level of competence has decreased. The debate is going on about the grade at which English should be introduced and the duration for which it should be taught and the trend is to advance the grade to start teaching of English, which is grade one in some States. This creates the problem of not having competent teachers of English lowering the standard of English. The increasing demand for English decreases its standard' (Annamalai 1988: 9).

The evidence is that this tenet, in combination with the other four, has been effective in maintaining the privileged position of English, and that the linguicist structure on which the tenets rest may actually have contributed to standards falling.

If an education system is expanding fast, large numbers of teachers are under-qualified, and few adequate textbooks are available, these are likely to be causal factors in standards falling. If, in addition, the monolingual fallacy, the native speaker fallacy, the early start fallacy, and the maximum exposure fallacy have influenced teacher training and educational language planning policy, it is scarcely surprising if educational results are poor, and that the familiar worry about standards is expressed. The educational system that is generated by English linguistic imperialism may indeed cause a decline of proficiency in English and inadequate learning of the language.

Such failure may or may not occur simultaneously with the rise of another language, with its elevation to greater status and use. It is fallacious to claim that the one is necessarily dependent on the other. It is the kind of subtractive fallacy that logically originates in a monolingual culture which is unfamiliar with the realities of multilingual societies. Thus the spread of literacy can lead to high levels of proficiency in more than one language, as has happened in much of the Soviet Union (Guboglo 1986b and

c) and bilingual parts of Yugoslavia (Institute for Ethnic Studies, Ljubljana 1986). At the individual level, the subtractive fallacy is a variant of the bilingual 'balance hypothesis', according to which addition to the one language involved subtraction of the other, a position which is no longer seriously countenanced in bilingualism research.

An analogy can also serve to point out the invalidity of the subtractive fallacy. Scandinavians are not worried that 'if English is used a lot, standards of Danish/Swedish/etc. will drop'. The increased use of English in Scandinavia has not led to standards of proficiency in Scandinavian languages dropping, even if the languages are being displaced by English in a number of domains (which of course has ideological and structural consequences) and there is a considerable amount of lexical borrowing.

The validity of a tenet which refers to English and other languages needs to be tested in the light of the power relations between languages. The tenet could be reformulated in terms of dominant and dominated languages: 'if dominated languages are used much, standards in the dominant language will drop'. This is still a subtractive fallacy, but the new wording leads logically to asking questions about whose the standards are and whose interests they serve. This in turn points to the need for educational language planning to clarify the purposes of language learning in relation to all the languages in the community.

Conclusions: the legacy of Makerere

This chapter can be concluded with some generalizations about the structure and ideology of ELT at the stage when it took upon itself a new expansionist missionary role. We shall also look at how one of the Makerere recommendations was followed up, as an example of the Centre-Periphery relationship.

The tenets which were widely subscribed to in the ELT profession and which were given a seal of approval at the Makerere conference were permeated by anglocentric attitudes. These served to strengthen the ideological dependence of the Periphery on Centre expertise, norms and definitions of what was important in language education, and, by implication, in language planning and policy. Structurally the recommendations served to strengthen the case for building up Centre expertise, and ensured 'aid' jobs for Centre inter-state actors in the Periphery. They secured a bridgehead for the Centre in the Periphery, thereby legitimating Centre export of 'experts', know-how, projects, books, etc., and securing imperialist penetration of the education systems of the emerging post-colonial states. The bridgehead is the base from which local élites are trained in the traditions, values, and tenets of the Centre, so that local people can take over as experts, teacher trainers, textbook-writers, etc. Scientific and educational imperialism ensure the continued exploitation of the material and immaterial resources of the Periphery. The continued development of the dominant language, English, to meet new challenges, contributes to the continued underdevelopment of dominated languages.

There was an almost exclusive concentration on English at the Makerere conference itself. The same was true of the teacher training and curriculum activities which sprang from it. The conference did not look at the overall educational needs of periphery-English children, or even their overall linguistic development, but at English and ways of strengthening English. This anglocentric focus, the professionalism endorsed at Makerere, and the structural and ideological consequences of adhering to the tenets amount to English linguistic imperialism.

The principle which was supposed to guide the deliberations of delegates at Makerere was 'efficiency' in English teaching, in accordance with the needs and wishes of the countries in question. English was assumed to lead to the promised land of 'progress' and prosperity. Efficiency requires professionalism, and this was what needed to be built up. The professionalism that did evolve over the next few years was inspired by the monolingual ELT tradition that had done service at home, in the colonies, and elsewhere in the EFL world, and by the new professionalism of applied linguistics.

The dangers of worshipping the God of efficiency were apparent quite soon, and some appreciated that the influence of linguistics and technology on language teaching had encouraged a technocratic approach to language teaching: 'in acquiring a new professional status . . . language-teaching technocracy shows the dangers inherent in conscious specialization', exemplified by the excessive concentration on isolated skills components in ELT, to such an extent that the purposes to which the language should be put were forgotten (Perren 1968: 179).

A number of circumstances conspired to make the ELT 'aid' effort a highly problematical one, despite the good intentions and devoted efforts that characterized it. Among the many factors, the following were perhaps the most significant:

- the fact that the key ELT academic institutions in the Centre were firmly rooted in Centre perceptions;
- the fact that the tenets endorsed at Makerere were at root quite false, and legitimated English linguistic imperialism;
- the trend towards an atomistic technocratic approach just noted;
- the fact that most newly independent periphery-English countries were in a hurry to expand education, and accepted foreign support in doing so.

The thread of this particular story will be picked up in the coming chapter, but prior to that it is important to probe into one more recommendation from Makerere. The way it was implemented reveals the structural nature of Centre-Periphery relations very clearly.

The organizers of the Makerere conference had had great difficulty in obtaining reliable information on English teaching throughout the world. At the conference itself it was apparent that delegates would benefit from closer familiarity with experience in other countries. This resulted in a proposal. 'It is, therefore, suggested that there be set up a Commonwealth English Language Information Centre (CELIC) whose task should be to collect and disseminate information about aspects of English as a second language. For this purpose it would maintain contact with government departments of education, universities, other research institutions and experimental departments, training colleges, and British Council offices all over the Commonwealth; and with similar institutions elsewhere, such as the Center for Applied Linguistics in Washington. The British Council has a good deal of unprocessed material, collected from all over the world, which would be most valuable to such a centre. The CELIC would pay special attention to research in progress and to the need for research projects. It would not itself normally conduct research, but would assist in the placing of research projects at appropriate institutions.' (*Makerere Report* 1961: 41)

The Nutford House conference was held a few months later, at the instigation of the British Council. It was also a British

Council officer who compiled and edited the report. The recommendations of this gathering of academics also contain a proposal for an ELT information centre, with precisely the same functions, though here it is seen as a purely British venture (Wayment 1961: 62). Within a matter of months the British Council had set up its own English-Teaching Information Centre (ETIC), which was to serve British Council career ELT staff and the ELT public for a quarter of a century, until it was reinserted into the British Council's internal information services in 1986. ETIC has an excellent language-teaching library, considerable archives of published and unpublished material on ELT worldwide, and publishes bibliographies and abstracts.[20]

According to Perren, its first director, the British Council was keen to establish such a centre so that no one else, for instance the Institute of Education at the University of London or another Commonwealth country, would get in first (Perren, interview). The idea of a co-ordinating centre in London and subsidiary centres overseas was floated, but to establish a network of this kind would have required financing by the British government, and the British Council rather pre-empted this by establishing a centre to which the interested public had access. It was probably not irrelevant that the Americans already had an equivalent centre, the Center for Applied Linguistics, as did the French, the Bureau pour l'Enseignement de la Langue et de la Civilisation Françaises à l'Étranger (BELC), a relatively modest set-up.

The effect of this action was to concentrate information and power in the Centre and maintain the rest of the Commonwealth in a peripheral role. Instead of sharing equitably in the collection and dissemination of information, plans for research projects, and the formation of strategy, the interests of the Periphery were fragmented and marginalized. British academics, publishers and administrators have had incomparably better access to information on ELT in all parts of the Periphery than their counterparts in the Periphery. In Galtung's theory of imperialism, fragmentation and marginalization are two of the four central processes in imperialism, along with exploitation and penetration. ELT fits into the overall pattern of imperialism in every respect.

Notes

1   There have always been in fact two relevant departments: EFL, now called ESOL (English to Speakers of Other

Languages—described by Perren, a student there in the 1940s, as too closely linked to English as a mother tongue then); and one concerned with education overseas, which has had a succession of titles, the Colonial Department, Department of Overseas Education, Education in Developing Countries, Comparative Education.

2   I am grateful to Peter Hill of the Institute of Education, London University, for drawing my attention to this, and lending me copies of Wingard's reports.

3   Monolingualism and insularity still seem to be professionally acceptable in some circles in Britain, witness the following comment in a review of the translation into English of a linguistics textbook by the German linguist, Dieter Wunderlich, in the (British) *Journal of Linguistics*: 'Cambridge University Press is to be commended for taking the trouble to commission a translation of a foreign book on linguistics, and it is to be hoped that more such ventures will make it easier for British readers to find out what their colleagues on the Continent are doing' (Sampson 1980: 168). It is difficult to imagine the reverse—a Continental scholar waiting for books from the USA, Britain, or Germany to be translated into Danish, German, etc., in order to find out what their colleagues are doing. But then linguistic and cultural imperialism are unidirectional. This said, it is my impression that many of the founding fathers of ELT were dedicated learners of foreign languages and far from insular, even if their teaching may have drawn on a monolingual doctrine.

4   At the Department of English for Speakers of Other Languages, Institute of Education, London University, there is a collection of taped talks recorded by some of the founding fathers of ELT (among them A. V. P. Elliott, L. A. Hill and L. G. Alexander). Dai Morgan's contribution provides a vivid student portrait of the first year of the Edinburgh applied linguistics course. I am grateful to the Department (in the person of John Norrish) for making them available to me.

5   The continuity in perceptions of what applied linguistics is for can be seen from an interview in *ELT Journal* with Professor Gillian Brown when she moved from Edinburgh to become head of a Centre for English as an International Language at Cambridge. She declares: 'The job of Applied

Linguistics is above all to define what the *content* of English Language Teaching is' and then states how such contributory disciplines as Education, Psychology, Linguistics, and Cognitive Science should be searched for insights into language teaching, methodology, and the description of language, for the benefit of ELT and teachers of English as a mother tongue, (Brown 1989: 169).

6   Some applied linguistics in Edinburgh became narrowly linguistic and psycholinguistic, in the pursuit of theoretical rigour (Corder 1973; Davies 1991), and evaded a direct link with teaching concerns. When these are more central it is more appropriate to refer to 'language pedagogy'.

7   The groundwork for this was laid by the Linguistics Panel of the British Council, which produced a Memorandum on University Training and Research in the Teaching of English as a Second/Foreign Language in December 1959. This identified needs and listed current resources. Among the members were Pattison (Institute of Education, London, chair), Catford, Firth, and Quirk.

8   For a striking sample of anglocentricity see the quotation from Holloway's contribution to the Nutford House conference in Chapter 9.

9   The legitimation is now more explicitly economic, reflecting Thatcherist developments. *The Economist Intelligence Unit Report* on ELT training (number 1166, 1989) warns against the risk of continental European countries intruding into this market.

10 For introductory reading, see Skutnabb-Kangas 1984a, and Hakuta 1986. For practical advice for parents of bilingual children see the *Bilingual Family Newsletter*, published by Multilingual Matters.

11 Official recognition of Zambian languages increased slightly in the early 1970s, as a direct result of the Ford Foundation Survey of Zambian Languages (one component of the Survey of Language Use and Language Teaching in Eastern Africa): this meant rather more school time for Zambian languages as a subject, secondment for the writing of teaching materials, and the appointment of some lecturers in teacher training colleges, (Ohannessian and Ansre 1975: 66).

12 For a state of the art survey article on ELT teacher training see Britten 1985, and for an integrated programme, Bowers 1987.

13   One can parody the native speaker tenet as follows: The ideal teacher is a native speaker. Teachers are born not made. Therefore, 1) those who are not born native speakers of English cannot be ideal teachers, and 2) since teachers are born not made, native speakers do not need any training to become teachers.

14   The following letter was published in *The Guardian Weekly* 23 July 1989:

>   I am involved in the recruiting and monitoring of staff in a large EFL school on the continent which employs both native and non-native English-speaking teachers.
>
>   In recent years we have become all too aware that, with the exception of those with degrees in modern languages, many young English graduates—in contrast to their Irish, Scots, North American, antipodean, and non-native English-speaking peers—are unaware of the most elemen-elementary points of the grammar they are supposed to be teaching and, in fact, have been known to correct students' perfectly accurate English to fit their own ungrammatical English usage. As most of these young teachers hold degrees in English or have 'A' level English, the alarming trend has made us quite as aware as Prince Charles that something indeed has gone wrong with the teaching of English in England and Wales.
>
>   Name and address supplied.

15   This tradition is aptly portrayed by William Empson, in his inaugural lecture as Professor of English at Sheffield University in 1953 (abridged and reprinted in the London Review of Books, 17 August 1989). Empson taught in Japan in the 1930s, in a post at Tokyo University for which he was recommended by his Cambridge tutor, I. A. Richards, and in China from 1947 to 1953. When legitimating his approach to the Communist authorities, he argued that 'If the teaching of English language to Chinese students was to be any use they must also be taught to understand the mind of the ordinary English speaker; and for that matter it was not only an effort of political understanding, but also a literary one, because unless a man (*sic*) had a certain amount of training in Shakespeare and all that, he could not always be trusted to get the point of a political leader in, let us say, *The New York Times*.'

16   Smith and Nelson 1985 contains a useful bibliography on intelligibility, and distinguishes between intelligibility, com-

prehensibility, and interpretability. Some empirical research has been done within foreign language pedagogy on 'tolerance testing', see for instance the coverage of this in Færch, Haastrup, and Phillipson 1984.

17 The Unesco delegate who attended the Makerere conference as an observer was a Frenchman from a teacher training college associated with the global dissemination of French (*Makerere Report* 1961: 52). Plus ça change . . .

18 Perren (ms) contests this, unless the reference is to the education of Asians. The Beecher Report in 1950 led to a three-tier system, four years of primary education using the vernacular, four years of intermediate education with the vernacular as the medium and English as a subject, and four years of secondary education with English as the medium. This policy led to an expansion in the provision and quality of intermediate education, and the education authorities were reluctant to heed African demands for English in the primary school.

19 There are detailed, vivid descriptions in Perren's set of three articles in the Colonial Office journal *Oversea Education*, 1959. On the origins of the project, undertaken when he was Inspector of English for Kenya, he states (ms) that there was no advance planning or costing of it, and he was given a free hand. This illustrates the *ad hoc* nature of 'research' in colonial education. Much was undertaken elsewhere but never reported on. A proximate motive was Asian dissatisfaction with 'standards' in government schools. The project was given a Ford Foundation grant in 1958, and was investigated by Unesco.

20 The language-teaching library was shared with the Centre for Information on Language Teaching and Research (CILT), which mainly served foreign language teaching in Britain. Perren left the British Council and ETIC to become first director of CILT in the late 1960s. In Perren's view, ETIC was good at collecting information, which was wanted for the British Council's own purposes, for publishers, universities, etc., but less successful in disseminating information. This was a major factor in the decision in 1986 to close ETIC to the public and concentrate its efforts on servicing British Council-recruited staff more effectively. The best known of its publications is the joint ETIC-CILT quarterly abstracting journal *Language Teaching*.

8   English language teaching in action

University departments of applied linguistics in Britain lead the world in the research and practice of the teaching of language, and especially English as both a foreign and second language.
(Overseas Development Administration 1990: 12)

This chapter looks at English language teaching in action and examines some of its consequences by considering ELT under two main headings, research, and 'aid' to education. The two are inextricably interwoven, because the same individuals and institutions have been involved in each. However, the division into 'research' and 'teaching/education' corresponds to the way higher education is organized and financed, and is a principled and practical one. Research itself is one way of analysing and reflecting on ongoing activities and relating them to theoretical perspectives. It also presupposes an explicit theoretical and methodological framework, as well as verifiable procedures of validity. Discussing the two areas separately should not obscure the unity of them in the overall ELT operation.

ELT research

The reports of the main conferences referred to in earlier chapters generally contain a section listing research needs. The Nutford House Conference states baldly that there is 'urgent need for research in all aspects of problems of teaching English', and notes the need for funding (Wayment 1961: 62). The Makerere Conference stresses that ELT research should be interdisciplinary, and that despite the urgent practical demands in the field, long-term research, preferably experimental work conducted on a regional basis, was 'essential' (*Makerere Report* 1961: 40–1). The report lists a wide range of research topics grouped under general linguistics, applied linguistics, psychological and social, testing and measurement, organization and method. The Anglo-American Conference in Cambridge the same year stressed that Britain and the USA should increase their provision for research and training in ELT and that this was a long-term commitment (Anglo-American Conference Report 1961: 8). Again a list of topics was appended, covering many basic matters related to the learning of English in periphery-English countries, communication misunderstandings, specialist registers, and the problems of foreign students in core-English countries.

How much of this research has actually been done? A comprehensive retrospective survey of the period from 1952 to 1974 was undertaken by the body which has funded more projects than any other in the area of language and development, the Ford Foundation. Their conclusion was that

> There is still a dearth of basic research in developing countries about the fundamental questions of learning and teaching in local languages, the language characteristics and behavior of children, the increasingly visible problems of bilingualism, and the related complexities involving reading. Where such re-search is being conducted, it is usually directed by expatriates . . . There is also a lack of middle-level research capabilities that are needed for a variety of implementation tasks. Finally, there is an almost total absence of the evaluative research indispensable for planning, for measuring achievement, and for comparing results among projects, and possibly reducing the high costs of failure.
> (Fox 1975: 121)

This sobering assessment mainly refers to American activity in the language and development field, much of which was in ELT. It also covers some British involvement, in two ways. Individual British scholars participated in Ford-funded projects in Eastern Africa. The British also worked closely with the Americans at the Central Institute of English and Foreign Languages (CIEFL) at Hyderabad, which was a major recipient of Ford and British Council support. The task of the Institute was nothing less than to reform English teaching throughout India. In Centre thinking, the aid efforts here and in Nigeria were regarded as flagships for ELT aid elsewhere in the Periphery. The Ford Foundation assessment of the results of Anglo-American efforts at Hyder-abad, which Braj Kachru was commissioned to undertake, is highly critical: 'at the outset the goals of the CIEFL were not well defined . . . This policy naturally resulted in . . . lack of serious, theoretically interesting and pedagogically useful research. In formulating these policies, the British Council was also responsible, since, in the beginning, the British Council provided the academic leadership for the institute. The British concept of TESOL did not go beyond what the Institute of Education (Program of TESOL) was doing in London' (Kachru 1975: 90).

British ELT aid or research work has never been reviewed comprehensively, though it is monitored constantly, particularly by the British Council, and aspects of it studied (in the *ELT Documents* series). The applied linguistics research community has tended to steer clear of analysing aid or wider policy issues (but see the contributions to Tiffen 1968). This area was notably absent from the agenda of the conference called to celebrate 50 years of British Council involvement in the field of 'English studies', reported in Quirk and Widdowson (eds.) 1985. The conference report contains a large number of papers describing different aspects of language and literature teaching, but no papers assessing particular ELT 'aid' projects or empirically-based research projects. Few of the contributions specifically attempt to take stock of successes and failures, except for allusions in the papers by Kachru, Brumfit (building on Candlin's ideas), and Swales. The concluding comments by Sinclair and Bowers raise serious policy issues, reiterate the need for more research, remind us that ELT is a 'new and relatively untried profession' (Sinclair 1985: 253), and call on ELT to 'recognize a multilingual world . . . our contemporary ethnic values and practices, to mediate between these and alternative ethics and ways of acting, both generally and in educational terms . . . to make common our knowledge and share our uncertainties' (Bowers 1985: 257). This comment, by a person at the top of the British Council ELT hierarchy, seems to acknowledge the need for a break with anglocentric professionalism.

In Britain, research capacity was created by the university expansion, producing an increased number of university teaching staff working on areas of interest to ELT. Research has also greatly increased our understanding of language learning, the structure of English, the levels of pragmatics and discourse, social functions and forms of language, syllabus development, etc. But in view of the unanimity in the ELT world on the magnitude of the research tasks that needed to be undertaken, one might have expected some major research projects to be set up. This never happened. 'The big questions, such as what the language policy ought to be in Nigeria, which are long-term questions, have not been tackled' (Perren, interview). Very few projects involving teamwork seem to have been undertaken, except for the Survey of English Usage project at University College, London, which was a language description rather than a language pedagogy project. In very few cases were long-term links between a British ELT department and overseas institutions established, whereas this kind of backstopping was frequently a feature of American development projects funded by foundations. Nor does there appear to have been serious campaigning for academic research to accompany the ELT 'aid effort'. There are of course major theoretical and logistic problems to be solved in conducting empirically-based educational research of this kind, but presumably the chorus of voices identifying the need for research included some soloists or even groups who had reason to believe the research could be done. It may well be that it would have been impossible to get funding for projects, but there does not seem to have been any serious effort to convert the identified research needs into actual projects.

The British Council has no funds specifically for research. The organization has never had a policy of identifying research needs, and then commissioning the research, except with regard to a few of its own operational activities.[1] What it has financed is the development of language proficiency tests for screening applicants for higher study in Britain.[2] The Ford Foundation financed the American equivalent, the TOEFL test.[3] The British Council has also detached some of its career ELT staff for doctoral research, some of which has been influential (Munby 1978), and has staff working on development activities, such as the use of computers in language learning.

American foundation funds were instrumental in establishing ELT departments in American universities (Cawston 1975: 430) and were heavily committed to ELT projects in many periphery-English countries (Fox 1975). In 1961, discussions were held between four British universities, Edinburgh, Bangor, Leeds, and University College, London and the Ford Foundation, which held out the prospect of a major grant for ELT work. Relatively small sums were in fact forthcoming, and the main consequence of this Ford involvement was to stimulate the provision of ELT training at these universities two or three years earlier than would otherwise have been possible (Cawston 1975: 417). (Edinburgh had started courses in 1957.) The number of universities or comparable institutions offering courses in ELT rose astronomically, to 28 by the mid-1970s, and nearly twice that number by 1990.

This university infrastructure was geared to teaching needs, and research was basically considered a matter for the individual. Many of these individuals were involved in consultancies, lecturing, short teaching assignments, and the like in the Periphery, which provided them with an opportunity to keep abreast of developments there. Such assignments were often planned, organized, and funded by the British Council, which still dispenses ELT patronage of this kind. Mostly the organization's links are with individual scholars, but a modest amount is channelled through the British Association of Applied Linguistics. All such Centre-Periphery contact involves the dissemination of Centre ideas. There are no ongoing research projects, where it might be a question of the Centre learning about something in the Periphery. Researchers from the Centre can of course learn a great deal during brief visits to the Periphery, but the general orientation and structure of 'aid' activities militates against hard research. The 'aid' effort tends to get channelled into teacher training, advisory work, and the like, rather than into research. As reported in Chapter 3, Haberland (1988) identified a similar pattern in the early development of sociolinguistics in the USA, with more money spent on 'development' than on 'hard-core research'. For research projects one has to look to occasional doctorates by British people, the trickle of doctorates by people from periphery-English countries, and the foundation-financed projects.

The Ford Foundation financed the surveys of language use and language teaching in Eastern Africa, which cover descriptions of the languages, sociolinguistic surveys of language use, and reviews of language in education. They were carried out between 1967 and 1971, for Ethiopia (Bender, Bowen, Cooper, and Ferguson 1976); Kenya (Whiteley 1974); Tanzania (Polomé and Hill 1980); Uganda (Ladefoged, Glick, and Criper 1972); and Zambia (Ohannessian and Kashoki 1978). The reports contain an impressive amount of documentation which provides insight into the complexity of the language scene in each country and is invaluable input to educational language planning. The fact that the sociolinguistic surveys cover all the languages of the countries, and that the language in education reviews cover all the languages used in the education system, rather than merely focusing on English, is a solid counterweight to the linguicism of much 'aid' work in this area.

Some of the spin-off was apparently a strengthening of indigenous, dominated languages, at least in the short-term, although this seems to have fitted into a pattern of dependency on the Centre, of scientific and educational imperialism. Ohannessian—who worked for the Center for Applied Linguistics—and Ansre (1975: 67) report that 'eight Zambian teachers and materials writers are receiving in-service training in language teaching at the University of London's Institute of Education, in collaboration with the School of Oriental and African Studies. (The scheme is under the auspices of the Commonwealth Education Study Fellowship Programs—1972/73). The impact of this training should be very important not only for the teaching of Zambian languages but for the teaching of English and French in Zambia'. Clearly such a programme can result in participants acquiring useful skills which may be unavailable locally (such as methods in field linguistics or syllabus design). At the same time it runs the risk of Zambian linguistic and educational thought being moulded by the perceptions and practices which are a hallmark of the dominant group and language, namely English in the Centre ('send them to London'). As in media imperialism, the process is one of the teaching of Zambian languages being 'modelled' on ELT so as to conform to Centre perceptions and precepts ('they know all about language teaching and Bantu linguistics in London'). Thus a programme which is possibly intended to combat the dominance of English, or at the least to give support to dominated languages, involves anglocentricity ('you can learn from how we do it for English') and professionalism derived from the ELT fountainhead ('we know how'). English is, needless to say, the medium for all this training.

In such a context, there is therefore a serious potential risk of the teaching of Zambian languages being appropriated by norms derived from ELT, and the over-arching structure of English linguistic imperialism remaining intact. Change can only be achieved if the new professionalism and favourable attitudes to Zambian languages are converted into positive structural changes, a larger role for Zambian languages in education, increased use of them in the media, etc. None of these follow necessarily from a training stint in London. It is possible that the eight Zambians returned from London fired with a desire to combat English linguistic dominance in Zambia (Kashoki, the Zambian linguist on the Ford project, has done much to legitimate and support Zambian languages, see Kashoki 1982), but the question then is whether the training acquired in London can serve to facilitate this, or whether it is not so socioculturally inappropriate that it is unlikely to impinge significantly on language policy. (The Zambian ELT experience will be described in more detail below, as well as some links between research and policy.)

The Ford Foundation also financed an *English-Language Policy Survey of Jordan. A Case Study in Language Planning* (Harrison, Prator, and Tucker (eds.) 1975). A detailed critique of the report is critical of the methodology of the survey: the questionnaire used is skewed in favour of English and pays inadequate attention to overall language planning; the authors operate with an unclear notion of 'needs' and seem to be insensitive to the social stratificational functions performed by English in Jordan, which their findings, for instance that there is a demand for general English as opposed to instrumental, special-purpose English, should have alerted them to (Jernudd 1977). Effectively what Jernudd reveals is the undeclared social and linguicist bias of the researchers.

Ford has supported work on African languages since the early 1970s, and part financed projects in West Africa on the use of African languages in the primary school. In the Rivers Readers Project a policy was adopted of providing initial literacy materials in as many as 20 languages in one Nigerian state (Williamson 1972 and 1976). The principle followed was that children should become literate in their mother tongues rather than in a state language which was artificially imposed on a population with a diversity of mother tongues. For the project the determining view of what was a language was the expressed feeling of a group that it constituted a distinct linguistic entity. The venture was successful because of the commitment to it of all those involved in the project, from the state government downwards. The project gives the lie to the notion that it is impracticable to produce literacy materials in anything more than a very restricted number of languages. Successful mother tongue education, as the Southern Sudan project also shows (Cjiko 1982), is contingent on adequate teaching materials,

relevant teacher preparation, and appropriate pedagogic exploitation of the available resources.

Another Ford-supported project was one for Yoruba-medium
education in Nigeria (Afolayan 1976). The Six-Year Primary
Project at Ife has shown 'most clearly that children can receive
their primary education in elementary science, mathematics, and
social and cultural studies through the medium of their mother-
tongue alone and yet most efficiently learn all lessons in
Secondary Class One without any intervening intensive English
language course after their primary education' (Afolayan 1984:
15). In other words, this project shows how fallacious the
earlier-the-better and the more-the-better tenets are. It is
significant for language education policy generally in Africa
because the dominant pattern in Nigeria, as elsewhere, is for
there to be 'an exaggerated notion of the importance of English',
a false belief that English is the only language suitable for formal
education, as in mathematics and science, backed up by
'specious arguments of the need for English for national unity,
and of therefore the necessity to use English as the medium of
secondary education' (ibid.: 15). Afolayan pleads for Nigerian
educational language planning to take a realistic view of English
as the nation's second language and for the national languages to
play a meaningful role side by side with it. Other Nigerian
linguists have argued along similar lines (Ikara 1987, who
notes that British colonial administrators and missionaries did a
lot more to promote and develop Nigerian languages than
independent Nigeria has done, and that absence of an appropriate language policy is at the root of Nigeria's political instability
and economic underdevelopment).

It is significant that research is increasingly being conducted in
the Periphery by *researchers* from the Periphery, and that it is
evaluative, critical research. For instance, the failings of education in Zambia, and in particular some of the effects of
choosing English as the medium of education, have been well
analysed. The ELT methodology promoted by the British
Council was unsuitable: the exercise types used in the Zambian
English Medium Scheme (permutation, transformation, etc.) and
the underlying psycholinguistic theory (behaviouristic analogical
reasoning) have trapped the children into a position where their
English can only be used for those purposes which are specific to
classroom interaction (Chishimba 1981: 174 and 176). In
addition the teaching materials do not reflect Zambian culture.

This is not surprising, as 101 out of the 103 readers for the scheme written from the mid-1960s to the early 1970s were written by non-Zambians (Higgs 1979 quoted in Chileshe 1982: 32). The cultural universe of the materials is consumerist and Western, and remote from that of most Zambians, who live in a rural environment. Several research studies document the failure of the scheme to provide Zambian children with adequate linguistic competence (Serpell 1978; Africa 1980). In addition, the priority accorded to English in education results in sharp social stratification and marks a dislocation between home and school ethics (Serpell 1978: 433). A linguicist language-in-education policy perpetuates social inequality.

A further disquieting factor about this particular example of Centre 'aid' is that although these teaching materials were originally intended as a pilot version, they were still in use in the late-1980s. Zambia's economy is in dire straits, partly because income from copper has shrunk drastically. A Finnish 'aid' project financed the reprinting of the same teaching materials in the mid-1980s as a rescue operation: the alternative was that no books would have been available.

The Zambian research findings raise serious questions about the nature of Centre influence in the Periphery. It was the British Council's 'experts' who were instrumental in persuading the Zambian government to adopt the English-medium scheme (Higgs 1979, quoted in Chileshe 1982: 27), and they have been active throughout its implementation. The question of the quality of such professionalism cannot be wished away by arguing that the decisions taken in the 1960s reflected the state of professional knowledge at the time. This would be to ignore the imperialist context which such 'aid' was part and parcel of. As the analysis of ELT tenets in Chapter 7 showed, there were major fallacies in the anglocentric professionalism of ELT. It is difficult to avoid the conclusion that English linguistic imperialism, channelled through educational 'aid', has perpetuated the underdevelopment of Zambian languages in a linguistic hierarchy through the maintenance of English as the dominant language. Even if the Centre's inter-state agents share responsibility with decision-makers in the Periphery, the causal role of the 'expert' cannot be ignored.

The legacy of Makerere appears to have weighed more heavily than the warning voices of some scholars from the Centre with extensive Periphery experience. Le Page ends his analysis of 'The national language question. Linguistic problems of newly independent states' by warning against expatriate experts in this area (1964: 81). The policy paper for the Third Commonwealth Education conference, Ottawa, 1964 also insists on sensitivity to local needs, and implicitly queries Centre expertise: 'An institute or organization devoted to the teaching of English throughout the world has far less educational validity than one which would embrace the teaching of Malay *and* English in Malaya, or French *and* English in Canada, Hindi *and* English in India, and so on. Academic vested interests in propagating a particular language can be as remote from the true interests of ordinary citizens as politically based linguistic chauvinism' (Perren and Holloway 1965: 23).

The research results reported here raise in an acute form the question of long-term accountability for projects. Even if the British Council is attempting to repair some of the damage inflicted by the first generation of 'aid' staff in Zambia by appointing an ELT expert to work on revising the primary materials, and even if this person has pointed out the need for initial literacy in the mother tongue (Constable 1984, English Curriculum Committee 1984), it is arguable that the 'aid' work in itself militates against finding authentic local solutions to the problems, and perpetuates dependency.

There seems to be little doubt that the *amount of research* done into ELT issues of the kind discussed here, by either Centre or Periphery scholars is *modest*. Reviewing a conference held in Edinburgh on Language in Education in Africa, Alan Davies suggests that two or three years of information-gathering and evaluation are needed before the state of the art in language in education in Africa can be properly assessed (Davies 1986: 13), which seems to imply that the topic has been seriously neglected.[4] A scholar from Kenya, Anna Obura, concluded as follows: 'Now, in dispersed institutions, a few lone national researchers, better qualified than in the sixties but possibly fewer in number than the transitory research body of those early years, face a vast array of urgent research questions in language in education, in societies which have been in rapid transformation, quantitatively and qualitatively, over the last twenty-five years. And the pace of research in language is slow. One simply has to ask why the research community in this field is so small; why the research outcome has been so disappointing, even marginal' (Obura 1986: 415).

The modest size of the research effort is surprising when one recalls the huge 'aid' effort in ELT, countless projects on materials development, teacher training, etc. Nor has there been any shortage of research into education. A great deal of this is done in the Periphery, but is little known outside it (Eisemon 1989). 'The 1984 issue of University Microfilms International (UMI) catalogue of doctoral dissertations on West and Central Africa lists well over seven hundred dissertations in education alone carried out in North American Universities' (Yoloye 1986:28). Language has not been high on lists of national priorities, as compared with mathematics and scientific and technological subjects, and has suffered in consequence. 'Aid donors and research granting bodies have advised potential applicants away from language research and training . . . The consequences of the subject-specific outlook have therefore contributed to a reduction in the number of qualified researchers in language-in-education and have isolated them from main-stream education concerns which bypass language issues' (Obura 1986:419). This has been compounded by other restrictions. 'For longer than a decade higher education has not been a priority area for either multilateral or bilateral aid' (King 1985). The American foundations no longer fund major projects in this area. In India the Ford Foundation funded projects in agriculture in the 1950s, languages and the humanities in the 1960s, whereas the beneficiaries in the 1980s are the traditional arts and folklore (Annamalai, personal communication).

It is therefore an inescapable conclusion that only small-scale research has been undertaken by Centre scholars on the ELT topics which were identified in 1961 as being essential questions for the new discipline to clarify. One has therefore to ask why the Centre has not conducted more research.

The commitment of the Centre to teaching and to 'aid' activities such as curriculum development and teacher training has not precluded research, but it has probably tied up much of the available professional energy, and diverted attention away from fundamental questions. Basic questioning of the content and form of ELT within ELT's own ranks seems to have been indulged in very seldom, apart from the isolated voices quoted in Chapter 1. There is in the profession a general ethos of reformism, which perhaps implies a dissatisfaction with some aspects of efforts hitherto, and an urge to innovate and extend theory development, but these may leave some more underlying issues, structural and ideological, unexplored.

Research which could query the whole basis of 'aid' activity might be unwelcome to those responsible for 'aid' policy. Seen from a structural point of view, what was important for the British and the Americans was to have a bridgehead in the Periphery, an influential voice in Ministries of Education, teacher training colleges, and so on. This the Centre has had in the entire post-colonial era, reflecting the fact that in the neo-colonial phase of imperialism, hegemony is maintained by means of ideas and structures rather than force. Strategically speaking, no research was needed. Research by fledgling Periphery scholars could best be influenced when it was conducted and 'supervised' as graduate study in Centre countries. And why should the British engage in research which might indicate that there ought to be quite different priorities in education? British universities and research councils, financed by the British taxpayer, were never likely to fund research purely for the benefit of a given Periphery country. In a sense, the ELT academic world did not need further research either, because their services were already in great demand, thereby creating the impression that the knowledge, skills, and methods for solving ELT problems already existed.

Another reason why the State may not be anxious to set up research in this area is that any research on priorities in ELT is likely to impinge on political questions and raise issues of cultural imperialism. Research into the export of university textbooks demonstrates clearly how embarrassing such research can be. American research has shown that American foreign aid programmes have played a crucial role in enabling American publishers to establish local subsidiaries; this is *literary colonialism* (Altbach 1975). Under the Indo-American Textbook Program millions of copies of more than 1000 different textbooks were distributed at subsidized prices for use by Indian higher education students.[5] In addition to many of the books being inappropriate to the Indian scene, the effect of the subsidized prices was to tend to drive their unsubsidized domestic counterparts off the market and to retard the development of indigenous Indian publishing.

The British Council administered a comparable scheme (1959–1990) financed by the Overseas Development Administration for subsidizing British books for sale in Third World countries, the Educational Low-priced Books Scheme.[6] This 'low-priced' books scheme has a mixture of political, commercial, and 'aid' motives. Any research into the operation of the scheme (which does not appear to have been investigated) would be likely to find that the operation perpetuates the dependence of the Periphery on the Centre, that many of the titles are culturally inappropriate (from the point of view of the recipient), and that it supports English linguistic imperialism.

It is of course an advantage for the student to have one book rather than no book, but this does not alter the fact that the British government's interest in the scheme is to ensure that the one book is British rather than American or Soviet. The presence of the foreign book has economic consequences, as it influences local production capacity. There is also the ideological consequence of ensuring the dissemination of Centre ideas, values, and methods. This dependence is of course precisely what the Centre intends.

There are also parallels between books for export and languages for export. 'Aid' in this field is inextricably interlocked with the political and commercial interests which it is the primary purpose of British diplomacy to promote (see Chapter 6). Research into the 'politically sensitive' question of the role of English *vis-à-vis* local languages in education could question the legitimacy of the entire ELT 'aid' operation, and this would damage Britain's political and commercial interests. The State's function is to protect the hegemonic interests mediated by English by financing Centre teaching staff in the Periphery, and providing scholarships for Periphery personnel, subsidized textbooks, etc., but not research that might question that hegemony.

Why then should the *foundations*, which are financed from the profits of the capitalist system and whose function is to promote the continuation of the 'free enterprise' system, be so keen to support research into language learning, including the learning of indigenous languages? The big money has mainly come from the American foundations, but the Nuffield Foundation was also involved in a small way in support for ELT research in Uganda and teacher training in India.

The convenience of educational aid appearing to be 'non-political' was referred to above (Chapter 4), as well as the role of the ideology of the American South in influencing the Phelps-Stokes foundation's involvement in colonial Africa (Chapter 5). When American foundations are the primary source of research funding, it is clear that the parameters for the type of research that ought to be done and the methods employed can in large measure be determined by the foundations. A study of the expansion of the social sciences in higher education in Britain in the inter-war period reveals the decisive role of the Rockefeller foundation as 'gatekeepers' who could decide what the content, methods, and goals of social science research should be (Fisher 1982). Rockefeller provided funds amounting to approximately twice what the University Grants Committee disbursed in the same period (ibid.: 240). The huge expenditure of American funds on research in the Periphery since the 1950s partly gives substantial numbers of Americans experience of the Periphery, which increases American professionalism, and partly exposes Periphery academics to the norms and values of the Centre. The institution-building which is central to scientific and educational imperialism serves to define the parameters of what gets studied and why. 'The direction of the research is thus heavily influenced by the policies and orientations of the donor agencies' (Yoloye 1986: 42).

ELT is no exception, as the Ford Foundation appreciated in the early days of the consolidation of the profession: 'The World Second Language Survey was undertaken as the first major task by the CAL (with separate Ford Foundation support) in co-operation with the British Council, and the then Bureau d'Étude et de Liaison pour l'Enseignement du Français dans le monde (BEL) . . . This program produced the first body of data on the worldwide role of English and French as second languages and significantly increased international contacts and co-operation and exchange of information and scholars. *It set the pattern for collaboration on the language problems of developing countries* that CAL sparked for almost a decade through co-operative establishment with the British and the French of annual meetings of the International Conferences on Second Language Problems.' (Fox 1975: 37; my italics)

This does not prevent foundations from funding projects that may be highly critical of the established order, as has happened, for instance, with theoreticians of dependency in Latin America (Arnove 1982c: 321). Such research is not threatening to the élites of the Periphery State, for three reasons: it is not comprehensible to the masses, the State can become better informed as a result of the research (as can the Centre), and there is no infrastructure for integrating research into policy formation or for the widespread dissemination of knowledge in terms understandable to the general public (ibid.: 322). If this is so, the Centre can only benefit from research which enlightens it, and which can point the way to policies for increased social justice and reformist improvements which do not threaten the overall power structure.

Arnove's analysis of the limited impact of research can be related specifically to ELT. It does not appear that the Zambian or Nigerian research referred to above has influenced the politicians and senior bureaucrats who decide on policy (Chileshe 1982: 22; Yoloye 1986: 45). This is so even when there may be an apparently democratic structure for consultation on educational policy, and lively debate in the media. The same applies in western countries in relation to minority groups who contest the established educational order, even when they back up their claims with research evidence (Keskitalo 1984; Skutnabb-Kangas 1985; Skutnabb-Kangas and Leporanta-Morley 1986). Educational reform in Periphery countries is more difficult to influence, because of the more limited infrastructure in education there, and the relative paucity and fragility of the institutions for the crystallization of public opinion as compared with those in western democracies (Habermas 1970). In Africa, as in the West, policy decisions demonstrate the complexity of hegemony being worked out, and may be unpredictable: 'Concerning the mechanisms which cause curricular change or language shift in education we can trace the development of language policy through various official documents but we also discern hiccups and sudden shifts: for example, the Tanzanian decision . . . to restrict Kiswahili medium to primary schools; the decision in Oyo State, Nigeria to expand the Yoruba medium project to 200 schools in 1985; the Kenyan decision in 1984 to make Kiswahili a compulsory component of the primary leaving examination' (Obura 1986: 435). Obura's conclusion is not that researchers cannot influence politicians, but that more glottopolitical research is needed, as well as research into all aspects of language in education.

Most research relevant to language in education is presumably intended to have an influence on the academic community that the researchers form part of, and also to have some social clout, to be incorporated into the decision-making process. It appears that this idea may be a delusion. Peter Strevens's extensive experience of ELT over more than 30 years leads him to conclude that 'in the last resort I don't know of a single country in the world which bases its English teaching policy on the results of research . . . it is a matter of administrative and political convenience' (Strevens, interview). Similarly, British Council policy on what ELT activities it should support does not originate in research findings: it is based either on openings identified locally by Centre specialists or on established Periphery policy in the country in question (Bowers, interview).

Clearly policy decisions on language in education *are* taken, and 'administrative and political convenience', however rigid education systems may be, is not immutable. If relatively little research into ELT has been done, it is not surprising that research has not been a major influence on policy-making. If there are grave doubts about the wisdom of past policies in ELT, which is a hypothesis that the rest of this chapter will explore, there is an urgent need for more research to clarify what has happened and why.

ELT in 'aid' to education

English teaching is such a huge operation worldwide, with great variation in the profession as a consequence, that it is presumptuous to attempt any review of it. On the other hand the ELT establishment in the Centre presumes to train people for high-level ELT work anywhere in the world. Centre 'experts' are despatched throughout the Periphery to train teachers, solve specialist training needs at higher education level, write teaching materials, and so on. Part of the professional identity and image of the Centre applied linguistics institutions is that their skills are universally relevant. An attempt to make a global assessment of the achievements of ELT in the field, even if limited to some of the aspects which are most relevant to an exploration of linguistic imperialism, is therefore in order.

The overall context of ELT 'aid'

Education in many underdeveloped countries is in crisis, the symptoms of which are shortage of books, high push-out rates, teacher disaffection (reflecting their low status and pay), stagnating enrolments, and in general failure to deliver the goods (World Bank 1988; Haddad *et al.* 1990). These factors have accompanied an impressive quantitative leap, so that in sub-Saharan Africa, from 1960 to 1983 the number of people in formal education quintupled, with major expansion in primary and higher education (ibid.). However, educational growth has not led to economic growth (Coombs 1985). Some researchers have suggested, on the basis of empirical study of the political and economic functions of education, that 'Formal education in Africa and Asia in its present form tends to impede economic growth and promote political instability; in short, education in Africa and Asia today is an obstacle to development' (Hanf *et al.* 1975). Educational expansion has not reduced inequities, nor dependency on Western 'aid'. The crisis in education has multiple causes. Our task is to attempt to pinpoint where language policies may have contributed to the problems, and to see what can be learnt from the ELT experience of the past quarter century.

The broader educational context of ELT needs to be remembered. At the start of the 1980s, the average ratio of expenditure on education between OECD countries and the most underdeveloped countries was about 50 to 1 (Heyneman 1982). Periphery children thus have immeasurably fewer resources devoted to their education than children in the Centre, even when their governments give education a high priority and devote as much as 40 per cent of their recurrent budget to education, as does Kenya for example (Eshiwani 1989). 'Students in developing countries' schools are . . . not only getting fewer years of education but are learning less in each of those years than students in higher-income countries' (Haddad *et al.* 1990: 69). Unesco figures for the entire developing world indicate that whereas primary school enrolments have increased 50 per cent from 1960–1985, tertiary education enrolments have quadrupled (Unesco, 1985). According to World Bank figures, funding of one tertiary education student in sub-Saharan Africa is, on average, equivalent to the cost of 60 primary school places (Foster 1989: 108).

These harsh economic realities make Centre expertise and practice of dubious relevance to quite different contexts. In the words of one ELT expert in Southern Africa (in private conversation) it may be professionally much more relevant and urgent to teach teachers to make paper from banana leaves than to write syllabuses for them.

The reality of African multilingualism has been referred to several times, but needs stressing. One large empirical study which investigated the question was the large secondary pupils' survey conducted in Tanzania in 1970 (reported in Hill 1986), which was a representative sample (20 per cent, randomly selected) of the entire first year secondary school population in the country. The *average* number of languages known by the pupils (self-report) was five. There was not a single one who claimed to be monolingual, and only 3 per cent claimed knowledge of as few as two languages. Thus 97 per cent of pupils could cope with three or more languages. (In the Tanzanian primary school, Swahili is the medium of education, and English is taught as a subject from the first grade. Swahili is a Bantu language, as is the mother tongue of most Tanzanians.)

Monolingually oriented Europeans seem to be blind to the implications of this linguistic richness. The following analysis by a British Africanist, summing up a recent conference on Language and Education in Africa, is not untypical. He considers as a crucial issue the question of 'how the state seeks to manage the transition from an élite secondary school system (where high quality English can be guaranteed)' to a 'mass secondary system (where there will necessarily be many children intellectually unable to cope with a foreign language)' (King 1986: 451). He is right that the transition from a mass school to a democratic one is demanding in many ways, but he seems to be implying that a substantial section of the population in Africa are intellectually incapable of learning a foreign language. It is of course true that in monolingual Britain a large part of the school population learns no foreign languages, but does this mean that children in, say Holland or Denmark, where all children learn at least one foreign language, are ascribed greater 'intelligence'? The scientific evidence is that any children with a 'normal' IQ can cope with foreign language learning. According to several studies (reviewed in Genesee 1976) on English-speaking children in French-immersion programmes in Canada, neither working class children nor children with special language difficulties had any difficulty in coping with the foreign language, in addition to developing their English. King's ascription of intellectual inadequacy to African children not only falls into the classic pattern of blaming the victim rather than the structural factors which disadvantage some children, it also ignores the African multilingual reality, and the cognitive advantages that flow from individual multilingualism. The quotation demonstrates how linguicism has taken over from racism as a more subtle way of hierarchizing social groups in the contemporary world.

The Organization of African Unity's Inter-African Bureau of Languages (OAU-BIL) sees the false emphasis in education on European values and languages as a major cause of the present crisis. 'The spirit of education is mainly oriented towards the acquisition of foreign languages, while the acquisition of other subjects necessary to technical and economic development is delayed, until these foreign languages are mastered' (OAU-BIL 1985: 10). This investment of effort only pays dividends for the relatively small numbers of children who continue into secondary education. As literacy is typically acquired almost exclusively in the education system, and in a foreign language, most children relapse into functional illiteracy (Chileshe 1982, a study of Zambia, echoing the conclusions of the Nuffield Foundation and Colonial Office 1953).

The ideological dependence on Europe continues in the secondary school and higher education: 'Being a student of literature in today's Kenya means being an English student. Our children are taught the history of English literature and language from the unknown author of Beowulf to T. S. Eliot' wrote Ngũgĩ during a debate on reform of the Kenyan literature curriculum as recently as in 1976 (Ngũgĩ 1981: 35; for an analysis of this struggle to redefine the curriculum see Lillis 1984, who reports that the state of curriculum dependency has not substantively changed, though some reforms have been introduced, ibid.: 56 and 79). 'Thus the teaching of only European literature, and mostly British imperialist literature in our schools, means that our students are daily being confronted with the European reflection of itself, the European image, in history. Our children are made to look, analyse, and evaluate the world as made and seen by Europeans' (Ngũgĩ 1981: 36). The old colonial system has given way to neo-colonialism: 'During the neo-colonial stage of imperialism education and culture play an even more important role as instruments of domination and oppression. European naming systems; European language; European theatre; European literature; European content in teaching materials; all these areas, so central to culture, are left intact' (Ngũgĩ 1983: 96).

This is the context in which ELT operates. The examples quoted here refer to all levels of the education system. Education plays a significant role in determining the individual's life chances in a world in which, as Pattanayak puts it (private communication), the world's 'have-nots' are fast becoming the 'never-to-haves'. Ngũgĩ's characterization of the education system fits into Galtung's prediction of the forms that Centre control over the Periphery will take under neo-neocolonialism. The 'educated' in the Periphery are internalizing Centre values and ways of thought to the point where the physical presence of Centre inter-state actors is no longer necessary and computers will ensure the Centre's control over the Periphery. The English language is essential in the new form that this structure takes, just as in education, English is still, as in colonial times, the key to success.

EFL, ESL, or . . .?

Clear thinking about different types of teaching and learning situations is impeded by a confusing use of terminology. The most common label for the adult education ELT tradition is 'EFL'—English as a Foreign Language. For instance, when talking of the sophistication of this branch of ELT, Peter Strevens, at the time chairperson of the International Association of Teachers of English as a Foreign Language, says 'the development of EFL, based in Britain, has outstripped in terms of effectiveness, classroom effectiveness, and methodology and so on, all other branches of second and foreign language teaching anywhere else in the world, in any other language' (Strevens, interview). This somewhat anglocentric claim might be modified if one considered several variants of successful bilingual education (Yugoslav bilingual schools, the bilingual lycées in major European cities, the immersion programmes in Canada and the United States, all of which are well analysed), but this is not central to the argument here. When referring to the EFL tradition, Strevens is thinking of the adult education work of private language schools in Britain and their equivalents abroad. Strevens uses the term in the way it is widely used in British ELT professional discourse (see Brumfit 1985b). The fortnightly paper serving this market, and much concerned with immigrant language teaching in Britain, is called the *EFL Gazette*.

Adult learners attending a language school in Britain are not in an EFL situation, but an ESL situation, as they are exposed to English constantly outside the classroom (see the presentation of

EFL and ESL in Chapter 2). This is a totally different situation from someone learning English as a *Foreign* Language in, say, Germany or Algeria, and requires different pedagogical strategies, just as the school child in these countries has different learning needs from the adult. The British adult ELT approach is monolingual, whereas when EFL is taught in schools, the approach is generally bilingual, either directly (through the use of translation, or specially relevant language practice) or indirectly (the teachers have an intimate knowledge of the mother tongue of the learners, a contrastive preparedness). It is therefore misleading that the label EFL is used in relation to both contexts. The British private language school situation is, like the minority-language immigrant one in Britain, an ESL one.

There is unfortunately also confusion in the term ESL, as it is used to cover two totally different groups of learners. The first is the foreign or immigrant learner in Britain, the USA, or some other core-English country. The *Swann Report* (1985) and Brumfit (1985c) use ESL in this sense. The second is the school child in countries such as Kenya or Hong Kong, where English is used widely in education and government and where English is not the mother tongue. The two contexts differ radically in the amount and type of support for learning English in the environment, and in the degree to which there is support for the mother tongue outside the home. The language learning needs of the two groups are thus completely different, and pedagogical strategies should reflect this. There is currently in Hong Kong an increasing realization that a monolingual English approach has failed, and that a bilingual approach, with a focus on the interface between English and Chinese is needed (Lord and T'sou 1985: 22). The monolingual approach for immigrant children in Britain is also increasingly under fire, but a quite different approach would be needed for children from the Chinese-speaking minority in London as compared with Hong Kong.

The effect of fuzziness in both terms, EFL and ESL, and the shifting borderline between them noted in Chapter 2 has been to blur the distinctions between the needs of adults and children, between learning situations inside and outside schools, and especially between learning a mother tongue, a second language, and a foreign language. The desire to avoid the multiple and conflicting meanings of the terms has also been a major reason for using the blanket term ELT throughout this study.

The imprecision of the terms justifies efforts to devise taxonomies for a more precise classification of English-using societies. Moag (1982) identifies 26 variables for this purpose, 17 of which are sociolinguistic (sets grouped under language policy, language use, language acquisition, language attitudes and bilingualism) and 9 linguistic (models, variation within English, interlanguage features). These permit more differentiation of the countries in the broad categories EFL and ESL. The taxonomy is however a somewhat cumbersome instrument, and Moag's major conclusion (ibid.: 45), that it is English-use patterns which 'condition features of language acquisition, language attitude, bilingualism' and the linguistic parameters is scarcely surprising, though it is not the whole story. The language-use factors have their own history, and in the present-day world they belong in a global capitalist system. Nor is it only English-use factors which determine language policy and planning decisions, as the theoretical coverage of these issues in Chapter 4 showed, and as the empirical study of the legitimation of English will demonstrate in Chapter 9.

Awareness of the inadequacy of the labels has also led to efforts to devise new ones for well-defined goals and learners. For instance, 'English as an International Language' (EIL) is now sometimes used to refer to the language used by non-native speakers of English of different nationalities for restricted communication purposes and which bears traces of their mother tongues (Smith 1983, an anthology in which several articles promote clarity in labelling English, Johnson 1990). EIL represents a laudable attempt to get away from the native speaker as the target, and to educate native speakers in interlanguage communication (Smith 1983: v). On the other hand EIL communication would be just as well covered by 'English as a lingua franca', which might have the effect of implicity putting English on a par with other languages. There is a risk of EIL fitting into the pattern of terms which glorify English and implicitly devalue other languages, of it being a linguicist label. Such terms as English as an International or Intranational Language can obscure the processes by which the global linguistic hegemony of English is created and maintained, and how English serves social stratificational purposes intranationally. Labels may indirectly contribute to a lack of awareness of these dimensions. For this reason the term 'English as a language of wider colonization' has been suggested, as an alternative to the familiar 'English as a language of wider communication', so as to highlight the processes of linguistic hegemonic control and structural incorporation (Phillipson and Skutnabb-Kangas 1986b). 'Colonization' may in fact be a historically inappropriate term, of which reason 'English as the language of wider incorporation' might be preferable.

The Director of the Organization of African Unity's Bureau of Inter-African Languages chooses to label English and French as *foreign* languages (Mateene 1985), so as to underline their historical imposition and alien nature. This is a conscious strategy for attempting to curb the dominance of the former colonial languages and create more positive conditions for the growth and spread of African languages. This involves rejecting the ESL label. The same applies if English is classified as an Indian language, on the premiss that the former colonial language has undergone a process of indigenization and should be regarded as being independent of British or American norms.

There is a strong case for expanding the number of categories in use to typologize different types of ELT learning situations.[7] This should be partly along the lines of Moag's study, but should also stress the different needs of the child and the adult, and the distinction between English as a second language in respectively core and periphery-English countries (these labels incorporating dimensions of sociolinguistic power, internationally and intra-nationally). Alternatively, if the norms of the Centre are rejected, English should be labelled as an indigenous language. The variables should be selected so as to serve to make target models and cultural emphasis explicit (as in Smith 1983: 15). Analyses based on such typological work could then make it easier to trace where ELT expertise originated and where it has expanded. If legitimacy is then made more visible, its relevance can be more effectively queried where this is necessary.

EFL and ESL are in reality often poles apart. Perren puts this vividly in a comment which begins by referring to the 'EFL' tradition: 'There is a very sophisticated line of development, with very able people, but how far that affected the business of teaching children in primary school classrooms where the teachers themselves were products of the same environment and woefully badly educated themselves, they are two different worlds . . . there are good ideas from Palmer, Mackin, Strevens, but what matters is how English is taught in 10,000 primary schools where the teachers themselves have had perhaps two more years than the children they are teaching' (Perren, interview). Nor does Chris Brumfit share Peter Strevens's optimism about the contribution of EFL: 'It may be very good for highly motivated small groups of middle class adults. I am not at all sure that it is having a good spin-off on EFL teaching as it typically is in normal state schools' (Brumfit, interview). One suspects that this remark also holds for schools in some EFL contexts and where English is a second language in periphery-English countries.

The effect of fuzziness in the labels has been to further the global promotion of ELT, as the assumption has been that it is universally relevant. We should now turn to the uses to which ELT has been put.

Principles for the analysis of ELT in 'aid'

ELT will be evaluated at a fairly abstract level, for several reasons. In the first place, ELT aid goals themselves have been formulated in very general terms (teacher training, curriculum development work, etc.). Secondly, the analysis is concerned with overall policy and its results, though informed by the conclusions of more detailed studies in the literature (some of which were reported in the consideration of ELT research, in particular the Zambian experience), and by the earlier parts of this study (policy formulation in colonial and post-colonial times, the Makerere tenets). Thirdly, the interviews undertaken for this study aimed at a clarification of broad policy issues as seen by some principal actors in the ELT drama. Their judgements carry considerable weight, in view of their extensive experience and involvement.

This constraint does not mean that detailed case study analysis of specific projects would not lead to more refinement in the analysis, if time had permitted. To some extent, such analysis is an ongoing concern within ELT (see, for instance the contributions to Brumfit 1983, the *ELT Documents* series, British Council house journals), and what one would expect from a lively profession. In recent years there has been a trickle of more critical articles in professional journals, some of which were referred to in Chapter 1. One purpose of this analysis is to stimulate further debate and reflection, and hopefully to see the theoretical framework applied and evaluated in other contexts.

The overall goal for this part of the analysis is to relate ELT to

English linguistic imperialism. The main criticisms of ELT (that ELT is not sensitive to its socio-political and economic contexts, and that it has not been explicitly anchored in general educational theory or practice) are characterizations that were suggested by the people I interviewed, and which confirmed some of my working hypotheses. These shortcomings are a logical consequence of the doctrine approved at Makerere and of the professional image of ELT as being a non-political activity. The analysis is structured around two postulates, namely that ELT has been politically disconnected, and that ELT has been narrowly technical. The evidence for these is assessed, explanation provided, awareness of the issue considered, and some of the consequences that follow identified.

There is no doubt that serious ELT professionalism has advanced theory-building and technical skills over the past quarter century. In many countries, European ones, for instance, an increased professionalism in foreign language teaching has occurred as a domestic development in parallel with influence from core English-speaking countries. In other countries, particularly periphery-English countries, there is a shortage of qualified English teachers, and there are therefore urgent demands for outside support both in the formal school system, and, for those who have not learnt enough English there, in special vocational courses both in higher education and in the private sector. ELT in its Anglo-American forms has had its greatest impact on periphery-English countries whose education systems have been most permeable and open to influence from outside, that is, in underdeveloped countres. The study of English in 102 countries (Fishman, Cooper, and Rosenbaum 1977: 105) noted that one consequence of a country being poor is a greater likelihood of dependence on English as a medium of instruction, and a probability of unequal access to the learning of English in formal schooling. Professionalism involves the creation and legitimation of a particular type of knowledge or expertise, and is exclusionary in that by definition those not certified as professionals are assumed not to have the same competence and are prevented from practising as authorized professionals do (Torstendahl and Burrage 1990). In an asymmetrical relationship, an ideology and structure of professionalism is bound to secure the interests of the Centre.

English has been associated with the new gods of efficiency, science and technology, modernity, etc. This demand for English is of course articulated on the premiss that English is needed in a given context, and, as the analysis of the tenets propounded at Makerere showed, educational policies are not necessarily well conceived on this score. The demand for English, wherever it originates, has been a reality for the past 30 years.

There has thus been a ready market for ELT skills from Britain and the USA. Increasingly this activity takes the form of projects with specified goals and time-scales. Some of this activity consists of aid packages, some is paid for at commercial rates to private ELT concerns like the Bell Educational Trust. Such activities now follow a well-established pattern and are closely planned and monitored (*Dunford Seminar Report* 1987, 1988; Bowers 1987, which describes a successful multi-faceted project).[8] From the analysis of the Makerere tenets and the description of the modesty of the research effort into broader aspects of ELT policy we have been able to glimpse something of the ELT teaching tradition that 'aid' activities have been cast in and which the core English-speaking countries' specialist departments train people in. If it is a correct diagnosis that ELT plots and plans have not always come to fruition, we need to know more about why not.

Such a perspective does not imply that we are looking for facile explanations for complex events. ELT is not being made a scapegoat for all the educational disasters of underdeveloped countries, although just this sort of monocausal analysis is not unknown in political circles. One of the principal legacies of colonial education was that language was perceived as a *panacea* for the solution of not only educational but also development problems. The arguments used to promote English (for instance at the Makerere conference) linked use of the master language to the promise of economic progress, enlightenment and so on, but that promised land is still for most an unredeemed promise. The pendulum has now swung, rather vigorously in certain countries whose governments had attempted to limit the scope of European languages and where there has since been a change of government. There is now the risk of language policies being made a *scapegoat* for deep-rooted educational, social, and economic problems.

Treffgarne, in a paper reviewing developments in francophone Africa reports the scapegoat syndrome after a change of government in Guinea; she also sees a risk of the same simplistic analysis and reaction occurring in Burkina Faso (Treffgarne

1986: 160). In French official 'aid' policy it has become expedient to recognize that other languages have some rights and to modify the claim that the French of France was the only acceptable one. The French now advocate a *francophonie* which is 'pluralist' (Haut Conseil de la Francophonie 1986: 344), which seems to imply a stance that there is no one Centre for the universalist language, and local variants reflect local cultures. The French provide some aid for the teaching of African languages, because a modicum of support for indigenous languages is a prudent way of ensuring influence, and allows the French to remain at the forefront of pedagogical innovation (which is where ELT conceives of itself). This French policy does not necessarily jeopardize the privileged position of French, as the linguistic hierarchy in the French-dominated African states remains unaffected (Treffgarne 1986: 156). The policy rather shows how linguistic hegemony is reconstituted in response to changed demands. Linguicism still operates to maintain French linguistic hegemony in such countries.

On the other hand, awareness of linguicism, or at least of the link between language and power, can be increased through programmes of literacy in the mother tongue. In Mali an adult education programme in Bambara is described as having a profound effect on the learners, who could no longer see the justification for having to communicate with the authorities in French (Calvet 1979). The learners wanted to use their new skills and appreciated that they were being deprived of their linguistic human rights. Conscientization, to use Paolo Freire's term, can in fact lead to the establishment of linguistic counter-hegemonies.

Obura also warns against false conclusions being drawn on language issues, exemplified by changes in Tanzania's Kiswahili-medium policy: 'It is possible that other African governments may point to the withdrawal of Kiswahili as proof of the failure of African-language-medium policies in general and of African-language-medium policy for secondary and higher education in particular. This would be a dangerous conclusion based on no evidence at all' (Obura 1986: 435). Among the factors that, according to Obura, could be causative variables for the Kiswahili goals not being met are inadequate financial resources, shortage of indigenous trained applied linguists, the likelihood that the Kiswahili-secondary-medium project did not last long enough to be evaluated properly, and that outside experts did not stay long enough to be useful (ibid.). There is detailed analysis of inconsistencies and inadequacies in Tanzanian language policies in Rubagumya 1990.

One conclusion that can be drawn from these warnings is that clear analysis of the strengths and weaknesses of language in education policy and practice is urgently needed. This is particularly so when conflicts on language policy tend to arouse strong emotions and to become explicit political issues. In relation to ELT, it means attempting to take stock of achievements and shortcomings, in the knowledge that ELT dovetails with many variables mentioned, but recalling that a substantial aid effort has gone into ELT. When attempting to see where ELT may have failed, and to identify the reasons why, it is therefore not a question of making ELT a scapegoat. That would be as fallacious as regarding ELT as a panacea.

Postulate 1: political disconnection

The first postulate is that despite a focus on language learning and teaching, *ELT has not been seen in a wider educational perspective*. This amounts to disconnecting ELT from the *structure* within which it operates. Ultimately it is therefore a *political* disconnection. Several informants saw the disconnection of ELT from its general educational context as a clear weakness. 'Where the British Council often fell down was in trying to make an artificial distinction between education and language teaching . . . this is partly historical because their background was language teaching outside the education system' (Perren, interview). 'Language teaching was seen to a very heavy extent as something that was a technical matter that could be isolated from the rest of education, and often it would ignore the general educational research' (Brumfit, interview). 'The notion of integrating English teaching with the general educational provision for language, I don't think has ever been British Council policy' (Widdowson, interview).

This did not deter the British and Americans from attempting to 'help' periphery-English nations to build up their *education systems*. The Americans naïvely believed they could transfer good American practice abroad *en bloc*, for example to Northern Nigeria in a major Ford Foundation/AID project from 1964 to 1969, which attempted institution-building and a transformation of teaching methodologies and materials for a whole school system. This project failed (Fox 1975: 83). The

Ford Foundation general review of aid projects in language and development (quoted in Chapter 1) attributes the failure of these projects to British and American ignorance of the local educational and linguistic context and to the inappropriateness of the Western development model for pre-university education.

It is likely that the British people involved would contest the claim that they lacked detailed knowledge of post-colonial educaton systems. However, they inevitably saw matters from a Centre perspective, and the chief problem in their eyes was that, as compared with the Americans, the British could only offer piecemeal help. In other words the problem was seen as a quantitative one. The Ford Foundation is right in stressing that in fact the issue is qualitative. Essentially, the wrong choices were made, and the role given to the English language was one of them. Part of the responsibility for the failure of efforts in places like Nigeria lies with those who formed the language-in-education policies, and educational planners like Ashby (see Chapter 5) who ignored indigenous languages altogether. (Nigeria is experiencing a 'virtual collapse of primary education' and 'severe difficulties' in the secondary system, Williams 1986: 41.) The fact that ELT was not seen in a wider educational context is symptomatic of the inappropriacy of the ELT contribution and difficulties in conceptualizing what was needed.

British ELT experts express the view, at least in private conversation, that *British* training for work overseas is more appropriate and successful than *American* training.[9] This comforting belief is probably based on a conviction that the teaching of linguistics, phonetics, and applied linguistics in Britain is more practically oriented, that there has been more creative thinking about teaching and learning activities, and that there is a more cosmopolitan orientation in British ELT departments. Empire and Commonwealth have tended to make the British ELT profession internationally aware, whereas their counterparts in the USA have been more domestically involved. British postgraduate students taking ELT qualifications often have experience abroad, and training or experience in the adult education sector. In the USA the major professional thrust has been towards second language acquisition problems within the country, with more concentration on linguistics and psycholinguistics than pedagogy. In Britain there tends to be a focus on educational problems, even if the approach and methods reflect a narrow ELT focus rather than a general educational one. These

Anglo-American differences are real enough, though they do not prevent successful teamwork in many parts of the world, and, as seen in Chapter 6, it was inter-governmental policy that efforts should be mutually supportive. The differences are, however, trivial in relation to the basic issue of whether the mainstream of ELT, dominated by anglocentric professionalism, and the structure of Centre-Periphery 'aid' made it possible for the ELT effort to achieve its goals.

Ann Hayes describes the fumbling nature of much British work in the field, the absence of 'thorough and thoughtful planning, with clear objectives open to evaluation at any stage, and detailed implementation schemes with realistic time-scales' (Hayes 1983: 15). These can be regarded as symptoms of political disconnection. Her sober assessment of the language-in-education project that she is involved in is that 'even if we only achieve half of what we set out to do, that half will count for more than something in Sierra Leone, which, as a typically African aid-worthy context, has seen more than its fair share of plans and projects, but precious little in the way of achieve-ments' (ibid.: 27).[10]

The April 1989 number of the British Council *English Teaching Information Circular* comments in the introduction that the first article 'provides a salutary reminder that in our field, as elsewhere, people are slow to benefit from the experience of others; one would have hoped that the lessons he offers from experience in China had been learned long ago.' The points made in the article (Morrison 1989) include stressing that familiarity with local culture and teaching context is crucial, that projects have suffered from the 'proselytizing zeal' of some teacher trainers and their failure to appreciate local conditions, that communication between host and expert has been deficient, and that the experts have disapproved of some of their counterparts. From this one can conclude that this particular ELT work in China has suffered from not being integrated adequately into the local context, meaning that it has been politically disconnected. Whether technocratic streamlining can remedy this, along the lines suggested in the article (better briefing, clearer definition of goals and roles, etc.) is debatable. The acquisition of cultural and linguistic insight adequate to such a context is not something that a few weeks of training or briefing can supply.

One example of the failure of ELT to respond to clear needs is that very little development work has been done in the area of *English across the curriculum*, in other words work to co-ordinate language learning across the subjects that are being taught through the medium of English and to see in what way the classes labelled 'English' can best support overall language learning. Apart from Ralph Isaacs' (1968) materials for this purpose in Tanzania, which represent only a short-term course, little effort seems to have been made to integrate the teaching of English with the use made of English by other subjects. Experienced textbook writers judiciously select material likely to be encountered in other subjects (Grant and Unoh 1976), but one would have expected 'English across the curriculum' to be regarded as an urgent task in all contexts where English was serving as the medium of instruction for other subjects. As it is, the imbalance between the vocabulary learnt in the subject 'English' and that of other subjects can be grotesque. Obura (1986: 432) reports that a study in Lesotho shows that primary school leavers have an active vocabulary of 800 words and that 12,000 words are needed for science in secondary school. 'This is by any standards a staggering discrepancy. The major significance however of this illustration is that Lesotho may be the only country to have documented this discrepancy in a systematic manner' (ibid.). This corroborates experience at an international conference in 1986 on educational language planning for Namibia, which endorsed the principle of English across the curriculum but found to its surprise that little work had been done in this area. The fact that ELT has traditionally operated in isolation from thought and practice in general education, is part of the explanation for this failure.

Another explanation for ELT failures is that blurring the contexts of ELT has served to legitimate the worldwide use of a monolingual methodology and monolingual teaching materials, irrespective of their origin—and, to judge by the evidence from Kenya, Zambia, Nigeria, and India referred to in this chapter, often irrespective of the cultural and linguistic needs of periphery-English children. This is a consequence of ELT being politically disconnected. As a result it has appeared that ELT experts were qualified to practise their technical skills anywhere in the world. Yet the only general educational experience that the British could draw on was the domestic tradition of teaching English as a mother tongue, a system exported to the colonies. The sophisticated adult education ELT tradition had been evolved in a quite different teaching environment, and should have been regarded as only indirectly relevant to school teaching in a multilingual environment.

One consequence of the expansion of facilities for applied linguistic degrees in Centre countries and the simultaneous creation of 'expert' posts in the Periphery was the rapid elevation to expert status of many native speakers of English, after a limited period of teaching experience, and with a strong likelihood that this experience was outside any education system. The outcome is predictable. 'There are already too many people designing syllabuses, writing materials, and advising with too little acquaintance with straightforward classroom teaching' (Brumfit 1985b: 101). This factor must also contribute to the failure of projects. It is compounded by anglocentricity and its corollary, lack of insight into the cultural and linguistic background of the learners they are supposed to be helping.

For a worldwide profession, backed up by the British publishing industry, it was logical that *monolingualism* should become an axiom. Monolingualism is the logical consequence of ELT neglecting the broader context of its operations. This is not only a question of linguicism, of promoting one language irrespective of the needs or claims of others. It is also a question of concentrating on technical skills irrespective of local and global factors of an economic, social, or ideological kind. 'The training and development of language teaching experts has been very insensitive to economic, social, and political implications of what happens' (Brumfit, interview). One of the few ESL books which addresses the issue directly (Ashworth 1985) recommends community involvement, and raises many political issues, but these are matters to which no answers are provided in mainstream ELT. Community involvement is also seldom practicable in the context of foreign as opposed to second language learning, and outside experts are not likely to be integrated into the local community.

It is instructive to contrast the significance of *local languages* for present-day experts with practice in colonial times. The monolingual approach legitimates the ignoring of local languages and the cultural universe that these languages mediate. Colonial education staff, by contrast, were obliged to learn a local language. It is now possible for ELT experts, for instance on British Council/ODA (Overseas Development Administration) projects, to be posted anywhere in the Periphery without any obligation to learn or be familiar with the local language or languages. Some such experts do, of course, learn the relevant languages (they are entitled to have tuition paid for, though they do not qualify for a language allowance if they reach a given level of proficiency, as do FCO and British Council employees), but there is no obligation to do so.

It is perhaps in periphery-English countries, particularly in Africa, where English is replacing other languages, that it is most urgent that ELT experts should learn, and be seen to learn, local languages. Otherwise they are inevitably contributing to linguicide, of which there is now plenty of evidence. A recent sociolinguistic survey in Zambia (where, it will be recalled, English is the sole medium of education from the first class) records that young Zambians lack a complete mastery of their own languages, no longer learn the local lingua franca of the Lusaka area (Nyanja) adequately, and that there is 'a breakdown of communication between them and their elderly relatives who do not speak English', this cultural dislocation being epitomized by children speaking to their elders in English, knowing full well that they neither speak nor understand the language (Siachitema 1986: 227). As the spread of English has occurred simultaneously with urbanization, the cultural disintegration is seen as a single process, that is, increased English and urbanization are not perceived as separate phenomena. It is also perfectly possible for the same individual to have negative attitudes to English, because of awareness of the negative developments mentioned above, as well as positive attitudes for instrumental reasons (ibid.: 228). Fishman too has observed mismatches between attitudes to a language and attitudes to the speakers of a language (1989: 250). This should make one sceptical about simple explanations for the ubiquitous 'demand' for English.

Unfortunately, in the present administrative and ideological climate, there is little likelihood of Centre ELT experts having to learn any local languages. Roger Bowers (interview), whose department administers the ODA/British Council scheme, agrees on the desirability of learning local languages but sees no possibility at all of ELT experts being encouraged to learn another language in an ESL context. The administrative justification for local language proficiency not being a requirement is that such posts are based on a two-year contract, and that this precludes long language training. Professionally, this monolingualism is indefensible, since ignoring local languages is fundamentally linguicist. It symbolizes and signals lack of respect for and interest in local culture, and it deprives the language expert of essential insight into local language learning difficulties and needs (teachers without a contrastive preparedness are bound to be less effective—advisers and materials producers and other 'experts' even more so). The anglocentricity and linguicism implicit in the attitudes towards local languages and the educational and structural consequences that follow from it are a clear reflection of the overall relationship between Centre and Periphery. The professionalism cannot but be disconnected.

Postulate 2: narrowly technical training

The second postulate is closely related to the first, but concentrates on the training provided to ELT experts. The claim is that this training is *narrowly technical*. This has already been touched on in considering the academic base on which ELT expanded. Applied linguistics drew heavily on linguistics, and only lightly on education, cultural theory, sociology, international relations, etc. This still appears to be the case. The current chief executive of the Centre for British Teachers, a private body which recruits teachers for many parts of the world and is involved in large projects in Brunei, Malaysia, Oman, and Germany, echoes the familiar analysis of ELT being dominated by linguistics: 'Maybe because of its historical links with linguistics, EFL has perhaps cut itself off from education' (Kennedy 1989). ELT teacher training concentrated on classroom techniques and materials production rather than on the social and cognitive prerequisites for learning.

The range of problems which are considered to be central to ELT aid can be seen from the choice of topics for the annual British Council seminars organized for ELT experts. Since 1978 they have covered the following topics, with an interesting move towards broader issues in recent years:

- ESP course design
- ELT course design
- communicative methodology
- design, evaluation, and testing in English language projects
- teacher training and the curriculum
- design and implementation of teacher training programmes
- curriculum and syllabus design in ELT
- communication skills in bilateral aid projects

- appropriate methodology
- ELT and development: the place of English language teaching in aid programmes
- ELT in development aid: defining aims and measuring results.
   (*Dunford Seminar Report* 1988/1989)

The Foreword to the 1988 seminar, by the Chief Education Adviser to the ODA, regrets that 'past seminars had involved participants in looking too narrowly at purely academic issues rather than at the broad context of their work overseas. ODA funds ELT activity because it believes that this is one means of furthering social and economic development' (Iredale 1989). For the ODA the context is one of ELT competing with other aid-worthy projects, and the need for ELT to demonstrate 'value for money'. The seminar itself focused on the monitoring and evaluation of educational aid projects, with little attempt to gauge in what way ELT might contribute to economic or social development. The latter would in any case be a difficult operation, granted the nature and time-scale of most projects, as a brief article on justifying and evaluating aid-based ELT shows (Chambers and Erith 1990), and unless the aid relationship itself was problematized and analysed. The inadequacies of existing frameworks for evaluating ELT projects have also been pointed out by Alan Beretta, who notes a mismatch between evaluation findings and their utility to policy-makers, his own experience being that he has been an 'ESL researcher without portfolio', unsure to whom he is answerable (1990: 1). The way forward is to bring 'scholarly enquiry to bear on real world policy' (ibid.: 11).

The evidence is therefore that there seems to be an increasing awareness of the need to reconnect politically, but the scholarly foundations for doing so are still being identified. One of the strengths of Centre-based ELT is that it can bring together experience from many diverse situations, and attempt to generalize and theorize on the basis of varied but comparable input. Nor is it necessary for any of the topics to be treated in a narrowly technical way, and indeed several of the contributions to Higgs 1986 (an annual seminar report) are set in a broad social perspective, partly because they are on ESP topics, partly because the seminar is designed to demonstrate enlightened practice. However the crucial issue here is the question of the initial training for the ELT profession, the overall theoretical framework within which such operations take place, the dominant paradigm for ELT activities, and the structure and ideology that has been exported to education systems in the Periphery.

The *linguistics* that has evolved in the Centre over the past century is anchored in Centre theories, with competing theoretical ships tugging in different directions. Very probably much of the speculation and sophistication of contemporary linguistics is of limited utility to ELT practitioners, and one can have grave doubts as to the utility of the linguistics and to some extent the applied linguistics that are on offer in the Centre. Björn Jernudd, with wide experience of Asia and the Islamic world, considers that the concerns and methods of western linguistics are inappropriate for the language problems of Third World countries (Jernudd 1981). Even within western societies, linguistics has had relatively little impact on such applied language tasks as terminological development, movements for plain language, minority education, mother tongue and foreign language teaching, translation, etc. Nevertheless linguistics is imported into Third World countries, often clashing with existing language cultivation traditions and causing pedagogic uncertainty. In addition the language that linguistics has been studied through, and that most work is done on, is English.

The native-language departments in the Anglo-American world (here: English departments) have a narrower approach to national language matters than have Continental ones, and are therefore of as little help in training people for applied language tasks as the linguistics departments. Jernudd provides a detailed example of the broad training offered in Swedish language departments in Sweden, which covers many applied language matters. He concludes that there must be a change of policy both in language cultivation structures in the Third World, and in aid policies designed to support such language work. 'Introduction of native-language departments to support indigenous language use through the study of history and current functions is essential to the development of emerging speech communities in the new nations' (ibid.: 47). Among his suggestions for combatting Anglo-American/English language domination are that 'universities in emerging speech communities could consider not accepting aid (or business contracts) for English teaching unless some aid is also offered for developing indigenous languages or for developing the national language treatment system' (ibid.: 50).

The situation is parallel in *applied linguistics*. This is securely ensconced at the Centre of the Centre-Periphery structure within which educational imperialism operates. Centre perceptions tend to define both the problems to be pursued and the proposed solutions. There is a risk of ELT operating with a narrow set of skills, sometimes dogmatically clung to, which are applied to a setting which has been imperfectly analysed, because it cannot come to grips with practical and ideological Periphery determinants. The training of ELT experts pays only superficial homage to social, political, and economic aspects which vitally affect language-in-education decisions, language planning in multilingual societies, and pedagogical innovation. It is likely that anglocentricity and professionalism effectively preclude the Periphery perspective from decisively influencing ELT decisions. The disconnection of ELT from the social context within which it operates combines with a focus on Centre technical professionalism to invalidate even the best designed and implemented plans. As Centre inter-state actors are supposed to liaise with counterparts who have been trained in Centre ways of thinking and who are generally in awe of Centre 'experts', the opportunity for effective dialogue with Periphery needs is precluded. The whole purpose of counterparting is to ensure that the Centre's ideas live on when the expert leaves. Time factors intervene to impose and rationalize a programme with definable short-term goals. The two-year contract syndrome ensures that results have to be visible fast, on terms that the Centre finds comprehensible. It is a top-down exercise, in which there is very little chance of those at the bottom benefiting.

Henry Widdowson brings many of these points together very lucidly:

> I think that what has developed quite impressively over the past 15 years or so has been if you like an expertise, an awareness of various aspects of language teaching . . . but where I think things have not been really effective has been in the mediation, the way in which these ideas have been integrated into local social, political, and educational conditions of the countries where they are applied, so that the overriding failure if you like has been that we have tended to get ideas which have hardened too readily into a paradigm, and people have shot off to various parts of the world and implemented various programmes. Whether this be the

Madras ELT snowball or the setting up of the KAAU project in Saudi Arabia or the development of study skills in Malaysia, we've tended always to make the same basic error, which is to assume that somehow it is the local conditions that have to be adjusted to the packaged set of concepts we bring with us rather than attempt to look into the real issues, practical as well as ideological, of implementation and innovation within those local contexts . . . I don't think we have brought into the operation an awareness of local conditions nor an effective involvement of local people, so that one can see these as in some sense, even though enlightened and benevolent, well-meaning, but nevertheless to some degree impositional.
(Widdowson, interview)

What Widdowson describes as a mediation problem relates in fact to the *Centre-Periphery structure within which educational imperialism takes place*, and which is intrinsically asymmetrical and 'impositional'. This structure is reinforced and perpetuated by the accumulation of technical expertise in the Centre, which keeps the Periphery in a dependent role. It is mediated by a monolingual doctrine, which the short-contract syndrome seeks to rationalize. Centre-Periphery dialogue is blocked by the focus on technical skills which only the Centre is supposed to be expert in. The power imbalance between Centre and Periphery enables the Centre to 'plug in aid' (to use Bernard Lott's term, interview) wherever it is policitically and economically most opportune for the Centre.

A number of voices critical of ELT were quoted in Chapter 1, in the section on professional and ethical aspects of aid. The relative failure of ELT to deliver the goods is part of a general failure of educational aid. A survey of theories of educational aid and dependency and the empirical evidence by a World Bank consultant ends with the bald statement that 'there is a good deal of evidence that much western educational curricula, technology, and institutions have failed in the Third World because of their inappropriateness' (Hurst 1984: 33). There seems little dispute about this fact, whereas there is no consensus among the theorists of educational dependency (where a major concern is the contribution of education to the economy) on the causes for the failure, or whether one can conclude that aid is harmful or merely irrelevant (ibid.: 28).

The widespread evidence of linguicism in educational aid is unambiguous, and can only be interpreted as harmful to the vast majority of the population in the Periphery and to their languages. Education systems in underdeveloped countries which follow a western model, like their western counterparts, qualify the few and disqualify the many. The allocation of material resources to English and not to other languages represents a structural favouring of English, which has the following consequences (with just a few representative sources given in the parentheses):

- school in underdeveloped periphery-English countries is dominated by English, pupils are taught by teachers with an inadequate command of English (Afolayan 1984), and the vast majority of children get little linguistic or content benefit from schooling (Mateene 1980)
- the focus on English stigmatizes local languages, prevents them from being regarded as equally valid, and thwarts local cultural and linguistic creativity (Ngũgĩ 1981)
- the Periphery looks to the Centre for professional guidance, instead of being self-reliant, but much Centre expertise is of dubious relevance to multilingual countries because of its linguistic, pedagogic, and cultural inappropriacy (Jernudd 1981; Kachru 1986a; Pattanayak 1986b).

The political disconnection and narrowly technical training associated with ELT contribute to each of these.

A related structural problem is that those who *teach* applied linguistics in the Centre are virtually excluded, because of the rigidity of career structures, from involvement in the direct teaching of a foreign or second language. Their first-hand experience of this inevitably recedes into the past year by year. This is not necessarily a disqualification, but it certainly increases the likelihood of academics being remote from everyday classroom realities. Conversely, the *experts in the field* are committed to a succession of practical projects, but are divorced from any ongoing theoretical analysis of ELT, whether at the broad level of language-in-education aid projects, or a narrower field such as intercultural communication analysis.[11] They are not expected to become integrated into the local community, which might lead to in-depth understanding of local cultural norms and patterns. Centre ELT experts are not encouraged to develop a regional specialization (Bowers, interview). The capacity of those based in the Centre to contribute usefully in the Periphery seems to be doubted by experts working in the Periphery (*Dunford Seminar Report* 1987: 130). Universally relevant professionalism is therefore likely to be 'narrowly technical'.

The concentration on technical ELT skills, both in initial training and in the field, means that *vital dimensions* of the ELT operation are left relatively *unexplored*. Among them are the following:

- the role of English internationally, cultural and linguistic imperialism, foreign 'aid', hegemony
- the role of English in particular Periphery countries, nativization, its local origins and local cultural values
- comparative educational theory and psychology
- intercultural communication, communication in non-Western cultures
- language learning, language planning and policy in bilingual and bicultural communities.

These are areas which are of general relevance to any ELT inter-state actor. Activating them in a specific context assumes detailed familiarity with and understanding of the particular cultural norms and values that form the starting-point of learners in that context. Individual applied linguists may be acutely aware of the relevance of these dimensions and incorporate elements from them into their theories and course work. An example of theoretical work at the micro level of intercultural interpretive strategies will be referred to in the next section. But awareness of the political, economic, social and cultural framework in which ELT operates should not be relegated to fringe exploration or to the private domain. They are factors that decisively affect the success or otherwise of the technical skills and the pursuit of valid pedagogic and social goals.

English for special and new purposes

One specialization within ELT which would appear to be sensitive to broader aspects of the use of English is English for Special Purposes (ESP). Much ELT expert work is of this kind, involving attachment to specialist higher education institutions. ESP was promoted in the 1970s as an administratively convenient way of attempting to customize syllabuses for learners whose needs could be unambiguously identified. It is probable that 'communicative' language syllabuses have been inspired by the clarification of discourse structure and communicative roles that theoretical work in ESP has contributed to. However, there is now rather less faith in the capacity of the needs analysis apparatus (in particular Munby 1978) to actually contribute to constructive language learning, and a feeling that the missionary innovation spirit induced large numbers of countries to embrace and apply ESP inappropriately (Brumfit, interview). In a thought-provoking review of ESP, John Swales assesses that it has been too closely linked to the language sciences and too divorced from 'a considerable range of disciplines in the Social Sciences and the Humanities' (Swales 1985: 220). On the other hand there is fertile theory-building in this area, in relation to both the target discourse and pedagogy (reviewed ibid.). Some are attempting to relate ESP to an explicit language planning and development planning model (Markee 1989). There is also increasing technical sophistication in implementing practical projects (Higgs 1986).

A crucial factor in the success of any ESP operation, as for ELT as a whole, is whether implementation is sensitive enough to the contexts in which it is to serve, and whether the staff in question have been trained in an adequate, critical, and theoretically valid way. ESP has the advantage of having limited objectives, learners who have completed general education, with mother tongues which are not at risk. The interesting question then arises as to whether some of the valid principles of ESP could be of direct relevance to mainstream ELT in periphery-English schools. If English is being learnt there for communication purposes, cannot the essential determinants be specified?

Candlin has brought together insights from many humanities and social sciences disciplines into a set of assumptions which underpin intercultural interpretive strategies and that should govern 'applied linguistic practice' (Candlin 1983: 144). The main elements are:

- to sensitize the learner to the cultural presuppositions which imbue particular utterances
- that the relationship between sense and force depends on continuous evaluation of the social views of speaker/hearers
- that there are culture-specific rules of discourse, and some pan-cultural rules, and these are the chief objective of language learning

- that such rules are realized in interaction—language learning data must therefore be transactional
- that the linguistic and paralinguistic signs necessary for such interaction are culturally and socially specific
- that the process of deriving meaning is one of dynamic inference
- that meanings are therefore plural and variable as communication proceeds
- that identifying strategies of interpretation can both serve to elucidate discourse and act as a language-learning objective.

As Candlin points out (ibid.), the effect of acting on these assumptions would dramatically alter the nature of most ELT materials in current use, except in the area of ESP, and alter many of our treasured methodologies. It is also clear that only bilingual, bicultural experts would be in a position to function adequately as teachers in such a cross-cultural learning context. Likewise that 'English' in many ESL contexts would be a nativized variant which reflected local cultural meanings. Furthermore the pedagogy associated with such an approach requires the learner to be the expert on what is learnt and to participate in deciding on, or at least monitoring, how it is learnt. Candlin's proposal thus challenges orthodoxy at many levels. Successful implementation of such a programme would lead not only to greater proficiency in English, but to increased metacommunicative and metacultural awareness. There is therefore a wider socio-political or macro dimension implicit in the proposal. This element is made more explicit in a teacher training programme designed to qualify teachers to teach according to these principles (Candlin 1985). One of the principles in this scheme is to make the ideological dimensions of the teaching-learning situation explicit, and situate them socially, culturally, educationally, and politically (ibid.: 115).

ELT conducted along such lines could make a break with anglocentric professionalism and serve to promote awareness of linguicism. It is one example of how ELT could potentially be used for quite new purposes. However linguicism, like racism, is not a 'problem' that will disappear if people are well-informed about it. Attitudes are embedded in structure, and structural change is also needed. This presupposes a redefinition of 'aid'.

Jernudd's suggestions for *reforming* language education practices and the content of 'aid' in the language field potentially strike at the heart of scientific and educational imperialism. At root they question the legitimacy and validity of a great deal of the pure and applied linguistic trainirĺg offered in the Centre. They attempt to correct the imbalance between the considerable support given to dominant languages and the relative neglect of dominated languages. A logical consequence of following Jernudd's suggestions would be that aid donor countries should, for instance in the case of Namibia, provide more support for teacher training and curriculum development work for Namibian languages than for English. Likewise, general educational and language planning theory should be firmly rooted in the problems of countries with grassroots multilingualism, rather than in the Western monolingual model.

This is in essence what the Nigerian researcher, Adebisi Afolayan recommends (1984: 4) when pleading for a restricted role for English and authentic development for local languages:

> . . . the English language now dominates the Nigerian educational system and through it the direction and success of the nation's multilingual and multicultural development. Until now, the role of English has not been proper and the national development, unwholesome. It is therefore time to place the English language in its proper place as a second language within the Nigerian educational system so that the colonially-enforced bilingualism/biculturalism may now be directed voluntarily along clearly identified and defined objectives and goals of self-respecting and nationally-inspired development.

It appears that very little British aid has been channelled into support for languages other than English. Few linguists from the Periphery have been brought over on scholarships for mother tongue training, for instance at the School of Oriental and African Studies in London. Roger Bowers has attempted to trace exact figures in British Council records, and found it difficult to elucidate. His estimate was that 'the number would be absolutely minute over the last twenty years' (Bowers, interview). Such training would in any case not be ideal, for the reasons given when training in Zambian languages in London was discussed. Expertise in teacher training with a multilingual focus and related theoretical work is manifestly in short supply both in Britain and in other Centre countries. There is more expertise in other parts of the Periphery, for instance at the Central Institute for Indian Languages in Mysore, India. In addition to working out their own solutions locally, there is a need for Periphery countries to strengthen their links with each other.

Those at the helm of ELT are fully aware of the need to improve what Centre universities offer and the practical management of aid projects. Roger Bowers (interview) would like to see an increased involvement of university ELT depart- ments in the management and monitoring of ELT aid projects, and feels that ODA ought to fund such activity so as to increase the expertise and insight of academics, and ultimately improve the training of recruits to ELT. Such a scheme could serve to consolidate institutional links between British and overseas institutions. Henry Widdowson (interview) feels that the present provision of postgraduate ELT training in Britain should be made more flexible, and that what should be aimed at is links with 'local universities, teacher training centres, educational ministries, and so on, so as to stimulate local operations and local continuing teacher development programmes . . . to enable them to call the tune and to develop the thing subsequently for themselves . . . MAs need to become critical, sceptical of any kind of solution that anyone might want to provide them from a laboratory or research library . . . local people have to be aware of how research should be interpreted, and one needs to breed a kind of scepticism, a kind of positive critical stance.'

This section has attempted a brief, and inevitably selective look at recent developments in ELT, and some examples of awareness of the issues connected with the 'professionalism' of ELT aid among leading ELT people. What emerges is the existence of a profession in which there is fertile academic discourse, revealing an urge to reform the dominant tradition and act innovatively. In principle the examples of teaching (ESP and Candlin's reformed applied linguistic practice) presuppose teachers who are qualified, culturally and linguistically, for each local socio-political context. Whether ELT 'experts' who have been trained in a narrow technical way and whose expertise is politically disconnected, would in fact be qualified to function in any given context is an open question. If linguicism or English linguistic imperialism are in operation, then the structure may assure that there is a 'demand' for Centre native-speakers, even if they are not ideally qualified. The nature of this 'demand' and the arguments used to legitimate English and ELT expertise will be discussed in the next chapter.

Although this section has some examples of the direction that change should move in if the linguistic human rights of learners in multilingual periphery-English contexts are to be respected, and more relevant professional aid provided, it has not explored at all the complex questions of how professional counter-hegemonies can be constituted and legitimated, nor the fundamental question of how structural change can be effected, and what sort of power needs to be acquired in order to permit change. These are major issues which need analysis in their own right, but which will have to wait for a future occasion. The same applies to aid that can support popular grassroots movements, which some Scandinavian projects now attempt. The British Council's commitment in South Africa is explicitly to provide educational aid to disadvantaged communities which are victims of apartheid (*British Council Annual Report* 1989/90: 25). In such contexts the role that English and ELT should play raises complex questions which revolve around the basic issue of what advantages and disadvantages follow if support is given to and through a dominant language. That English can be successfully projected as a language of liberation is clearly demonstrated by the example of Namibia. The role of ELT experts in legitimating English specifically in the Namibian context will be explored in the coming chapter.

Notes

1   Bernard Lott (interview), who headed the British Council's ELT operations from the mid-1960s to the mid-1970s, reports that on a couple of occasions high-ranking academics were commissioned to analyse a given problem, and that their reports were voluminous but concluded that not enough was known about the situation. The lesson drawn was that it was not the Council's job to foster large-scale studies. This description fits exactly with Beretta's analysis (1990) of the mismatch between scholarly evaluation and the policy-shaping community.

2   The first test was the 'Davies' test, named after its progenitor, Alan Davies, which later appeared in a revised edition, and gave way in 1980 to an English Language Testing Service more oriented towards English for Special Purposes.

3   Bernard Spolsky is currently researching into the origins of testing on both sides of the Atlantic (personal communication).

4   The research needs identified by Davies remain within a
    fairly narrow conception of applied linguistics. His list of
    research topics covers classroom processes, teacher pre-
    paredness, the role of L1s and languages of wider commun-
    ication (implicitly within education only), attitudes to
    languages and education, the dissemination of research
    findings, and costs (Davies 1986: 12). This list is conserv-
    ative and scarcely lives up to his own specification of what
    is needed within a multidisciplinary applied linguistics
    approach to the issues. His reasoning, when situating
    language in education in applied linguistics, is also circular:
    'From our point of view language in education is an
    Applied Linguistics interest. The value of thus locating
    language in education within Applied Linguistics is that it
    allows us to recognize that language in education is not a
    problem that belongs elsewhere but that it is a language
    issue and can and must be tackled from considerations of
    sociolinguistics, language planning, language in relation to
    politics and general questions of language teaching studies,
    all matters that belong within the concerns of Applied
    Linguistics' (ibid.: 2).

5   The sheer volume of this operation is staggering. Between
    1950 and 1964 the USIA assisted in the production of 9,000
    editions and printed 80 million copies in 51 languages
    (Altbach 1975: 233, quoting figures from the National
    Foreign Trade Council).

6   A complete catalogue of books in the Educational Low-
    priced Books Scheme is published by International Book
    Development Ltd. It also lists the nearly 90 countries in
    which the books are available.

7   Obura also notes the need to develop terminology in this
    area. She suggests dividing Second Language learning into
    SLI (*immigrant* context) and SLS (Third World *school*
    context) (Obura 1986: 438). Her suggested binary pair fails
    to distinguish adequately between child and adult learners,
    and clearly 'school' and 'immigrant' do not exclude each
    other. This demonstrates the need for more detailed labels.

8   John Webb and John Sinclair report 'an almost universal
    feeling among those involved in aid training projects that
    the relationship is in a curious way unsatisfying. It is a
    commonly held view that resources are wasted in one way
    or another . . . The need to avoid any waste on a tight

budget is reinforced by the pressure to demonstrate success in a notoriously capricious and unpredictable area of human endeavour, namely teaching and learning' (Webb and Sinclair 1986: 7). Such projects generally take place outside formal education systems. Their conclusion is that there is a need for ELT experts to be trained as effective managers and administrators. This tallies with British Council policy *vis-à-vis* their own teaching operations and the 'aid' projects that they oversee. Roger Bowers reports that as compared with a few years ago there is now a 'more managed set of projects in the sense that there are objectives, time scales, balances written in between the external expertise and local inputs, the training of counterparts, and so on' (Bowers, interview).

9   There have always been differences of style between the British and the Americans. According to Bernard Lott, the British 'didn't have a sufficiently developed set of tenets to take them out with missionary zeal, whereas in the early to mid-1950s Georgetown was sending out young Americans to teach EFL convinced with religious zeal that there was only one way—structural mim-mem' (Lott, interview). Peter Strevens is reported to have summed up the differences in the British and American approaches at the 1986 conference of the International Association of Teachers of English as a Foreign Language by saying 'there is a tendency for the American approach to look for an answer and then apply it, and for the British approach to recognize that there are no answers and try everything' (Bowers, interview). Strevens's clarification of British eclecticism was that 'in Britain and Europe we are taught that anyone who thinks he has a monopoly of the truth is probably a charlatan, and we will find bits of the truth in different places, and part of our training is to make syntheses which we develop as we go along' (Strevens, interview).

10 In the context of the language-in-education project in Sierra Leone that Hayes describes, she identifies many causal factors accounting for poor English learning (Hayes 1983: 17), and discovers that the 'Sierra Leoneans have the professional expertise to remedy the ELT situation by themselves. They have a framework whereby the remedy can be administered.' She overcomes her doubts as to whether she ought to be there at all, and as a result the

policy becomes 'to help the Sierra Leoneans in what they are already doing in ELT and co-ordinate their efforts' (ibid.: 18). If 'aid' projects are increasingly to take the form of managerial work of this kind, which traditional ELT training does not cover, one wonders whether it is not the Sierra Leoneans who ought to be given the necessary management training rather than Centre experts who come and go.

11   Intercultural communication is naturally a topic that some 'aid' work is sensitive to. See for instance the brief presentation of 'Cross-cultural differences in the Arab World' by Clive Holes (in Higgs 1986: 192). The project deals with communication difficulties between native speakers of English and native speakers of Arabic, examples of which are given. The title of the project is revealingly anglocentric. What is implicit in it is that we are regarded as the norm, whereas the Arabs are different (otherwise the name of the project leads one to believe that it deals with differences between Arabs from different parts of the Arab world when communicating with each other). See also the description by Maurice Broughton of a Thai distance-education project (in Higgs 1986: 166) which appropriately builds on 'socio-cultural and linguistic differences between Thai and English, from a Thai perspective'. On differences in learning style in higher education in India and Britain, see Hasan 1976.

9 Arguments in linguistic imperialist discourse

> ... the latest ideas in English teaching. Where best, after all, to get the latest ideas on this than in the English-speaking countries.
> (Quirk 1990: 8)

Types of argument and types of power

We shall now look in more depth at typical arguments that are used to promote English, and relate them to a theory of power.[1] The examples to be analysed say something about how English is 'sold'. They attribute characteristics to the English language, describe the resources that follow with the language, or suggest a promise of what will ensue if more English is used in a given country, in an education system, or in personal or professional life.

The arguments are articulated in academic and political discourse. They also interact with popular sentiment so that such arguments become part of and draw nourishment from the 'common sense' that typifies hegemonic beliefs and practices. Arguments show applied linguists making statements which legitimate English in a wider context. The arguments are put forward from a professional platform, but they exemplify applied linguists entering the wider political arena. The arguments demonstrate the legitimation of English linguistic imperialism in the wider context of a hierarchy of languages and the crystallization of official language policy.

The arguments used to promote English can be classified into three sets, relating to

- capacities: English-intrinsic arguments, what English *is*
- resources: English-extrinsic arguments, what English *has*
- uses: English-functional arguments, what English *does*.

English-intrinsic arguments describe English as rich, varied, noble, well adapted for change, interesting, etc. English-extrinsic

arguments refer to textbooks, dictionaries, grammar books, a
rich literature, trained teachers, experts, etc. English-functional
arguments credit English with real or potential access to
modernization, science, technology, etc., with the capacity to
unite people within a country and across nations, or with the
furthering of international understanding.

The conceptual framework for analysing power developed by
Galtung (1980: 62) identifies three types of power, innate
power, resource power, and structural power. The means used
to assert power are respectively persuasion, bargaining, or force.
Power requires senders and receivers, as 'power is a relation, not
a property or attribute of somebody or something' (ibid.: 63).
For persuasion to work presupposes some kind of submissive-
ness, bargaining some kind of dependency, and force an element
of fear. But underpinning the discourse in which power is
negotiated, constituted, and affirmed is the structure which
supports the actors whose pronouncements we shall be analysing. This structure is an imperialist world order, in which
English is the dominant world language. The supremacy of
English needs to be constantly reasserted in the hierarchical
ordering of languages, in which there are competing dominant
languages, both internationally and intranationally, and in
which even dominated languages may be able to assert their
rights, especially intra-nationally.

So far as the power of English is concerned, the actors we shall
be concerned with are the language itself, and the resources it
commands (materials, people, for instance teachers and applied
linguists, intra- and inter-state actors) which serve to reproduce
or create knowledge of English. The uses to which the language
is put, the functions it serves, form part of the structure in which
the actors operate.

The advocates for English have successfully projected an idea
of the community which English speakers make up, both a local
and an international community. Establishing the idea of such a
community involves an active feat of the imagination, and in this
way parallels the way a sense of nationalism is created
(Anderson 1983). Nations are actively 'constructed' by being
imagined. 'All communities larger than primordial villages of
face-to-face contact (and perhaps even these) are imagined . . .
(The nation) is imagined as a *community*, because, regardless of
the actual inequality and exploitation that may prevail in each,
the nation is always conceived as a deep, horizontal comrade-

ship' (ibid.: 15–6). The community of English is imagined similarly, and comradeship is created in an ascription process equating English with bounty and other languages with the opposite. The promise of English is increasingly identified with a community of English users who are economically privileged, in a world of inequalities and exploitation. This privilege is due to the structural favouring of English, nationally and internationally.

Galtung's three types of power are listed in the first two columns of Table 1. The remaining two columns juxtapose the arguments for English in the three categories:

Innate power	being-power	English *is*	English-intrinsic
Resource power	having-power	English *has*	English-extrinsic
Structural power	position-power	English *does*	English-functional

Table 1   Types of power and arguments for English

Structural power can, according to Galtung, lead to resource power, and vice versa. One form of power 'is convertible to another: structural power into accumulation of resources, resource power into sufficient command of the structure to get into positions of structural power' (ibid.: 64). The analysis of the discourse of English linguistic imperialism will attempt to trace the interconnections between the resource and structural power of English.

The arguments in each category will now be analysed as symptoms of the power inherent in the discourse in which they appear.

English-intrinsic arguments

Innate power derives from exceptional qualities which permit the power sender to influence many receivers. But just as exceptional muscles or charisma are not God-given, but to some extent the product of socialization, what English *is* is not God-given either, even if it is sometimes described as such (as seen in the observation by the Chairman of the British Council about English as a 'God-given asset', quoted in Chapter 6).

Linguists also invoke the supernatural, probably more metaphorically:

In becoming something close to a universal language English
has accomplished something close to a linguistic miracle.
(Kachru and Quirk 1981: xiv)

Next best to divine intervention is a God-given civilizing
mission, the white man's burden. In the heyday of imperialism,
the English felt 'genuinely confident in the superior fitness of
England for any work she may essay in the civilization of the
world' (Hobson 1902: 160), a sentiment that patriotic French-
men, Germans, and Russians each also ascribed to themselves
(ibid.: 159). In direct continuation of this tradition, the civilizing
mission for teachers of English, the educated native speaker's
burden, was formulated, as recently as 1961, at the Nutford
House conference:

> . . . we have to remember that the major reason for supporting
> and sustaining the study of our literature in African or Asian
> countries, the major reason which lies outside the usefulness
> of literary studies as improving competence in language, is
> that our literature is itself the major product of a great
> civilization. It is this which our literature has to offer to
> Africans and Asians.
>
> Many of the nationalities we are concerned with have no
> literature of their own. A language like Persian, of course,
> does have its own literature. But we should have in mind, I
> think, that even with, say, Asian nations which have a
> literature of their own, it is often the case that this literature is
> of a thoroughly different kind from our own or from any
> major European literature; and it does not offer many great
> things that those literatures do offer. An Asiatic literature
> which consists of devotional mystical prose and fifteenth
> century court poems using a specially allusive diction is
> obviously going to offer something quite different from the
> languages in which there are great novels of the contemporary
> world.
> (Holloway 1961: 45–6)

This pretentious argument for what English (literature) *is* —the
innate power of English—is in the same vein as English as a
'vehicle of the entire developing human tradition', past, present
and future, in the words of I. A. Richards at the Anglo-American
Conference on English Teaching Abroad, also in 1961. Of
similar ilk is the equation made between English and deprivation
by Burchfield (1985), quoted in Chapter 1. Holloway's legitim-

ation for English is an echo of the century-old tradition of Macaulay. Having 'analysed' how his compatriots, the Orientalists, were construing other cultures, he concluded:

> I have no knowledge of either Sanskrit or Arabic. But I have done what I could to form a correct estimate of their value . . . I am quite ready to take the Oriental learning at the valuation of the Orientalists themselves. I have never found one among them who could deny that a single shelf of a good European library was worth the whole native literature of India and Arabia.
> (quoted in Sharp 1920; see also equivalent passages in Trevelyan 1881: 290)

Influential linguists, past and present, have also been effusive when describing the innate qualities of what English *is*:

> It must be a source of gratification to mankind that the tongue spoken by two of the greatest powers of the world is so noble, so rich, so pliant, so expressive, and so interesting.
> (Jespersen 1905: 234)

> English possesses a great range of rules for the formation of new words . . . English, it would seem, is well adapted for development and change.
> (Strevens 1980: 85)

> English has moved beyond its traditional home in the North Atlantic towards a unique non-national, non-regional, non-ethnic stature as the world's first truly global language. It has even been spoken on the moon. (Editorial comment in the preview issue of *English Today: the international review of the English language*, 1984).

> . . . since no cultural requirements are tied to the learning of English, you can learn it without having to subscribe to another set of values . . . tied to no particular social, political, economic, or religious system, nor to a specific racial or cultural group, English belongs to everyone or to no one, or it at least is quite often regarded as having this property.
> (Wardhaugh 1987: 15)

> I have never doubted the existence of a universal interest in the English language . . . The language seems to provide a talking-point for everyone.
> (Crystal 1984)

If one conflates the English-intrinsic arguments, one can conclude that English *is* God-given, civilizing, noble, a vehicle of the entire developing human tradition, well adapted for change and development, not ethnic or ideological, the world's first truly global language, of universal interest. The conclusion would seem to be that you are in a very real sense deprived if you do not know it.

As power is relational, the arguments for the innate qualities of English are generally marshalled in discourse which also categorizes the power of other languages, as several of the examples quoted below will demonstrate. Other languages are either explicitly or implicitly identified as not being endowed with equivalent qualities; for instance other languages are ideological or nationalistic, whereas it is argued that English is not (as in the British Cabinet Report analysed in Chapter 6). Apologists for English are inconsistent here: arguments for the non-ethnic nature of English rub shoulders with the 'opportunity' or 'responsibility' of the British to meet the demand for English; likewise, English can scarcely be tied to no system and simultaneously symbolize progress.

Some of the English-intrinsic arguments may be plausible *vis-à-vis* most languages (non-national, for instance), but even they are less easy to sustain in relation to competing 'international' languages such as French, whose protagonists invoke equally linguicist arguments for it (French as logical, elegant, the language of human rights, etc).[2] Linguists are trained to see any language as potentially fulfilling any function, hence not intrinsically superior or inferior to any other language. Other languages are equally 'well adapted for change and development', and may indeed have a simpler structure, morphological, syntactic or phonetic, which renders them more flexible and productive, and arguably easier to learn. Even if English-intrinsic arguments are therefore not often accorded much prominence, the examples demonstrate that the underlying linguicism of innateness is still very much alive and kicking. There is also a tendency for English-intrinsic arguments to blend into arguments of the other two types.

English-extrinsic arguments

Material resources (a gun, books, capital) are often deployed along with immaterial resources (knowledge and skills). Material resources, for instance wealth, can be converted into immaterial resources, such as formal knowledge and skills.

As we know, English *has* both material resources (trained teachers, teacher trainers, teaching materials, literature, dictionaries, multinational publishers, computers and software, BBC English by Radio and TV, low-priced books schemes, etc.) and immaterial resources (knowledge, skills, know-how via its 'experts', etc.). The following quotation illuminates how English-extrinsic resources are displayed, in a planning document written by 'aid' experts for an underdeveloped country, Namibia, when about to choose an official language. The extract also anticipates several of the English-functional arguments of the following section, which enumerate further 'possessions' of English:

> . . . well-established techniques of implementing the use of English exist both for foreign students in Britain and other English speaking countries and in countries where English is learnt as a foreign or second language (EFL-ESL) through organizations such as the British Council and Unesco, as well as many university departments. Furthermore, there are many professionals available with long experience in teaching and developing English programmes throughout the world, and in using or adapting the wealth of English learning materials developed in past years . . . The latest published sources concerning scientific and technological development are printed in English, worldwide, and make English probably the leading international library language for reference and research.
> (UNIN 1981: 40)[3]

Publicity from organizations involved in the teaching of English or of applied linguistics necessarily specifies what physical and intellectual resources they have available. Because of the purpose of such documentation, it declares, faithfully one presumes, what English *has*.

Publicity material for books has a similar legitimatory function, with resources often explicitly linked to learning. Randolph Quirk, the eminent grammarian, in a preface to the recent *Longman Dictionary of Contemporary English* (1987), declares that bilingual dictionaries are a need in the initial stages of foreign language learning, whereas a monolingual dictionary is essential for 'free creative expression'. These are highly disputable propositions, on which the views of experts on foreign language learning might be more relevant than those of a grammarian. His claim about progression from a bilingual to a monolingual dictionary is also in fact in conflict with research evidence quoted elsewhere by Della Summers, the Editorial Director of the same Longman dictionary, namely that 'most students prefer to use a bilingual dictionary no matter how small or old, either exclusively or in addition to a good monolingual' (1988: 11). Quirk's pronouncements may appear to be insignificant sales blurb, but they faithfully reflect the ELT professionalism endorsed at Makerere (and which Quirk regards himself as having been only peripherally involved in, interview). In the same vein, teaching materials published by Longman for West Africa specifically warn against the use of bilingual dictionaries, and recommend monolingual dictionaries from Britain (Bevan and Grant 1983: 12). These examples of professional advocacy when marketing the resources of English are of dubious scientific and ethical quality. Nor are they isolated aberrations. They fit into the wider picture of global monolingualism which is central to English linguistic imperialism.

English-extrinsic arguments frequently dovetail with descriptions of the inadequacy of other languages, this reflecting the relational aspect of the power of languages. Gilbert Ansre, the Ghanaian linguist, has analysed the falsity of 'Four rationalizations for maintaining European languages in education in Africa'. He has distilled the rationalizations from statements from a cross-section of educated West Africans, 'officials of Ministries of Education and other civil servants, military personnel, economists, political scientists, teachers, businessmen, and erstwhile politicians' (1979: 11). He also stresses that the number of highly-placed people who subscribe to the rationalizations is 'very substantial and the conviction with which they hold them is very deep-rooted' (ibid.).

One of the rationalizations is: 'Since we need rapid technological development and yet since none of the languages is "developed" enough for use in giving modern technological education, we must teach in the languages which have a highly developed technical and scientific terminology and concepts' (ibid.). He refutes the argument by pointing out that European languages were once 'barbaric', that the language planning experience for Swahili and Hebrew is instructive, and that the terminology issue is irrelevant to the real needs of children in elementary education.

English-extrinsic arguments are frequently linked to the inordinate cost of building up equivalent resources in other languages. A second of the rationalizations in Ansre's study is: 'The cost of producing educational material in indigenous languages is excessive in both money and human effort' (ibid.). He rejects the argument, partly on the grounds that it reflects an internalization of linguistic imperialist attitudes, partly because the cost argument cannot be divorced from the inappropriacy of both current education and the economic models that underpin it. One consequence of these is that '. . . a great deal of drop-outs and failure cases in schools in Africa are due to lack of ability to manipulate the language of education adequately' (ibid.: 13).

The English *has* arguments glorify English, and the resources which other languages and multilingual countries have are either made invisible or regarded as handicaps rather than riches. The parlous state of publishing in Africa is a direct consequence of the relative dominance of British publishing in Africa, and a reflection of the material and immaterial resources that have been allocated to each.

It is an incontrovertible fact that English has a lot of resources, and there are clear historical reasons for this being so. The structural power of English has generated English-extrinsic resources, just as the English-extrinsic resources have consolidated the structural power of English. Present-day English-extrinsic resources are a direct result of the planning papers and conferences of the decade from the mid-1950s which triggered the expansion of ELT worldwide, and ensured that the agenda was decided on by the Centre. The unequal resources of the Centre and the Periphery reflect the pattern of English linguistic imperialism in the past. Moreover it is the present-day imperialist structure which perpetuates the development of English and the underdevelopment of other languages. The continued unequal allocation of resources to English prevents other languages from developing their own resources. English-extrinsic arguments which refer to English as the language of technology or to the prohibitive cost of developing other languages serve the linguicist purpose of maintaining the inequalities between English as a dominant language and the dominated state of others. They obscure the fact, as Ansre points out, that many of the English-extrinsic resources may be inappropriate for deployment in a Periphery education system with learners from a multilingual background whose basic need is that resources should be allocated to their own languages.

English-functional arguments

The third type of argument refers to what English *does*. The functions carried out through English reflect the structural power of the position of English in the hierarchy of languages, nationally and internationally. The position of English as the international language *par excellence* was sketched out in Chapter 1. Something of the structural power of English, what English *does* or *can do*, can be gleaned from the following quotations. (In addition, parts of the arguments cited earlier have included elements of the English-functional arguments.) Along with the resources that English *has*, underdeveloped countries also need what English *gives access to*.

The first quotation comes from the *Makerere Report*, 1961. English was portrayed as a panacea:

> to improve and extend the use of English as a gateway to better communications, better education, and so a higher standard of living and better understanding.
> (*Makerere Report* 1961: 47)

The next two arguments come from papers on language policy for Namibia, the second of which describes relevant Zambian experience:

> In all branches of science and technology, including medicine, English is paramount as an international medium for offering direct access to workers and specialists in these areas.
> (UNIN 1981: 40)

> . . . we have found it necessary in Zambia to adopt English as the official language in order to facilitate the administration of the country and the transfer of personnel from one language zone to another . . . here in Zambia, English is used as the medium of instruction in all our educational institutions. In addition, it is the language of the civil service, of business, industry and commerce. It is pertinent to mention also the requirement that all candidates in the general election taking place next week must be proficient in English, and any candidate who is found lacking in that respect can be disqualified from standing. We have found this provision

necessary in order to provide a neutral language for communication within the National Assembly, which helps
overcome regional differences and ensures that no particular
advantage is given to one language group.
(Nalumino Mundia, Prime Minister of Zambia, in Commonwealth Secretariat and SWAPO 1983: 6–7)

These quotations fit into the pattern of the remaining two
rationalizations cited by Ansre:

The world is 'shrinking' and pupils need an international
language to be able to have dealings with people from
different countries and large groups. With so many languages
and tribes in the country, there are tendencies towards
tribalism and divisiveness and therefore it is better to use a
neutral foreign language to achieve national unity.
(1979: 11)

He refutes the 'shrinking world' argument by showing that
elementary education does not have the function of making
children international personages, and that it is essential to
educate them in a local language first. On the 'detribalization'
argument his rejoinder is that multilingual realities should
provide a foundation for sound education and nation-building,
that there is no causal relationship between lack of ability to
speak African languages and the presence or absence of
'tribalism', and that foreign languages create an élite alienated
from the rest of the population.

The labels currently used in political and academic discourse
to describe English are almost invariably positive ascriptions. By
implication other languages lack these properties or are inferior.[4]
In Table 2, the first column lists labels commonly attributed to
English, and the second column possible implications for other
languages. Significantly, all the labels are English-functional.
What is dangerous about the labels is the assumed isomorphy
between English and the ascriptions, and the concomitant
exclusion of other languages. For instance, English is not the
only 'language of wider communication'. You can get further
with a south Slavic language like Serbocroatian in Central Asia,
or with Finnish in northern Norway, than with English. Equally,
many languages are international link languages. A second
objection to the labels is that calling English a 'world' language
falsely implies that English is universally relevant. Under the

Glorifying English	Devaluing other languages
– World language	– Localized language
– International language	– (Intra-) national language
– Language of wider communication	– Language of narrower communication
– Auxiliary language	– Unhelpful language
– Additional language	– Incomplete language
– Link language	– Confining language
– Window onto the world	– Closed language
– Neutral language	– Biased language

Table 2 The labelling of English and other languages

pressure of such labels and arguments, what is happening in some ESL contexts is that English is displacing and replacing local languages rather than functioning as an 'auxiliary' or 'additional' language.

Kachru too has brought together a number of labels and classified them as positive or negative (1986b: 136):

Positive	Negative
– National identity	– Anti-nationalism
– Literary renaissance	– Anti-native culture
– Cultural mirror (for native cultures)	– Materialism
– Modernization	– Westernization
– Liberalism	– Rootlessness
– Universalism	– Ethnocentricism
– Technology	– Permissiveness
– Science	– Divisiveness
– Mobility	– Alienation
– Access code	

Table 3 Labels used to symbolize power of English

Again, virtually all the labels are English-functional, although the context of their use is an intranational one. Kachru concedes that some labels, such as 'Westernization', can belong in either category, depending on who is using them. There is a similar problem with several of his 'negative' labels. In some contexts, English is legitimated precisely because it is supposed to unite the various people who make up a nation, whereas here it is associated with 'divisiveness'. 'Alienation' and 'rootlessness' (negatives) are symptomatic of 'modern' culture (positive). English is marketed as 'non-ethnic' and 'national' (positive), but here linked to 'ethnocentricism' (negative). With so many conflicting ascriptions, it is perhaps not surprising that Kachru diagnoses linguistic schizophrenia (1984: 193), with many individuals protesting against the exploitative nature of English but ensuring that they benefit from the language structurally themselves.

Whereas with English-extrinsic arguments, there was no doubt about the existence of the resource power in question, with English-functional arguments there is a more problematical relationship between the claims put forward in the arguments and the structural power of English. The discussion so far has indicated how subjective the connotations of each label are, and that, as with Ansre's 'shrinking world' and 'tribalism' arguments, they may be irrelevant or false. There are significant biases in many of the English-functional arguments. 'International' or 'global' links are of greater significance for élites than the child in primary school or even secondary school. 'National unity' is not something that any language can guarantee, just as proclaiming a single official language cannot wish away a multilingual reality. English-functional arguments need therefore to be examined critically whenever they are used, and this will be done in a specific context below. On the face of it, because of their inherent vagueness (and untestability) and the implicit or even explicit stigmatization of other languages, there is a strong likelihood of the arguments being used to legitimate English linguistic imperialism.

The means used to exert linguistic power

We can now consider these arguments in relation to Galtung's tripartite classification of power being based on ideas (persuasion), carrots (bargaining), or sticks (force).

Most of the arguments try to *persuade* us of the superior merits of English and the failings of other languages. This type of argumentation has a long pedigree, going back at least to the

Greeks. When French became the dominant European language, there was a strong tradition, from du Bellay onwards, of linguicist discourse (Calvet 1987). The British, as the quotations from Lord Macaulay and Matthew Arnold in the nineteenth century and Holloway in the twentieth show, have not lagged far behind.

Other arguments *promise* goods and services to those who accept English—science and technology, modernity, efficiency, rationality, progress, a great civilization. These tempting 'carrots' are often compared with what other languages can offer. These offerings are presented as a negative counterpart to what English offers: traditionalism instead of modernity, superstition instead of rationality, divisiveness instead of unity, etc. The way English and underdeveloped languages were treated in the *Makerere Report* is typical of this discourse. An unstated assumption of the Zambian Prime Minister is that benefits accrue to a 'modern' state from the use of English.

In some of the arguments quoted there are also covert or even overt *threats*. They hint at what is going to happen if people stick to their own languages and reject the gospel of English. For instance, refusal to back English is often associated with conflict, and the fact that English as a common language has not created harmony in Northern Ireland, Uganda, or Nigeria is conveniently ignored. The Prime Minister of Zambia, when congratulating SWAPO of Namibia on their choice of English as an official language, uses both the cost and conflict arguments:

> I am glad that SWAPO has opted for English as an official language, for basic practical reasons. It has, I feel, been correct in resisting the costly, futile, and potentially divisive option of giving pre-eminence to one local African language.
> (Nalumino Mundia, in Commonwealth Secretariat and SWAPO 1983: 6)

Threats also characterize the right-wing backlash against any recognition of immigrant languages in core-English countries. Thus, according to Senator Huddleston, the purpose of bilingual education in the USA is 'to deliberately fragment the Nation into separate, unassimilated groups', whereas 'our common meeting ground, namely the English language' ensures that Americans will not 'suffer the bitterness of ethnic confrontations and cultural separation'. This is because '. . . in countless places, differences in languages have either caused or contributed significantly to political, social, and economic instability' (quoted in Marshall 1986: 60). Marshall and 17 other scholars in the same issue of the *International Journal of the Sociology of Language* refute such claims by adherents of the English Language Amendment (ELA) to the US Constitution (the 'US English' movement) convincingly. Most of them point out that there are undeclared political and economic interests behind such claims.

Another protagonist argues that 'most international and intranational wars have been caused primarily by differences in religions, political philosophies, races, and cultures—and languages. Language diversity has been a major cause of conflict' (Imhoff 1987: 40). This is a myth, which Fishman in extensive cross-polity studies has been concerned to debunk: 'the widespread journalistic and popular political wisdom that linguistic heterogeneity *per se* is necessarily conducive to civil strife has been shown, by our analysis, to be more myth than reality' (Fishman 1989: 622). Similarly Pattanayak (1988) has incisively rebutted the myth that many languages divide a nation.

Senator Hayakawa, Honorary Chairman of US English, has also used false arguments in support of the ELA: 'The longer they (non-English-speaking children) are instructed in the native tongue (through bilingual education programs) the more difficult it becomes for them to learn English in their later years' (quoted in Guerra 1988). It is unlikely that members of the general public, or many members of the Senate, will know that such a claim is contradicted by well-documented research evidence (see Cummins 1984; Skutnabb-Kangas 1987, 1991) and totally false.

Pressure from the IMF or World Bank for a particular type of economic reform may be accompanied by a demand that more focus should be placed on English. In the Philippines the export-oriented industrialization strategy has been linked to strengthening English, the result being disastrous for the Filipinos but effective in protecting US neo-colonial interests (Enriquez and Marcelino 1984: 4).

All these arguments represent various ways of exerting and legitimating power. Not surprisingly, those who represent English linguistic hegemony do *not* come with arguments which stress what English *is not*, does *not have* and does *not do*. For children whose mother tongue is not English, English is *not* the language of their cultural heritage, *not* the language of intense personal feelings and the community, *not* the language most appropriate for learning to solve problems in cognitively demanding decontextualized situations, etc. English does *not* necessarily have teaching materials which are culturally appropriate, *nor* experts with the appropriate linguistic and cultural understanding for all learning contexts. In multi-ethnic, multilingual situations, English does *not* do what is claimed for it, often quite the opposite. Rather than uniting an entire country or helping to form a national identity, it is used for 'élite formation and preservation, intranational and international links between élites, and international identity' (Annamalai 1986: 9).

False arguments are articulated by representatives of the Periphery as well as the Centre, by élites who share common interests. The advocacy of the norms of the Centre by 'educated persons tutored in the modes of western thinking' (Pattanayak 1986d: vi) in language policy has had harmful effects on dominated languages and societies: 'These societies are then made permanent parasites on the developed countries for knowledge and information. By destroying interdependent self-directed societies, the élites in these countries achieve what colonialism failed to achieve through coercive occupation' (ibid.: vi). For Kashoki the explanation is simple: 'Africans have been psychologically conditioned to believe that only European languages are structured to aid development' (UNIN 1981: 41).

The sophistication of the arguments grows on a scale advancing from the use of force to the use of carrots to the use of ideas. At one stage, the colonial power could use coercion when selling one of its products, English. When the counterpart became slightly more equal, and brute force could no longer be applied or was no longer an ethically acceptable alternative, carrots were more suitable. But the ideal way to make people do what you want is of course to make them want it themselves, and to make them believe that it is good for them. This simplifies the role of the 'seller', who then can appear as 'helping' or 'giving aid', rather than 'forcing' or 'bargaining with' the victim. And this is what has happened in selling English too, as the quotation from the chairman of the British Council so pithily showed. When the British 'do not have the power we once had to impose our will' ('sticks'), cultural diplomacy must see to it that people see the benefits of English ('carrots') and the drawbacks with their own languages, and then, consequently, want English themselves for their own benefit ('ideas'): 'the demand is insatiable'. And that means that British influence, British power has not diminished, because Britain has this 'invisible, God-given asset'. Thus, 'Britain's influence endures, out of all proportion to her economic or military resources' (*British Council Annual Report* 1983/84: 9, see pp. 144-5).

What typically happens with this growing sophistication in 'selling' English is that the structures (that is, a capitalist world order) to be sold with the language are marketed with the help of cultural arguments, at the same time as this culture is disconnected from structure. The sellers of English use cultural, 'neutral' arguments and normally claim that what they are doing has nothing to do with political, economic, or military power. The cultural 'product', the 'goods' to be sold (English) is technicalized and professionalized. What is sold is presented as a technical instrument (like a tractor), not a world order. The instrument, the tool, can be used for better or for worse, and it is up to the buyer to decide on the use. Once the seller has handed over the product, it bears no trace of the context where it was developed. As an instrument it is presented as being completely neutral towards the uses to which it can be put. A tractor is a tractor, and you can transport a Muslim or a Hindu on it as well as a Christian. The tractor does not restrict you to transporting only certain types of load. English is an instrument, and you can speak or write whatever you want in it. Is not the point proven when texts which query English linguistic hegemony are written in English? Does it not show that English lends itself to any use?

Referring to a language as an instrument or tool, like a tractor, involves 'reifying one aspect of language, and not necessarily the most important . . . When linguists refer to language as an instrument, they are not describing its essential nature, only its purpose. "Instrument" or "tool" is merely a metaphor that is synonymous with "means" and contrasted with "end" or "purpose"' (Haugen 1971: 283).

Claiming that English is neutral (a tool, an instrument) involves a disconnection between what English *is* ('culture') from its structural basis (from what it *has* and *does*). It disconnects the *means* from *ends* or *purposes*, from what English is being used for. The type of reasoning we are dealing with here (and which Haugen also criticizes) is part of the rationalization process whereby the unequal power relations between English and other languages are explained and legitimated. It fits into the

familiar linguicist pattern of the dominant language creating an
exalted image of itself, other languages being devalued, and the
relationship between the two rationalized in favour of the
dominant language. This applies to each type of argument,
whether persuasion, bargaining, or threats are used, all of which
serve to reproduce English linguistic hegemony.

Arguments in language planning for Namibia

The case of language planning for Namibia will now be analysed,
in particular the key document, 'Toward a language policy for
Namibia. English as the official language: perspectives and
strategies' (UNIN 1981: 123). This contains an extremely
thorough survey of the language and educational scene in
Namibia, a distillation of relevant experience in adjacent
countries, a description of the options open to Namibia and
strategies for achieving language planning goals. The title page
states that the text is based on the work of three named scholars
attached to the United Nations Institute for Namibia (UNIN),
but not that one of them was a British Council employee, one an
American, and the third an Indian. The document was written
after an international conference, with strong British and
African representation, which was held to consider the implications of the choice of English as an official language for
Namibia. The Ford Foundation financed the publication.

Few underdeveloped countries have been in a position to plan
language policy properly in advance of independence, and to
learn from the experience of other countries. Namibia, until
1990 illegally occupied by South Africa, has, because of the
delayed advent of independence and major United Nations
support over two decades, been able to plan more thoroughly
than most countries.

Policy and plans for a liberated Namibia were articulated in a
series of publications from UNIN, an independent research and
teaching centre established to train a cadre of people to take over
the administration of the country after liberation. SWAPO
decided that English should be *an* official language in independent Namibia—though this became *the* official language in the
title of the report under analysis—and that the mother tongues
would be the medium of education at the lower primary level
and not neglected thereafter (SWAPO 1982: 40; Commonwealth Secretariat and SWAPO 1984). The intention was to

replace Afrikaans, then the dominant language in Namibia and the medium of education from upper primary level and sometimes even earlier, which was seen as the language of oppression, with English, which was seen paradoxically as a language of liberation. Less than 1 per cent of the population (mostly whites) have English as their mother tongue, while 15 per cent have Afrikaans. Only a small proportion are fluent in English as a second or foreign language. There are seven main language groups. The largest, Oshiwambo, accounts for more than 46 per cent of Namibians (UNIN, 1981: 3). Several of the languages were alphabetized a century ago. The vast majority of Namibians drop out of the education system and 60 per cent of the population is illiterate.

The criteria to be used when choosing an official language for independent Namibia are spelled out in UNIN 1981 (pp. 37–8). In a section setting out a rationale for English, it is stated that a major priority in post-independence Namibia for the new government will be 'to minimize any divisive tendencies and practices in the country on the one hand, and on the other hand, to reinforce all such factors that may contribute to national unity, i.e. to create conditions conducive to national unity, whether in the realm of politics, economics, religion, culture, race, or language' (ibid.: 37). It is also stated that South Africa has 'capitalized on and exploited the existence of various languages in Namibia . . . It has used language differences to create ethnic divisiveness. It has attempted to drive the people to focus on linguo-tribal affiliations and differences instead of national unity' (ibid.). The criteria have been chosen 'in view of the factors related to this perspective and the needs of an independent nation' (ibid.).

The full list of the criteria, selected as 'the most significant ones', for choosing an official language for Namibia can be seen in Table 4 below. The content of most of them is self-evident, but the following descriptions exemplify the way the language planners saw the criteria:

2 Acceptability: The chosen language should be one which in the specific case of Namibia has positive rather than negative associations for the people. This would mean avoiding languages that may be associated with the oppression and injustices which have characterized Namibian history, and which are still being perpetrated.

3 Familiarity: The language chosen should be one with

which Namibians both inside and outside the country have some familiarity and with which there has preferably been some experience in the educational system.

4 Feasibility, has to do with 'cost and effort involved in promoting a language to official status', 'whether the necessary resources are available', 'learning programmes . . . books and materials readily available', 'sufficient expatriate professionals . . . for teaching, teacher training, crash courses, curriculum design, educational administration', and 'training facilities'.
(UNIN 1981: 37)

After discussing the criteria *vis-à-vis* several possible languages or groups of languages, the conclusion is drawn that 'the choice of English as the main official language seems to be well supported' (ibid.: 40). Table 4 extracts and correlates the assessments in the text (in which they are not tabulated in any way) on the extent to which the various languages fulfill the demands of each criterion. The quantification system at the bottom of the table is not used in the report, but has been added so as to provide a more objective measure of the merits of each option. Three points have been allotted for a +, two points for a +/−, one point for a −/+, and no points for −. The result is a clear

	Indigenous languages	Afrikaans	German	French	English
1 Unity	−	−	−	+	+
2 Acceptability	+	−	−	+	+
3 Familiarity	+	+	+	−	+
4 Feasibility	−	+	+	+	+
5 Science and technology	−	−	+	+	+
6 Pan Africanism	−	−	−	−/+	+
7 Wider Communication	−	−	+	+	+
8 United Nations	−	−	−	+	+
Total points	**6**	**6**	**12**	**19**	**24**

Table 4 The suitability of selected languages as an official language for Namibia

progression from left to right, reflecting a hierarchy which could equally well have been established by totting up the number of states in which the respective languages are used.

The most striking feature of the exercise is the imbalance between giving separate treatment to three European languages (English, French, German) and one European-based language (Afrikaans), whereas all Namibia's own languages are lumped together into one category and none is given proper scrutiny. Other potentially relevant African languages, such as the major languages of southern Africa or Swahili, are not even considered. 'The two most widely spoken languages of South Africa are not Afrikaans and English, but Nguni (= isizulu + isixhosa + isiswati) and Sotho (= sesotho + setswana + sepedi), spoken as mother tongues by two thirds of the total population of South Africa, as well as by almost the entire populations of Botswana, Lesotho, and Swaziland, and by almost a third of the population of Zimbwabwe. Ethnic and dialectal divisions within each of these languages have been exploited in the interests of white rule' (Dalby 1985: 32). The languages chosen in the Namibian language planning exercise reflect this linguicist 'white rule' perspective.

The criteria used in the Namibian planning document now need to be related to the framework for analysing the type of arguments used to legitimate the spread of English, and the means used.

The criteria look sober and sound. None are a question of the intrinsic qualities of any language. The only extrinsic criterion is the feasibility criterion. Most of the criteria (1, 5–8) are functional. These deal with what the language should give access to (Science and technology, Wider Communication, United Nations) or be able to achieve (Unity, Pan-Africanism). This leaves two criteria which are difficult to place, because they relate to attitudes and exposure, namely *Acceptability* and *Familiarity*. Being acceptable or familiar to a group is not anything 'inherent' in a language. Nor can they be properly characterized as a resource, unless one looks at them as resources acquired through the structural position that the language has had relative to other languages. Attitudes to English are instrumental in the spread of the language, as many scholars have noted, but they are as much to do with images or projections of reality as with objective facts or structural realities. If illiterate peasants can be regarded as rating English highly on Acceptability or Feasibility (as is done in the report), this presumably reflects their submission to prevalent hegemonic ideas.

Turning to the second set of analytical tools, the means for exerting power (ideas, carrots, sticks), all three are used in the argumentation. 'Threats' come in when discussing the possible choice of a Namibian language:

> . . . choosing one of the local languages as the official language could arouse unnecessary intra-linguistic competition and strife. It is conceivable that other Namibians whose languages are not strong enough candidates for national status on a numerical basis might oppose the claims of this language. (UNIN 1981: 39)

Here one can see the familiar false rationalization of potential conflict, and flight from multilingual realities.

As regards 'carrots' and 'ideas', English is a clear winner, whereas the other languages all fall down on one or more counts. For instance, in relation to 'familiarity', English is said to be 'pre-eminently suitable' (ibid.: 40), while a local language is merely 'a satisfactory choice' (ibid.: 39). This argumentation in favour of English is unconvincing. The experience of migrant labour and refugee exile has probably served to make major Namibian languages, particularly Oshiwambo, more 'familiar' to many Namibians than English, even if SWAPO uses English for official purposes. Otherwise English is 'at present taught only minimally and cursorily in schools', '. . . purely as a foreign language subject . . .', and 'students are not expected to use it as a language of real communication' (ibid.: 8). The report also notes that 'English used to be considered by most Namibians as the language of the élite' (ibid.), and even if these attitudes have changed in recent years and Namibians want to learn English, that scarcely seems to warrant a conclusion that English is more familiar than any of the Namibian languages.

Even if some of the 'carrots' and many of the 'ideas' carry more convincing weight than does the coverage of 'familiarity', their use still conforms to the linguicist pattern, in that English is glorified and African languages are devalued, both in what *is* said about them and in what is *not* said. The way European languages are favoured and Namibian languages devalued can be seen in the choice of criteria. Criteria which are of extreme relevance but which are not used are *Ease of Learning,*

Namibian Cultural Authenticity, *Empowering the Underprivi-leged* (which could include *Democratization*) and *Self-Reliance*. Each of these would upset the pattern that emerges from the criteria actually selected, for the following reasons (presented here in highly compressed form). Any Bantu language is likely to be easier for Namibians to learn than English, as the experience of East Africans learning Swahili as a second language shows. No language other than a Namibian language is likely to be able to convey the authentic cultural heritage of the various ethnic groups of Namibia. A policy of empowering the underprivileged is certain to take the language(s) that the Namibian child knows from home as the starting-point. Self-reliance presupposes an educational system (including adult education) without wastage, and which gives democratic access to knowledge through languages known well by the learners. This is of course seldom the case in African countries. In the words of the then Director of the OAU's Inter-African Bureau of Languages, Kahombo Mateene, '. . . the educational authorities have continued to grant English a privileged position. The consequences have been a waste of educational resources, the exclusion of the vast majority from effective participation in government and a failure to popularize basic scientific concepts' (*Daily Nation*, Kampala, 22 July 1986).

Another criticism of the criteria is that they overlap each other. The *United Nations* criterion could be included under *Wider Communication*, as could *Pan-Africanism*.

It is difficult to avoid the conclusion that the criteria seem to have been selected so as to make English emerge as the absolute winner. Postulating eight distinct criteria as the yardstick against which choice of an official language should be made has rationalized the complex real world into a selective checklist which is skewed in favour of English. According to the report, choosing an official language has two related purposes: the need to combat South African-engineered divisiveness, and the unity of Namibians. These factors are national rather than international. Even so, international factors get more prominence than national ones when the criteria are operationalized. For most Namibians, international contacts will not be a pressing concern (as Ansre points out in his analysis of the same issue in West Africa). The criteria chosen thus seem to fit with Pattanayak's analysis that 'in the post-colonial developing countries, educated persons tutored in the modes of western thinking consider (1) transnational communication more important than national communication, (2) standardization and uniformity more important than transmission of knowledge and information within the country, and (3) translation and transference of knowledge more important than creation of knowledge' (Pattanayak 1986a: vi).

The eurocentric approach is evident in one of the inexplicit assumptions of the report which has already been mentioned, namely that the exercise was designed to identify *one* official language. This reveals a policy to retrace the steps of European powers with a single official language, and of those African states that have followed suit and ostensibly given precedence to nationism rather than the development of local linguistic and cultural resources. An alternative strategy for the report would have been to focus on language needs at the local and district levels as well as the national level, and seek inspiration from such multilingual countries as India and Switzerland. This would have led to less focus on the international functions of the official language and more focus on political, economic, sociocultural, and educational factors as part of an overall multilingual policy.

What this part of the report has done, then, is to 'view multilingualism with a monolingually conditioned perception' which is bound to 'distort the perspective and result in bias' (Srivastava 1986: 45). 'The western model of language planning seems to aim at the replacement of many languages by one' (Pattanayak 1986b: 23). This model 'promotes a view of development that equates modernization with westernization and projects a mono-model as the only way through which planned societies can operate' (Pattanayak 1986a: vii). The report as a whole describes the reality of Namibia as a multilingual, multi-ethnic country, and stresses that language planning should respect this, but the decisive section which covers the issue of choice of an official language does not do so. The issue becomes one of selecting a single language, as opposed to formulating a multilingual policy that could lead to the goals that SWAPO has identified.

One problem with the report is therefore that the value judgements of its architects have not been made clear and public. This was identified in Chapter 4 as being an essential requirement for socially responsible language planning. In the report, both the criteria themselves and beliefs about what the languages in question can do are presented as though they are derived exclusively from knowledge, and not from value judgements. An impression is created of objective presentation of all the various options (the parliamentary theory of knowledge). Elsewhere in the report many of the hazards involved in choosing English are recorded, and awkward questions asked, for instance whether the choice of English could lead to eurocentric planning and attitudes, to which the bland response is given: 'Not if Namibian cadres committed to the needs of the country are politically motivated and trained early enough' (UNIN 1981: 46). Such a soothing response shows little awareness of structural factors, linguicism, cultural imperialism, or even the hazards of 'modernization'. But then this is not surprising, since the framework for the report as a whole is not directly anchored in any theory, and since the value judgments which have guided the selection of issues and criteria are not explicitly declared.

The linguistic imperialism which in fact underpinned the whole operation comes out very clearly in the last of the thirteen chapters of the report. This is entitled 'Specific project areas for further research'. Eight research areas are identified, but the areas have already been confined to matters dealing with the 'implementation of *English* for Namibia' (ibid.: 111, my italics). In five of the eight areas, ELT figures explicitly in the rubric (those for personnel needs, training, syllabus and course design, materials preparation, and administrative needs). Two of the remaining three are also directly related to ELT (language needs and use surveys, distance teaching), while the final one is on linguistic research. Under this heading, what is specifically proposed is contrastive analysis of Namibian languages and English, error analysis with English as the target language, bilingual dictionaries, and a Namibian ELT journal.

This is what concludes a report, the main title of which is *Toward a language policy for Namibia*. History thus repeats itself in the 1980s, with an almost uncanny replication of the linguicist pattern of equivalent reports in earlier decades. In colonial days, as was seen in the 1953 report analysed in Chapter 5, African education was narrowed down to a linguicist primary focus on English, at the cost of African languages. In like fashion, in the post-colonial educational language planning of the Makerere conference in 1961, as seen in Chapter 7, English was the sole concern.

The packaging of the linguicist programme for Namibia is vastly more subtle, as the report reveals considerable awareness of the issues involved in educational language planning. This is not surprising in view of the fact that champions of African languages (Kashoki, Ansre) participated in the conference on which the report is partly based. There are chapters on sociopolitical and sociocultural aspects of the relationship between English and local languages and on the 'medium of instruction dilemma'. The experience of similar countries was analysed, and one of the contributors to the report favoured a much greater focus on Namibian languages.[5] A set of 19 'general pointers' in Chapter 12, prior to an elaboration of possible ways of organizing educational language policy, contains many eminently sound propositions (for instance, that there is a tendency to emphasize the non-indigenous language at the expense of indigenous ones, that there is a risk of diglossia with English for the educated and local languages for the masses). The Makerere tenets are barely discernible, though the monolingual fallacy implicitly underlies much of the focus on ELT training and expertise, and concomitant dependence on expatriates. The early start fallacy is also supported, in a discreetly metamorphosed form: 'A foreign language as medium of instruction at primary level could be a hindrance to concept formation. But if it (English) is the official language, and Namibians are expected to be able to communicate in it, then its introduction as medium cannot be delayed' (ibid.: 46). What seems to be lacking is any clear awareness of the implications of pushing English in the ways recommended, or of the structural favouring of English through the allocation of resources and a privileged status.

What language policy will be followed in independent Namibia remains to be seen. Clearly the overall starting-point is inauspicious, after decades of apartheid and war, with economic policies geared towards minerals extraction and the needs of the white minority, and a civil service inherited from the previous incumbents. While in exile, SWAPO was totally dependent on international 'charity', with the United Nations, and Scandinavian organizations playing an important role. A substantial effort went into devising appropriate strategies for the English Language Programme for Namibians (Commonwealth Secretariat and SWAPO 1983) and its implementation (Commonwealth Secretariat 1985), the latter a report mainly produced by the British Council. This sets out a 'linked set of activity areas and project outlines' in the form of a catalogue of proposals to strengthen the capacity of Namibians in exile to implement

English as a national language. The authors display a creditably balanced view of the needs of Namibian languages and English throughout, and the need for adequate co-ordination, planning, and follow-up is impressively documented. However, the decisive premiss on which the proposals are based is the belief that western training is appropriate and can be sensitive to the context of Namibian languages and cultures. In the light of the experience of other African countries which have been heavily dependent on western aid, one can only be sceptical as to whether this is the case. Counterparting is an essential component, and again experience elsewhere is not encouraging. There needs to be careful attention to how a counterpart model can serve the interests of the Periphery.

In an article entitled 'Educational language planning for Namibia: English for liberation or neocolonialism?' (Phillipson, Skutnabb-Kangas, and Africa 1985), published by the OAU, some relevant international experience is analysed and conclusions drawn. These are summed up as follows (ibid.: 93):

1 English as an official language will be assisted if Namibian languages are used maximally inside and outside the education system.

2 Resistance to the use of mother tongues is an expression of a colonized consciousness, which serves the interests of global capitalism and South Africa, and the bourgeoisie and petty bourgeoisie who are most dependent on capitalist interests.

3 Namibia should follow the example of those states which have alternative language programmes leading to bilingualism.

4 Educational aid from 'donors' should be long-term and explicitly accept Namibian multilingual goals.

While struggling for the liberation of their country, there is substantial evidence of leading SWAPO educationalists forming policy in an informed, sophisticated way (Angula in Commonwealth Secretariat and SWAPO 1983). As victims of oppression, they are in a better position to understand the workings of linguicism and to resist it.

Notes

1 Much of the theoretical and empirical work for this chapter derives from two articles written jointly with Tove

Skutnabb-Kangas (Phillipson and Skutnabb-Kangas 1985 and Skutnabb-Kangas and Phillipson 1986b). The section on labels for English also draws on a joint article (Phillipson and Skutnabb-Kangas 1986b). Two of these papers were given at the 11th World Congress of Sociology, New Delhi, August 1986, and the Post Congress Session on 'Ethnocentrism in Sociolinguistics', at the Central Institute for Indian Languages, Mysore. We are particularly grateful for inspiring feedback from Annamalai, Lachman Khubchandani, Chris Mullard, Debi Pattanayak, and R. N. Srivastava. The description of educational language planning for Namibia also draws on Phillipson, Skutnabb-Kangas, and Africa 1985.

2 When pleading for French as a major international language, similar French-intrinsic arguments are used. For instance, 'The French language . . . is a logical and subtle language, rich by virtue of its aerated and very articulated syntax, . . . through its rigorous capacity for distinguishing concepts and ordering pronouncements, discourse, argumentation and narrative . . .' (Haut Conseil de la francophonie 1986: 343). French is also seen as bearer of the ideals of human rights (ibid.: 22), and the mission of French is to counteract the degradation and 'uniformization' of language that the spread of English, particularly American English, is leading to (ibid.: 341). Advocates for English can probably see through these arguments without necessarily applying their insights to English.

3 I am intrigued by Unesco being paired off with the British Council, as though it also deployed resources for English learning. To my knowledge, this has not been the case.

4 Danish administrative regulations often distinguish between publication in Danish and in a 'main language' (Danish: 'hovedsprog'), meaning English and occasionally French or German. For instance, the regulations on the dissemination of doctoral theses ('Vejledning om fremstilling og udgivelse af videnskabelige publikationer', A Guide to the Preparation and Publication of Scientific Texts, Forskningssekretariatet, the Secretariat of the Danish Research Councils, 1984) state that it is 'natural' to write theses in the humanities and social sciences in Danish, with a summary in a 'main language'. In other fields the intended audience is assumed to be international, and it is 'appropriate' to write theses in a 'main language'. 'Main language' is not defined in such public-

ations, nor is any particular language named. It is 'natural' for the language to be English. The term seems to have become established without the demeaning and stigmatizing effect of the label 'main language' on Danish having been considered.

5 This was E. J. John, the Indian applied linguist.

10 Linguistic imperialism and ELT

ELT: master-minded?

The picture of ELT that has emerged is one of a boom subject expanding on the narrow professional base that was the only one available to it, and developing sophisticated technical expertise, paralleled and nourished by the equally specialized discipline of linguistics. This professionalism was monolingual and anglocentric, and tended to ignore the wider context of its operations. The question then arises as to who decided on policy, and who was ultimately responsible for what happened?

Formal academic training for ELT was the responsibility of the universities, where applied linguistics in its contemporary guise was nursed into life by the British Council. The British Council was domestically the key link between the state, private interests, and the academic establishment. Their overseas offices selected local nationals for further training in Britain and identified openings abroad for the newly-created 'expert' products of the university applied linguistics departments. The British Council has not had unlimited funds at its disposal, and was initially as short of expertise as were British universities, but as the organization was so centrally placed, it is relevant to ask whether it or its paymasters had a master plan for extending ELT and through it, maintaining British influence worldwide.

Bernard Lott was in charge of the British Council's English teaching operations for a decade from the mid-1960s. His analysis is that Britain 'did not really make policies at all in the areas you are interested in. Far from wanting to ram English down the throats of people who did not want it, everything by way of post-colonial support was done because, as near as makes no odds, everybody thought it was the right thing to do' (Lott, interview). The guiding principle was to find out what was required and 'plug in aid', generally in much smaller amounts than what was asked for, because of limited resources. What this assessment by a key policy-maker and administrator seems to indicate is that there was always a greater 'demand' for ELT than could be met, and that the response was to meet this demand by spreading the limited 'supply' of professionals over as wide a field of operations as possible. In this sense ELT efforts have been determined by supply rather than demand, with the limitations, quantitative and qualitative, that this entailed.

Lott's analysis is influenced by the fact that demands were articulated by Periphery leaders who were attempting to find solutions to urgent educational problems. It ignores the fact that, as seen in the analysis of the Makerere and other conference reports, and of the 'arguments' used to promote English, the demand was largely created and orchestrated by the Centre, and reflected Centre perceptions of what was needed in the Periphery. However it is doubtless correct that no blueprint for the exercise as a whole was ever *explicitly* formulated (and Lott's statement on the absence of policy is revealing) except in the most general of terms (of the 'good for Britain and good for them' type), after the policy documents of the 1950s, in particular the Cabinet paper of 1956. This was a secret document which was kept away from public scrutiny for 30 years. So far as the expression of Periphery demands and needs is concerned, there is certainly much wider scope nowadays, with more tightly managed programmes, for more informed negotiations and planning. Many of the symptoms of malaise noted in earlier chapters have been matters that Centre and Periphery representatives have been aware of, though not perhaps of the underlying weaknesses of anglocentricity and professionalism.

The spread of English, and the growth of a profession to serve it, was reported regularly in the *British Council Annual Reports*, whose lead articles accurately reflect this trend: 1955–56 'The English Language', 1958–59 'The Main Tasks', 1960–61 'The English Language Abroad', 1961–62 'Teaching Overseas', etc. A more explicit plan was probably superfluous, and might be internationally damaging. There is also no doubt that the allies in the international promotion of English, Britain and the USA, have always suspected each other's motives and been careful to check what the other was doing. The joint conferences and high-level talks were initially held in order to avoid friction and competition in the field. The guidelines to ensure collaboration, irrespective of methodological or personality quirks, were more a defensive strategy than a recipe for an integrated approach. Diplomacy, even cultural diplomacy, requires discretion.

George Perren (interview), like Bernard Lott, reckons that policy did not follow a specific plan, whether on the part of the Foreign Office or the British Council, although clearly the Council had a vested interest in ensuring expansion in this area. This interpretation tallies with views from virtually all the informants on the role of the English-Teaching Advisory Committee, the official link between the academic profession and the British Council. According to them, the committee has never exerted any major policy influence. It has served as a sounding-board for ideas, and clearly both parties to the arrangement, the universities and the international cultural bureaucrats, have a common interest, personal and institutional, in amicable relations (which have at times been distant). Both are engaged in operations which are profitable for the other.

The absence of any policy or plan, other than a general wish to promote English through ELT professionalism, was no serious impediment to expansion. There was no reason for the foreign policy agenda of ELT to be articulated more explicitly. ELT professionals regard language teaching and learning as their business, and they did not have the training to put their expertise into a wider economic or political analysis. This is one of the essential characteristics of the profession, as we have seen. Even the British Council has only very general, abstract goals. Its staff have never been trained in policy formation in relation to, say, international cultural relations or 'aid' (except at the level of managerial skills and university postgraduate degrees, which tend to be theory- rather than policy-oriented, and are unlikely to qualify them to analyse policy—though this may be changing now, with closer cost control of Council activities). In a hybrid organization of this kind, the considerable initiative allowed to individual offices, and even individual members of staff, permits diversity and creativity, just as it also permits inefficiency and irrelevance.

However, irrespective of the degree of explicit articulation of official policy, all inter-state actors and activities have implications of a structural and ideological kind. The tenets enunciated at Makerere, on the surface the profound deliberations of devoted professionals, had far-reaching economic and cultural consequences. British Council promotion of ELT, ranging from minor matters like book presentations or an air ticket for a conference to major schemes for teacher training, is part of a structure which facilitates the operation of English linguistic hegemony.

Higher up in the British Council hierarchy, policy has to be co-ordinated with the FCO, and here it is the interpretation of where British economic, political, and military interests lie which directly determines ELT policy. It is at this level that decisions are taken on whether the British Council should be represented in a country or not, on the placing of ELT experts predominantly in countries which are strategically important for British investments and commercial links (currently the Middle East and Africa), on book promotion (it is the Overseas Development Administration which funds the Educational Low-Priced Books Scheme) (ELBS), on whether aid should be spent on an ELT project or on agriculture, and so on. At this level, all inter-state ELT activity forms part of a wider policy. ELT professionals are deluding themselves if they choose to ignore this dimension.

Most of the empirical analysis for this book stems from the formative years of ELT, as a result of an attempt to chart how the profession emerged and to identify the structure which it forms part of. It has obviously not been possible to analyse the evolution of the entire profession, or even of all its main wings. Thus the adult education market worldwide, which is expanding very rapidly in such places as Japan and Southern Europe, has barely been touched on. This was a justifiable exclusion for two reasons. Firstly, in this field learners are adding a language to their repertoire, and there is no risk of subtractive bilingualism taking place (Lambert 1975). It is therefore less like second language learning and more akin to foreign language learning in schools (another field which has not been of central concern to the study). There is though the difference that success in a language school may be of personal and professional benefit, while success in an obligatory school subject may decisively influence one's chance to climb up the educational ladder. Secondly, virtually all teaching of this kind is self-financing, rather than being government or aid-financed. Thus British Council teaching centres generate income, while also aiming to set standards for good pedagogical practice. Possibly further studies in this area could contribute to an unpicking of the intimate links between linguistic imperialism and educational imperialism, which in 'aid' contexts are indissolubly interwoven. This would presuppose that linguicism is in operation, which may well not be the case in many adult education situations. It would also be interesting to explore the viability of the monolingual and native speaker tenets/fallacies in this context.

The recent report on cultural diplomacy by the Foreign Affairs Committee of the House of Commons (extracts of which and analysis are reported in *Britain Abroad*, the British Council magazine, issue 4, October 1987) reveals that, so far as the FCO is concerned, cultural diplomacy is 'not pursued by the FCO for its own sake, but only as an instrument by which the pursuit of other activities may be assisted' (political and economic activities). There was no explicit FCO or Government policy for cultural diplomacy proper. This the parliamentary committee would like to see remedied, and the budget for cultural diplomacy expanded, so that policy should conform to the FCO's own proposition that 'we should share a culture which enriches the human spirit, enhances international understanding, and expands the horizons of men and women throughout the world.' The FCO thus wishes to project an image of Britain and its culture which draws on a blend of English-intrinsic and English-functional arguments, and uses the same type of rhetoric as that of the foreign policy élite in the USA (discussed in Chapter 6). Interestingly, the committee report wishes international arts promotion activities to be disconnected from narrow commercial motives, while at the same time recognizing that all aspects of diplomacy interlock. The report also echoes the verdict of an earlier review committee of British Council activities, the Seebohm Report (1981), that in the promotion of English there is no clear dividing-line between cultural diplomacy and aid.

Formally speaking these British Council activities are funded separately, FCO money going to information and cultural representation work, which is specifically connected to commercial and political benefits, and ODA money to aid, which is regarded as 'disinterested and humanitarian' (ibid.), a formulation which diverts attention away from the structural context of aid. Perren notes (ms) that internal debates in the British Council in the 1960s on distinctions between 'information' and 'aid' functions attained a subtlety and complexity worthy of medieval scholastics. According to the Seebohm committee, both types of activity are still expected to contribute to 'creating abroad an understanding and appreciation of Britain', just as English teaching is not only profitable but 'an excellent way of establishing the Council's presence overseas, and can be a useful gateway to the other services it has to offer. As a cultural vehicle, as opposed to a mere instrument of international communication, its importance to Britain is inestimable if it is properly used to transmit our national values' (ibid.: 45). 'It is the Council's strength that it is regarded overseas primarily as a cultural, non-political organization; any system of funding which ties its work in any country too exclusively to aid programmes must in the long term reduce its value to the Overseas Development Administration as an effective agent' (Seebohm Report 1981: 18).

In view of these multiple pressures and goals, it is not surprising that there has never been a blueprint for expansion of ELT or 'linguistic diplomacy', and that this gap parallels the absence of an explicit policy for cultural diplomacy. There has presumably been no need for either. At least so far as ELT is concerned, the structures established from the mid-1950s and the professionalism that evolved seem to have served the purpose of protecting the interests of the Centre effectively enough. One wonders whether recipients of 'aid' are aware that the donors find it difficult to clearly demarcate cultural diplomacy or promotion on the one hand, and 'aid' on the other. Perhaps the current trend towards multilateral aid projects[1] and the increasing role of non-governmental organizations in underdeveloped countries will counteract the blending of aid with the promotion of national interests. Whether structural relations between Centre and Periphery will be substantially changed is more disputable.

One might then ask who runs the Centre, who ELT policy is determined by. Clearly there are the external pressures of foreign policy already referred to, representing an external constraint on the profession. The ELT policy-makers themselves, in Centre and Periphery, in Ministries of Education, universities, curriculum development centres and the like are part of a hegemonic structure. They have shared interests and beliefs, a shared stake in the scientific and educational status quo, a shared perception of what the central internal constraints are. The structure of academic imperialism has ensured that Centre training and expertise have been disseminated worldwide, with change and innovative professionalism tending to be generated by the Centre.

The focus in this book on the historical and structural determinants of ELT and aid policies enables us to avoid accusations of personal incompetence or ill-will on the part of individual inter-state actors. In general they have not been trained well enough for what they were doing, and may well have contributed constructively in an untenable situation. This however in no way absolves us from responsibility. Hopefully some of the familiar complaints (frustration with their task and dissatisfaction with their predecessors' achievements) combined with more awareness of the structural context of their activities and the ethics of aid could permit a link-up between the role and functions of the 'expert' and the wider structural framework. Applied linguists can choose to address or to ignore the structural aspects of the spread of English, but they and their professional activities are no more 'neutral' than the English language that their professionalism mediates. As one scholar aptly puts it: 'Applied Linguistics must by its very nature take sides . . . There is no such thing as neutral Applied Linguistics' (Christophersen 1989: 46).

There is another sense in which hiding behind a claim that ELT has never been forced on people (one of Bernard Lott's points, quoted earlier) is rather too facile an argument. When the professionalism of ELT is essentially anglocentric, which monolingualism is the clearest expression of, there is almost inevitably a linguicist devaluing of local languages and cultures. When there are programmes for teacher training and curriculum development in English, but not in local languages, linguicism is in operation. Structural factors ensure that English advances at the expense of local languages, and ELT professionalism is a key link in this process. The situation is one of subtractive rather than additive bilingualism (Lambert 1975). This is something that scholars from underdeveloped countries have no illusions about. The neglect of African languages is integrally linked to the maintenance and consolidation of English as the dominant language (Mateene 1985a). In India the dominance of English perverts the efforts of education, diverts funds wastefully, and thwarts the natural multilingual developmental process (Pattanayak 1986b). If English linguistic imperialism had not been in operation, other languages would have had much more scope for development in periphery-English countries, and these languages might have followed the course of the languages of many European countries over the past century. In which case English might in such countries be an additive rather than a subtractive language. The 'not-forcing-English-on-anyone' argument ignores the position of English in each local linguistic hierarchy and the determinants of these hierarchies.

Stating this does *not* imply that if English were to vanish (a highly improbable hypothesis in the present world), other languages would live in equity. Dominant languages in multilingual communities and in a multilingual world are dominant because their speakers have the power to secure advantages for their own group, among them linguistic advantages. Thus linguicism serves to maintain the dominant position of French in a substantial number of countries which are linked to France in an imperialist structure in much the same way as English linguistic imperialism operates. In India there are many regionally dominant languages in a complex linguistic hierarchy, and many more dominated ones. In both core-English and periphery-English countries hegemonic beliefs are constantly contested and a reordering of linguistic hierarchies may ensue, as speakers of dominated languages succeed in asserting their linguistic human rights, generally in conjunction with economic and political rights. This is precisely what is happening in the Soviet Union at present, with Russian losing its legitimacy as the Soviet system disintegrates, and as other languages assert their rights. Under the Soviet system many languages were cultivated or maintained to the point where they can serve all essential societal purposes. Even if there has been a linguicist favouring of Russian in many domains (scientific research, the army), most Soviet citizens other than those with Russian as a mother tongue are functionally bilingual, as they have had most of their education through the medium of the mother tongue. This is a very different position from that in virtually all periphery-English former colonies. The fact that linguicism is not smoothly functional, and that both democratic and more violent means may permit change, does not however exonerate those associated with the promotion of English from identifying what the structural factors are which impell English forward and which produce benefits for speakers of English, whether as a first or second language.

One can conclude that ELT has not been promoted globally as a result of a master-minded plan. It is in the nature of hegemony that it is not static and rigid, but is reconstituted continually in lived experience. This means that at the ideological level it adapts dialectically to challenge and change. It is also, as we saw in Chapter 3, functional for an ideology of the superiority of a language or of a particular brand of professionalism to project values over and above those of the discipline proper, to project moral and ethical leadership, in the same way as hegemony is exercised in political discourse. This ELT has done by formulating arguments for the values associated with the dominant language, those of modernization, progress, unity, and similar 'English-functional' arguments. One aspect of the successful legitimation of English linguistic imperialism is that the ELT profession has held out such promises, and these appear to have been redeemed for some. It needs to be remembered that education is an activity on the borderline between the dictates of the state (which can through funding and policy decrees decisively influence the parameters of what is seen as legitimate activity) and the free-for-all of civil society (where norms and social values are negotiated). ELT has appeared to be detached from the interests of the State, both in the Centre and the Periphery. This increases the sense of those involved that they are 'free agents', and that in turn increases the apparent legitimacy of a profession as an independent self-monitoring body. This political disconnection can of course blind the actors involved to the structural context of their activities. Clearly those in the Centre who shape this structure have no wish to alter one which is so effective in defending Centre interests.

On the force of the evidence

This book has attempted to integrate evidence from several sources, primarily written material, eight interviews, and ongoing activities in English language education, in particular for Scandinavia and for SWAPO of Namibia. The advantage of having several sources of input is that each type can be cross-checked, and that theoretical and empirical issues interact dialectically. At the conclusion, it is important to consider how the various types of data have served the purposes of the book and to consider their validity.

A general point is that it was easier to trace written sources originating from the Centre than the Periphery. This is scarcely surprising, as most of the source material is British, but the issue is part of the more general one of the proliferation of Centre journals and books tending to define problems and monopolize academic discourse. This is bound to over-represent the perspective of one party. This imbalance has hopefully been rectified to some extent by my frequent reference to Periphery sources, though there are certainly Periphery sources in languages I can read that I am unaware of, and even more certainly sources in languages which I cannot read.

Secondly, it is important to recall that the 'Centre' and 'Periphery' concepts are metaphors for a rich variety of lived experience. They are a convenient form of shorthand which appropriately reflects the power relationships in force, and should not be interpreted as underplaying the diversity and specificity of each individual context.

This relates to another problem of selection. In looking at the history and origins of ELT, it was essential to probe into both British and American sources and to attempt to clarify the contribution of each nation to professional doctrine. For the empirical analyses it was necessary to concentrate on British source material. This was partly a matter of time and logistics, but more importantly it reflected a belief that the book would benefit from a concentration on the tradition that I have most direct, inside experience of. I also hypothesized that the underlying structural forces operate in similar ways in each of the key Centre set-ups, and nothing in the study would seem to contradict such an analysis. There are differences of degree in the weighting of British and American 'aid' work, and differences of professional emphasis, but linguicism seems to be as much a defining characteristic of both establishments. The inter-state actors from both sources seem to be part and parcel of the structure of English linguistic imperialism.

Interviewing some of the chief protagonists in the ELT drama made it possible to check the dry brevity of academic written discourse against lively personal involvement and commitment. The brief extracts from the interviews inevitably do less than full justice to the richness of these contributions. (The interviews contain enough material for a small book in its own right.) No attempt was made to pursue with the informants the question of how to characterize or operationalize linguicism or English linguicist imperialism. At that stage of the study it had been possible to hypothesize about the specific processes that determined the historical development of ELT, for instance that certain tenets had been disseminated uncritically (a position that not all the informants agreed with).

One example of the dovetailing of spoken and written data is the analysis of the Anglo-American Conference on English teaching abroad (1961). George Perren compiled the report which contains the extremely revealing comments by I. A. Richards on ELT 'restructuring' the students' world in ESL contexts (quoted in Chapter 6). What became clear in the interview, and which is not hinted at in the written report, is that Richards (of *Basic English* fame) was brought in to the conference in order to impress the literary mandarins in British universities, who regarded ELT as *infra dig.* ELT had to be made academically respectable. The hidden addressee for the entire exercise was the conservative 'Eng.Lit.' establishment, a few of whose number were invited to attend. Perren's view of the conference was that, except for social purposes, it was 'not worth a row of beans', presumably a reference to the academic quality of the gathering. A report on the other hand was essential in order to impress the funding authorities on both sides of the Atlantic. The arguments in the report are therefore far from of limited utility, as they directly express the kind of legitimation that was thought necessary in order to impress senior people in the British Council and the FCO and their American counterparts. The document provides a very clear image of the dominant ideology of those who were working to expand the ELT field, at the interface of the professionals and the state bureaucrats.

Another interesting point made by Perren was that despite it being government policy that English should be promoted, ELT did not rank high in FCO priorities. As the bulk of the British Council's funding came over the FCO grant, it was natural that the British Council should have the FCO as an indirect addressee for all of its reports stressing the importance of ELT. For the State Department too, ELT has been a rather minor concern, but in the American context it is important to recall that many governmental and private organizations are involved in the promotion of English. If the FCO and the State Department have tended to under-rate cultural diplomatic activities, and ELT in particular, this may reflect a lack of awareness of the role of language or even of the potential of English linguistic imperialism. However, even if ELT had a low priority as compared with other foreign policy activities, official support for ELT has in fact increased steadily over the past 50 years, as the narrative of the evolution of the British Council indicated. In effect the flowering of ELT has been the direct result of state support.

All the reports analysed in this study are likely to have had multiple addressees in the same way as the Anglo-American Conference report. The genre is at the interface of political discourse and academic discourse, and may be of some broad public interest. The *Makerere Report* was prepared for the

Commonwealth Education Liaison Committee, which represented Commonwealth governments, and which was based, predictably, in London. The main body of the report is highly technical, and not likely to be read by people outside ELT. The effect of such a specialized text was undoubtedly to create the impression on policy-makers in the Centre and the Periphery that the professionalism necessary to solve the Periphery's educational problems already existed. As demonstrated in the description of the ELT academic base at the time and of the tenets endorsed at Makerere, this was a pre-emptive bid by the Centre to define the parameters of education and development in the Periphery countries. The motives of all concerned in planning and implementing 'aid' of this kind may have been pure and altruistic (as Bernard Lott put it, 'our hearts were in the right place', interview), but appreciating this merely serves to underline the disconnection of ELT from structural factors, and the fact that the professionalism available was not fully competent to the task. The tasks actually undertaken served to promote Centre interests, which is what the professional politicians and senior bureaucrats in the Centre were concerned to ensure. The *Makerere Report* provided ideal legitimation for the Centre bridgehead in education in the Periphery.

One topic considered in Chapter 8 is ELT research. Analysis of the interview responses, and the written evidence, led to the conclusion that relatively little research was done into the problems which ELT aid work was supposed to be solving. The oral responses reveal a unanimity about the paucity of the research effort, but diverge in relation to the causes. The suggested explanations can be taken one by one, and commented on, in order to demonstrate how conclusions were drawn on the basis of information elicited in the interviews.

One informant said he had difficulty in conceptualizing what form such research could actually take, and stressed the difficulty of controlling the variables in educational research. However, the practical objections have in fact been overcome in comparable situations, as in the Nigerian projects referred to in Chapter 8, and in bilingual education projects in such places as North America and Sweden. It is desirable that such research should be conducted mainly by nationals of the countries in question or members of the ethnolinguistic group under investigation. If this principle were applied in ELT research, it would inevitably make Centre expertise ancillary rather than central to the exercise.

One informant reacted by saying that no British university would do research purely for the benefit of an overseas country. This view may accurately reflect the way limitations on research funding were perceived, but on the other hand a good deal of research was undertaken in the Centre into Periphery problems, in areas other than ELT. In any case, research of this kind in fact benefits the Centre, which increases its expertise. This response, like the first one, leads to the conclusion that little effort was made to get research going in this area. A related point is that British university applied linguistics departments have tended not to specialize in particular Periphery countries or areas.

A third informant saw research into the forms of the contemporary language and into the language learning and teaching process as being the main concern of ELT. (As the discussion in Chapter 8 indicated, it is true that there was a huge gap to be filled there, one which has been impressively filled, on both sides of the Atlantic.) He felt though that organizational and educational policy fell outside the field of ELT. This attitude conforms to the model of ELT being divorced from its wider educational context. It is also inconsistent with what was identified in a succession of reports (at the Makerere Conference, for example) as being research needs in the ELT field.

On the basis of these divergent responses, the conclusion is drawn that the ELT establishment failed to undertake research into areas that were of central concern, and which had been identified as in need of research. Of the three explanations, the first refers to an internal constraint, a methodology problem, the second to external constraints, while the third one on the surface of it is also an internal constraint but also has to do with where the boundaries of a profession are drawn. This could imply an acceptance of a remit prepared by others (externally) or a wish to exclude matters which are seen to be outside professional competence (an internal motive). The motives of the state and of foundations in commissioning research were also explored in Chapter 8.

One consequence of the relatively narrow basis of research has been that Periphery ELT experts sent for training in the Centre have learnt many useful skills but have tended not to be familiarized with research methodology that would be relevant for many applied language tasks on their return home. Applied linguistics seems to fall down as does theoretical linguistics, in not equipping those who travel to the Centre for high level training with the skills necessary to meet the applied linguistic needs of their own countries.

This highlights a basic dilemma for the ELT establishment in the Centre. Applied language research logically implies involvement in the community around a university. What then is the community or constituency of ELT, if a defining characteristic of it is its global relevance, implying mainly an involvement in the Periphery? There are of course many applied language problems to be solved domestically, and some ELT departments in the Centre are moving in that direction (into ESL or social work), but is this likely to resolve the problem of the relevance of Centre expertise and experience to Periphery problems? It is an open question.

I have drawn on much of the relevant written evidence accessible to a scholar who is resident in the Centre, and have also drawn on others' experience through interviews. These were a practical way of approaching a vast and complex topic and delimiting the field. In an exploratory study of this kind, which attempts to look at the historical record within a provisional theoretical framework, the study can do little more than come up with a tentative description of a field which tends to be explored in a more atomistic way, and where there is still a manifest need for better theoretically-based understanding of the issues.

Studying ELT and imperialism

I have attempted in this book to unravel some of the links between ELT and imperialism. There is no doubt that research into the issues raised would benefit if a larger number of empirical studies were undertaken. These should ideally be carried out by mutli-disciplinary teams, primarily of researchers from the Periphery. This would facilitate the elaboration of a more refined theoretical framework. Such work should draw more strongly on ongoing work in such fields as race, class, gender, and ethnicity; development studies, with particular reference to strategies for alternative development, grassroots mobilization, and social movements; political science, in particular the role of the state and policy implementation studies; the sociology of language, particularly attitudes to language, and language and identity in multilingual societies; educational sociology, particularly multilingual education in social movement-directed revitalization situations. Such an enlarged study would permit clearer demonstration of the interaction between linguicism and other mechanisms of exploitation, between linguicism and other hegemonic ideologies. It could help to clarify the relationship in a range of contexts between ELT 'experts' and the state policies of which their work is an integral part, and the contribution of ELT at the micro level (linguicism in social-psychological processes) and at the macro level (the evolution of educational language policy, and through this the constitution of linguistic hierarchies).

Many of the main concepts used for this study are extremely broad and diffuse—for instance, a monolingual norm, anglocentricity, and professionalism—and the phenomena they relate to evolve over time, just as the macro level structures are constantly evolving. They might profitably be broken down into further parts or sub-types. Likewise their realization in different periphery-English contexts should be specified. Some of the more detailed parts of the present study, for instance the analysis of the Makerere tenets, have demonstrated the complexity of the issues involved.

One question that needs confronting is the adequacy of the existing theoretical framework for the study that has been undertaken. There are many relevant questions which further studies might clarify, for instance, are there periphery-English countries where an increased use of English has been accompanied by less exploitation, more democratization, and prosperity? In what contexts does ELT not involve linguicism or English linguicist imperialism? If English linguistic imperialism in this study has related to two dimensions, linguistic imperialism and educational imperialism, can one envisage studies which separate these out and where the one might hold but not the other? All that can be attempted here is to ask whether there is counter-evidence that has been overlooked because of the framework adopted, or whether a different theoretical framework would have led to quite different conclusions.

We could consider Singapore as an example of an under-developed country which has accorded pride of place to English and has a relatively thriving economy, where 'modernization' seems to be working. (The language situation in Singapore was described briefly in Chapter 2; for a more detailed description, see Kuo and Jernudd 1988.) Is it possible that in a country such as Singapore English actually extends what is promised to most of the population, that the language is facilitating the attainment of societal and individual goals, and that it does not involve a pattern of English linguistic imperialism? To provide properly researched answers to such questions would require a detailed study, but some of the variables that would need investigation can be highlighted.

Present policy aims at the de-ethnicization of Singaporeans through English but at the maintenance of Asian values (ibid.: 10). The Prime Minister has recently summed this up (quoted ibid.) by stating that 'foreign talents can impart their skills, not their values, to Singaporeans'. Another argument used in official discourse is that English has been opted for as a way of avoiding 'racial tension'.

The variables that could well indicate the operation of English linguistic imperialism in Singapore are:

– that there is a structural favouring of English in the education system that can only be described as linguicist (possibly languages other than English are learnt effectively too, despite being marginalized)
– that English is a major instrument for social stratification
– that there are many Centre representatives active in promoting proficiency in English, including a strong Centre ELT presence
– that most of these inter-state actors presumably function monolingually
– that structurally English is favoured in all activities in the 'modern' sector, and that this sector is intimately integrated into the western capitalist order.

To investigate whether 'modernization' has succeeded would involve correlating economic and political variables for different groups in society with the above indicators of linguistic penetration and dependence. The language-related variables are compatible with an analysis of the language situation of Singapore being one of English linguistic imperialism. This does not mean that consumerist Singapore is a 'victim' of westernization. It is a dynamic society which is trying to make a synthesis of western and Asian values, reflecting a multitude of influences at the national, group, and individual levels. But it is false to maintain, as the Prime Minister seems to be doing, that it is possible to adopt English without assimilating the values embedded in the language, particularly if those values are reinforced in many societal domains. The 'racial tension' argument is also false: where there is inter-ethnic tension, this is to a large extent the result of perceived injustice, with ethnicity or language as a mediating variable rather than a causal factor.

English linguistic imperialism is functional in maximizing the chances of the Singapore élite to benefit from participation in the capitalist world order. The élite also attempt to direct a process of democratization and re-linguification (by, for instance, people who are dominant in Malay or Chinese becoming dominant in English) from the top downwards in the society. The evidence thus is of a structural context of imperialism, with linguicism serving to allocate more power and resources to those who are proficient in English. By contrast the linguistic hierarchy is more complex in Malaysia, with which Singapore once formed a federation, in that there are competing claims between English as a language of power, and Malay, which is much more actively promoted as a national language than in Singapore.

This analysis is also compatible with the existence of counter-hegemonic tendencies, ranging from celebrating the unique form that English literature takes locally (Thumboo 1985), to querying native-speaker English as the norm for Singaporeans (Wong 1982). Such moves could ultimately lead to a declaration of partial linguistic independence, when local professionalism can dispense with Centre norms. By then English linguistic imperialism will have served its purpose in contributing to the establishment and maintenance of the dominance of English. To gauge the precise contribution of ELT to this process would require a detailed analysis of the history of language policy and language in education in Singapore.

The evidence from Singapore in fact appears to support the theory of English linguistic imperialism. If it also seems to be compatible with a 'modernization' paradigm, in that Singapore, unlike other underdeveloped periphery-English countries referred to in this study seems to be retracing the route of western countries towards prosperity (but not to parliamentary democracy), then this is due to the uniqueness of the state itself (which has a few, minor affinities with Hong Kong), with the city, port, and base as pre-eminently a colonial creation and later a partner of the West. The modernization strategy is relatively more likely to succeed in a country in which the entire economy can be modelled on the West, and if there is no competing economy (which is the case in many underdeveloped countries, the 'economy of affection' as Hyden, 1983, terms it). Another conclusion would be that 'modernization' intrinsically involves modelling underdeveloped countries on western lines, and that an extreme form of this would involve taking over the western language as well.

By contrast, in Scandinavia English teaching influence from Anglo-American ELT is slight. As Scandinavia is a Centre country, it is in a position to generate the professionalism it needs to solve its own language teaching problems with recourse to primarily local resources. Scandinavia can also attempt to influence the cultural and scientific imperialism that emanates from the Anglo-American Centre, and which it is simultaneously a recipient of and a competitive participant in. As 'north' countries, the Scandinavian countries benefit from their privileged position in the imperialist world order. English can be learnt as a second language in Scandinavian schools without the Scandinavian languages being underdeveloped (though there is slight displacement, particularly in vocabulary for new concepts). The advance of English is mainly associated with media imperialism, business, and politics. In higher education there is a tendency towards an increased use of English, not only in the choice of textbooks but also as the medium of education, at undergraduate and postgraduate levels. The implications of this development are at present unclear, but even with more use made of English in Scandinavia, ELT plays a more marginal role in education as compared with its role in underdeveloped countries.

The importance of historical factors for the success of linguistic decolonization strategies can be seen in the Nordic countries. In Norway a popular movement to develop a form of Norwegian from local dialects and distinct from the Danish-influenced language used by the élite (Denmark being the former colonial power) gradually resulted in the legitimation of this new variant over a period of several decades of intense controversy. The compromise evolved attempts to please all parties and is essentially tolerant of linguistic diversity. Local solutions were evolved within a local democratic tradition, and without interference from the former colonial power or any other external power.

Finland was a colony of Sweden for 650 years, and then a Russian Grand Duchy from 1809 until 1917. The main language planning efforts that went into developing Finnish for formal purposes from the 1860s onwards, including a 'finnicization' of large parts of the Swedish-speaking élites, took place as an autonomous development in an atmosphere of strong nationalist sentiment, such as also existed among speakers of the two languages, Swedish and Russian, which otherwise might have exerted an imperialist influence similar to that of English. In the same period there were language movements elsewhere in Europe, for instance in Serbia and Hungary. One can speculate that if the developments in Finland had been delayed for a century, Finland might be in an equivalent position to that of many African countries now.

Nothing that I have written here disputes the fact that the English language can be used for good or bad purposes, both by native speakers and second language users. It is a truism that English can be used to either promote or fight capitalism (which is itself full of contradictions), to liberate people or oppress them. But this argument ignores the structural power of English nationally and internationally.[2]

The aim of this book has been to try to clarify linguistic imperialism past and present, to unpick some of the relevant strands, and to make some significant connections. It has hopefully shed some light on how the 'white man's burden' became the English native-speaking teacher's burden, and how the role played by ELT is integral to the functioning of the contemporary world order.

Linguicism has been evolved as a construct for understanding how language decisions effect unequal resource and power allocation. It seems highly likely that in many neo-colonial contexts linguicism has taken over from racism as an ideology which legitimates an unequal division of power and resources. Linguicism is a neologism which has been applied in the present study to the question of the global dissemination of a language. It has also been elaborated in parallel in minority education studies as a concept for capturing the relationship between the language of the dominant group and dominated (indigenous and immigrant) groups.[3] Even though the concept is still a somewhat broad and amorphous one, it is hoped that the present study has shown that it is useful, and potentially of theoretical and practical significance, in order to single out in what way language contributes to certain types of inequality, in the contemporary world as much as in the colonial one.

This is a modest goal compared with the more major issue of

attempting to analyse what role language can play in facilitating a change of the structure in a more equitable direction. This would be a topic for a further study, which would raise many new issues. Among the key issues would be the new forms that linguicism will take in a changing world; whether a shift in the international linguistic hierarchy will take place in view of the increased economic power of Japan or Germany, and the implications this might have for English as the dominant 'international' language in a neo-neo-colonial period; whether there will be more or less monolingualism in future;[4] whether speakers of underdeveloped languages will abandon 'moderniz-ation' efforts *vis-à-vis* their own languages and use English instead[5] or succeed in establishing linguistic human rights for dominated languages; alternative 'aid' strategies.[6] Can ELT contribute constructively to greater linguistic and social equality, and if so, how could a critical ELT be committed, theoretically and practically, to combating linguicism?[7]

Notes

1   Technical assistance in education is increasingly funded by international bodies such as the World Bank, the regional development bodies, United Nations agencies, rather than by bilateral bodies. Such projects tend to be the sole source of innovation in education in Third World countries (Arnove 1982b: 456). The trend towards multilateral control concentrates power in the Centre in fewer hands. For a Periphery view, with examples of innovation, see Obura 1986.

2   Occasionally applied linguists explicitly refuse to relate their professionalism to the structure in which they operate: 'I must admit I don't know how or why English has become an international auxiliary language of frequent use but I do know that it has', writes Larry Smith (1983) in a book edited by him and called *Readings in English as an International Language*. This amounts to treating English as a tool, the falsity of which was demonstrated in Chapter 8.

3   A perspective from minority education that could be useful and relevant for the study of linguistic imperialism, is 'deficit' theories. They are revealing in relation to the successive phases that immigrant education has gone through—immigrants lack the L2, their culture is deficient, their L1 is

deficient, etc. (Skutnabb-Kangas 1984a). Equally fundamentally false is the misapprehension that learners of English
in underdeveloped countries are suffering from a deficiency
called lack of English. They do lack English, but probably
only in the same way as a child brought up in Denmark or
France lacks English, and no one would brand such children
negatively in relation to their 'need' of a foreign language.
Deficiency-based theories reveal how dominant groups
stigmatize and define the dominated (as in Orientalism) in
order to control them and to impose the dominator's view of
social reality. This is probably true of western models of
educational language planning for underdeveloped multilingual societies.

Deficiency-based explanations for the difficulties experienced by dominated groups transform the relationship of
exploitation into one where the dominated are made to
appear responsible for these societally-imposed handicaps.
They then appear to be in need of help or 'aid', and the
neglect of their linguistic human rights can continue. When
the dominated have internalized this message, physical
coercion can be replaced by ideological coercion, sticks by
carrots, first, then ideas. Linguicism is an effective means of
ideological coercion. Linguistic underdevelopment parallels
economic underdevelopment.

4   Lenin (1951: 9) in his *Critical Remarks on the National
    Question*, written in 1913, is adamantly opposed to the
    belief that a single dominant language is essential for each
    nation, this being bourgeois thinking. The national pro-
    gramme of working-class democracy is: 'absolutely no
    privileges for any one nation or any one language' (ibid.: 10).
    'No democrat, and certainly no Marxist, denies that all
    languages should have equal status' (ibid.: 13).

5   Some protagonists of English from underdeveloped countries
    seem to think that other languages should withdraw from the
    unequal struggle with English:

    The development of a language from a premodern
    language into a modern one—i.e. into a vehicle of modern
    science and technology—requires a complex and time-
    consuming effort to create thousands of modern terms and
    to provide the language with books and other reading
    materials. I can say that until now none of the languages of

the new nations has achieved this aim satisfactorily, neither the Hindi language of India, the Urdu of Pakistan, nor the Mandarin of China or the Indonesian language of Indonesia . . . Most of (these languages) are still lacking not only the necessary modern vocabulary of science, technology and economic progress but also the totality of human thought, ideas and experiences through the centuries . . . Will these languages still be able to catch up with the existing advanced modern languages such as English, French, German, Russian and Japanese, through an extensive programme of translation and through the writings of native scholars? Is it still worthwhile to achieve this gigantic task, or, to put it differently: Is it not easier and more efficient for these nations to take the existing modern languages as the languages of their modern culture, which is dominated by the progress of science, technology and economics?

(Alisjahbana 1984: 50–4)

6   Each Periphery context needs its own experts. There must be a break with the counterparting model which assumes a unidirectional transfer of skills and know-how from Centre to Periphery. More experimentation is needed rather than the dissemination of a Centre-patented solution. This presupposes a recognition of the diversity of periphery-English contexts. In ESL contexts, recognition of the reality of nativized forms of English can serve as a source of strength for the Periphery, as it can lead to increased self-reliance.

7   A critical applied linguistics can draw inspiration from critical linguistics (Mey 1985; Fairclough 1989; van Dijk 1990) and critical pedagogy (Freire 1972; Giroux 1988). (For a rationale, with a focus on scientific method, see Pennycook 1990; for a practical example of English empowering oppressed groups in South Africa see Peirce 1989.)

Bibliography

Abdulaziz, M. H. 1982. 'Patterns of language acquisition and use in Kenya: rural-urban differences.' *International Journal of the Sociology of Language* 34: 95–120.

Achard, P. 1986. 'The Development of Language Empires.' Paper presented at the post-congress session on Ethnocentrism in Sociolinguistics, Central Institute of Indian Languages, Mysore, August 1986.

Achebe, C. 1975. *Morning Yet on Creation Day: Essays*. London: Heinemann.

Adams, K. L. and D. T. Brink (eds.) 1990. *Perspectives on Official English. The Campaign for English as the Official Language of the USA*. Berlin: Mouton de Gruyter.

Adiseshiah, M. S. 1980. 'Future Asian education: the challenge of numbers.' *Prospects* X/4: 471–81.

Afolayan, A. 1976. 'The six-year primary project in Nigeria' in Bamgbose (ed.) 1976: 113–34.

Afolayan, A. 1984. 'The English language in Nigerian education as an agent of proper multilingual and multicultural development.' *Journal of Multilingual and Multicultural Development* 5/1: 1–22.

Africa, H. 1980. 'Language in Education in a Multilingual State: A Case Study of the Role of English in the Educational System of Zambia.' Ph.D. dissertation, University of Toronto.

Alatis, J. (ed.) 1978. *International Dimensions of Bilingual Education*. Washington, D.C.: Georgetown University Press.

Alavi, H. and T. Shanin (eds.) 1982. *Introduction to the Sociology of 'Developing' Societies*. Basingstoke: Macmillan.

Alisjahbana, S. T. 1984. 'The problem of minority languages in the overall linguistic problems of our time' in Coulmas (ed.) 1984: 47–55.

Allen, H. B. (ed.) 1965. *Teaching English as a Second Language. A Book of Readings*. New York: McGraw-Hill.

Altbach, P. G. 1975. 'Literary colonialism: books in the Third World.' *Harvard Educational Review* 45/2: 226–36.

Altbach, P. G. 1982. 'Servitude of the mind? Education, dependency, and neocolonialism' in Altbach, Arnove, and Kelly (eds.) 1982: 469–84.

Altbach, P. G., R. F. Arnove, and G. P. Kelly (eds.) 1982. *Comparative Education.* New York: Macmillan.

Altbach, P. G. and G. P. Kelly (eds.) 1978. *Education and Colonialism.* New York and London: Longman.

Ammon, U. (ed.) 1989. *Status and Function of Languages and Language Varieties.* Berlin/New York: de Gruyter.

Ammon, U., N. Dittmar, and K. J. Mattheier (eds.) 1988. *Sociolinguistics: An International Handbook of the Science of Language and Society.* Berlin: de Gruyter.

Andersen, L. and D. M. Windham (eds.) 1982. *Education and Development: Issues in the Analysis and Planning of Postcolonial Societies.* Lexington: Heath.

Anderson, B. 1983. *Imagined Communities. Reflections on the Origin and Spread of Nationalism.* London: Verso.

Anglo-American Conference Report 1961. 'Anglo-American Conference on English Teaching Abroad.' Jesus College, Cambridge. London: British Council (mimeo).

Angula, N. 1983. 'English as a Medium of Communication for Namibia: Trends and Possibilities' in Commonwealth Secretariat and SWAPO 1983: 9–12.

Annamalai, E. 1986a. 'The sociolinguistic scene in India.' *Sociolinguistics* XVI/1: 2–8.

Annamalai, E. 1986b. 'A typology of language movements and their relation to language planning' in Annamalai, Jernudd, and Rubin (eds.) 1986: 6–17.

Annamalai, E. 1988. 'English in India: Unplanned Development.' Paper at the Regional Seminar on Language Planning in a Multilingual Setting: the Role of English. National Unversity of Singapore, September 6–8, 1988.

Annamalai, E., B. Jernudd, and J. Rubin (eds.) 1986. *Language Planning. Proceedings of an Institute.* Mysore: Central Institute of Indian Languages, and Honolulu: East-West Center.

Ansre, G. 1975. 'Madina: three polyglots and some implications for Ghana' in Ohanessian *et al.* 1975: 159–78.

Ansre, G. 1979. 'Four rationalisations for maintaining European languages in education in Africa.' *African Languages.* 5/2: 10–17.

Apple, M. W. 1979. *Ideology and Curriculum.* London: Routledge and Kegan Paul.

Apple, M. W. (ed.) 1982. *Cultural and Economic Reproducton in Education. Essays on Class, Ideology and the State.* London: Routledge and Kegan Paul.

Arnove, R. F. (ed.) 1982a. *Philanthropy and Cultural Imperialism:*

Bibliography

The Foundations at Home and Abroad. Bloomington: Indiana University Press.

Arnove, R. F. 1982b. 'Comparative education and world-systems analysis' in Altbach, Arnove, and Kelly (eds.) 1982: 453–68.

Arnove, R. F. 1982c. 'Foundations and the transfer of knowledge' in Arnove (ed.) 1982a: 305–30.

Arutiunian, Y. V. (ed.) 1986. *Multilingualism: Aspects of Interpersonal Communication in Pluricultural Societies*. Moscow: Institute of Ethnography of the Academy of Sciences of the USSR.

Ashby, E. 1966. *Universities: British, Indian, African. A Study in the Ecology of Higher Education*. Cambridge, Mass.: Harvard University Press.

Ashworth, M. 1985. *Beyond Methodology*. Cambridge: Cambridge University Press.

Asquith Report 1945. *Report of the Commission on Higher Education in the Colonies*. London: HMSO (Command 6647/IV: 673).

Awoniyi, T. A. 1976. 'Mother tongue education in West Africa: a historical account' in Bamgbose (ed.) 1976: 27–42.

Bailey, R. W. and M. Görlach (eds.) 1982. *English as a World Language*. Ann Arbor: University of Michigan Press.

Bamgbose, A. (ed.) 1976. *Mother Tongue Education. The West African Experience*. London: Hodder and Stoughton, and Paris: Unesco.

Battestini, S. (ed.) 1987. *Developments in Linguistics and Semiotics, Langugage teaching and Learning, Communication Across Cultures*. Washington, D. C.: Georgetown University Press.

Bayer, J. M. 1986. *A Sociolinguistic Investigation of the English Spoken by the Anglo-Indians in Mysore City*. Mysore: Central Institute of Indian Languages.

Bender, M. L., J. D. Bowen, R. L. Cooper, and C. A. Ferguson (eds.) 1976. *Language in Ethiopia*. London: Oxford University Press.

Benson, P. 1990. 'A language in decline?' *English Today* 6/4: 19–23.

Benton, R. A. 1986. 'Schools as agents for language revival in Ireland and New Zealand' in Spolsky (ed.) 1986: 53–76.

Beretta, A. 1990. 'The program evaluator: the ESL researcher without portfolio.' *Applied Linguistics* 11/1: 1–15.

Berman, E. H. 1982a. 'Educational colonialism in Africa: the role of American foundations, 1910–1945' in Arnove (ed.) 1982a: 179–202.

Berman, E. H. 1982b. 'The foundations' role in American foreign policy: the case of Africa, post 1945' in Arnove (ed.) 1982a: 203–32.

Bericht. 1985. *Bericht der Bundesregierung über die deutsche Sprache in der Welt.* Bonn: Drucksache 10/3784.

Bernstein, B. 1970. 'Education cannot compensate for society' in Rubinstein and Stoneman (eds.) 1970: 104–16.

Bevan, R. and **N. Grant.** 1983. *Secondary English Project for Botswana, Lesotho and Swaziland.* Harlow: Longman.

Bierbach, C. 1989. 'La lengua, compañera del imperio?' ou 'la filología, compañera del imperialismo?' – 'Nebrija (1492) au service de la politique linguistique du Franquisme' in Py, Bernard, and René Jeanneret (eds.) 'Minorisation linguistique et interaction', papers from an AILA Symposium, Neuchâtel, 16–18 September 1987. Neuchâtel: Faculté des lettres.

Bocock, R. 1986. *Hegemony.* Chichester, and London: Ellis Horwood and Tavistock.

Bokamba, E. G. 1983. 'The Africanisation of English' in Kachru (ed.) 1983b: 77–98.

Bokamba, E. G. and **J. S. Tlou.** 1980. 'The consequences of the language policies of African states vis-à-vis education' in Mateene and Kalema (eds.) 1980: 45–66.

Bourdieu, P. 1982. *Ce que parler veut dire: l'économie des échanges linguistiques.* Paris: Fayard.

Bourhis, R. Y. (ed.) 1984. *Conflict and Language Planning in Quebec.* Clevedon: Multilingual Matters.

Boyd-Barrett, O. 1977. 'Media imperialism: towards an international framework for the analysis of media systems' in Curran, Gurewitch, and Woollacott (eds.) 1977: 116–35.

Bowers, R. 1983. 'Project planning and performance' in Brumfit (ed.) 1983: 99–120.

Bowers, R. 1985. 'General issues' in Quirk and Widdowson (eds.) 1985: 255–57.

Bowers, R. (ed.) 1987. *Language Teacher Education: An Integrated Programme for EFL Teacher Training.* London: Modern English Publications in association with the British Council, ELT Documents 125.

Brandt Commission 1980. *North-South: A Programme for Survival.* London: Pan.

Brandt Commission 1983. *Common Crisis: Cooperation for World Recovery.* London: Pan.

Bright, J. A. 1968. 'The training of teachers of English as a second language in Africa' in Perren (ed.) 1968: 14–43.

British Council, India 1950. 'The Teaching of English as a Foreign Language', a report on the British Council Summer Conference, Mahableshwar, 3–13 May 1950.

British Council Annual Reports 1940–41 to 1989–90.

Britten, D. 1985. 'Teacher training in ELT.' *Language Teaching*, Part 1, April 1985: 112–28; Part 2, July 1985: 220–38.

Bromley, Y. V. 1984. *Theoretical Ethnography*. Moscow: Nauka.

Bromley, Y. V. and V. I. Kozlov 1981. 'Present-day ethnic processes in the intellectual culture of the peoples of the USSR' in Grigulevich and Kozlov (eds.) 1981: 19–38.

Brown, G. 1989. 'Sitting on a rocket.' An interview with Gillian Brown. *ELT Journal* 43/3: 167–72.

Brumfit, C. J. (ed.) 1983. *Language Teaching Projects for the Third World*. Oxford: Pergamon, in association with the British Council, ELT Documents 116.

Brumfit, C. J. 1984. *Communicative Methodology in Language Teaching. The Roles of Fluency and Accuracy*, Cambridge: Cambridge University Press.

Brumfit, C. J. 1985a. 'Creativity and constraint in the language classroom' in Quirk and Widdowson (eds.) 1985: 148–57.

Brumfit, C. J. 1985b. *Language and Literature Teaching: from Practice to Principle*. Oxford: Pergamon.

Brumfit, C. J. 1985c. Preface, in Brumfit *et al.* (eds.) 1985: v.

Brumfit, C. J., R. Ellis, and J. Levine (eds.) 1985. *English as a Second Language in the UK. Linguistic and Educational Contexts*. Oxford: Pergamon, in association with the British Council, ELT Documents 121.

Bugarski, R. 1987. 'Language policy and planning in Yugoslavia' in J. Maurais (ed.) *L'aménagement linguistique comparé*. Québec and Paris: Conseil de la langue française, le Robert: 417–52.

Burchfield, R. 1985. *The English language*. Oxford: Oxford University Press.

Burgh, J. 1985. Foreword, in Quirk and Widdowson (eds.) 1985: vii–ix.

Calvet, L. -J. 1974. *Linguistique et colonialisme: petit traité de glottophagie*. Paris: Payot.

Calvet, L. -J. 1979. *Langue, corps, société*. Paris: Payot.

Calvet, L. -J. 1982. 'The spread of Mandingo: military, commercial and colonial influence on a linguistic datum' in Cooper 1982a: 184–97.

Calvet, L. -J. 1985. 'Mehrsprachige Märkte und Vehikularsprachen: Geld und Sprache' in Pleines (ed.) 1985: 91–101.

Calvet, L. -J. 1987. *La guerre des languages et les politiques linguistiques*. Paris: Payot.

Cameron, D. and J. Bourne 1989. 'Grammar, Nation and Citizenship: Kingman in Linguistic and Historical Perspective.' London:

Institute of Education, University of London, Department of English and Media Studies, Occasional Paper No. 1, and *Language and education* 2/3: 147–60.

Candlin, C. N. 1983. 'Discoursal patterning and the equalizing of interpretive opportunity' in Smith (ed.) 1983: 125–46.

Candlin, C. N. 1985. 'Teacher-centred training: costing the process' in Quirk and Widdowson (eds.) 1985: 107–20.

Capotorti, F. 1979. *Study on the rights of persons belonging to ethnic, religious and linguistic minorities.* New York: United Nations.

Carnoy, M. 1982. 'Education, economy and the State' in Apple (ed.) 1982: 79–126.

Catford, J. C. 1961. 'Training in the teaching of English' in Wayment (ed.) 1961: 33–7.

Catford, J. C. 1981. 'First AL landmark dates from 1871.' *The Linguistic Reporter* 23/5: 13.

Cawson, F. 1975. 'The international activities of the Center for Applied Linguistics' in Fox 1975 Volume 2: 385–434.

Center for Applied Linguistics 1959. *Proceedings of the Conference on Teaching English Abroad, May 1959.* Washington, D. C.: Center for Applied Linguistics.

Center for Applied Linguistics 1964. *Report on the Fifth Meeting of the International Conference on Second Language Problems.* Rome, March 1964. Washington, D.C.: Center for Applied Linguistics.

Center of African Studies 1986. 'Language in Education in Africa'. Seminar proceedings 26; proceedings of a seminar at the Centre of African Studies, University of Edinburgh, 29–30 November, 1985. Edinburgh: Centre of African Studies.

Centre for British Teachers 1989. *Pilot Study of the Career Paths of EFL Teachers.* London: Centre for British Teachers.

Chambers, F. and P. Erith 1990. 'On justifying and evaluating aid-based ELT.' *ELT Journal* 44/2: 138–43.

Chileshe, J. 1982. 'Literacy, Dependence, and Ideological Formation: The Zambian Experience.' Unpublished paper, University of Sussex.

Chinebuah, I. K. 1981. 'Language policy and practice in education in Ghana.' *AILA Bulletin* 2/30: 8–36.

Chinweizu, O., I. Jemie, and Madubuike 1983. *Toward the Decolonization of African Literature.* Washington, D. C.: Howard University.Press.

Chishimba, M. M. 1981. 'Language teaching and literacy: East Africa.' *Annual Review of Applied Linguistics* II: 168–88.

Chomsky, N. 1982. *Towards a New Cold War: Essays on the Current Crisis and How we Got There.* London: Sinclair Browne.

Christensen, P. K., B. S. Hansen, A. Haugbølle, and I. H. Østergaard

1983. *Amerikanisering af det danske kulturliv i perioden 1948–1958.* Aalborg: Aalborg Universitetsforlag.

Christophersen, P. 1958. Correspondence to the editor, *English Language Teaching* XII/4: 151–2.

Christophersen, P. 1989. 'The prescriptive bugbear.' *English Today* 19: 46–7.

Chrystal, J. A. 1988. *Engelskan i svensk dagspress* (English in Swedish daily newspapers), Skrifter utgivna av Svenska språknämnden 74, Stockholm: Esselte.

Churchill, S. 1984. *The Education of Linguistic and Cultural Minorities in the OECD Countries.* Clevedon: Multilingual Matters.

Clarke, D. 1988. 'The project approach to bilateral ELT aid programmes.' English Teaching Information Circular 22: 25–9.

Cleghorn, A., M. Merritt, and J. O. Abagi 1989. 'Language policy and science instruction in Kenyan primary schools.' *Comparative education review* 33/1: 21–39.

Clive, J. 1973. *Macaulay: The Shaping of the Historian.* New York: Knopf.

Clyne, M. 1982. *Multilingual Australia.* Melbourne: River Seine.

Clyne, M. 1986. 'Comment from "down under".' *International Journal of the Sociology of Language*: The question of an official language, language rights and the English Language Amendment 60: 134–44.

Cobarrubias, J. and J. A. Fishman (eds.) 1983. *Progress in Language Planning: International Perspectives.* Berlin: Mouton.

Colonna, F. 1975. *Instituteurs algériens: 1883–1939.* Alger: Office des publications universitaires.

Commission on Security and Economic Assistance 1983. A Report to the Secretary of State. Washington, D.C.: Department of State.

Commonwealth Relations Office 1959. *Report of the Commonwealth Education Conference, Oxford, 15–28 July.* London: HMSO (Command 841).

Commonwealth Secretariat 1982. *The Declaration of Commonwealth Principles,* brochure in Notes on the Commonwealth series. London: Commonwealth Secretariat.

Commonwealth Secretariat 1985. *Implementing an English Language Programme for Namibians.* London: Commonwealth Secretariat.

Commonwealth Secretariat and SWAPO 1983. *English Language Programme for Namibians.* Seminar Report, Lusaka, 19–27 October 1983.

Conrad, A. W. and J. A. Fishman 1977. 'English as a world language: the evidence' in Fishman, Cooper, and Conrad 1977: 3–76.

Constable, P. 1984. 'The case for teaching initial reading in Zambian languages.' *Nkrumah Education Review* 3: 13–17.

Coombs, P. H. 1964. *The Fourth Dimension of Foreign Policy: Educational and Cultural Affairs.* New York: Harper and Row, for the Council on Foreign Relations.

Coombs, P. H. 1985. *The World Crisis in Education – The View from the Eighties.* New York: Oxford University Press.

Cooper, R. L. (ed.) 1982a. *Language Spread: Studies in Diffusion and Social Change.* Bloomington: Indiana University Press, for the Center for Applied Linguistics.

Cooper, R. L. 1982b. 'A framework for the study of language spread' in Cooper 1982a: 5–36.

Cooper, R. L. 1988. 'Planning language acquisition' in Lowenberg (ed.) 1988a: 140–51.

Corder, S. Pit 1973. *Introducing Applied Linguistics.* Harmondsworth: Penguin.

Coste, D. (ed.) 1984. *Aspects d'une politique de diffusion du français langue étrangère depuis 1945, matériaux pour une histoire.* Paris: Hatier.

Coulmas, F. (ed.) 1981. *A festschrift for native speaker.* The Hague: Mouton.

Coulmas, F. (ed.) 1984. *Linguistic Minorities and Literacy: Language Policy Issues in Developing Countries.* Berlin: Mouton.

Coulmas, F. (ed.) 1988. *With Forked Tongues. What are National Languages Good For?* Singapore: Karoma.

Coulmas, F. (ed.) 1991. *A Language Policy for the European Community: Quandaries and Prospects.* Berlin: de Gruyter.

Court D. and D. P. Ghai (eds.) 1974. *Education, Society and Development.* Nairobi: Oxford University Press.

Cox Report 1989. *English from ages 5 to 16.* London: Department of Education and Science and Welsh Office.

Crystal, D. 1985. 'How many millions? The statistics of English today.' *English Today* 1: 7–9.

Cummins, J. 1979. 'Cognitive/academic language proficiency, linguistic interdependence, the optimal age question, and some other matters.' *Working Papers on Bilinguilism* 19: 197–205.

Cummins, J. 1984. *Bilingualism and Special Education: Issues in Assessment and Pedagogy.* Clevedon: Multilingual Matters.

Cummins, J. and M. Danesi 1990. *Heritage Languages: The Development and Denial of Canada's Linguistic Resources.* Toronto: Our Schools/Our Selves Education Foundation.

Curran, J., M. Gurevitch, and J. Woollacott (eds.) 1977. *Mass Communication and Society.* London: Arnold.

Cziko, G. A. 1982. 'Vernacular education in the Southern Sudan: a test case for literacy.' *Journal of Multilingual and Multicultural Development* 3:4: 293–314.

Dakin, J., B. Tiffen, and H. G. Widdowson 1968. *Language in Education: The Problem in Commonwealth Africa and the Indo-Pakistan Sub-continent.* London: Oxford University Press.

Dalby, D. 1985. 'The life and vitality of African languages: a charter for the future' in Mateene, Kalema, and Chomba (eds.) 1985: 29–34.

Dale, R. 1982a. 'Education and the capitalist state: contributions and contradictions' in Apple (ed.) 1982: 127–61.

Dale, R. 1982b. 'Learning to be . . . what? Shaping education in "developing societies"' in Alavi and Shanin (eds.) 1982: 408–21.

Dale, R. and A. Wickham 1984. 'International organizations and educational dependency' in Treffgarne (ed.) 1984a: 38–51.

D'anglejan, A. 1986. 'Multilingualism in the Canadian context.' *Annual Review of Applied Linguistics* 6 (1985): 113–31.

Davidson, B. 1982. 'Ideology and identity: an approach from history' in Alavi and Shanin (eds.) 1982: 435–56.

Davies, A. 1986. Introduction, in Center of African Studies, 1986: 1–18.

Davies, A. 1991. 'British applied linguistics: the contribution of S. Pit Corder' in Phillipson *et al.* (eds.) 1991: 52–60.

Davis, A., C. Criper, and A. P. R. Howatt (eds.) 1984. *Interlanguage.* Edinburgh: Edinburgh University Press.

Day, R. R. 1981. 'ESL: a factor in linguistic genocide?' in Fisher *et al.* (eds.) 1981: 73–8.

Defoe, D. 1965. *Robinson Crusoe.* Harmondsworth: Penguin (first published 1719).

de la Warr Commission 1937. *Report of the commission appointed by the Secretary of State for the Colonies.* London: HMSO (Colonial no. 142).

Department of Education and Science 1983. *Foreign Languages in the School Curriculum*, a consultative paper. London: DES.

Development Issues 1985. *US Actions Affecting Developing Countries.* Annual Report of the Chairman of the Development Coordination Committee, Washington, D. C.: US International Development Cooperation Agency.

Devonish, H. 1986. *Language and Liberation. Creole Language Politics in the Caribbean.* London: Karia Press.

de Witte, B. 1991. 'The impact of European Community rules on linguistic policies of the member states' in Coulmas 1991.

Donaldson, F. 1984. *The British Council: The First 50 Years.* London: Cape.

Dorman, A. and **A. Mattelart** 1975. *How to Read Donald Duck: Imperialist Ideology in the Disney Comic.* New York: International General.

Drogheda Report Summary 1954. *Report of the Independent Committee of Enquiry into the Overseas Information Services.* London: HMSO (Command 9138).

Duncan Report 1969. *The Report of the Review Committee on Overseas Representation, 1968–69.* London: HMSO (Command 4107).

Dunford House Seminar Report 1986. London: The British Council.

Dunford Seminar Report 1987. 1988. London: The British Council.

Dunford Seminar Report 1988. 1989. London: The British Council.

Durmüller, U. 1984. 'English for International and Intranational Purposes in Multilingual Switzerland, A Research Project Report'. Paper at the AILA World Conference, Brussels, August 4–11, 1984.

Edwards, J. 1984a. 'Irish: planning and preservation.' *Journal of Multilingual and Multicultural Development* 5/3 and 4: 267–76.

Edwards, J. (ed.) 1984b. *Linguistic Minorities, Policies and Pluralism.* London: Academic Press.

Eisemon, T. O. 1989. 'Educational reconstruction in Africa.' *Comparative Education Review* 33/2: 110–6.

Elliot Report 1945. *Report of the Commission on Higher Education in West Africa.* London: HMSO (Command 6655, V, 593).

English Curriculum Committee 1984. *First Steps in Reading: In English or in a Zambian Language.* Lusaka: Ministry of Higher Education.

English Today. Cambridge: Cambridge University Press.

Enriquez, V. G. and **E. P. Marcelino** 1984. *Neocolonial Politics and the Language Struggle in the Philippines.* Quezon City: Philippine Psychology Research House.

Eriksen, K. E. and **E. Niemi** 1981. *Den finske fare: sikkerhetsproblemer og minoritetspolitik i nord 1860–1940.* Oslo: Universitetsforlaget.

Eshiwani, G. S. 1989. 'The World Bank document revisited.' *Comparative Education Review* 33/2: 116–25.

Fabian, J. 1986. *Language and Colonial Power: The Appropriation of Swahili in the Former Belgian Congo 1880–1938.* Cambridge: Cambridge University Press.

Færch, C., K. Haastrup, and R. Phillipson 1984. *Learner Language and Language Learning*. Clevedon: Multilingual Matters, and Copenhagen: Gyldendal.

Færch, C. and G. Kasper (eds.) 1983. *Strategies in Interlanguage Communication*. Harlow: Longman.

Færch, C. and G. Kasper (eds.) 1987. *Introspection in Second Language Research*. Clevedon: Multilingual Matters.

Fairclough, N. 1989. *Language and Power*. Harlow: Longman.

Fanon, F. 1952. *Peau noire, masques blancs*. Paris: Seuil.

Fanon, F. 1961. *Les damnés de la terre*. Paris: Maspero.

Featherstone, M. (ed.) 1990. *Global Culture. Nationalism, Globalization and Modernity*. London: Sage.

Ferguson, C. A. 1983. Foreword, in Kachru (ed.) 1983b: vii-xi.

Filipović, R. (ed.) 1982. *The English Element in European Languages: Reports and Studies*. Zagreb: Institute of Linguistics, University of Zagreb.

FIPLV 1988. *FIPLV's 1988 Report to Unesco*. A combined response to the Director General's Circular (Ref: DG/8.2/049) and report identifying future trends and needs in language education, with special reference to foreign languages. London: FIPLV.

Firth, J. R. 1961. 'The study and teaching of English at home and abroad' in Wayment (ed.) 1961: 11–21.

Firth, J. R. 1964. *The Tongues of Men and Speech*. London: Oxford University Press (first published 1930).

Fisher, D. 1982. 'American philanthropy and the social sciences: the reproduction of a conservative ideology' in Arnove (ed.) 1982a: 233–68.

Fisher, J. C., M. A. Clarke, and J. Schachter (eds.) 1981. *On TESOL '80. Building Bridges: Research and Practice in Teaching English as a Second Language*. Washington, D. C.: TESOL.

Fishman, J. A. (ed.) 1968. *Readings in the Sociology of Language*. The Hague: Mouton.

Fishman, J. A. 1972. *Language in Sociocultural Change*. Essays by J. A. Fishman selected and introduced by A. S. Dil. Stanford: Stanford University Press.

Fishman, J. A. 1976. *Bilingual Education. An International Sociological Perspective*. Rowley, Mass.: Newbury House.

Fishman, J. A. 1977. 'The spread of English as a new perspective for the study of "Language maintenance and language shift"' in Fishman, Cooper, and Conrad 1977: 108–33.

Fishman, J. A. 1987. 'English: neutral tool or ideological protagonist? A 19th century East-Central European Jewish intellectual views English from afar.' *English World-Wide* 8/1: 1–10.

Fishman, J. A. 1989a. *Language and Ethnicity in Minority*

Language Perspective. Clevedon: Multilingual Matters.

Fishman, J. A. 1989b. 'Bias and anti-intellectualism: the frenzied fiction of "English Only" ' in Fishman 1989a: 638–54.

Fishman, J. A. 1990. 'What is reversing language shift (RLS) and how can it succeed?' *Journal of Multicultural and Multilingual Development* 11/1 and 2: 5–36.

Fishman, J. A., R. L. Cooper, and A. W. Conrad 1977. *The Spread of English: The Sociology of English as an Additional Language.* Rowley, Mass.: Newbury House.

Fishman, J. A., R. L. Cooper, and Y. Rosenbaum 1977. 'English around the world' in Fishman, Cooper, and Conrad 1977: 77–107.

Fishman, J. A., C. A. Ferguson, and J. Das Gupta (eds.) 1968. *Language Problems of Developing Nations.* New York: Wiley.

Flaitz, J. 1988. *The Ideology of English: French Perceptions of English as a World Language.* Berlin: Mouton de Gruyter.

Foster, B. 1968. *The Changing English Language.* London: Macmillan.

Foster, P. 1975. 'Dilemmas of educational development: what we might learn from the past.' *Comparative Education Review* 19/3: 375–92.

Foster, P. 1977. 'The vocational school fallacy in educational planning' in Karabel and Halsey (eds.) 1977.

Foster, P. 1989. 'Some hard choices to be made.' *Comparative Education Review* 33/2: 104–10.

Fox, M. 1975. *Language and Development: A Retrospective Survey of Ford Foundation Language Projects, 1952–1974.* New York: Ford Foundation (Volume 1, report; volume 2, case studies).

Fox, M. 1979. 'The Ford Foundation and CAL.' *The Linguistic Reporter* 21/7: 4.

Frank, A. G. 1969. *Latin America: Underdevelopment or Revolution?* New York: Monthly Review Press.

Freire, P. 1972. *Pedagogy of the Oppressed.* Harmondsworth: Penguin.

French, M. 1986. *Beyond Power: On Women, Men and Morals.* London: Cape.

Fries, C. C. 1945. *Teaching and Learning English as a Foreign Language.* Ann Arbor: University of Michigan Press.

Gage, W. W. and S. Ohannessian 1974. 'ESOL enrollments throughout the world.' *The Linguistic Reporter* 16/9: 13–16.

Galtung, J. 1980. *The True Worlds. A Transnational Perspective.*

New York: The Free Press.

Galtung, J. 1988. *Methodology and Development*. Essays in methodology, volume 3. Copenhagen: Christian Ejlers.

Gandhi, M. 1929. *The Story of my Experiments with Truth*(English edition, 1949). London: Cape.

García, O. and R. Otheguy, (eds) 1989. *English Across Cultures: Cultures Across English. A Reader in Cross-cultural Communication*. Berlin: Mouton de Gruyter.

Gaski, H. 1986. *Den samiske litteraturens røtter. Om samenes episk poetiske diktning*. Tromsø: Magistergradsafhandling, Institutt for Sprog og Litteratur, Universitetet i Tromsø.

Gass, S. and L. Selinker (eds.) 1983. *Language Transfer in Language Learning*. Rowley, Mass.: Newbury House.

Gatenby, E. V. 1965. 'Conditions for success in language learning' in Allen (ed.) 1965: 9–14.

Genesee, F. 1976. 'The suitability of immersion programmes for all children.' *Canadian Modern Language Review* 32/5: 494–515.

Gilroy, P. 1987. *There ain't no Black in the Union Jack*. London: Hutchinson.

Giordan, H. (ed.) 1992. 'Language Rights/Human Rights.' Papers from the Council of Europe colloquium, Strasbourg, 15–17 November 1990.

Giordan, H. (ed.) 1991. *Les Minorités en Europe: Droits Linguistiques et Droits de l'Homme*. Paris: Kimé.

Giroux, H. 1988. *Teachers as Intellectuals: Toward a Critical Pedagogy of Learning*. Granby: Bergin and Garvey.

Golding, P. 1977. 'Media professionalism in the Third World: the transfer of an ideology' in Curran, Gurevitch, and Woollacott (eds.) 1977: 291–308.

Gomes de Matos, F. 1985. 'The linguistic rights of language learners.' *Language Planning Newsletter* 11/3: 1–2.

Goodman, E. R. 1968. 'World state and world language' in Fishman (ed.) 1968: 717–36.

Görlach, M. 1988. 'English as a world language—the state of the art.' *English World-Wide* 9/1: 1–32.

Gorter, D., J. F. Hoekstra, L. G. Jansma, and J. Ytsma (eds.) 1990. *Fourth International Conference on Minority Languages, Volume II, Western and Eastern European Papers*. Clevedon: Multilingual Matters.

Gramsci, A. 1971. *Selections from the Prison Notebooks*. London: Lawrence and Wishart.

Grant, N. J. H. and S. O. Unoh 1976. *Reading for a Purpose*, Book 1. Harlow: Longman.

Gregersen, F. 1991. 'Relationships between linguistics and applied linguistics: some Danish examples' in Phillipson *et al.* 1991: 11–28.

Grigulevich, I. R. and V. I. Kozlov (eds.) 1981. *Ethnocultural Processes and National Problems in the Modern World.* Moscow: Progress.

Grillo, R. D. 1989. *Dominant Languages: Language and Hierarchy in Britain and France.* Cambridge: Cambridge University Press.

Guboglo, M. N. 1986a. 'Factors affecting bilingualism in national languages and Russian in a developed socialist society' in Spolsky (ed.) 1986: 23–31.

Guboglo, M. N. 1986b. 'Languages and communication in Soviet society' in Arutiunian (ed.) 1986: 3–18.

Guboglo, M. N. 1986c. 'National and language policy in the Soviet Union at present' in Arutiunian (ed.) 1986: 47–64.

Guerra, S. 1988. 'Voting rights and the Constitution: the disenfranchisement of non-English speaking citizens.' *Yale Law Journal* 97: 1419–37.

Haarmann, H. 1990. 'Language planning in the light of a general theory of language: a methodological framework.' *International Journal of the Sociology of Language* 86: 103–26.

Haberland, H. 1988. 'Research policy' in Ammon *et al.* (eds.) 1988: 1814–26.

Haddad, W. D., M. Carnoy, R. Rinaldi, and O. Regel 1990. 'Education and Development: Evidence for New Priorities.' Washington, D. C.: World Bank (Discussion paper 95).

Haigh, A. 1974. *Cultural Diplomacy in Europe.* Strasbourg: Council of Europe.

Hakuta, K. 1986. *Mirror of Language: The Debate on Bilingualism.* New York: Harper and Row, Basic Books.

Halliday, M. A. K., A. McIntosh, and P. Strevens 1964. *The Linguistic Sciences and Language Teaching.* London: Longman.

Hamel, R. E. 1990. 'Language and Education for Indian Peoples in Latin America.' Paper at the AILA World Congress, Thessaloniki, April 1990. To appear in Skutnabb-Kangas and Phillipson (forthcoming).

Hamelink, C. 1983. *Cultural Autonomy in Global Communications.* New York and London: Longman.

Hancock, G. 1989. *Lords of Poverty. The Free-wheeling Lifestyles, Power, Prestige and Corruption of the Multi-billion Dollar Aid Business.* London: Macmillan.

Hanf, T., K. Ammann, P. V. Dias, M. Fremerey, and H. Weiland 1975. 'Education: an obstacle to development? Some remarks about the political functions of education in Asia and Africa.' *Comparative Education Review* 19: 68–87.

Harding, S. 1986. *The Science Question in Feminism*. Ithaca, NY: Cornell University Press.

Harrison, W., C. Prator, and G. R. Tucker 1975. *English-Language Policy Survey of Jordan. A Case Study in Language Planning*. Arlington: Center for Applied Linguistics.

Hasan, R. 1976. 'Socialization and cross-cultural education.' *International Journal of the Sociology of Language* 8: 7–26.

Haugen, E. 1971. 'Instrumentalism in language planning' in Rubin and Jernudd (eds.) 1971: 281–9.

Haut Conseil de la Francophonie 1986. *État de la francophonie dans le monde. Rapport 1985*. Paris: La documentation française.

Hayes, A. 1983. 'Planning a project' in Brumfit (ed.) 1983: 15–28.

Hayter, T. and C. Watson 1985. *Aid: Rhetoric and Reality*. London: Pluto.

Heath, S. B. and F. Mandabach 1983. 'Language status decisions and the law in the United States' in Cobarrubias and Fishman (eds.) 1983: 87–106.

Henriksen, C. 1990. 'The Danish Language in the European Community.' Proceedings of the Twelfth Scandinavian Conference of Linguistics, Reykjavik.

Hernández-Chávez, E. 1978. 'Language maintenance, bilingual education, and philosophies of bilingualism in the United States' in Alatis (ed.) 1978: 527–50.

Hernández-Chávez, E. 1988. 'Language policy and language rights in the United States: issues in bilingualism' in Skutnabb-Kangas and Cummins (eds.) 1988: 45–56.

Heyneman, S. D. 1982. 'Resource availability, equality, and educational opportunity among nations' in Andersen and Windham (eds.) 1982.

Higgs, D. (ed.) 1986. *Communications Skills Training in Bilateral Aid Projects. Dunford House Seminar Report 1985*. London: The British Council.

Higgs, P. 1979. 'Culture and Value Changes in Zambian School Literature'. Ph.D. thesis, University of California at Los Angeles.

Hill, C. P. 1980. 'Some developments in language and education in Tanzania since 1969' in Polomé and Hill (eds.) 1980: 362–409.

Hill, C. P. 1986. 'Patterns of language use among Tanzanian secondary school pupils 1970: a benchmark' in Centre of African Studies 1986: 231–76.

Hindley, R. 1990. *The Death of the Irish Language, a Qualified Obituary*. London: Routledge.

Hobson, J. A. 1902. *Imperialism, a Study*. London: Allen and Unwin.

Holloway, J. 1961. 'Contribution to a session on English Language and Literature' in Wayment (ed.) 1961: 45–7.

Hollqvist, H. 1984. *The Use of English in Three Large Swedish Companies.* Uppsala: Acta Universitatis Upsaliensis, Studia Anglistica Upsaliensia 55.

Holmstrand, L. 1980. Effekterna pa kundskaber, färdigheter och attityder av tidigt pabörjad undervisning i engelska. Uppsala: Pædagogisk forskning i Uppsala 18.

Hollis, R. 1990. 'A national languages policy for New Zealand.' *New Settlers and Multicultural Education Issues* 7/3: 12–14.

Honkala, T., P. Leporanta-Morley, L. Ljukka, and E. Rougle 1988. 'Finnish children in Sweden strike for better education' in Skutnabb-Kangas and Cummins (eds.) 1988: 238–50.

Hoogveldt, A. M. M. 1982. *The Third World in Global Development.* Basingstoke: Macmillan.

Howatt, A. P. R. 1984. *A History of English Language Teaching.* Oxford: Oxford University Press.

Huiser, G. and B. Mannheim (eds.) 1979. *The Politics of Anthropology.* The Hague: Mouton.

Hurst, P. 1984. 'Educational aid and dependency' in Treffgarne (ed.) 1984a: 23–37.

Hvalkof, P. and S. Aaby 1981. *Is God an American? An Anthropological Perspective on the Work of the Summer Institute of Linguistics.* Copenhagen: International Work Group for Indigenous Affairs, and London: Survival International.

Hyden, G. 1983. *No Shortcuts to Progress: African Development Management in Perspective.* London: Heinemann.

Hymes, D. H. 1985. Preface, in Wolfson and Manes (eds.) 1985: v–viii.

Ikara, B. 1987. *Minority Languages and Lingua Francas in Nigeria.* Maiduguri: University of Maiduguri.

Illich, I. 1981. *Shadow Work.* Boston and London: Marion Boyars.

Imhoff, G. 1987. 'Partisans of language.' *English Today* 11: 37–40.

Institute for Ethnic Studies 1986. *Education in Multicultural Societies*, Treatises and Documents 18. Ljubljana: Institute for Ethnic Studies.

Iredale, R. O. 1986 'The English language as aid' in Dunford House Seminar Report 1986: 41–6.

Iredale, R. O. 1989. Foreword in Dunford House Seminar Report 1988: 7.

Isaacs, R. 1968. *Learning Through Language.* Dar es Salaam: Tanzania Publishing House.

Jakobovits, L. A. 1970. *Foreign Language Learning: A Psycho-linguistic Analysis of the Issues.* Rowley, Mass.: Newbury House.

Jernudd, B. 1977. 'Review of Harrison, Prator, and Tucker (eds.) 1975.' *Sudan Research Information Bulletin* February 1977 (revised version in *Language in Society* 8/1: 1979).

Jernudd, B. 1981. 'Planning language treatment: linguistics for the Third World.' *Language in Society* 10: 43–52.

Jernudd, B. and J. V. Neustupny 1986. 'Language Planning: for Whom?' Paper at the International Colloquium on Language Planning. Ottawa, May 1986.

Jespersen, O. 1905. *Growth and Structure of the English Language.* Oxford: Blackwell, ninth edition 1967.

Johnson, R. K. (ed.) 1989. *The Second Language Curriculum.* Cambridge: Cambridge University Press.

Johnson, R. K. 1990. 'International English: towards an acceptable, teachable target variety.' *World Englishes* 9/3: 301–15.

Jolly, R. (ed.) 1969. *Education in Africa—Research and Action.* Nairobi: East African Publishing House.

Jones, D. 1983. 'The Purposes for which English is Used in Sweden.' Stockholm: English Department, English in Sweden project report 5.

Jones, D. G. 1973. 'The Welsh language movement' in Stephens (ed.) 1973.

Jones, T. J. 1922. *Education in Africa: A Study of West, South and Equatorial Africa by the African Education Commission under the Auspices of the Phelps-Stokes Fund and the Foreign Missions Societies of N. America and Europe.* New York: Phelps-Stokes Fund.

Jones, T. J. 1925. *Education in East Africa: a study of East, Central and South Africa by the Second African Education Commission under the Auspices of the Phelps-Stokes Fund, in cooperation with the International Education Board.* New York: Phelps-Stokes Fund.

Jordan, D. F. 1987a. 'Aborigines and Education' in Keeves (ed.) 1987.

Jordan, D. F. 1987b. 'Aboriginal identity: the management of a minority group by the mainstream society.' *Canadian Journal of Native Studies.*

Jordan, D. F. 1988. 'Rights and claims of indigenous people—education and the reclaiming of identity; the case of the Canadian natives, the Sami, and Australian aborigines' in Skutnabb-Kangas and Cummins (eds.) 1988: 189–222.

Joseph, G. G., V. Reddy, and M. Searle-Chatterjee 1990. 'Euro-centrism in the social sciences.' *Race and Class* 31/4: 1–26.

Kachru, B. B. 1975. 'A retrospective study of the Central Institute of English and Foreign Languages and its relation to Indian Universities' in Fox 1975, volume 2: 27–94.

Kachru, B. B. 1981. 'An overview of language policy and planning.' *Annual Review of Applied Linguistics* II: 2–7.

Kachru, B. B. 1983a. *The Indianization of English: the English Language in India*. Delhi: Oxford University Press.

Kachru, B. B. (ed.) 1983b. *The Other Tongue: English Across Cultures*. Oxford: Pergamon.

Kachru, B. B. 1984. 'The alchemy of English: social and functional power of non-native varieties' in Kramarae *et al.* (eds.) 1984: 176–93.

Kachru, B. B. 1985. 'Standards, codification and sociolinguistic realism' in Quirk and Widdowson (eds.) 1985: 11–30.

Kachru, B. B. 1986a *The Alchemy of English: The Spread, Functions and Models of Non-native Englishes*. Oxford: Pergamon.

Kachru, B. B. 1986b. 'The power and politics of English.' *World Englishes* 5/2–3: 121–40.

Kachru, B. B. 1991. 'Liberation linguistics and the Quirk concern.' *English Today* 25 (7/1:3–13).

Kachru, B. B. and R. Quirk 1981. Introduction in Smith (ed.) 1981a: xiii–xx.

Kalema, J. 1980. 'Report on functions and activites of the OAU Inter-African Bureau of Languages' in Mateene and Kalema (eds.) 1980: 1–8.

Kalema, J. 1985. Introduction in Mateene, Kalema, and Chomba (eds.) 1985: 1–6.

Karabel, J. and A. Halsey (eds.) 1977. *Power and Ideology in Education*. New York: Oxford University Press.

Karetu, T. (forthcoming). 'The Maori language in New Zealand' in Skutnabb-Kangas and Phillipson (eds.) forthcoming.

Kashoki, M. E., 1982. 'Rural and urban multilingualism in Zambia: some trends.' *International Journal of the Sociology of Language* 34: 137–66.

Kasper, G. 1981. *Pragmatische Aspekte in der Interimsprache: eine Untersuching des Englischen fortgeschrittener deutscher Lerner*. Tübingen: Günter Narr.

Keeves, J. (ed.) 1987. *Research and Studies in Australian Education, A Trend Report in Education*. Canberra: Academy of Social Sciences.

Kelly, G. and P. G. Altbach 1978. Introduction in Altbach and Kelly (eds.) 1978. 1–49.

Kennedy, C. *et al.* 1989. 'Talking shop. Teacher development: an employer's view.' *English Language Teaching Journal* 43/2: 127–32.

Kennedy, P. 1981. *The Realities behind Diplomacy: Background Influences on British External Policy 1865–1980.* Glasgow: Fontana.

Kenyatta, J. 1979. *Facing Mount Kenya.* London: Heinemann.

Keskitalo, J. H. 1984. *Samisk eller norsk?* Oslo: Statens speciallaererhogskole.

Khan, V. S. 1985. 'Language education for all?' Chapter 7 of the Swann Report. London: University of London Institute of Education, Centre for Multicultural Education, working paper 6.

Khubchandani, L. M. 1983. *Plural Languages, Plural Cultures: Communication, Identity, and Sociopolitical Change in Contemporary India.* Honolulu: University of Hawaii, for East-West Center.

Kidron, M. and **R. Segal** 1981. *The State of the World Atlas.* London: Pan.

King, A. H. 1961. 'The nature of the demand for English in the world today, as it affects British universities' in Wayment (ed.) 1961: 22–5.

King, E. W. and **C. Vallejo** 1986. 'Training teachers in the United States for a multilingual society: some comparisons to the United Kingdom.' *Journal of Multilingual and Multicultural Development* 7/1: 71–6.

King, K. 1985. *North-South collaboration in higher education, Academic links between Britain and the developing world,* Occasional papers 8, Edinburgh: Center of African Studies, Edinburgh University.

King, K. 1986. Postscript in Centre for African Studies 1986: 445–54.

Kingman Report 1988. *Report of the Committee of Enquiry into the Teaching of English Language.* London: HMSO.

Kivikuru, U. 1985. 'From Import to Modelling: Cultural Dependency and Finnish Mass Communications.' Paper to VII Nordic Conference for Mass Communication Research, Knebel, Denmark.

Kolinsky, M. 1983. 'The demise of the Inter-University Council for Higher Education Overseas: a chapter in the history of the idea of the university.' *Minerva* XXI/1: 37–80.

Krag, H. L. 1983. *Die Sowjetunion – Staat, Nationalitätenfrage und Sprachenpolitik.* Wien: Sprache und Herrschaft 13/II.

Kramarae, C., M. Schulz, and **W. M. O'Barr** (eds.) 1984. *Language and Power.* Beverly Hills and London: Sage.

Krashen, S. 1981. *Second Language Acquisition and Second Language Teaching.* Oxford: Pergamon.

Krasnick, H. 1986. 'Images of ELT.' *English Language Teaching Journal* 40/3: 191–5.

Kuo, E. C. Y. and B. H. Jernudd 1988. 'Language Management in a Multilingual State: The Case of Planning in Singapore.' Paper for the National University of Singapore Seminar on Language planning in a multilingual setting: the role of English, 6–8 September 1988.

Kuparinen, E. and K. Virtanen (eds.) 1983. *The Impact of American Culture*. Turku: General History, University of Turku, publication 10.

Ladefoged, P., R. Glick, and C. Criper 1972. *Language in Uganda*. London: Oxford University Press.

Lado, R. 1957. *Linguistics across Cultures: Applied Linguistics for Language Teachers*. Ann Arbor: University of Michigan Press.

Lambert, W. 1975. 'Culture and language as factors in learning and education' in Wolfgang (ed.) *Education of Immigrant Students*. Toronto: OISE.

Lebovic, J. H. 1988. 'National interests and US foreign aid: the Carter and Reagan years.' *Journal of Peace Research* 25/2: 115–37.

Lenin, V. I. 1951. *Critical Remarks on the National Question*. Moscow: Progress Publishers.

Lenin, V. I. 1973. *On Imperialism and Imperialists*. Moscow: Progress Publishers.

Le Page, R. B. 1964. *The National Language Question. Linguistic Problems of Newly Independent States*. London: Oxford University Press.

Lewis, E. G. 1982. 'Movements and agencies of language spread: Wales and the Soviet Union compared' in Cooper 1982a: 217–59.

Leys, C. 1982. 'Samuel Huntington and the end of classical modernization theory' in Alavi and Shanin (eds.) 1982: 332–49.

Lieberson, S. J. 1982. 'Forces affecting language spread: some basic propositions' in Cooper (ed.) 1982a: 37–62.

Lieberson, S. J. and E. J. McCabe 1982. 'Domains of language usage and mother-tongue shift in Nairobi.' *International Journal of the Sociology of Language* 34: 83–94.

Lightbown, P. M. 1987. 'The influence of linguistic theory on language acquisition research: now you see it, now you don't' in Battestini (ed.) 1987: 130–42.

Lillis, K. M. 1984. 'Africanising the school literature curriculum in Kenya: a case-study in curriculum dependency' in Treffgarne (ed.) 1984b: 56–80.

Linguistic Minorities Project 1985. *The Other Languages of England*. London: Routledge and Kegan Paul.

Ljung, M. 1982. 'Social Determinants of the Use of English in Sweden.' Stockholm: English Department, English in Sweden project report 2.

Lo Bianco, J. 1987. *National Policy on Languages*, Canberra: Commonwealth Department of Education.

Longboat, D. 1984. 'First Nations' Jurisdiction over Education: The Path to Survival as Nations.' Ottawa: mimeo.

Lord, R. and **B. K. T'sou** 1985. *The Language Bomb. The Language Issue in Hong Kong.* Hong Kong: Longman.

Lowenberg, P. H. (ed.) 1988a. *Language Spread and Language Policy: Issues, Implications, and Case Studies.* Washington, D.C.: Georgetown University Press.

Lowenberg, P. H. 1988b. 'Malay in Indonesia, Malaysia, and Singapore: three faces of a national language' in Coulmas (ed.) 1988: 146–79.

MacCabe, C. 1985. 'English literature in a global context' in Quirk and Widdowson (eds.) 1985: 37–46.

Mackey, W. 1970. Foreword in Jakobovits 1970.

MacKinnon, K. 1990. 'Language maintenance and viability in the contemporary Scottish Gaelic speech-community: some social and demographic factors' in Gorter *et al.* (eds.) 1990: 69–90.

McCallen, B. 1989. *English: a World Commodity. The International Market for Training in English as a Foreign Language.* Special Report 1166, London: The Economist Intelligence Unit.

Maher, J. 1986. 'The development of English as an international language of medicine.' *Applied Linguistics* 7/2: 206–18.

Makerere Report 1961. *Report on the Conference on the Teaching of English as a Second Language.* Entebbe: Commonwealth Education Liaison Committee.

Malinowski, B. 1936. 'Native education and culture contact.' *International Review of Missions* 25: 480–515.

Malinowski, B. 1979. Introduction in Kenyatta 1979: vii–xiv.

Mamdani, M. 1976. *Politics and Class Formation in Uganda.* New York: Monthly Review Press.

Marckwardt, A. H. 1965. 'English as a second language and English as a foreign language' in Allen (ed.) 1965: 3–8.

Marckwardt, A. H. 1967. 'Teaching English as a foreign language: a survey of the past decade.' *The Linguistic Reporter*, supplement 19: 1–8.

Markee, N. 1989. 'ESP within a new descriptive framework.' *World Englishes* 8/2: 133–46.

Marshall, D. F. 1986. 'The question of an official language: language rights and the English Language Amendment.' *Inter-*

national Journal of the Sociology of Language 60: 7–75.

Mateene, K. 1980a. Introduction in Mateene and Kalema (eds.) 1980: vi–vii.

Mateene, K. 1980b. 'Failure in the obligatory use of European languages in Africa and the advantages of a policy of linguistic independence' in Mateene and Kalema (eds.) 1980: 9–41.

Mateene, K. 1985a. 'Colonial languages as compulsory means of domination, and indigenous languages, as necessary factors of liberation and development' in Mateene, Kalema, and Chomba (eds.) 1985: 60–9.

Mateene, K. 1985b. 'Reconsideration of the official status of colonial languages in Africa' in Mateene, Kalema, and Chomba (eds.) 1985: 18–28.

Mateene, K. and J. Kalema (eds.) 1980. *Reconsideration of African Linguistic Policies*. Kampala: OAU Bureau of Languages, OAU/BIL Publication 3.

Mateene, K., J. Kalema, and B. Chomba (eds.) 1985. *Linguistic Liberation and Unity of Africa*. Kampala: OAU Bureau of Languages, OAU/BIL Publication 6.

Maxwell, I. C. M. 1980. *Universities in Partnership*. Edinburgh: Scottish Academic Press.

Mayhew, A. 1926. *The Education of India*. London: Faber and Gwyer.

Mazrui, A. A. 1968. 'Some sociopolitical functions of English literature in Africa' in Fishman, Ferguson, and Das Gupta (eds.) 1968: 183–98.

Mazrui, A. A. 1975. *The Political Sociology of the English Language. An African Perspective*. The Hague: Mouton.

Mazrui, A. A. 1978a. 'The African university as a multinational corporation' in Altbach and Kelly (eds.) 1978: 331–54.

Mazrui, A. A. 1978b. *Political Values and the Educated Class in Africa*. Berkeley and Los Angeles: University of California Press.

McCallen, B. 1989. *English: a world commodity. The international market for training in English as a foreign language*. Special Report 1166. London: The Economist Intelligence Unit.

McDonough, S. H. 1981. *The Psychology of Foreign Language Learning*. London: George Allen and Unwin.

McLaughlin, B. 1987. *Second Language Acquisition*. London: Edward Arnold.

Merritt, M. and M. Abdudaziz 1988. 'Swahili as a national language in East Africa' in Coulmas (ed.) 1988: 48–67.

Mey, J. 1985. *Whose language? A Study in Linguistic Pragmatics*. Amsterdam: John Benjamin.

Miles, R. 1989. *Racism*. London: Routledge.

Ministry of Education 1956. *Report of the Official Committee on the Teaching of English Overseas*. London: Minstry of Education.

Misra, B. G. 1982. 'Language spread in a multilingual setting: the spread of Hindi as a case study' in Cooper 1982a: 148–57.

Moag, R. F. 1982. 'English as a foreign, second, native and basal language: a new taxonomy for English-using societies' in Pride (ed.) 1982b: 11–40.

Morrison, B. 1989. 'TEFL training—some Chinese lessons.' London: *English Teaching Information Circular*. British Council 23: 4–9.

Moussirou-Mouyama, A. 1985. 'Die einführung der französischen Sprache in Gabun: die Philosophie der Glottophagie' in Pleines (ed.) 1985: 75–90.

Mullard, C. 1980. 'Racism in society and schools: history, policy, and practice.' London: University of London Institute of Education, Centre for Multicultural Education Occasional Paper no. 1.

Mullard, C. 1984. 'The Social Dynamic of Migrant Groups: From Progressive to Transformative Policy in Education.' Paper prepared for OECD/CERI. Paris, July 1984.

Mullard, C. 1985. *Race, Power and Resistance*. London: Routledge and Kegan Paul.

Mullard, C. 1988. 'Racism, ethnicism, and etharcy or not? The principles of progressive control and transformative change' in Skutnabb-Kangas and Cummins (eds.) 1988: 359–78.

Munby, J. 1978. *Communicative Syllabus Design*. Cambridge: Cambridge University Press.

National Council for Mother Tongue Teaching 1985. 'The Swann Report: education for all?' *Journal of Multilingual and Multicultural Development* 6/6: 497–508.

Neustupny, J. V. 1983. 'Towards a paradigm for language planning.' *Language Planning Newsletter* 9/4: 1–4.

Ngũgĩ wa Thiong'o 1972. *Homecoming: Essays on African and Caribbean Literature, Culture and Politics*. London: Heinemann.

Ngũgĩ wa Thiong'o 1981. *Writers in Politics*. London: Heinemann.

Ngũgĩ wa Thiong'o 1982. *Devil on the Cross*. London: Heinemann.

Ngũgĩ wa Thiong'o 1983. *Barrel of a Pen*. London: New Beacon Books.

Ngũgĩ wa Thiong'o 1985. 'The language of African literature.' *New Left Review* April-June 1985: 109–27.

Ngũgĩ wa Thiong'o 1986. *Decolonising the Mind: the Politics of Language in African Literature*. London: James Currey.

Nicolson, H. 1955. 'The British Council 1934–1955' in *Report on the Work of the British Council 1934–1955*. London: The British Council: 4–30.

Nilsen, A. P., H. Bosmajian, H. L. Gershuny, and J. P. Stanley 1977. *Sexism and Language*. Urbana: National Council of Teachers of English.

Ninkovich, F. A. 1981. *The Diplomacy of Ideas. US Foreign Policy and Cultural Relations, 1938–1950*. Cambridge: Cambridge University Press.

Njoroge, Kimani wa' 1986. 'Multilingualism and some of its implications for language policy and practices in Kenya' in Centre of African Studies 1986: 327–54.

Nuffield Foundation and the Colonial Office 1953. *African Education: A Study of Educational Policy and Practice in British Tropical Africa*. Oxford: Oxford University Press.

Obura, A. P. 1986. 'Research issues and perspectives in language in education in Africa: an agenda for the next decade' in Centre of African Studies 1986: 413–44.

Ohannessian, S. 1978. 'Historical background' in Ohannessian and Kashoki (eds.) 1978: 271–91.

Ohannessian, S. and G. Ansre 1975. 'Some reflections on the uses of sociolinguistically oriented language surveys' in Ohannessian, Ferguson, and Polomé (eds.) 1975: 51–70.

Ohannessian, S., C. A. Ferguson, and E. C. Polomé (eds.) 1975. *Language Surveys in Developing Nations*. Washington, D. C.: Center for Applied Linguistics.

Ohannessian, S. and M. E. Kashoki (eds.) 1978. *Language in Zambia*. London: International African Institute.

Okonkwo, C. E. 1983. 'Le bilinguisme dans l'enseignment: réexamen de l'expérience nigériane.' *Perspectives* XIII/3: 403–9.

Onoge, O. F. 1979. 'The counterrevolutionary tradition in African studies: the case of applied anthropology' in Huiser and Mannheim (eds.) 1979: 45–66.

Open University 1983. *Third World Atlas* (Ben Crow, Alan Thomas *et al*). Milton Keynes: Open University Press.

Organization for African Unity Inter-African Bureau of Languages (OAU-BIL) 1985. 'Linguistic liberation and unity of Africa' in Mateene, Kalema, and Chomba (eds.) 1985: 7–17.

Overseas Development Administration 1985. *A Guide to the Key English Language Teaching (KELT) Scheme*. London: ODA, Education Division.

Overseas Development Administration 1990. *Into the Nineties: an Education Policy for British Aid*. London: ODA.

Overseas Information Services 1957. London: HMSO (Command 225).

Overseas Information Services 1959. London: HMSO (Command 685).

Palmberg, R. 1985. 'How much English vocabulary do Swedish-speaking primary-school pupils know before starting to learn English at school?' in Ringbom (ed.) 1985: 89–98.

Palmer, H. E. 1964. *The Principles of Language Study*. London: Oxford University Press.

Paternost, J. 1985. 'A sociolinguistic tug of war between language value and language reality in contemporary Slovenia.' *International Journal of the Sociology of Language* 52: 9–30.

Pattanayak, D. P. 1981. *Multilingualism and Mother Tongue Education*. Delhi: Oxford University Press.

Pattanayak, D. P. 1985. 'Diversity in communication and languages; predicament of a multilingual nation state: India, a case study' in Wolfson and Manes (eds.) 1985: 399–407.

Pattanayak, D. P. 1986a. 'Educational use of the mother tongue' in Spolsky (ed.) 1986: 5–15.

Pattanayak, D. P. 1986b. 'Language, politics, region formation, and regional planning' in Annamalai, Jernudd, and Rubin (eds.) 1986: 18–42.

Pattanayak, D. P. 1986c. *Ethnicity in Plural Societies: A Study of Two Cultures*. London: Centre for Multicultural Education.

Pattanayak, D. P. 1986d. Foreword in Annamalai, Jernudd, and Rubin (eds.) 1986: v-vii.

Pattanayak, D. P. 1988. 'Monolingual myopia and the petals of the Indian lotus: do many languages divide or unite a nation?' in Skutnabb-Kangas and Cummins (eds.) 1988: 379–89.

Patthey, G. G. 1989. 'Mexican language policy.' *New Language Planning Newsletter* 3/3: 1–6.

Peirce, B. N. 1989. 'Toward a pedagogy of possibility in the teaching of English internationally: people's English in South Africa.' *TESOL Quarterly* 23/2: 401–20.

Pennycook, A. 1990. 'Towards a critical applied linguistics for the 1990s.' *Issues in Applied Linguistics* 1/1: 8–28.

Perren, G. E. 1958. 'Bilingualism, or replacement? English in East Africa.' *English Language Teaching* XIII/1: 18–22.

Perren, G. E. 1959. 'Training and research in English teaching. The work of the Special Centre in Nairobi.' *Oversea Education* vol. XXXI: 50–7. 125–33, 156–65.

Perren, G. E. 1963. 'Teaching English literature overseas: historical notes and present instances' in press (ed.) 1963: 9–18.

Perren, G. E. (ed.) 1968. *Teachers of English as a Second Language*. Cambridge: Cambridge University Press.

Perren, G. E. 1969. 'Education through a second language: an

African dilemma' in Jolly (ed.) 1969: 197–207.
Perren, G. E. and **M. F. Holloway** 1965. *Language and Communication in the Commonwealth*. London: HMSO (for Commonwealth Education Liaison Committee).
Pfeiffer, A. B. 1975. 'Designing a bilingual curriculum' in Troike and Modiano (eds.) 1975: 132–9.
Phillipson, R. 1988. 'Linguicism: structures and ideologies in linguistic imperialism' in Skutnabb-Kangas and Cummins (eds.) 1988: 339–58.
Phillipson, R. 1990. Book review of Calvet 1987 and Wardhaugh 1987. *World Englishes* 9/1: 85–94.
Phillipson, R., E. Kellerman, L. Selinker, M. Sharwood Smith, and **M. Swain** (eds.) 1991. *Foreign/Second language Pedagogy Research: A Commemorative Volume for Claus Færch*. Clevedon: Multilingual Matters.
Phillipson, R. and **T. Skutnabb-Kangas** 1983. *'Cultilingualism— Papers in Cultural and Communicative (In)competence.'* ROLIG-papir 28, Roskilde Universitetscenter.
Phillipson, R. and **T. Skutnabb-Kangas** 1985. 'Applied linguistics as agents of wider colonisation: the gospel of International English' in Pleines (ed.) 1985: 159–79.
Phillipson, R. and **T. Skutnabb-Kangas** 1986a. *Linguicism Rules in Education*. Roskilde: Institute VI, Roskilde University Centre (3 volumes).
Phillipson, R. and **T. Skutnabb-Kangas** 1986b. 'English: The Language of Wider Colonisation.' Paper at the XIth World Congress of Sociology. New Delhi, India, August 1986.
Phillipson, R., T. Skutnabb-Kangas, and **H. Africa** 1985. 'Namibian educational language planning: English for liberation or neo-colonialism?' in Mateene, Kalema, and Chomba (eds.) 1985: 42–59; also in Spolsky (ed.) 1986: 77–95.
Platt, J., H. Weber, and **M. L. Ho** 1984. *The New Englishes*. London: Routledge and Kegan Paul.
Pleines, J. (ed.) 1985. *Sprachenkonkurrenz und gesellschaftliche Planung. Das Erbe des Kolonialismus*. Osnabrück: Osnabrücker Beiträge zur Sprachtheorie 31.
Politi, J. 1985. Comment in Quirk and Widdowson (eds.) 1985: 195–6.
Polomé, E. C. and **C. P. Hill** (eds.) 1980. *Language in Tanzania*. Oxford: Oxford University Press, for the International African Institute.
Prator, C. H. 1968. 'The British heresy in TEFL' in Fishman, Ferguson, and Das Gupta (eds.) 1968: 459–76.
Preiswerk, R. 1978. 'The place of intercultural relations in the study

of international relations.' *Yearbook of World Affairs*, 1978: 251–67.

Preiswerk, R. (ed.) 1980. *The Slant of the Pen: Racism in Children's Books*. Geneva: World Council of Churches.

President's Commission on Foreign Languages and International Studies 1979. *Strength through Wisdom: A Critique of US Capability*. Washington, D. C.: US Government Printing Office.

Press, J. (ed.) 1963. *The Teaching of English Literature Overseas*. London: Methuen.

Prewitt, K. 1974. 'Educational and social equality in Kenya' in Court and Ghai (eds.) 1974: 199–216.

Price, G. 1985. *Languages of Britain*. London: Arnold.

Pride, J. B. 1982a. 'The appeal of the new Englishes' in Pride (ed.) 1982b: 1–7.

Pride, J. B. (ed.) 1982b. *New Englishes*. Rowley, Mass.: Newbury House.

Pride, J. B. and **Liu Ru-Shan** 1988. 'Some aspects of the spread of English in China since 1949.' *International Journal of the Sociology of Language* 74: 41–70.

Prodromou, L. 1988. 'English as cultural action.' *ELT Journal* 42/2: 73–83.

Pupier, P. and **J. Woehrling** (eds.) 1989. *Langue et droit*. Montreal: Wilson and Lafleur.

Quirk, R. 1985. 'The English language in a global context' in Quirk and Widdowson (eds.) 1985: 1–6.

Quirk, R. 1989. 'Separated by a common dilemma.' *The Times Higher Education Supplement* 10.2.1989.

Quirk, R. 1990. 'Language varieties and standard langauge.' *English Today* 21 (6/1): 3–10.

Quirk, R., S. Greenbaum, G. Leech, and **J. Svartvik** 1985. *A Comprehensive Grammar of the English Language*. Harlow: Longman.

Quirk, R. and **H. G. Widdowson** (eds.) 1985. *English in the World: Teaching and Learning the Language and Literatures*. Cambridge: Cambridge University Press, for the British Council.

Rabinow, P. (ed.) 1984. *The Foucault Reader*. New York: Pantheon.

Rajyashree, K. S. 1986. *An Ethnolinguistic Study of Dharavi, a Slum in Bombay*. Mysore: Central Institute of Indian Languages.

Rampton, M. B. H. 1990. 'Displacing the "native speaker": expertise, affiliation, and inheritance.' *ELT Journal* 44/2: 97–101.

Rannut, M. 1989. 'Language Conflict in Estonia.' Paper at the Fourth International Conference on Minority Languages, Ljouwert, June 1989.

Rannut, M. (forthcoming). 'Beyond the linguistic policy of the Soviet Union: Estonian cultural autonomy and linguistic rights' in Skutnabb-Kangas and Phillipson (eds.) forthcoming.

Richards, I. A. 1961. 'An impression of the Conference.' Appendix II, Anglo-American Conference on English Teaching Abroad, Cambridge 1961 (British Council internal report).

Richards, J. 1984. 'The secret life of methods.' *TESOL Quarterly* 18/1: 7–24.

Richards, J., J. Platt, and **H. Weber** 1985. *Longman Dictionary of Applied Linguistics*. Harlow: Longman.

Riggs, F. W. 1986. 'What is ethnic? What is national? Let's turn the tables.' *Canadian Review of Studies in Nationalism*.

Ringbom, H. (ed.) 1985. *Foreign Language Learning and Bilingualism*. Åbo: The research institute of Åbo Akademi.

Rodgers, T. S. 1989. 'Syllabus design, curriculum development and polity determination' in Johnson (ed.) 1989: 24–34.

Rodney, W. 1973. *How Europe Underdeveloped Africa*. London: Bogle l'ouverture.

Rogers, J. 1982. 'The world for sick proper.' *English Language Teaching Journal* 36/3: 144–51.

Rosen, H. and **T. Burgess** 1980. *Languages and Dialects of London School Children: an investigation*. London: Ward Lock.

Rubagumya, C. M. (ed.) 1990. *Language in Education in Africa: A Tanzanian Perspective*. Clevedon: Multilingual Matters.

Rubin, J. and **B. Jernudd** (eds.) 1971. *Can Language be Planned?* Hawaii: University Press of Hawaii.

Rubinstein, D. and **C. Stoneman** (eds.) 1970. *Education and Democracy*. Harmondsworth: Penguin.

Said, E. W. 1978. *Orientalism*. Harmondsworth: Penguin.

Said, E. W. 1990. 'Figures, configurations, transfigurations.' *Race and Class* 32/1: 1–16.

Sajavaara, K. 1983. 'Anglo-American influence on Finnish' in Kuparinen and Virtanen (eds.) 1983: 36–49.

Sampson, G. 1980. 'Review of Dieter Wunderlich, Foundations of Linguistics.' *Journal of Linguistics* 16: 166–8.

Sancheti, N. 1984. 'Ford philanthropy and Indian education: some issues of motives and power' in Treffgarne (ed.) 1984b: 1–14.

Schiller, H. I. 1969. *Mass Communications and American Empire*. New York: Augustus M. Kelley.

Schiller, H. I. 1976. *Communication and Cultural Domination*. White Plains, N. Y.: Sharpe.

Scotton, C. M. 1981. 'The linguistic situation and language policy in East Africa.' *Annual Review of Applied Linguistics* II: 8–20.

Scotton, C. M. 1982. 'Learning lingua francas and socioeconomic integration' in Cooper (ed.) 1982a: 63–94.

Sebeok, T. A. 1971. *Current Trends in Linguistics. Volume 7. Linguistics in sub-Saharan Africa*. Mouton: The Hague.

Seebohm Report 1981. Review of the British Council, by Lord Seebohm, Lord Chorley, and Richard Auty. London: British Council.

Selinker, L. 1991. 'Early language transfer experimental thought' in Phillipson *et al.* (eds.) 1991: 29–37.

Serpell, R. 1978. 'Some developments in Zambia since 1971' in Ohannessian and Kashoki (eds.) 1978: 424–47.

Shield, L. E. 1984. 'Unified Cornish—fiction or fact? An examination of the death and resurrection of the Cornish language.' *Journal of Multilingual and Multicultural Development*, 5/3 and 4: 329–38.

Siachitema, A. 1986. 'Attitudes towards the use of English in three neighbourhoods of Lusaka' in Centre of African Studies 1986: 199–230.

Sieghart, P. 1983. *The International Law of Human Rights*. Oxford: Oxford University Press.

Sigurd, B. (ed.) 1977. *De nordiska språkens framtid*. Stockholm: Skrifter utgivna av Svenska Språknämnden 61.

Sinclair, J. 1985. Selected issues in Quirk and Widdowson (eds.) 1985: 248–54.

Skutnabb-Kangas, T. 1984a. *Bilingualism or not—The Education of Minorities*. Clevedon: Multilingual Matters.

Skutnabb-Kangas, T. 1984b. 'Barns mänskliga språkliga rättigheter. Om finsk frigörelsekamp på den svenska skolfronten. (Children's linguistic human rights. On Finnish liberation struggle on the Swedish school front)'. *Kritisk Psykologi* 1–2: 38–46.

Skutnabb-Kangas, T. 1984c. 'Children of guest workers and immigrants: linguistic and educational issues' in Edwards (ed.) 1984b: 17–48.

Skutnabb-Kangas, T. 1986. 'Who wants to change what and why—conflicting paradigms in minority education research' in Spolsky (ed.) 1986: 153–81.

Skutnabb-Kangas, T. 1987. 'Are the Finns in Sweden an Ethnic Minority? Finnish Parents Talk about Finland and Sweden.' Working Paper 1. Research project: The education of the Finnish minority in Sweden. Roskilde: Roskilde University Centre.

Skutnabb-Kangas, T. 1988. 'Multilingualism and the education of minority children' in Skutnabb-Kangas and Cummins (eds.) 1988: 9–44. First published in Phillipson and Skutnabb-Kangas 1986a: 42–72.

Skutnabb-Kangas, T. (1991). 'Bilingual competence and strategies for negotiating ethnic identity' in Phillipson *et al* (eds.). 1991: 307–32.

Skutnabb-Kangas, T. and S. Bucak (forthcoming). 'Killing a mother tongue—how the Kurds are deprived of linguistic human rights' in Skutnabb-Kangas and Phillipson (forthcoming).

Skutnabb-Kangas, T. and J. Cummins (eds.) 1988. *Minority Education: From Shame to Struggle.* Clevedon: Multilingual Matters.

Skutnabb-Kangas, T. and P. Leporanta-Morley 1986. 'Migrant women and education' in S. Lie (ed.) *Scandinavian Journal for Development Alternatives.* Special issue, December: 83–112.

Skutnabb-Kangas, T. and R. Phillipson 1983. 'Intercommunicative and intercultural competence' in Phillipson and Skutnabb-Kangas 1983: 43–77.

Skutnabb-Kangas, T. and R. Phillipson 1985a. *Educational Strategies in Multilingual Contexts.* ROLIG-papir 35. Roskilde: Roskilde Universitscenter.

Skutnabb-Kangas, T. and R. Phillipson. 1985b. 'Cultilinguistic imperialism—what can Scandinavia learn from the second and third worlds?' in Skutnabb-Kangas and Phillipson 1985a: 27–55; also in Wande *et al.* (eds.) 1987: 167–90.

Skutnabb-Kangas, T. and R. Phillipson 1986a. 'Denial of Linguistic Rights: The New Mental Slavery.' Paper presented at the XIth World Congress of Sociology. New Delhi, August 1986.

Skutnabb-Kangas, T. and R. Phillipson 1986b. 'The Legitimacy of the Arguments for the Spread of English.' Paper presented at the post-congress session on Ethnocentrism in Sociolinguistics. Central Institute of Indian Languages: Mysore, August 1986.

Skutnabb-Kangas, T. and R. Phillipson 1989a. ' "Mother tongue": the theoretical and sociopolitical construction of a concept' in Ammon (ed.) 1989: 450–77.

Skutnabb-Kangas, T. and R. Phillipson. 1989b. *Wanted! Linguistic Human Rights.* ROLIG-papir 44. Roskilde: Roskilde Universitscenter.

Skutnabb-Kangas, T. and R. Phillipson 1990. 'Kurdish—A Prohibited Language. On How the Kurds are Deprived of Linguistic Human Rights in Turkey.' Bremen: Initiative for Human Rights in Kurdistan.

Skutnabb-Kangas, T. and R. Phillipson (eds.) (forthcoming). *Linguistic Human Rights.*

Skutnabb-Kangas, T. and P. Toukomaa. 1976. *Teaching Migrant Children's Mother Tongue and Learning the Language of the Host Country in the Context of the Socio-cultural Situation of the Migrant Family.* A report prepared for Unesco. Tampere: Department of Sociology and Social Psychology. University of Tampere: Research reports 15.

Sørensen, K. 1973. *Engelske lån i dansk*. Copenhagen: Dansk Sprognævns Skrifter 8.

Smith, L. E. (ed.) 1983. *Readings in English as an International Language*. Oxford: Pergamon.

Smith, L. E. and C. L. Nelson 1985. 'International intelligibility of English: directions and resources.' *World Englishes* 4/3: 333–42.

Smolicz, J. J. (forthcoming). 'The "monolingual urge" and minority rights: Australia's language policies from an international perspective' in Skutnabb-Kangas and Phillipson (eds.) forthcoming.

Spencer, J. 1971. 'Colonial language policies and their legacies' in Sebeok (ed.) 1971: 537–47.

Spolsky, B. (ed.) 1986. *Language and Education in Multilingual Settings*. Clevedon: Multilingual Matters.

Spolsky, B. 1989. *Conditions for Second Language Learning*. Oxford: Oxford University Press.

Sridhar, K. K. and S. N. Sridhar 1986. 'Bridging the paradigm gap: second language acquisition theory and indigenized varieties of English.' *World Englishes* 5/1: 3–14.

Srivastava, A. K. 1986. 'Language planning in multilingual contexts: educational and psychological implication' in Annamalai, Jernudd, and Rubin (eds.) 1986: 43–72.

Stairs, A. 1988. 'Beyond cultural inclusion: an Inuit example of indigenous educational development' in Skutnabb-Kangas and Cummins (eds.) 1988: 308–27.

Stephens, M. 1982. *The Welsh Language Today*. Llandysul: Gomer Press.

Stern, H. H. 1983. *Fundamental Concepts of Language Teaching*. Oxford: Oxford University Press.

Sternagel, P. 1984. 'Kann auswärtige Kulturpolitik in Entwicklungsländern Selbstbestimmung stimulieren? Vom Dilemma des Goethe Instituts' in Pleines and Wigger (eds.) *Sprachen aus Europa: sprachpolitische Folgen des Kolonialismus*. Osnabrück: Osnabrücker Beiträge zur Sprachtheorie 25: 10–23.

Stone, G. W. 1959. 'The pattern of language interest in the MLA' in Center for Applied Linguistics 1959: 11–19.

Strevens, P. 1976. 'A theoretical model of the language learning/teaching process.' *Working Papers in Bilingualism* 11: 129–52.

Strevens, P. 1980. *Teaching English as an International Language: from Practice to Principle*. Oxford: Pergamon.

Stubbs, M. 1991. 'Educational language planning in England and Wales: Multi-cultural rhetoric and assimilationist assumptions', in Coulmas (ed.) 1991.

Sutherland, G. (ed.) 1973. *Arnold on Education*. Harmondsworth: Penguin.

Summers, D. 1988. 'English Language Teaching dictionaries: past, present, and future.' *English Today* 14: 10–16.

Swain, M. and S. Lapkin 1982. *Evaluating Bilingual Education: A Canadian Case Study*. Clevedon: Multilingual Matters.

Swann Report 1985. *Education for All*. Report of the committee of enquiry into the education of children from ethnic minority groups. London: HMSO (Command 9453).

SWAPO 1982. *Preliminary Perspectives into an Emergent Educational system for Namibia*. Luanda: Department of Education and Culture, SWAPO of Namibia.

SWAPO 1983. *Education for the Future: Programmes, Prospects and Needs*. Luanda: Department of Education and Culture, SWAPO of Namibia.

SWAPO 1984. *Education: for all! National integrated educational system for emergent Namibia*. Luanda: SWAPO of Namibia.

Tadadjeu, M. 1980. *A Model for Functional Trilingual Education Planning in Africa*. Paris: Unesco.

Taleb Ibrahimi, A. 1973. *De la décolonisation à la révolution culturelle*. Alger: Societé nationale d'édition et de diffusion.

Thierfelder, F. 1940. *Englischer Kulturimperialismus. Der "British Council" als Werkzeug der geistigen Einkreisung Deutschlands*. Berlin: Junker und Dünnhaupt (Schriften des Deutschen Instituts für Aussenpolitische Forschung).

Thumboo, E. 1985. 'Twin perspectives and multi-ecosystems: tradition for a commonwealth writer.' *World Englishes* 4/2: 213–21.

Tiffen, B. 1968. 'Language and education in Commonwealth Africa' in Dakin, Tiffen, and Widdowson 1968: 63–113.

Torstendahl, R. and M. Burrage (eds.) 1990. *The Formation of Professions. Knowledge, State and Strategy*. London: Sage.

Tosi, A. 1984. *Immigration and Bilingual Education*. Oxford: Pergamon.

Tosi, A. 1988. 'A new jewel in the crown of the modern prince. The changing patterns of language education for ethnic minorites in England' in Skutnabb-Kangas and Cummins (eds.) 1988: 79–102.

Toukomaa, P. and T. Skutnabb-Kangas 1977. *The Intensive Teaching of the Mother Tongue to Migrant Children at Preschool Age*. Tampere: Department of Sociology and Social Psychology. University of Tampere Research reports 26.

Treffgarne, C. B. W. (ed.) 1984a. *Contributions to the Workshop* on '*Reproduction and Dependency in Education*', part 1. London: Department of Education in Developing Countries. University of London Institute of Education (EDC occasional papers 6).

Treffgarne, C. B. W. (ed.) 1984b. *Contributions to the Workshop on 'Reproduction and Dependency in Education*', part 2. London: Department of Education in Developing Countries. University of London Institute of Education (EDC occasional papers 7).

Treffgarne, C. B. W. 1986. 'Language policy in francophone Africa: scapegoat or panacea?' in Centre of African Studies 1986: 141–70.

Trevelyan, G. O. 1881. *The Life and Letters of Lord Macaulay*. London: Longmans, Green.

Troike, R. C. 1977. 'The future of English.' Editorial, *The Linguistic Reporter* 19/8: 2.

Troike, R. C. and N. Modiano (eds.) 1975. *Proceedings of the First Inter-American Conference on Bilingual Education*. Arlington: Center for Applied Linguistics.

Trudgill, P. (ed.) 1984. *Language in the British Isles*. Cambridge: Cambridge University Press.

Turi, J. G. (forthcoming). 'Typology of language legislation' in Skutnabb-Kangas and Phillipson (eds.) forthcoming.

Unesco 1953. *The Use of the Vernacular Languages in Education*. Paris: Unesco.

Unesco 1969. *Educational Development in Africa* (I.The planning process; II.Costing and financing; III.Integration and administration). Paris: Unesco, International Institute for Educational Planning.

UNIN (United Nations Institute for Namibia) 1981. *Toward a Language Policy for Namibia. English as the Official Language: Perspectives and Strategies*. Lusaka: UNIN.

United States Advisory Commission on Public Diplomacy 1986. Washington, D. C.: State Department.

Usher, G. 1989. 'English as a second language, language support and anti-racist education: language policies in further and adult education.' *Language Issues* 3/1: 31–5.

Van Dijk, T. 1990. 'Discourse and society: a new journal for a new research focus.' *Discourse and Society* 1/1: 5–16.

Verma, M. 1986. 'From Macaulay to Michael Swann: The Language Education of South Asian Children.' Paper presented at the 11th World Congress of Sociology. New Delhi, August 1986.

Verschueren, J. 1989. 'English as object and medium of (mis)understanding', in García and Otheguy (eds.) 1989: 31–54.
Viereck, W. and W. -D. Bald (eds.) 1986. *English in Contact with Other Languages*. Budapest: Akademiai Kiado.
Viikberg, J. 1989. 'The Siberian Estonians and language policy' in Görter *et al.* (eds.) 1990: 175–80.
Vinje, F.- E. 1977. 'Språksituationen i Norge' in Sigurd (ed.) 1977: 26–40.

Wagner, J. 1991. 'Innovation in foreign language teaching' in Phillipson *et al.* (eds.) 1991: 288–306.
Wande, E., J. Anward, B. Nordberg, L. Steensland, and M.Thelander (eds.) 1987. *Aspects of Multilingualism, Proceedings from the Fourth Nordic Symposium on Bilingualism, 1984*. Uppsala: Acta Universitatis Upsaliensis, Studia Multietnica Upsaliensia 2.
Wardhaugh, R. 1987. *Languages in Competition: Dominance, Diversity and Decline*. Oxford: Blackwell.
Warner, A. 1958. 'African students and the English background.' *English Language Teaching* XIII:1: 3–7.
Wayment, H. G. (ed.) 1961. *English Teaching Abroad and the British Universities*. London: Methuen.
Webb, J. and J. Sinclair 1986. 'Educational project management: survey of communications skills requirements in aid projects in Indonesia' in Higgs (ed.) 1986: 7–32.
Weinreich, U. 1963. *Languages in Contact. Findings and Problems*. The Hague: Mouton.
West, M. 1958. 'Bilingualism.' *English Language Teaching* XII/3: 94–7.
White, A. J. S. 1965. *The British Council: The First 25 Years, 1934–1959*. London: British Council.
White, J. 1980. 'The historical background to national education in Tanzania' in Polomé and Hill (eds.) 1980: 261–82.
Whiteley, W. H. (ed.) 1974. *Language in Kenya*. Nairobi: Oxford University Press.
Widdowson, H. G. 1968. 'The teaching of English through science' in Dakin, Tiffen, and Widdowson 1968: 115–75.
Wigzell, R. 1983. 'The role and status of English as a subject in the Zambian English-medium context' in Brumfit (ed.) 1983: 1–14.
Williams, C. H. 1990. 'The United Kingdom's Celtic Languages: a Socio-linguistic Profile.' Paper at the International Colloquium on Language Rights/Human Rights, Council of Europe, Strasbourg, 15–17 November 1990, in Giordan 1992.
Williams, R. 1986. 'Extract from a report on an ESP seminar at Kaduna Polytechnic, Nigeria' in Higgs (ed.) 1986: 41–3.

Williams, R. 1973. 'Base and superstructure in Marxist cultural theory.' *New Left Review* 82: 3–16.

Williams, R. 1977. *Marxism and Literature*. Oxford: Oxford University Press.

Williams, R. 1983. *Keywords*. London: Flamingo/Fontana.

Williamson, K. 1972. 'The Nigerian Rivers Readers Project.' *The Linguistic Reporter* 14/6: 1–2.

Williamson, K. 1976. 'The Rivers Readers Project in Nigeria' in Bamgbose (ed.) 1976: 135–53.

Wingard, P. 1958. Nuffield Research Project in the Teaching of English. Fourth Progress report. Makerere, stencil.

de Witte, B. (in press). 'The impact of European Community rules on linguistic policies of the member states' in Coulmas (ed.).

Woehrling, J.-M. 1990. 'Les institutions européennes et la promotion des droits linguistiques des minorités. Le project de Charte européenne des langues régionales et minoritaires.' Paper at the International Colloquium on Language Rights/Human Rights, Council of Europe, Strasbourg, 15–17 November 1990 (in Giordan 1992).

Wolfson, N. and J. Manes (eds.) 1985. *Language of Inequality*. Berlin: Mouton.

Wong, I. 1982. 'Native-speaker English for the Third World today?' in Pride (ed.) 1982: 259–86.

World Bank 1988. *Education in sub-Saharan Africa: Policies for Adjustment, Revitalization and Expansion*. Washington, D. C.: World Bank (summarized in *Comparative Education Review*, February 1989).

Worsley, P. 1990. 'Models of the modern world-system' in Featherstone (ed.) 1990: 83–96.

Yoloye, E. A. 1986. *The Role of Research in Curriculum Development in Anglophone Africa*. Occasional papers 15. Edinburgh: Centre of African Studies, Edinburgh University.

Index

Entries for many of the frequently used concepts refer mainly to the initial presentation of the concept.